CONTROLLING SMALL WARS:

A Strategy for the 1970's

CONTROLLING
SMALL WARS:
A Strategy for the 1970's

BY LINCOLN P. BLOOMFIELD

AND

AMELIA C. LEISS

ALFRED · A · KNOPF

NEW YORK

1969

A Study from the Center for International Studies
Massachusetts Institute of Technology

————————————

THIS IS A BORZOI BOOK
PUBLISHED BY ALFRED A. KNOPF, INC.

————————————

anon.

FIRST EDITION

Copyright © 1969 by Massachusetts Institute of Technology

Library of Congress Catalog Card Number: 68–26491

Manufactured in the United States of America

Preface

This work is the outgrowth of a series of research studies conducted by the Arms Control Project of the MIT Center for International Studies on the problems of arms and security in the developing regions of the world. The war in Vietnam gave special point to our research. More generally, as the 1960's yield to the 1970's, Americans with concern for the future cannot help but be sobered by examination of the multitude of small wars the world over in which the United States has either been playing a part, or believed lay within the ambit of its concern as a great power with extensive—but ill-defined—responsibilities. Our own approach to this broad range of issues has been primarily as scholars. But as concerned citizens we have the strong conviction that the recent past teaches crucially important lessons about the future, which the United States will ignore at its peril.

In our research we were fortunate to have the willing and indeed indispensable collaboration of a number of associates. In the historical-analytical case studies that we devised, the better to comprehend the dynamic history of conflicts, we are indebted to the following individuals who drafted the first part of each, i.e. the historical narrative from which we derived the systematic catalog of factors, measures of control, and the like. Mrs. Jane K. Holland drafted virtually the entire first part of Chapter 5 on the Soviet-Iranian Conflict. Miss Priscilla A. Clapp did the same with Chapter 6 on the Bay of Pigs, and Mr. R. Lucas

Fischer prepared the bulk of the first part of Chapter 8 on the Indonesian War of Independence. Conflict in the Middle East was initially researched by Mr. Philip Raup, Miss Clapp, and Mrs. Irirangi C. Bloomfield, who also helped with the general editing.

The WEAPONS sections of the chapters in question were prepared by Miss Clapp for the Bay of Pigs, Conflict in the Middle East, and the Soviet-Iranian Conflict; Mr. Lewis Frank assisted with the WEAPONS sections of the Greek Insurgency and the Indonesian War of Independence.

A very special debt of gratitude is owed to our closest collaborator throughout the entire research, Colonel Laurence J. Legere, USA (Ret.). Colonel Legere contributed much to the present work and in addition served as a source of advice and judgment without which we would have been the poorer.

We also benefitted at all stages of the research from the imaginative and sympathetic collaboration of Dr. Richard E. Barringer and Mr. John H. Hoagland, as well as from the helpful assistance of Miss Janet Fraser and Mr. Robert K. Ramers.

This book is based in part on research prepared under a contract with the United States Arms Control and Disarmament Agency. The judgments expressed herein are those of the authors, and they do not necessarily reflect the views of the United States Arms Control and Disarmament Agency or any other department or agency of the United States Government.

At the same time, we would be derelict in not paying tribute to two public servants of high competence—Lieutenant-General John J. Davis, USA, and Mr. Edmund S. Finegold, whose wise, understanding, and encouraging sponsorship of our research could serve as a model for government-university relations.

LPB / ACL

Cambridge, Mass.
April 1969

Contents

Maps

Introduction

Since the 1940's, United States policy, when faced with a foreign conflict in which Communism seemed involved or serious instability threatened, has reacted with a certain consistency. Toward such local conflicts—and there have been many —the guiding assumption has been that someone, whether collective security agencies such as the United Nations or if necessary this country alone, must be prepared to intervene to repel aggression, restore order, or both. Vietnam is only the latest example. The U.S. attitude has been that of a strong and responsible power which regretted its irresponsible isolationism during the rise of Fascism, Nazism, and Japanese militarism. It has also been that of a rich status-quo power with worldwide interests which felt itself threatened by violent and convulsive changes virtually anywhere in the world. And it has been that of the leading proponent of universal collective security and international organization. We expected the newly re-created world order to function, and, when it could not, we created new organizations on a regional scale; when these could not cope, it became natural for us to consider unilateral intervention.

On occasion since the end of World War II, the peace of the world has probably been saved by the willingness of the United States to act in this unilateral fashion. For the 1970's, however, this nation may need a rather different approach.

It is not that the fundamental problems will be radically different. As the world moves into the 1970's, aggressive international behavior will remain, as before, a virulent danger to world peace. It will still be true that unless someone discourages such behavior, it will tend to flourish. And some Communists, however homegrown, will remain committed to political means that profoundly violate the central traditions of Western ethics and democratic life.

But some other things *have* altered. Today, we surely know that social change in developing societies, though it often looks like instability, may, in the long run, be the only sure road to stability. Also, we have observed that contemporary revolution is as often as not non-Communist, however frequently Communists may seek to manipulate it. And we have noticed that Communist intervention can frequently be as much of a headache for them as our own variety can be for us. Furthermore, Communism itself has become a congeries of feuding powers. And in this epoch of thermonuclear arsenals, strategic delivery systems, and sophisticated nuclear warheads, the possible price of direct great-power military involvement in local conflict has gone steadily up. Perhaps most to the point, the United States of America is long overdue in refurbishing its own social order, a task deserving the highest priority in both resources and attention.

For all of these reasons the 1970's call for an alternative strategy to unilateral military intervention. Intervention may still be found necessary when vital interests are threatened. But the peace—and U.S. national interests—may be better served at most times by a purposeful strategy of *conflict control*. The prime aim of this strategy would be neither to win nor to guide local conflicts; it would be to prevent, contain, or terminate them. It would seek, in short, to make them less threatening to regional and world peace by applying American brains, energy, and resources to the minimizing of violence by deliberate, purposeful policies.

We do not allege that the United States government has been unmindful of the growing incidence of internal conflict and conflict among smaller powers. It has been trying hard to educate itself about insurgency situations, good and bad, Communist and other. It has at times sought to damp down small wars between nations. But faced with both types of prevalent local conflicts—internal insurgencies and interstate wars in regions that are developing—the United States has given the impression it lacked coherent policy doctrines, did not always know what kinds of policies would best serve its interests, and had failed to anticipate conflicts intelligently.

Two policy failures have been in evidence. One is failure to take advantage of such patterns and uniformities as may exist among local conflicts. The other is failure to anticipate and prevent embryonic conflicts. The United States has appeared to lurch with pained surprise from crisis to crisis; the central preoccupation of American decision makers has often been keeping up with unanticipated squabbles abroad. Perhaps because they never have caught up, and there has never been time or energy for analysis, the notion persists that such conflicts are random and individually unique phenomena calling typically for traditional diplomatic and military treatment—and that only if they become sufficiently menacing.

Failure to anticipate and prevent is a great handicap in coping with internal conflict—revolutions, civil wars, and guerrilla uprisings. Even more to the point, the United States has been looking at these internal struggles primarily from the standpoint of producing an outcome favorable to itself, although even when "our" side "wins" it is by no means clear that the ultimate outcome will truly favor U.S. interests, let alone the larger common interest in regional and world peace. To date, the dominant questions have been how to deny the area in question to those nations hostile to the United States and how best to apply friendly resources and power to produce an outcome favorable to the United States.

It seems both relevant and timely to ask an additional question. If, instead of "winning," one's objective were *to bring a given conflict under control with the prime aim of avoiding or minimizing violence,* what would have to be done?

It is another matter whether one wants to carry out such a policy. There may well be local conflicts that the United States is legitimately more interested in winning than in controlling. On occasion the United States might choose even to foment a local conflict rather than accept the moral or strategic consequences of keeping the conflict suppressed (although the Bay of Pigs and the Suez Conflict of 1956 illustrate both the great political costs and the agonizing practical difficulties of wars—particularly "limited wars"—generated by democracies). Other values than minimizing violence or keeping down the potential risk of intensification may frequently be preferred. The overarching goal may legitimately be victory for one side, the serving of justice, the defeat of Communism, the downfall of oppressors, the ousting of colonial rulers, etc. There will continue to be times when these latter ends are, by any but doctrinaire pacifist standards, more to be valued than the exclusive end of avoiding or minimizing violence. But might it not be well to develop a set of prescriptions for those times when minimizing violence *is*—or *should be*—the determinant of policy? We are profoundly convinced it would.

PART ONE

PART ONE

CHAPTER 1

The Age of Local Conflict

For two decades the world has lived in the shadow of a nuclear war. The driving ambitions of first the Soviet Union and then Communist China, as well as the determined opposition of the West, gave such a war every reason for happening. But only a madman could regard a general thermonuclear exchange as a rational means of gaining political ends. Because of this fearsome realization, local quarrels and disorders far from the capitals of the great powers have become in a sense substitutes for "general war." Small wars do get fought in this era. In case after case, they have posed at least potential threats of intensification to wider areas and of use of more destructive weapons.

Two consequences follow. Now that fear of intensification has generally inhibited the intervention of superpowers, local conflicts have been more free to take place. And today the most powerful nations on earth have found themselves entangled with small-scale conflicts to a degree that is unique in political history. Post-World War II conflicts of the local variety thus pose a problem of growing magnitude for the superpowers. They have also acutely complicated the process of modernization for developing nations in the regions outside Europe. So far, over 95 per cent of the little wars of our age have taken place in the great southern, underdeveloped half of the world.

Some of these local conflicts resemble the traditional type of warfare between states. But over half have been internal insurrections, insurgencies, civil wars, and guerrilla-type conflicts.

All have been "limited," most in the sense of taking place within the frontiers of a single state. Even the largest-scale, such as Korea and Vietnam, have been tied to restricted objectives. Along with the general decline in international wars for conquest and colonization has come an increase in the proportion of wars for psychologically coercive purposes. Furthermore, formal declarations of war are almost completely out of fashion. Therefore, if we define "conflicts" as disputes in or between nations that involve the threat or use of significant violence, some fifty-four have taken place since 1945.

The forces that generate local conflicts show no sign of diminishing. To the extent that the incidence of local conflict is a function of economic, social, and political change, one can confidently predict a steepening of the curve as the change processes accelerate. A familiar historic process of geopolitical consolidation is taking place; this process includes conflict. In the case of the East:

Insurgency really springs out of the fact that Asia is entering, shall we say, the nineteenth century. Stronger central governments imbued with nationalist concepts have arisen since World War II. They are in the process of extending their authority to areas hitherto only claimed on maps. . . . It's like the rise of national European powers in the nineteenth century. It's always the hill people who are last to be brought under control.[1]

The same description may be applied equally to parts of Africa where independent governments face the problem of maintaining internal security against a variety of domestic dissidents.

The sundering of the nineteenth-century colonial map into fragments of independent political life has produced a multitude of states without settled boundaries, viable economies, or adequately trained personnel. Add to these instabilities the population and technological explosions, as well as the spread of mass communications preaching a message of human rights and individual freedom, and all the ingredients exist for revolutionary change.

[1] Statement by a Chinese-born diplomat in Bangkok, cited in Harrison E. Salisbury: "Unrest in the Hills Besets South Asia," *The New York Times*, June 26, 1966.

Whatever the color of a given revolution, conflict arises from the very nature of revolutionary change. Danton's apothegm that "revolution devours its children" has proved no less true of a Nkrumah or Sukarno than of a Trotsky, Zinoviev, Peng Teng-hua, or Liu Shao-ch'i. Future victims are not hard to discern.

In the southern half of Africa there are several potentially explosive colonial situations. Despite surface calm, the continued domination of a black population by a white minority puts a slow but sputtering fuse on the Portuguese territories of Angola and Mozambique, as well as on South West Africa, where the United Nations has declared its competence to lead the inhabitants to independence but has yet to solve the problem of wresting control from the South African government. Racial conflagrations could develop in South Africa or Rhodesia and perhaps in the Congo or any other place where white settlers or mercenaries continue to defy the aspirations of a black majority. Continued white-minority domination has created a widespread commitment to violence by Africans inside and outside these areas.

Future conflicts *between* states should not be written off either. The absence of clearly demarcated boundaries in Africa looms as another source of local conflict—between Algeria and Morocco, Morocco and Mauretania, Ethiopia and Somalia, and some other areas where the issue is not yet acute. Nor is this problem confined to Africa. There are border disputes in the Arab world, such as between Saudi Arabia, Yemen, and the recently created South Yemen. In the Himalayan foothills, India has yet to solve border differences with China that have already had at least one violent phase.

Rivalries for leadership in the Arab world seem to be sharpening. An ideological void has followed the rejection of colonial and tribal political concepts; a legitimate basis for authority is often lacking, and what one faction claims, another may challenge until force becomes the final arbiter. Only where one leader can claim leadership through the charisma of his person, such as Gamal Abdel Nasser in Egypt, has there been internal stability, however fragile. Stability may materialize in

South and Southeast Asia as an accompaniment of efforts to organize the nations on a regional basis. But the hardy perennial trouble spots of Kashmir, Palestine, and Cyprus are chronic Middle Eastern conflicts that remain dangerously unresolved.

It is the rivalries between the superpowers that make local conflicts matter so much to those not directly involved. Changes, however, are taking place in these rivalries. Relations between the United States and the Soviet Union have seemed to be undergoing a shift toward improved understanding and recognition of limited common interests. Moscow's role as peacemaker in the Indian-Pakistani fighting in 1965 contrasted with two decades of dogmatic Soviet support in and out of the United Nations for the Indian side. Likewise, despite its drive for influence and control in the Middle East, Soviet diplomacy strongly favored an end to fighting when the guns finally spoke there in 1956 and in 1967.

Nevertheless, continuing international dangers inhere even in *controlled* Soviet troublemaking around the world. In developing regions the Sino-Soviet split may now generate conflicts by competition for the allegiance of local radical movements; such intra-Communist conflicts may be exacerbated by rivalry with leftist *non*-Communist revolutionary groups in Latin America and elsewhere. Chinese nuclear diplomacy will doubtless endow some such issues in the future with an apocalyptic note of terror. Alongside all of this may of course be increasing collisions within Moscow's Eastern European empire.

All local conflicts are now potentially subject to the use of nuclear weapons. It takes little effort to imagine what may happen when fanatical local leaders possess crude nuclear weapons and perhaps a willingness to use them. Unfortunately, the instabilities that lie behind local conflicts will be little affected by great-power arms control and disarmament agreements, with the notable exception of the nuclear nonproliferation treaty.

For the developing regions, then, the preconditions for continued conflict exist in abundance. Nothing seems safer than the prediction that the decade of the 1970's, because it will be one of revolution, modernization, and change, will be one of local conflict. The ingredients are likely to exist in the foreseeable future, as they do now, for local conflicts to flourish, to draw in the great powers, and to intensify.

In the face of these prospects, it is our thesis that a more purposeful effort is required—as a matter of high urgency and concern—to prevent, contain, and terminate such conflicts with a minimum of violence and with the least chance of their intensifying or spreading. It is our further conviction, based on a fine-grained analysis of "small wars" in the postwar period, that much can be learned from recent history for present and future application. We believe that significant elements of a *strategy of conflict control* can now be derived and be set alongside past strategies of "win" that all too often involved belated, politically costly, and sometimes bloody unilateral military intervention.

Lest our assertions seem overly pretentious, let it be admitted at once that, even if a purposeful conflict-control policy is to be studied and adopted for maximum use, in few other areas of foreign policy are there more formidable difficulties and obstacles. Even in terms of available information on which to base a new look at local-conflict control, one starts from a surprisingly thin base of organized knowledge; for a generation, substantial American intellectual energy has been devoted to understanding and calculating the prospect of general war between the superpowers. We now know a great deal about the theory of superpower wars, happily still in the realm of theory.

As a mutual desire to avoid thermonuclear war created a built-in strategy of caution in Moscow, Washington, and probably Peking as well, strategic theory lowered its gaze to the subject of limited war, in the sense of less than general nuclear clashes between the United States and the Soviet Union in Europe and elsewhere. Virtually all the limited-war literature deals with this less than all-out nuclear exchange between the superpowers. Henry A. Kissinger, in his pioneering work on nuclear warfare, established the characteristics of such a conflict: specific rather than unlimited objectives and the intention of affecting rather than crushing the will of one's opponent. Thomas C. Schelling illuminated the bargaining utility of unused force. Both writers emphasized the fact of not using all of one's power and thus not fighting a "general war" on the model of World Wars I and II (or of, presumably, III). This genre of analysis is of great value. The control of what we here call "local conflict" can benefit from the ideas of deliberate restraints, symbolic communications, and tacit bargaining that are now a part of superpower relations. But specific new policies are now needed to cope with the "cat-and-dog" fights that often take place far from the heart of Soviet or U.S. military power.

Even the definition of "limited" becomes blurred when removed from the familiar superpower lexicon, which is why we will call such lower-level conflicts "local." In many of them (although less so, for example, in the Korean and Vietnam wars) the discrepancy between the potential power of the belligerents and the actual force exerted by one or more of them is much less than in skirmishes or proxy wars among the superpowers. The relative "limitation" of local wars has not generally been brought about by deliberate self-denial, typical of current superpower policy. What has kept them limited, and sometimes kept them local, was not always lack of physical capabilities; but it was rather consideration of the nature and value of war aims, possible costs of the war, and prospects of achieving aims at a particular level of effort—a consideration that is by no means always affected by capabilities.

Just because local conflicts have tended to remain confined and rather low-level from a superpower standpoint, it does not follow that either the passions involved, the intensity of commitment, or the ideological component were necessarily less. Some conflicts are of a low order of intensity even by local standards. But sometimes this was only because they lacked the capacity to be intercontinental, rather than because they were purposefully modest in their aims.

There is thus a range of points of view from which one can consider conflict "limited." What looks to Washington like a brushfire may from the standpoint of the combatants appear total. To those who were involved, unlimited annihilation may have seemed an accurate description for an Alamo, a Little Big Horn, a Carthage—or an Asian village that was leveled, its crops destroyed, and its population decimated. That such conflict stands low on the scale of thermonuclear casualties is irrelevant to the local perspective.

By the same token, the seeming inability of non-great-power countries to carry their struggles to the point of exhaustion or annihilation does not necessarily carry with it a willingness on their part to reach any kind of settlement, other than perhaps an armed truce (as examples: Palestine, Cyprus, and Kashmir). The Nasserite Arabs, the black-majority-ruled African states (vis-à-vis South Africa and the white Rhodesian regime), and Ho Chi Minh's North Vietnam, even if deprived of sophisticated means, in theory could with will and organization conduct war without end. Rome, as Robert Osgood has pointed out, did not need nuclear bombs to annihilate Carthage. The most intractable conflicts are often the most local of all—especially those that occur within the boundaries of a new state (or newly divided state) in which the issue is control over the machinery of internal rule; by virtue of the potency and universality of internal instability in developing regions, this sort of conflict may range very high in intensity and commitment. For this reason, the temptations to *external* involvement on ideological grounds may be extensive, as they were in the Spanish Civil War, the Greek Insurgency of the late 1940's, the Vietnam War, the Bay of Pigs fiasco in Cuba, the 1960 Congo collapse, and the Nigerian civil war that began in 1966. In such cases, one danger of intensification is a possible spread of war to the general neighborhood. Another danger is that the involved outside powers will wind up fighting each other. The indivisibility of security in the world of the last third of the twentieth century has come to imply a built-in potential for what is commonly called "escalation" in its attempts at peacekeeping and peace-making. The aim should be to make security *divisible*.

It should be clear that, whatever great powers may decide, by no means all local conflicts are equally controllable, ranging as they do from, say, a potential Asian nuclear war to guerrilla warfare in one province of a Latin American country. More-over, for control-policy purposes superpowers must also con-sider the difference between what has been an inadvertent stumbling into an unwanted local war and the local conflict that has been planned, initiated, and will be persisted in until death or victory.

China, for example, claims to see itself in a continuing worldwide conflict in which stimulated "wars of national libera-tion" are to be viewed as battles in a prolonged revolutionary war of global sweep. On a somewhat lower order, Nasser's Egypt holds aims that at times have appeared to embrace all of the African continent. Fidel Castro acts as if he has unlimited aims with regard to the whole of Latin America. In previous years Sukarno's ambitions extended to wherever the Malay race was found in Southeast Asia; Kwame Nkrumah's, to a mystical notion of "pan-Africa." Certainly some African states would, if they could, draw all of Europe and North America into a war to the end against white-ruled governments in such places as Rhodesia and South Africa. Even discounting the occasional tendency of local leaders rhetorically to invoke World War III and threaten thermonuclear exchanges and all the other apoca-lyptic extravagances they evidently wish they had available, indigenous self-restraint cannot always be counted on to keep local conflicts either local or limited.

Thus, there are many hindrances to a conflict-control ap-proach. But, as we propose to show, there are also some poten-tial levers or handles available to the would-be conflict con-troller that are not always remembered, used, or used well or intelligently. A closer look at the detailed life cycles of postwar local conflicts reveals that, far from being totally unique and unsusceptible to any general rules, they conform surprisingly to common patterns of structure and have common factors at work at different points along their lifelines (factors identifiable as either promoting or limiting violence). Thus, some elements exist for a positive approach that, within the limits of realism, may hold promise for influencing events which frequently seem unavoidable.

CHAPTER 2

An Anatomy of Conflict

To move toward greater understanding of a strategy for controlling future conflicts, one must be more systematic and precise about lessons drawn from past experience than is possible by relying solely on memory and general impressions. Using *traditional* methods, a great deal can be learned about a particular conflict, even about a number of conflicts, but without moving toward a better understanding of the phenomenon of conflict itself—its structure, its mechanism, the pressures that drive it—or how those pressures can be controlled. What is, therefore, required is a device to enable us to observe the *internal dynamics* of conflicts. For this we need a concept of the anatomy and bone structure of conflict.

Essential to unearthing such an anatomy is recognition that conflict is a dynamic process, not a single, unchanging state of affairs. People tend to refer to the "Kashmir Conflict," for example, as a convenient shorthand for the whole history of Indian-Pakistani quarrels over this piece of beautiful but tortured territory. Within the "Kashmir Conflict"—and all others —there have been many different stages or phases, some characterized by bellicose language, some characterized by saber rattling, some characterized by bloody war. If we wish to learn more about conflict with the central purpose of developing a catalog of conflict-control measures, it is essential that such stages or phases be studied separately.

We start, then, with a basic concept of conflict as a sequence of *phases*. Within each phase exist *factors*—conditions, perceptions, or events—that generate pressures. Some of these pressures tend toward increased violence and some tend away from violence. Their relative strength during the phase determines whether or not the conflict worsens. Within each phase the factors interact in such a way as to push the conflict ultimately across a series of *thresholds* toward or away from violence. The transition across thresholds is a function of the combined interaction of the factors of the previous phase.

Conflict originally arises out of a substantive *dispute,* which may be over territory, borders, legitimacy, ideology, power, race, or whatever. This quarrel or dispute over an issue is at first not necessarily perceived in military terms by either party. It is waged at the polls, in the courts, in the press, through UN exchanges or other diplomatic media, economically, politically—anything but militarily. But if one or more parties makes it military—introduces a *military option*—a threshold has then been crossed to a second phase, in which hostilities are potentially likely or at least reasonably expectable; a *conflict* has been generated, starting when the dispute comes to be regarded in military terms by one or both parties.

This condition which we define as "conflict" can come about when one side acquires military matériel—for example, when a disaffected group in a given society acquires arms and thus equips itself with the option of pressing its demands by force. Or the military option can be introduced when one or both sides—in a situation, say, of an interstate conflict where both parties from the outset have standing military establishments—decide that the force they possess is specifically relevant to their dispute. The introduction of a military option does not mean that hostilities have actually occurred, just that they are likely or possible. The conflict is still in a *pre-hostilities* stage.

If *hostilities* break out, intended or accidental, a third phase is entered. *Intensification* (usually, but imprecisely, called "escalation") may take place during this phase. That is, the hostilities may spread to wider geographic areas; new parties may become engaged; small-scale skirmishes may burgeon into pitched battles; or a war begun with small arms may develop into one in which the full panoply of weapons in the adversaries' inventories is hurled against opposing forces and perhaps civilian and economic targets as well.

If hostilities are *terminated,* another threshold is crossed to a fourth phase, in which the conflict may well continue, but without fighting necessarily being resumed. The conflict remains if at least one party continues to view the quarrel in potentially military terms. The conflict ceases when the dispute is no longer perceived significantly in military terms, real or potential. A fifth phase may then be entered, in which the military option is discarded but the issues in dispute remain unresolved; in which case it can be said that the conflict is ended, but not the dispute. If the parties manage to resolve the issues, or if they just cease to care, the dispute is *settled*.

The resulting continuum can thus be assigned these general phases:

Dispute → Pre-hos-tilities → Hostilities → Post-hos-tilities → Dispute → Settlement

C O N F L I C T

For convenience, these various phases can be numbered. Phase I is the dispute stage, where a divisive issue exists but has not yet been cast by either disputant in terms to which military power becomes importantly relevant. Phase II is the pre-hostilities phase, where no shooting takes place but it begins to "look like war": a military build-up starts, or an arms race develops, or military forces are deployed with serious intent to use them at some point. In general, the conflict is now perceived more in military than non-military terms. Phase III—the hostilities phase—is when the disputants have crossed the threshold to actual fighting. Phase IV—the cessation of hostilities phase—is an armed truce, so to speak, but with no end to the conflict, let alone a settlement of the underlying dispute. Phase V is a phase beyond conflict, where the situation is no longer perceived in military terms but the dispute persists. Finally, there is another stage beyond, a final stage where the underlying dispute and, *a fortiori,* the conflict are settled. This stage is *Settlement* (S).

The notion of thresholds separating different phases of conflict needs some explanation. One might think that thresholds are the really crucial points to study and understand; these moments of execution, as it were, might appear the centrally important ones, particularly since decisions leading to the succeeding phases can be changed right up to a threshold. For example, the decision to attack is reversible until the attack is actually launched. By this reasoning, one might think we should concentrate here on thresholds of transition, rather than on phases, as sources of identifiable points of possible policy leverage in our quest for conflict control.

Exact moments of transition from one threshold to another are often difficult to identify precisely. In addition, as we have said, they misleadingly suggest that, if one is looking for policy handles, the important moment of change is when an event becomes visible—when hostilities break out, an arms deal is publicly consummated, negotiations succeed, etc. But the moment of conception may be really more significant than the transitional moment of birth; it is at the former that events are, so to speak, foreordained. The point is that violence-producing factors and those tending away from violent outcomes in fact have their interactions *during* phases rather than exactly at moments of transition. At a threshold, they have accumulated to a point where the change visibly takes place. In short, thresholds are merely convenient points of demarcation at which to separate phases; the event of transition is itself a product of forces that have been at work throughout the phase.

Several intriguing hypotheses about the nature and course of local conflicts are implicit in the picture we have drawn so far:

(1) Local conflicts have a general, common structure rather than being always unique and random phenomena.

(2) All conflicts go through a preliminary dispute phase (Phase I) and one or more of three basic conflict phases.

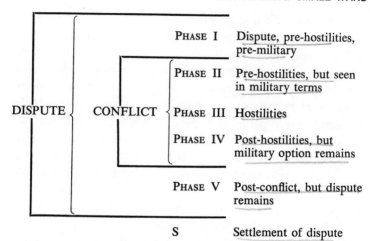

		PHASE I	Dispute, pre-hostilities, pre-military
DISPUTE {	CONFLICT {	PHASE II	Pre-hostilities, but seen in military terms
		PHASE III	Hostilities
		PHASE IV	Post-hostilities, but military option remains
		PHASE V	Post-conflict, but dispute remains
		S	Settlement of dispute

(3) In each phase identifiable factors generate pressures that tend to push the conflict across a threshold of transition into another phase; these factors are countered by other factors that can be regarded as tending toward the prevention of that transition—or toward Settlement.[1]

With these three hypotheses in mind, we can now propose that change in the relationship among factors will alter the likelihood of a conflict's undergoing transition from one phase to another. This last hypothesis is at the very center of the quest for a strategy of conflict control. We assert that: (4) *The course of local conflicts can be significantly altered by policy measures aimed at reinforcing violence-minimizing factors and offsetting violence-generating factors, as appropriate for the phase in question.*

In short, this kind of four-part analysis can suggest specific policy measures that may tend to control conflicts. Once said, this kind of analysis and logic may appear obvious. But it seems not to have been obvious in an age that must increasingly feel itself the victim of forces beyond its control.

An important insight emerges from the above fourfold line of reasoning. Just as conflict is a dynamic process and not a single

[1] This interrelationship of the dynamic process of conflict and the operative pressure factors may be represented in the form of a matrix, as shown in Appendix A.

state of affairs, so also conflict control cannot be a single policy objective. Control is composed of *several* related but distinct objectives which differ from phase to phase. One control objective is common to every phase: to settle the underlying dispute. But, failing that, there are additional objectives to work toward. Initially, the objective is to keep a dispute (Phase I) nonmilitary. Once a military option has been introduced (Phase II), the objective is to prevent the outbreak of hostilities and to contain (i.e., restrict the scope/scale of) potential hostilities. If hostilities break out (Phase III), the objective is to contain (i.e., moderate) them or terminate them. Once open hostilities are terminated (Phase IV), it is necessary to prevent their resumption and, once more, to restrict the scale of a potential resumption. If the disputants are pacified to a point where there is no longer any intention by either to seek a military solution (Phase V), the objective is to keep it that way.[2] Many of these objectives are pursued every day by responsible governments and by international organizations, and they will come as no surprise. What is perhaps suprising is that they can be brought into a coherent theory. Can it be put to use?

The analytic representation of conflict and policies of conflict control described in the preceding pages is based on pure deduction. Like many models, it is an abstract, generalized, even idealized picture—in this case, of a common and all too pervasive phenomenon—and will rarely be followed in exact detail by any real-life conflict. Some cases of conflict fortunately never cross the threshold of outbreak of hostilities. Others stay for a mercifully brief time in the hostilities phase and then are either pacified while moving through Phase IV, where the conflict is still sharp but not openly violent, perhaps go through Phase V, where there is no longer any intention to resolve the dispute by military means, and on to S. Some may even go directly from the battlefield to Settlement if results of battle are

---

[2] A comprehensive model of the structure of local conflict, including the definitions and interrelations among phases, factors, and conflict-control policy objectives, appears in Appendix B.

decisive enough, although what happened to Carthage hardly qualifies as a satisfactory avoidance of Phases IV and V. Another, less Punic example would be the end of a resistance movement in occupied territory when occupation forces surrender or withdraw. A depressing number of conflicts linger in the hostilities phase, moving through sub-phases representing intensification of hostilities (escalation), or perhaps resting in a tenuous, cease-fire "peace" (Phase IV) until—with renewed wind and limb—hostilities resume. There is, furthermore, no time limit on any single phase. The U.S.–Soviet Cold War is an example of a decades-long Phase II conflict, hopefully always to stay pre-hostilities. In 1947, the Kashmir Conflict between India and Pakistan remained in Phase II only a matter of days before plunging into open hostilities.

The conflict structure we have described is not, of course, the only possible one; other devices may be chosen for dissecting the course of conflict. Mao Tse-tung's three stages of guerrilla warfare, for example, are in a crude sense analogous to our Phases II and III, although his emphasis is on the degree to which terrorism becomes organized into ever larger military formations. Another scale[3] involves four stages: an initial conspiratorial phase (our Phase II); a violent stage (our Phase III); a "revolutionary stage"; and lastly, a "final victory stage," which presumably corresponds either to our Phase V, if the issue remains, or our S, if it has disappeared.

There are, in short, a variety of possible pictures of the general conflict process. Their utility depends on the kinds of questions they are best suited to illustrate. Those just mentioned

[3] A. J. Thomas, Jr., Ann V. Thomas, and Oscar A. Salas: *The International Law of Indirect Aggression and Subversion,* Report Prepared for the U.S. Arms Control and Disarmament Agency Under Contract No. ACDA/GC–41, June 30, 1966.
A related attempt to refine stages or subprocesses of insurgencies, civil wars, and nationalist movements lists ten: initial alienation; organization of revolutionary organizations; mass revolutionary appeals; revolutionary coalition and movement-building; non-violent revolutionary politics; the outbreak of revolutionary violence; rule of the moderates; accession of the extremists; reigns of terror; Thermidor. David C. Schwartz: *A Theory of Revolutionary Behavior* (University of Pennsylvania, Document 6–28–66–86), pp. 9–10.

apply most directly to internal insurgency situations. Since our interest is in *both* internal and interstate conflict and our goal is to make more coherent a purposeful conflict-control policy, we elected to construct a model that seemed applicable to a wider range of types of conflict and appeared to hold most promise of illuminating the real policy problem of conflict control.

Before showing what policy-relevant lessons may be learned by using our model, some further preliminary questions need to be posed. How far back toward the roots of conflict need one go to develop a comprehensive catalog of conflict-control measures? And what is the relative importance for conflict-control purposes of the several phases?

The answer depends on one's particular angle of vision. The historian usually wishes to comprehend as much as he can of the total sequence of events, tracking them through until their eventual termination. The philosopher is generally concerned with "first causes"—the innate and often concealed bases for later actions. The peacemaker focuses most often on the later stages of the conflict, bent on seeing how the belligerent parties may be moved toward settlement. And the senior American policy maker typically starts to focus seriously on a local conflict only when it reaches a stage of volatility sufficient to warrant assigning it a priority among a range of other threatening disturbances.

Furthermore, in order to develop a coherent strategy of conflict control, one needs to learn as much as possible about the larger process within which international or internal political differences move across thresholds toward and away from "war." Such an effort requires, of course, an explicit understanding of all the pressures and factors generating conflict.

A model only does part of the job of identifying causal elements. Because a complex phenomenon can be portrayed schematically does not mean that all operative elements can be identified or that the cause-effect relationships that link them can be clearly understood. It is important to understand enough of the cause-effect relationships only to be sure that a given policy activity will in fact reinforce or offset any given combination of factors. This might raise a larger question: Can *historic* causes ever be identified, with real confidence, as the basis for later effects?

This question poses anew some of the vexing philosophic problems that are inherent in the search for "causes of war." Apart from a few hardy souls in the peace-research field, few still research today in the fashion of, for example, Sidney Fay, in his monumental—and dubious—attempt to learn the true causes of World War I. The beginnings of a conflict stretch back into time, originating from causes that are only imperfectly knowable. Various situations, occurrences, and constellations of pressures can be identified along the route toward a conflict. Some of them are obviously causes. But it is equally true that a conflict may have exploded into hostilities because of some hitherto undetected situation—or because a new condition was suddenly introduced. Not all pressures along the time-space continuum are man-made, or visible at the time, or "always there." Some even represent gathered momentum, just as some barriers to intensification represent sheer inertia rather than purposeful policy.[4] Social scientists have been probing into conditions that seem to generate conflict *within* nations. But, with regard to interstate conflict, the policy maker and the student of policy will probably always have to content themselves with proximate causes, with no assurance that the basic forces generating conflict are fully revealed.

A related intellectual hazard is believing that all conflicts are "determined," in the sense that, given the appropriate ingredients, they will proceed in certain inevitable ways. Our thesis rests on the conviction that conflicts are *not* fatally irreversible. All in all, causality appears to be embodied in a combination of

[4] For evidence of the presence at critical choice points of nonrational factors of pressures, acceleration, and a sense of fatality, a classic example may be the World War I case. See especially Barbara W. Tuchman: *The Guns of August* (New York: Macmillan; 1962) and recent social-science experiments in simulating that event, notably Robert North's at Stanford, reported in Appendix B in Robert C. North et al.: *Content Analysis* (Chicago: Northwestern University Press; 1963).

environmental situations, willful intentions, and triggering
events, all reaching critical mass at the point a conflict becomes
acute. But within these boundaries, some probable cause-effect
relationships can be discerned.

One basis for this discernment is simple historical correlation. In one sense, every significant correlation between a given
set of circumstances and a given action may be interpreted as
embodying either an explanation or a prediction about probable
cause and effect. In our own conflict model, correlations can be
made between transitions and the presence of factors in the pre-
transition stage which in a limited, but important, sense imply
cause and effect. With caveats similar to those of the historical
correlator, some medical scientists, for example, implicate
blood cholesterol in coronary-artery disease and tobacco in lung
cancer. Likewise, the factors that are present during the identifiable phases of a conflict correlate with transitions in the course
of a conflict. Only in this sense do they add up to a body of
causation.

Ideally, then, _all_ factors should be identified in order that all
elements of probable causality may be translated into relevant
conflict-control measures. The process of identification and
correlation becomes increasingly difficult, however, the further
one tracks a dispute back in time. More remote causes are
embedded in factors that are increasingly difficult to discern.

What all this suggests is that there are actually _two_ pre-
conflict phases. One is the Phase I of our model, where a
discernible dispute exists. The other is a _pre-dispute_ phase—
"Phase Minus-One," so to speak—during which the preconditions for the dispute are maturing.

Is not that "seedbed" phase the one in which to concentrate
for the application of measures to prevent conflict? Ideally, yes.
But where? The UNESCO constitution asserts that "wars begin
in the minds of men," and this is undeniable. Without much
doubt there is a general built-in cause in the human proclivity for
conflict, along the lines suggested by William James when he
wrote that "our ancestors have bred pugnacity into our bones
and marrow, and thousands of years of peace won't breed it out

of us."[5] Clearly, policy must be considered in a shorter and more manageable focus.

An important root cause of internal conflict is implied in the increasingly demonstrated correlation of insurgency with economic conditions (and Communist exploitation of those conditions to seize power). Persuasive statistics have been adduced to support the argument that, as one newspaper put it after Secretary of Defense Robert McNamara's notable Montreal speech in May 1966 on this topic, "Where the Poverty Is, Is Where the Insurgency Is."[6] Direct connections have also become increasingly evident between the incidence of conflict and the stresses of the modernization process. A general strategy aimed at minimizing conflict over a long future period quite correctly should focus on measures related to basic factors along the path to modernity. But, again, clearly only some of these factors lend themselves to purposeful current policy likely to control a given conflict.

If the pre-dispute "Phase Minus-One" stage is essentially unmanageable for our analytical purposes, the same can by no means be said of the second pre-conflict phase—the dispute phase—where a specific quarrel has started (Phase I). This phase is of vital importance for better understanding of how to prevent the transition from dispute to conflict, i.e., to Phase II. A few contemporary examples can make this point. Social

---

[5] This view of man as susceptible, regardless of culture, to militarism has had a recent public revival at the hands of the ethologists, led by the celebrated Viennese Konrad Lorenz. See particularly Konrad Lorenz: *On Aggression* (New York: Harcourt, Brace; 1963); and Robert Ardrey: *African Genesis* (New York: Dell; 1963) and *The Territorial Imperative* (New York: Atheneum; 1966). For the view that violence is a "chronic disease of society," see Kenneth Boulding: *Conflict and Defense* (New York: Harper & Row; 1962), p. 323.

[6] *The New York Times,* May 22, 1966.

In his Montreal speech, McNamara pointed out that, since 1958, 87 per cent of the world's "very poor" countries, 69 per cent of its "poor" countries, and 48 per cent of its "middle income" countries had suffered significant conflicts, whereas only one out of twenty-seven "rich" countries had experienced "major internal upheaval on its own territory." Ibid., May 19, 1966. The Secretary was using "rich," "poor," etc., as defined by the International Bank for Reconstruction and Development (which he now heads).

justice in Cuba during the Batista years might have prevented guerrilla warfare from developing in Cuba. Purposeful religious and ethnic collaboration—or separation—would perhaps have averted the strife on the Indian subcontinent and in Cyprus and Palestine. Preventive diplomacy remains the ideal of diplomacy itself.

Nevertheless, it is not entirely realistic to ask diplomacy to focus even on Phase I rather than on Phase II. In principle, massive diplomatic efforts ought to be employed for preventive diplomacy as early as possible in the life of a dispute. To be realistic, the world is fortunate when policy focuses on conflicts even in their Phase II stage, when hostilities have become more likely but have not yet actually broken out.

In fact, the closer one is in time to the actual threshold of hostilities, the more pertinent are concrete policy measures bearing on the conflict itself—and the less relevant are the sorts of measures that might have prevented the conflict from arising in the first place. As the threshold of war gets closer, the policy measures need increasingly to focus on such tangible present realities as arms and external support, as well as on the various forms of diplomatic influence that can be applied to control the conflict.[7]

What happens when we apply our abstract model of local conflict to real-life events?[8] Do the definitions and hypotheses

[7] A striking "laboratory" example of the diminishing relevance of first causes at points well along the conflict-control scale was suggested in a policy-type MIT political-military exercise. The U.S. team sought to head off the hypothetical outbreak of violent revolution in a Middle Eastern country through activation of measures of economic reform and aid that had long been recognized as a means of getting at some of the root causes of strife in the area. But such measures turned out to be far too long-range in impact to affect management of the crisis and had no appreciable bearing on the violent events that unfolded to carry the situation across the threshold from Phase II to Phase III. Lincoln P. Bloomfield et al.: *Political Exercise II—The U.S. and the U.S.S.R. in Iran* (Cambridge: MIT Center for International Studies; December 1960).

[8] A more detailed description of the analytic technique used in this study is contained in Chapter 4, and five examples of its application appear in Chapters 5 through 9.

that make it up still appear meaningful? Does it reveal patterns and consistencies? Or are individual conflicts so different that no useful generalizations can be made? Above all, can the process teach us anything about what ought to be done? In short, can these hypotheses about the way conflicts behave be combined with facts from real local conflicts to move us closer to a set of policy prescriptions that might be helpful in getting through the predictably turbulent 1970's?

To assist in the search for answers to these questions, detailed studies were made of fourteen post–World War II local conflicts.[9] These fourteen conflicts were selected as a representative sample out of fifty-four cases.[1] The choice of them was based on the importance of their geographic locus; a desire to have some distribution among colonial, internal, and interstate types, and the different degrees of successful control demonstrated among them. The first task was to examine the history of each conflict in detail in order to find the transitions or sharp changes that distinguished the different phases hypothesized in our abstract model. At what point was a military option introduced into a dispute, giving it a new character of conflict? When, if at all, did hostilities break out? Were there distinct points at which the hostilities intensified or moderated? When did they cease? And so forth, through whatever pattern of transitions each particular conflict passed.

Once the phases had been isolated in each conflict, they were searched for factors that could be identified as bearing on the

[9] Algerian-Moroccan Conflict, 1962–1963
  Angola Conflict, 1950–1961
  Arab-Israeli Conflict, 1956–1967 (See Chapter 9.)
  Bay of Pigs, 1960–1961 (See Chapter 6.)
  Conflict on Cyprus, 1952–1964
  Greek Insurgency, 1944–1949 (See Chapter 7.)
  India-China Border Conflict, 1954–1962
  Indonesian War of Independence, 1945–1949 (See Chapter 8.)
  Indonesian-Malaysian Confrontation, 1963–1965
  Kashmir Conflict, 1947–1965
  Malayan Emergency, 1948–1960
  Somalian-Ethiopian-Kenyan Conflict, 1960–1964
  Soviet-Iranian Conflict, 1941–1947 (See Chapter 5.)
  Suez (or British-French-Egyptian) Conflict, 1956 (See Chapter 9.)
[1] The list of fifty-four cases is found in Appendix C.

way the conflict developed, that is, on the transitions to new phases. These factors took the form, not of abstractions about conflict, but of economic, political, military, or social events, conditions, or perceptions that could reasonably be shown to have exerted pressures, in varying degree, on the future course of the conflict.

The detailed list of factors is long, as the case studies in this volume will illustrate. The following general categories of significant factors emerged from the fourteen cases; we feel they include many and perhaps most of the influential variables that may be found in an over-all hypothesis about the internal dynamics of local conflict:

(1) *Degree of commitment.* Included here are answers to the following kinds of questions: What proportion of available military force is engaged in the conflict? Is the conduct of hostilities limited—e.g., are the strategies being pursued more modest than either party is capable of pursuing? How widespread or restricted is the issue at stake? for example, does it involve only points on the border, or certain sections of the country? or is the issue one of national survival? Are the populations of the parties united behind their leaders in the conflict?

(2) *Autonomy of action.* This refers to factors that affect the degree to which the parties to local conflicts are subject to outside influences constraining their freedom of action. Factors concerning general dependence on external military or economic aid and political assistance, as well on as specific matériel support in the conflict, are included here. Also found in this category of factors are the controversies that can arise among allies and coalitions as to how the conflict should be conducted.

(3) *Environment.* The physical nature of the locale can profoundly influence the way in which a conflict unfolds. The actions of the parties themselves are influenced by the ease with which each of them can project its power and influence into the critical area. For this reason, geographic and weather factors are important, as are roads, railroads, airports, rivers, and harbors. Whether the country is flat and open or mountainous or jungle and whether borders are defined and controllable can

also be significant. These factors also affect the accessibility of the area to those external powers—other states or international organizations—that might contemplate intervention.

(4) *Information.* The speed and accuracy with which information about developments within a conflict reaches the parties and interested outside powers can also have a major bearing on the conflict. And the channels of communications—how and from whom information is received—can help determine whether or not information is to be believed. Included here are factors, therefore, relating to reliable reports on immediate events as well as to long-range assessments of capabilities and intentions.

(5) *Time.* In many conflicts, one can observe pressures that are generated by time: Is there time to await clarification of events or are things moving so rapidly that action must be taken immediately if it is to be taken at all? Does the future appear to hold promise of an improvement or a deterioration in the relative balance of power between the parties? Are there specific anticipated events that may affect the prospects of one or both parties, such as an election, the arrival of arms, actions taken by international organizations, interventions by external powers? Such time factors have a bearing on the way in which parties to a local conflict behave and, hence, on the course the conflict takes.

(6) *Military relationship.* One obvious category of factors relates to the relative military power of the parties. And what the military balance between them is *believed* to be can be just as critical as what it actually is. Furthermore, what people think the future balance will be can help determine their decisions about *how vigorously* and *when* to take action. Included in this category are factors relating to the numbers in the armed forces, how much and what kinds of equipment they have, how well they are trained, how rapidly they can be moved about to meet new challenges or capitalize on new opportunities, and how many threats they must be prepared to meet simultaneously. Related to all these issues are the kinds of strategy and tactics

both sides are employing and whether the military doctrines of the parties are suitable to the challenges they face.

(7) *Internal cohesion.* The stability and unity of the people of a state are, of course, prime factors in internal conflicts. (By definition, it is the absence of such stability and unity that makes internal strife possible.) There are, as well, a number of ways in which the internal cohesion of states can influence the course of *interstate* conflict. We have already mentioned that pressures from powerful groups in a divided nation can alter the freedom of action of its leaders. Equally, foreign adventures are a classic way in which weak leaders seek to unite their followers and distract them from problems at home. The degree of obvious internal cohesion also helps to determine each side's perceptions of the other's "staying power" and can reveal the possible existence of active or potential "allies" within the enemy camp.

(8) *Internal control.* The authority of central leadership over segments of its nominal following is often clearly absent in internal conflict. But there can be found within opposing camps of contestants, in both internal and interstate conflicts, factors that reflect the degree of their strong, united leadership. Included in this category, therefore, is knowledge of the level of authority that can be exercised over local activists, including at times the military.

(9) *Ethnic relationships.* Both within each side to a local conflict and between them a variety of factors can at times be found that reflect basic racial, tribal, religious, or linguistic factors. Such factors can produce a volatile situation when the issues in the conflict tend to take shape along ethnic lines.

(10) *Ideology.* Ideologies are also factors affecting the course of local conflict. Democracy, monarchism, Communism, socialism, colonialism, traditionalism, self-determination, nationalism—all these can be banners behind which opposing forces rally, as well as factors conditioning their perceptions and expectations.

(11) *Past relationships.* Many of the issues in contention between local adversaries have had their genesis in the past

history of their relations—issues such as disputed boundaries, irredentist claims, and other general historic animosities. At issue can be a long history. This category of factors therefore includes not only the memories that conflicting parties carry with them into their new quarrel but also the manner in which each will interpret or perceive the other's words, deeds, and intentions. Furthermore, actions which the parties have taken in earlier phases of the conflict can help condition their own, their supporters', and their adversaries' present outlooks and expectations. Men often learn from history, but sometimes they learn the wrong lessons.

(12) *Actions of international organizations.* Since the states of the world have provided themselves with instruments for keeping the peace, it is not surprising that a large number of factors found to be operating within conflicts involve these organizations in some way. Included in this category are not only the United Nations but also various regional security arrangements such as the Organization of American States, the Arab League, and the Organization of African Unity. Factors here relate to past actions the organizations have taken—the precise kinds of action, the speed and harmony with which they proceeded, the success they had—and to the parties' expectations about the role these bodies might play in the unfolding conflict.

(13) *Great-power interests, commitments, and actions.* This major cluster of factors encompasses the variety of impacts great powers can have—or have had—on the course of local conflicts. Each of the great powers has acquired obligations toward the developing countries or regions that color the former's assessment of its stake in the outcomes of local quarrels and the latter's expectations about the role the great power will play. Ideological ties, formal treaty commitments, historic spheres of interest or responsibility, base rights, economic interests—all these can affect local conflicts. Whether local conflicts are sparked by competitive great-power interests or whether local adversaries themselves seek to draw in friendly great powers, the fact remains that time and again the great

powers play critical roles in other people's quarrels. Once again, specific timing of action is equally important. Also of special importance is whether the great powers act in concert or in competition. Finally, the general state of relations among the great powers generally provides the broad setting within which local conflicts take place.

The above categories encompass all the factors we identified as exerting a force on the development of local conflicts. They are not, to be sure, exclusive categories. In the context of a specific conflict, a particular significant event might have in it elements of several categories. For example, the imminent arrival of large quantities of Soviet arms in Cuba in 1961 represented competitive great-power involvement that appeared likely to strengthen Castro militarily to the point where no low-key exile invasion could succeed, and this in turn was used by those who argued for prompt U.S. action while opportunity still existed. But although, historically, factors seldom fall neatly into single categories, the ones listed above underscore the very wide range of factors we found in local conflicts.

Another necessary caveat is that no factor or category of factors will always exert pressure in one direction only, that is, as a conflict-controlling pressure or a pressure worsening the conflict. When we ask what kind of pressure a given factor or category generated in a specific conflict in a particular phase, the answer must be complex in order to be accurate.

In the Soviet-Iranian Conflict in the late 1940's, for example, the relative weakness of the Iranian central government was, during pre-hostilities (Phase II), a factor tending to encourage the Soviet Union and its Azerbaijani separatist cohorts to resort to force to wrest Azerbaijan from Iranian control. At a comparable stage in the Bay of Pigs crisis the apparent weakness of Castro's control—evidenced by the mass exodus from Cuba of his early supporters and by continued anti-Castro guerrilla activities in Cuba—led the United States to believe that a very low-level use of force (the exile invasion) could topple the government. Real or apparent weakness of the central government was, in both cases at this phase, a factor tending toward violence. However, once hostilities had broken out in Iran, this weakness had a reverse effect: It permitted a rapid, relatively bloodless Azerbaijani-Soviet victory that quickly terminated hostilities (but was undesirable and subsequently reversed).

In Cuba the presumed weakness turned out to be an illusion, posing for the United States the agonizing dilemma of accepting the rapid defeat of its proxy or of committing its own forces and, thus, seriously intensifying the hostilities.

Finally, in our study of the fourteen conflicts, there remained the most demanding—and perhaps most controversial—task of all: *to identify all possible policy measures that might have had the effect of strengthening factors promoting control or the effect of countering or weakening factors tending to push the conflict toward violence.* The number of measures (or actions) to be identified was limited only by the imagination of the authors. Any action by any agent—the United Nations, the great powers, or the parties themselves—that could reasonably be expected to have the desired effect was included. The question we asked ourselves was not: What measures would have controlled this conflict? It was rather: What measures would have strengthened (or countered) this particular factor exerting this kind of pressure? We believe that to answer the second question helps to answer the first.

It is also important to keep in mind that we were, at this stage, trying to answer the above question when the policy objective *was* conflict control. Some of the measures that might have been taken to control conflict are politically ludicrous. For example, with regard to the "weak central government" factor, a measure aimed only at violence avoidance would have sought to strengthen the internal regimes of anti-Soviet Iran—and of pro-Soviet Cuba—the latter hardly an acceptable U.S. policy objective.

In the real world, all interested parties to conflicts in fact pursue a complex set of objectives in which conflict control is, at best, only one of the desired ends and, at worst, is actively opposed. Our objective in going through the exercise just described was neither to replay history in the most realistic manner possible nor to second-guess policy makers or castigate them for their lack of foresight and imagination (although at times the evidence is too persuasive to avoid such conclusions). It was rather to compile as large and imaginative a list as possible of policy measures that belong on an agenda of conflict control, and that might, above all, enable diplomacy to do better in those future conflicts *where the minimizing of violence is the prime objective being sought.* The list of conflict-control measures that emerged from this process includes some that would have been politically unacceptable in the real circumstances of the conflict in question or would have been impossible to achieve in time to be effective, even some that—because we deliberately looked at factors in isolation—were at times mutually inconsistent.

But from this approach to the fourteen actual conflicts emerged, first, a substantial list of the types of factors that have in fact been operating in contemporary local conflict, and second, a rich agenda of the types of policy measures and capabilities that belong in the armory of those who would control such local conflicts in the future.

CHAPTER 3

Lessons from Recent History

Let us now turn from *how* we tried to learn from history about conflict control to *what* we learned. We shall look first at some general control-policy implications we saw in the fourteen conflicts and then at the implications derived from five selected cases.

SOME GENERAL CONTROL-POLICY IMPLICATIONS

The number of instances in our fourteen cases in which control measures of one kind or another might in a given situation have reinforced factors favoring a movement away from hostilities or might have offset factors favoring a movement toward hostilities exceeded 425. (If we had examined more cases, the number would obviously have been larger.) These instances were, in other words, theoretical *opportunities* to take purposeful policy action of some sort aimed at conflict control. Some were in fact taken at the time; most were not.

The bare total of theoretical opportunities for conflict-control measures may not tell very much. Nevertheless, it is not uninteresting, since it shows how many measures emerged, through a systematic analytical process, as precisely matched to particular significant factors or pressures at particular phases in the lives of given conflicts. These were the "tourniquets" applicable at key pressure-points in the conflicts.

These "instances-opportunities" were distributed very unevenly among the phases of conflict. Of the total, 149, or 36 per cent, occurred in the first, or pre-conflict, phase (Phase I). This has extraordinary implications; it suggests that *between one third and one half of all relevant violence-controlling policy activity may be applicable before a dispute has even turned into a "conflict."*

This is not to say that all such measures as we have suggested could be taken today in comparable cases. What it does say is that there are a large number of measures to be taken that may go far to prevent a dispute from turning into a later war. Lamentably, statesmen and diplomats do not usually take notice of a potential conflict until it has been perceived by at least one party in primarily military terms and begins to frighten people.

Let us examine further these 425 instances of conflict-control opportunities. After a startlingly large concentration of them for the pre-conflict phase, the total number of suggested conflict-control measures declined through the phases of actual conflict (pre-hostilities, actual fighting, and the post-hostilities stages). Compared to 149 suggested instances in Phase I, a total of 94 were identified for Phase II, 83 for the first round of hostilities (Phase III), 75 for Phase IV, and 24 for Phase III_2 (resumed hostilities, when they occurred). The research method itself placed no special weight on any particular phase. But what happened was that the process of deriving conflict-control measures from factors yielded fewer and fewer steps that policy makers might take to avert violence as conflict progressed along its path through actual bloodshed to termination. The range and variety of such measures declined as options began to close, attitudes hardened, and perceptions increasingly narrowed down to a preoccupation with the violent bands of the spectrum of political conduct. Even if guns are silenced, the task of moving toward a lasting solution is vastly more difficult than it is before they speak!

But what types of conflict-control measures are we talking about? By far the largest number (146, or 34 per cent of the total) were peacemaking and peacekeeping diplomatic measures by international organizations, especially the use of the machinery of the United Nations and/or such regional organizations as the Organization of American States and the Organization of African Unity. Measures in this category ranged from assisting local efforts to resettle or control refugees to active peacekeeping efforts in the form of border patrols, interposed forces, and the like. Under this heading were some measures involving the use of *available* international machinery and other measures calling for *improved* capabilities—standing peacekeeping forces, for example, able to be dispatched quickly to areas of trouble and equipped with such adjuncts as reconnaissance aircraft and other technical devices to make their presence most effective.

The next largest category of measures that can be conveniently grouped were those that states external to the issues in conflict—great powers, neighboring states, and others—could have taken. These numbered eighty-five (20 per cent). One of the ironies that clearly emerged is that, while malevolent or maladroit meddling by outside powers is perhaps the most pervasive local-conflict-*promoting* factor, at the same time these same external powers emerge time and again as crucial potential sources of pressure for conflict *control*. The measures included in this category ranged from such fundamentals as avoiding or composing the great-power conflicts that spawn and feed local tensions, to using such levers of influence as external powers may have to encourage local forces toward moderation and accommodation.

The third and fourth broad categories of measures—military forces and strategy, and internal political measures—were equal in number (sixty-two, or 14 per cent). The measures relating to military forces and strategy ranged from such specifics as improved command and control within the armed forces of the local contestants, to the adoption by the great powers of military strategies that both minimize the need for overseas bases and deter other great-power meddling that might instigate and encourage local dissidents. Internal political measures included those affecting the cohesiveness and stability of the government, civilian control of the military establishment, clarity of objectives, and rationality of decision making.

A fifth category of measures (twenty-nine, or 6.8 per cent) did not apply to some of the fourteen conflicts studied but lies so close to the central nature of conflict as to merit special attention. These were measures relating directly to the arms and other military matériel available or used in the conflicts. A nearly equal number of measures (twenty-six, or 6 per cent) could be grouped as economic and technical. Here were found such basic measures as general economic and technical assistance, as well as specific actions such as developing the technology in order to lessen great-power reliance on bases (e.g., by developing long-range air-lift capabilities) and thereby reduce such vested interests in the outcomes of local quarrels.

A last category, measures relating to communication and information, yielded a small number of instances (sixteen, or 4 per cent). But the types of measures included under this heading were not unimportant. Better facilities for rapid and secure communication between adversaries might, in some instances, have avoided hasty responses based on misperception of intentions. More adequate intelligence as to the facts might, at other times, have prevented one side from plunging into a situation only to find that a much greater commitment of force was required in order to protect its initial modest commitment. And a more accurate long-term assessment of the capabilities of a quarrelsome neighbor could have helped alleviate the types of exaggerated and often unjustified fears that set off spiraling arms races.

The possibility of use of these several categories of conflict-

control measures *across the phases of conflict*[1] may be meaningful at this point:

Type of Measure	Ph. I	Ph. II	Ph. III	Ph. IV	Ph. III$_2$
International-organization	53	33	25	31	4
External-political	33	17	15	16	4
Military & strategic	16	17	16	10	3
Internal-political	24	13	11	9	5
Arms & other matériel	6	8	5	5	5
Economic & technological	15	0	6	3	2
Communications & information	2	6	5	1	2

A relatively large incidence of international-organization
measures—ways in which such institutions might have been
used by the parties themselves or by external powers (including
the great powers)—appeared to be appropriate and needed in
the pre-conflict stage of dispute. Almost twice the number of
measures were found to be relevant there as in the next preventive stage (conflict, but pre-hostilities) and considerably
more than the number available and relevant *after* fighting
broke out—which is precisely where most actual policy activity
has unfortunately been focused.

The incidence of external-political measures was also greatest
in the dispute phase and next greatest in the second preventive
phase (Phase II). Measures of military and strategic policy
followed the same pattern. Here again the largest proportions of
suggested measures emerged in Phases I and II and tended to
center around deterrence postures and policies. The same was
true of economic and technological measures; that no such
measures could have been appropriate in the simmering, Phase
II stage and very few in subsequent stages (save for those that
merely repeated the desirability of substitutes for bases already

---

[1] It may be convenient to recapitulate that phase structure:

PHASE I	Dispute, pre-hostilities, pre-military
PHASE II	Pre-hostilities, but seen in military terms
PHASE III	Hostilities (Resumed hostilities are designated III$_2$, III$_3$, etc.)
PHASE IV	Post-hostilities, but military option remains
PHASE V	Post-conflict, but dispute remains
S	Settlement of dispute

covered under the military and strategic category) may reflect our lack of expertise or imagination; all that can be said is that they were not obvious to us. However, great-power and related political influence continued to be relevant during hostilities and after.

Much the same was true of internal-political measures: preventive activity, chiefly in the form of building sound socioeconomic bases for effective political governance, outnumbered later action by a significant margin. Save for out-and-out repression, which a strong government can apply any time (and a weak one can try to, usually expediting its own demise), the best time to carry on nation-building is clearly before the nation is engaged in a serious quarrel with another nation or has a genuine insurgency movement on its hands.

Arms and hardware measures (i.e., those most directly bearing on potential arms-control policy), appeared not surprisingly to have more applications early in the conflict process rather than later; by a small margin, specific opportunities for measures of arms control were more numerous in Phase II, when arms build-ups were underway, than in any other phase.

The final conclusions we drew from our list of possible control measures were concerned with the distinction between interstate and internal conflicts. Of the total of 425 measures, 250 were for conflicts of the interstate variety, 175 for those of the internal variety. These appear to be roughly comparable when adjusted for the slight difference between the number of internal and interstate cases analyzed.[2] But if the internal group is boiled down to "pure" subversion insurgencies, there would then be about twice as many measures suggested proportionately for interstate conflicts as for internal. That striking differential might merely show a paucity of imagination. But it may equally show the difficulty of thinking up strategies to deal with internal insurgency-type situations—unfortunately not a new difficulty for the Western mind.

In the arms and hardware measures category, out of the total

---

[2] Eight of the fourteen conflicts studied came to be classified as interstate, six as internal (some with significant external involvement).

of 29 instances-opportunities, across all phases, 20 surfaced for interstate conflicts and only 9 for internal. The numbers of military and strategic opportunities emphasized internal conflict control (26 for interstate, 36 for internal), chiefly because of great-power involvement. Of possible international-organization measures, interstate incidences outnumbered internal by well over two to one (104 to 42), a commentary on the limitations of the international juridical order when it comes to the mounting problems of insurgency and internal defense. Externally sponsored political measures showed almost identical incidence (45 for interstate and 40 for internal).

Economic and technological measures were three to two in favor of interstate (16 to 10). This was doubtless a further reflection of our failure to be more imaginative about the possible relevance of these two types of nonpolitical measures for internal conflicts. But it was also due to the fact that the best time to conceive and initiate economic development and modernization programs is in Phase Minus-One, *before* forces of division and subversion can begin seriously to threaten the internal fabric of inchoate societies.

In the category of policy measures of an internal-political sort, not surprisingly somewhat more incidences emerged for internal conflicts than for interstate (34 to 28). As for measures involving better communications and intelligence, these overwhelmingly (12 to 4) were deemed relevant to interstate conflicts, where there are two "sides" usually willing to get in touch, rather than to internal ones, where passions for total victory run highest.

One of the most profound political ironies of our times is thrown into sharp relief when the theoretical opportunities for conflict control are compared with the opportunities actually seized in these same cases. And though our figures have no profound statistical value, it surely is no coincidence that the *number* of measures of all types actually taken in these cases was roughly *in inverse proportion* to those that, with the benefit of hindsight, might have been taken in pursuit of a purposeful conflict-control strategy: In the dispute phase, 9 measures were actually taken, out of 149 possible; in Phase II also, 9 out of a possible 94; only when violence broke out in Phase III were there real signs of conflict-control activity—31 measures out of 83 "possible" were taken; when hostilities ceased in Phase IV, interest began to flag—14 measures were taken, out of 75 seen by us as possible; and where hostilities were resumed, 11 were taken, out of 25 identified as relevant; furthermore, when it came to shortcomings in preventive arms control, economic, diplomatic, and virtually every other conflict-controlling activity, there was no more than a modest difference between interstate and internal cases.

As for *types* of control measures actually taken, by far the most numerous were in the realms of military and strategic action and UN cognizance (18 and 20 instances each). Not surprisingly, both peaked after hostilities actually broke out. Next was external-political action (16 instances), also focused heavily on the hostilities phases. As for internal-political action, 6 of 12 instances noted were acts of repression by the Portuguese authorities in Angola—policies that in the longer run seem certain to produce more severe conflict. Apart from these, the number of measures taken in the areas of economic aid, arms control, and improvement of communications is insignificant.

The fourteen cases were, as explained earlier, all conflicts, but not all became equally severe or intense. No significant relationship could be deduced between the number of measures actually taken and the inclination of the conflicts to intensify. But it should be emphasized again that most conflict-control effort was made *after* things became too volatile to ignore. In general, conflict-controlling policy activity pursued in the fourteen representative cases of local conflict was almost in inverse proportion to the chances of influencing events.

PART TWO

PART TWO

CHAPTER 4

Learning from Experience: A Technique

It is an axiom of the historian that the crucial characteristics of all events are unique and that the circumstances in which one episode in the human chronicle is imbedded are never duplicated, despite superficial resemblances. Thus, efforts to divine from the past the precise nature of future events are doomed to failure; the detailed structure and timing of a given event defies any but accidental prediction. Even the historians writing of past events cannot fully encompass and describe, let alone account for, all of the elements that came into play.

It is equally axiomatic that, at some level of abstraction, valid generalizations can be made about any class of events, even the most complex. The philosopher deals with such large abstractions as *truth, beauty,* and *the meaning of life*—levels of generalization that seek to encompass all human experience. At a much less global level, the policy planner brings to bear on his problems his understanding of how the events he deals with behave; his understanding can, of course, be arrived at intuitively or systematically. But the planner who would design policy to meet future contingencies is acting on the assumption that there are in human experience discernible patterns that are valid beyond each unique event and at the same time specific enough to be operationally useful.

This chapter sets forth one technique for examining a special class of events: the local conflicts outside Europe since World War II in which armed forces of the Soviet Union and of the United States were not *both* directly involved. Our technique was, of course, designed with the conscious purpose of developing a catalog of policy measures relevant to the control of such local conflicts in the future. The policy implications derived from the application of this technique to recent history have been recorded in Chapter 3; the posture they suggest the United States adopt will be set forth in Chapter 12. Our purpose here is to elaborate the ways in which we used the model of conflict sketched in Chapter 2 to lay the foundations for those policy implications.

We call the series of steps by which we proceeded from the study of past conflicts to an agenda of measures for controlling future conflicts the historic-analytic approach. These steps, in brief, were as follows: (a) to impose on real conflict data the phase structure postulated in our model of conflict; (b) to extract from each phase all identifiable factors deemed to have some relationship to that particular pattern; (c) to specify for each such factor a policy-relevant control measure; and (d) finally to extract from the specific statements of those measures the generalized lesson for future conflict control. This was a systematic way of using the realities and complexities of the real world to generate widely applicable policy insights; it is at many stages highly subjective, hence not "scientific" in the purest meaning of the word. The crucial test—which must be left to the reader—is whether the process has taught us anything useful about conflict and about its control.

STRUCTURING THE DATA

As noted earlier, we began with a total of fifty-four conflicts in the developing world since the end of World War II, all of which had involved a serious threat of violence or actual violence.

From these, fourteen were selected for more intense study. Since we were interested in ensuring that the sample cover as many different types of conflict as possible, we wanted to be sure that certain gross characteristics were adequately represented in the sample.

First of all, we sought to select conflicts with wide geographic distribution. To have selected all the conflicts from one area—say, Latin America—might have raised doubts that the conclusions were valid for conflicts in other regions. Latin America shares some characteristics with the rest of the developing world, but it is Spanish in cultural heritage, has a relatively low incidence of interstate conflict, has since the Monroe Doctrine enjoyed virtual immunity from European intervention, and has fallen for 150 years within the U.S. sphere of influence. Other geographic regions of the world have their own distinguishing characteristics, too. So geographic spread was important if we were to limit the possible bias of "Asianness," or "African-ness," or "Latin American-ness" in our conclusions.

In terms of the kinds of warfare that had taken place in those of our fifty-four which *had* entered hostilities, we wanted to include the two broad types: wars between units of the regular armed forces—so-called conventional warfare; and wars in which one side used irregular units and guerrilla tactics—so-called unconventional warfare. Other conflict characteristics that we wanted to include were internal conflicts, interstate conflicts, and—a common type after World War II—colonial conflicts.

In addition, we wanted cases in our sample that represented different degrees of controllability. Had hostilities dragged on, or were they ended quickly? How intense were they, in terms of the proportion of available forces committed, the geographic spread of the fighting, the kinds of weapons used? And did these features change while the fighting was going on, or did the war begin at a moderate level and stay there irrespective of how long the fighting lasted. Finally, we wanted to look at some conflicts in which at least one of the superpowers was directly involved, some in which the superpower role was indirect, and some in which they remained disengaged.

The fourteen conflicts finally chosen combined the above characteristics in a variety of ways:

(1) *The Indonesian War of Independence, 1945–1949,* was a colonial conflict in Southeast Asia in which hostilities broke out three times before the conflict was finally resolved. The hostilities, which did not intensify, proved hard to terminate. They involved conventional tactics on the part of the Dutch and unconventional (guerrilla) tactics on the part of the Indonesian nationalists.

(2) *The Indonesian-Malaysian Confrontation, 1963–1965,* also took place in Southeast Asia. It was an interstate conflict in which Indonesia employed largely unconventional warfare tactics. Britain, Australia, and New Zealand were also actively involved. In the course of long hostilities there was a marked intensification in the form of a geographic expansion of the conflict.

(3) *The Malayan Emergency, 1948–1960,* was the third Southeast Asian conflict in our sample. There was significant external involvement in this internal conflict, and the guerrilla warfare lasted over ten years but at a very low level.

(4) *The Kashmir Conflict, 1947–1965,* took place in South Asia and was of the conventional, interstate type. In the first round of hostilities in the late 1940's fighting was hard to stop, whereas when fighting broke out again in 1965 it was quickly ended. In both instances the fighting intensified. The latter period of the conflict saw the Chinese become indirectly involved.

(5) *The India-China Border Conflict, 1954–1962,* also in South Asia, was an interstate conflict in which hostilities were fought by conventional tactics. While the fighting covered a fairly long period before it was ended, the hostilities did not intensify. This case was also interesting to us because it interacted with the Indian-Pakistani conflict over Kashmir. It was therefore possible to see in some detail the way in which one conflict affected the course of another.

(6) *The Bay of Pigs, 1960–1961,* was the only Latin American conflict on which a detailed case study was made. That conflict can be viewed either as an interstate conflict between the United States and Cuba, in which the Cuban exiles were U.S. pawns, or as an internal conflict among Cubans, which the United States exploited for its own ends. In either event, the U.S. role was clearly that of conflict fomenter. The hostilities ended quickly, without intensifying.

(7) *The Algerian-Moroccan Conflict, 1962–1963,* was selected as a North African example. This interstate border clash involved the use of regular armed forces in hostilities that ended quickly and with no intensification.

(8) *The Somalian-Ethiopian-Kenyan Conflict, 1960–1964,* is one of the sub-Saharan African cases in our selection. Again it can be viewed as two internal conflicts—in Ethiopia and in Kenya between Somali-speaking minorities and the governments —that were exploited by an external power, Somalia, and led ultimately to armed clashes across interstate boundaries between units of the regular armed forces. The internal aspects of the conflict were fought by unconventional guerrilla tactics, the interstate aspects by conventional military tactics. The internal wars have proved hard to terminate, whereas the interstate hostilities ended quickly. But both remained moderate.

(9) *The Angola Conflict, 1950–1961,* is a sub-Saharan colonial conflict that has broad racial implications as well. The hostilities that have broken out on several occasions between Portugal and black Angolan nationalists have been low-level guerrilla warfare in nature and have been terminated relatively quickly.

(10) *The Soviet-Iranian Conflict, 1941–1947,* was selected as one of the Middle Eastern cases in our sample. It, too, combined internal and interstate features—an internal struggle between the central government and the Azerbaijani separatists that took place within the larger context of a Soviet-Iranian conflict. The hostilities that occurred involved conventional military tactics; they were low-level and very short-lived.

(11) *The Arab-Israeli Conflict, 1956–1967,* refers to the

continuing Middle Eastern conflict that erupted into open interstate warfare in 1948, in 1956, and again in 1967. We looked
at the conflict beginning with the period leading up to the 1956
war and continuing through the 1967 war. In both cases
hostilities ended quickly. In 1956 fighting intensified with the
entry of additional states into the war (France and Britain); in
1967 the war spread geographically to include the Israeli-
Jordan and Israeli-Syrian fronts as well as the Israeli-Egyptian
front.

(12) *The Suez (or British-French-Egyptian) Conflict, 1956,*
was selected as a separate case for study but was analyzed
together with the Arab-Israeli Conflict just described, from
which it grew and to which it contributed. The combined
conflicts are analyzed here (see Chapter 9) under the broader
heading Conflict in the Middle East. The hostilities of 1956
were common to both conflicts, but the courses of the two
conflicts, both before and after that event, were markedly
different.

(13) *The Greek Insurgency, 1944–1949,* took place on
continental Europe. One of our major interests in this case was
the uncanny resemblance it has to the war in Vietnam. For this
reason, we included it in our sample even though our main
interest was not in European conflict. The conflict involved two
hostilities phases, the first of them a short, urban guerrilla
uprising, the second a long guerrilla war that saw the hostilities
intensify on several occasions, ending with the guerrillas attempting a conventional military campaign.

(14) *The Conflict on Cyprus, 1952–1964,* took place, along
with the Greek Insurgency, in the eastern Mediterranean. The
first part of the conflict was a colonial struggle to oust the
British; then, once independence had been achieved, internal
communal tensions on the island, which had been an important
subtheme during the earlier parts of the conflict, became the
predominant theme in a new round of hostilities. The first
hostilities (1952–1960) were drawn out and intensified from
urban terrorism to guerrilla warfare in the countryside; the

second round of fighting (1960–1964) began at a more intense level but did not further intensify and was quickly ended.

For each of these fourteen cases a chronological history was prepared and our conflict model was imposed on it. The phases of that model were outlined in Chapter 2 (see p. 16).

Our objective in examining this historical record was neither to develop new information nor to write exhaustive histories. It was rather to identify in each case the phase structure and the points of transition from one phase to another. To prepare our chronological histories we relied almost exclusively on secondary sources, though in the case of the Greek Insurgency we used a single secondary source as a substitute for preparing our own narrative account. For the other thirteen cases, no single previous study proved sufficiently comprehensive for our needs. Most histories of these conflicts deal almost exclusively with their political and diplomatic aspects, to the virtual exclusion of the military side of their story.

On the whole, it was possible to identify with considerable precision the points of transition that marked the entry of a conflict into a new phase. As might be expected, the most difficult transition to locate was that into Phase II (when a conflict was generated by the introduction of a military option). At times the beginning of Phase II was clearly visible, as when Soviet troops occupied northern Iran during World War II and placed Soviet military power in a position to influence directly the longstanding Soviet-Iranian dispute; in some cases there was widespread agreement on the actual date—such as when the United States in the Bay of Pigs conflict began to equip itself with a proxy military option in its dispute with Castro's Cuba; other transitions to Phase II were marked by the sudden capacity to use force that already existed—for example, when the Somali Republic became independent and thus acquired the capacity to employ force in its drive to unify the Somali-speaking peoples of the Horn of Africa. In most cases, however, the point of transition from dispute to conflict was more problematical. One could find a period of, say, several months, before which the dispute was clearly still in Phase I but after which it emerged as a Phase II conflict.

Transitions to later phases were more readily pinpointed. Certainly hostilities were usually highly visible. Even here, however, there could be difficulty. It is a matter of judgment at what point in 1947 the mounting crescendo of violence in Kashmir by Pathan tribesmen and among Kashmiris should be said to have involved Indian-Pakistani hostilities. And how low a level did hostilities in a situation such as the Malayan Emergency have to reach before one could have considered Phase III at an end?

In some cases it was possible to refine the process by dividing phases into sub-phases in which the conflict moved perceptibly toward a transition. The decision of the United States to recruit and equip a force of exiled Cubans in order to have the option of using them against Castro marked the transition of the U.S.–Cuban dispute to the pre-hostilities Phase II. The later decision to exercise that option, on the other hand, was a major step *within* Phase II toward the actual outbreak of hostilities, that is, when the forces landed on the beaches of the ill-famed Bay of Pigs.

Similarly, in the hostilities phase (Phase III) it was sometimes possible to identify intensifications and moderations of the hostilities—that is, points at which there were changes in the "rules of the game" governing the conduct and limitations of hostilities. Illustrative here were the successive extensions of hostilities in Kashmir in 1965 from clashes within Indian-controlled portions of Kashmir between infiltrating irregulars and Indian forces, to clashes across the 1949 cease-fire line between Indian and Pakistani regulars, to invasions across the fixed international boundary between the two states.

Once the phases and sub-phases had been determined, each was searched for factors that appeared to have had an effect, however slight, on the course the conflict took. These factors were seen as events, perceptions, or conditions of an economic, political, diplomatic, or military nature.

DERIVING MEASURES

It was not enough merely to identify a list of factors for each phase (or sub-phase) of each case. These factors håd to be further grouped in terms of their relationship to a given control objective; it will be recalled that one insight we earlier derived from our model was that what "controlling the conflict" means can differ from phase to phase. The phases and their appropriate control objectives can be stated as follows:

In PHASE I	To Settle the Dispute
	To Keep the Dispute Nonmilitary
In PHASE II	To Settle the Dispute
	To Prevent the Outbreak of Hostilities
	To Restrict the Scale/Scope of Potential Hostilities
In PHASE III	To Settle the Dispute
	To Terminate Hostilities
	To Moderate Hostilities
In PHASE IV	To Settle the Dispute
	To Prevent the Resumption of Hostilities
	To Restrict the Scale/Scope of Potential Hostilities
In PHASE V	To Settle the Dispute
	To Keep the Dispute Nonmilitary

It was essential to our method of analysis that the factors not just be identified but also be defined in terms of supporting the accomplishment of a control objective or of making that goal more difficult to achieve.

This task in our analysis made clear one of the central problems of conflict control: The control objectives both within phases and among phases are not necessarily compatible; furthermore, there is no consistent pattern of goals that are more or less likely to be compatible. Let us clarify these basic but complex assertions by a few illustrations. In Phase III of the Bay of Pigs conflict, the invasion by the exile forces was quickly contained by Castro's forces. For the United States, whatever pressures existed to continue the hostilities were also, in those circumstances, pressures to intensify the fighting by the direct commitment of U.S. forces. In this case, therefore, the control objectives of terminating the hostilities and of keeping them moderate were compatible. Or, put more generally, the factors tending to moderate hostilities coincided with or complemented those tending toward termination. On the contrary, in the Greek Insurgency and Malayan Emergency, and perhaps latterly in Vietnam, the goal of speedy termination of hostilities tended to be antithetical to the goal of moderating them. In Malaya, the Malayan and British authorities elected to keep their military response to the guerrilla challenge relatively low-level, and the guerrillas themselves were unable to intensify their operations. But, in part as a result, the war dragged on for a decade. In Greece, on the other hand, both sides repeatedly intensified the hostilities—each in an effort to terminate the war by winning it.

Similar incompatibilities are found within other phases. Within Phases II and IV, for example, the control objective of preventing the outbreak or resumption of hostilities may be at odds with the control objective of keeping future hostilities moderate if they nonetheless occur. This dilemma is particularly evident where arms levels are raised in Phases II and IV in an effort to secure "peace" by maintaining military "balance" or a "deterrent" posture.

Once all the factors that could be identified were classified in terms of their bearing—positive or negative—on a given control objective, it was possible to ask what types of policy activity might have served to reinforce conflict-controlling factors or to offset conflict-promoting factors. Here the only limit to the numbers and types of measure identified was our imagination.

It must be stressed that it was each separate factor that we were looking at, not the conflict as a whole. In other words, our initial question was not, for example: What measures would have been required to control the Indonesian War of Independence? The question was rather: If a lack of strong control authority over various paramilitary formations in Indonesia was pushing the conflict toward hostilities, what kinds of measures would have been relevant to offset that pressure? These measures might have included steps to strengthen the central government's position as well as steps to neutralize or counter the impact a lack of authority was having on the conflict.

There are cases in which the time perspective with which the problem of control is viewed can influence the control measures that suggest themselves. In a conflict such as that in Angola, for example, one set of measures (efficient and ruthless Portuguese suppression of Angolan nationalists) might have seemed effective for dealing with immediate threat, whereas a completely different set (accommodation to demands for liberalization and eventual independence) might have been far more appropriate to the longer-run goal of settling the dispute. The policy dilemma becomes even more acute when the likelihood is recognized that this latter course might have itself been conflict promoting in the short run. We feel it is important to make this dilemma clear.

Because the only objective considered was conflict control, other policy objectives were ignored. The result of tagging each separate factor with a policy measure was that at times the measures were inconsistent when read in sequence. Rather than seeking to discuss control of the whole conflict, our focus was only on measures offsetting or reinforcing each specific factor.

We realize that the individual policy activities or measures identified by this method as relevant may have been quite unachievable in the actual context of the conflict or may have been achievable only within a time span that made them unlikely to have the desired effect quickly enough. But our over-all purpose was to develop insight into the potentials as well as the problems and dilemmas of controlling future local conflicts. While some ot our specific measures may thus appear inapplicable or even bizarre in isolation, developing them in this manner was not wholly unrealistic. In reality, goals often do conflict, steps taken to achieve one objective often do have undesired side consequences, and things that might have been righted a generation ago often turn out to be generators of today's troubles.

In the five chapters that follow, illustrations are given of the application of this technique to five of our fourteen cases of recent local conflict. The conflict-control lessons derived from these five cases are contained in Chapter 10.

CHAPTER 5

The Soviet-Iranian Conflict, 1941-1947[1]

THE PHASES OF CONFLICT

PHASE I   *Background of the Conflict*

During the century and a half preceding World War I, Iran was a battleground, virtually passive itself, on which the imperial struggles of the great powers were carried out. Russia and Britain were the constant factors: Russian policy had traditionally been to expand toward the Dardanelles, Turkey, and the Middle East; British policy had traditionally focused on Iran as a protective buffer for India and on the preservation of economic advantages gained in Iran during the struggle against Russian expansion.

Previous Soviet-Iranian Conflicts

In 1920 the Red Army regained control in Georgia, Armenia, and Azerbaijan, three parts of Russia that had proclaimed their independence at the time of the Bolshevik revolution. Large numbers of refugees fled to Turkey and Iran, including many who left Soviet Azerbaijan to take refuge in the Iranian province of Azerbaijan.[2]

---

[1] The authors wish to acknowledge the contributions to this chapter of Mrs. Jane K. Holland and Miss Priscilla A. Clapp.

[2] George Lenczowski: *Russia and the West in Iran, 1918–1948: A Study in Big-Power Rivalry* (Ithaca: Cornell University Press; 1949), p. 26. The author was with the Polish Legation in Iran from 1942 to 1945.

At the same time, the Soviets gave significant military aid to several local rebel governments established in northern Iran—broadly speaking, in the same area that was to be involved in the 1941–1947 Soviet-Iranian Conflict. In May 1920 the Soviet fleet bombarded the Iranian port of Enzeli on the Caspian as the Red Army pursued remnants of the White Russian army under British protection there. A Soviet expeditionary force, composed of regular Red Army units, sailors from Kronstadt,

Soviet Azerbaijani troops, and armed Persian oil workers from Baku, soon occupied most of the coastal Iranian province of Gilan. The Soviets alleged that this was a security measure undertaken by the independent Soviet Republic of Azerbaijan, over whose actions and policies Moscow had no influence.[3] In 1921 the Soviet Republic of Gilan, with the support of Soviet advisers and troops, launched an unsuccessful attack on Tehran. Following the failure of this effort, the Soviets withdrew aid from Gilan, and Iran easily regained control of that territory. After this period of semi-open conflict, Soviet-Iranian relations became relatively stabilized.

A treaty that was to play a role in the 1941–1947 conflict was concluded between Iran and the Soviet Union in 1921, "a genuine 'leave-me-alone' treaty made by two very weak nations on the defensive who were both anxious to have time to recuperate."[4] Each nation agreed to prohibit activity on its territory by groups that had designs on the other. A key provision stated that if a third party attempted armed intervention in Iran or sought to use Iranian territory as a base of operations against any of the Soviet republics and if the Iranian government were not able to deal with the situation, the Soviets would have the right to move their troops into the Iranian interior.[5]

The long history of the Russian threat to Iranian territorial integrity and of Iranian suspicion of Russia was fortified by the many differences between the two societies. The Moslem clergy and the devout in general in Iran were anti-Communist; the difficulties faced by Moslems inside the Soviet Union increased this feeling. During World War II the left-wing Tudeh ("masses") party gained considerable strength in Iran, appealing to some real grievances and supported by many liberal intellectuals. The Tudeh lost strength, however, as its connection with the Soviet Union became clearer and as Soviet and Iranian national aims came into direct conflict.

---

[3] Ibid., pp. 52–3, 59.
[4] Richard W. Van Wagenen, in consultation with T. Cuyler Young: *The Iranian Case 1946* (New York: Carnegie Endowment for International Peace; 1952), p. 10.   [5] Ibid., pp. 10–11.

Geographic and Physical Factors

The Iranian province of Azerbaijan, focus of the 1941–1947 conflict, borders on the Soviet Union. Tabriz, the provincial capital, is only sixty miles from the Soviet Union. The border area is mountainous and difficult, but crossed by well-developed railways and paved roads built as lend-lease supply routes during World War II. Natural barriers between Azerbaijan and the rest of Iran do not offer serious obstacles to military movement, at least on a limited scale. The geography and terrain of the area thus offered no real advantages to either party in the conflict.

PHASE II   *August 1941–August 1945*

Britain and the Soviet Union occupied Iran in August 1941 to prevent its falling under pro-German control. The Soviets occupied the northern provinces (including Azerbaijan), and the British the larger southern and central regions, with a neutral zone including Tehran in the middle. In January 1942 the situation was formalized in a tripartite treaty among Britain, the Soviet Union, and Iran, in which Britain and the Soviet Union promised to withdraw their forces no later than six months after the end of all hostilities. It was also agreed that the occupying forces were to disturb as little as possible the internal affairs of Iran.[6]

Subsequently, U.S. forces also entered Iran to help move lend-lease shipments to the Soviet Union. The United States never formally became a party to the tripartite agreement but informally operated under its provisions. At the Tehran Big Three meeting in November 1943 the Soviet Union, the United States, and Britain signed a Declaration on Iran which reaffirmed Iran's independence, sovereignty, and territorial integrity.[7]

---

[6] *U.S. Army Area Handbook for Iran* (Washington: Department of the Army; 1963), pp. 174–5.   [7] Ibid., p. 176.

Soviet Wartime Pressures

The exact time is not clear at which the Soviet Union began to perceive that its occupying military force would be useful in achieving its postwar objectives in Iran. While the occasion for the introduction of Soviet forces into Iran arose from broad requirements of World War II strategy, the Soviets quickly began to exert pressures directly and indirectly on internal Iranian politics. For example, the Tudeh, formed in January 1942 as a legal political party, had a hard core of Moscow-trained leaders. The party played a major role in Tehran politics as well as in the attempted communization of Azerbaijan.[8] The Soviet military presence thus provided a shield for the development of a Communist movement which the Soviets sought to use to influence and possibly eventually control the government of all Iran.

In October 1944 the Soviet Union made broad and vague demands for an oil concession in the five northern provinces of Iran. Iranian Premier Mohammad Saed Maragnej announced that no concessions would be granted to any foreign parties until after the war. The Soviets, however, were able to keep up sufficient pressure, through the Tudeh and a press campaign, so that Premier Saed finally had to resign. The Soviet demands were not dropped until the Iranian national assembly, the Majles, passed a law making it a crime for any government official to enter any negotiations with any foreign government or oil company.[9]

---

[8] During the wartime period, Iranian political life reflected the lifting of restrictions on political activity. Politics became a crazy quilt of parties and interest groups, with a rapid turnover of governments. With the exception of the Tudeh, however, all political parties were in agreement on the objective of regaining complete control of all the territory of Iran and on the complete evacuation of Soviet troops.

[9] Benjamin Shwadran: *The Middle East, Oil and the Great Powers* (2nd edn. rev.; New York: Council for Middle Eastern Affairs Press; 1959), pp. 65–7.

Iranian Reactions

During World War II the Iranians were concerned that the Soviets were using their position as an occupying power to pursue their long-term goals vis-à-vis Iran. The Iranians responded to Soviet pressure by utilizing the U.S. military mission in an advisory capacity to reorganize and strengthen their army and gendarmerie. With this U.S. aid, the Iranian gendarmerie became an efficient force "whose loyalty to the government often proved to be of decisive significance. . . . The calm and determined attitude of the gendarmerie at the time of the Azerbaijan crisis in 1945–1946 . . . prevented panic and riots in the capital at a most critical moment."[1]

The Iranian army was generally loyal to the institution of the monarchy, although there was some infiltration by the Tudeh.[2] Iranian Chief of Staff General Hassan Arfa states that the army consisted of about 100,000 men (though this may be an exaggeration). There was some local production of small arms and ammunition (before the war, at least), and the Iranian forces had some modern offensive weaponry.

During the wartime occupation, the over-all military balance in Iran between Iranian and Soviet forces was overwhelmingly in favor of the Soviets. Before March 2, 1946, there was reported to be in Iran a "garrison force" of about three Soviet divisions—one infantry and two cavalry—with supporting armor.[3] The Soviets had a barracks area in Tabriz and presum-

---

[1] Lenczowski, op. cit., p. 304.

[2] Hassan Arfa: *Under Five Shahs* (London: John Murray; 1964), p. 354. General Arfa, Iranian Chief of Staff until February 1946, claims to have uncovered a plot for a military rising in Tehran late in 1945, in which between fifty and one hundred subversive officers were involved; he also states that the defense of Tehran was complicated for him because of "Communist secret agents, whose presence was suspected within the General Staff itself." There was also some defection to the forces of the Azerbaijani army during the course of the conflict.

[3] Robert Rossow, Jr.: "The Battle of Azerbaijan, 1946," *Middle East Journal,* Vol. X, No. 1 (Winter 1946), p. 19. Rossow was U.S. Consul in Tabriz December 1945–July 1946, then chief of the political section of the U.S. embassy in Tehran until January 1947.

ably facilities for maintenance of their military equipment. All this personnel and matériel was brought in openly as part of the wartime occupation. (See the WEAPONS section of this chapter for details.)

British military posture in the Middle East, while weakened as a result of war exhaustion, was of a continuing nature. The British were still in India and Egypt and had bases in Aden, Kuwait, and Bahrein; they also had effective control of the Jordanian and Iraqi armies. Whereas the Iranians needed British support against the Soviets, they regarded it, however, as something of a Trojan horse. Suspicion of British motives was widespread and it was feared that Britain and the Soviet Union would divide Iran between themselves.[4]

Iran's important relationship with the United States began during World War II as an outgrowth of the presence of the Persian Gulf Command forces in Iran. U.S. backing of Iran was not vigorous in the early days of the conflict, although the Iranian ambassador seems to have had no difficulty in being heard in Washington.[5]

The End of the War in Europe

With the end of the war in Europe, Iran made repeated and unsuccessful efforts to persuade the Soviet Union to cease interfering in internal Iranian politics and asked the British and the Soviets to withdraw altogether. In reply, both the British and Soviets pointed out that they were not legally obliged to leave before the agreed deadline—six months after the end of hostilities. In the spring of 1945, however, the British did begin partial withdrawal and fruitlessly sought Soviet agreement for simultaneous action. The Soviets refused, but did agree to the early evacuation of the Tehran area. The Tehran evacuation began on August 7, 1945, but the Soviets replaced their uniformed troops with NKVD plainclothesmen, estimated at several thousand. Thus the possibility of Soviet military action in

[4] Nasrollah Saifpour Fatemi: *Oil Diplomacy: Powderkeg in Iran* (New York: Whittier Books; 1954), p. xv.   [5] Ibid., pp. 270, 279 *ff*.

the capital remained.[6] Soviet propaganda pressure on Iran
increased during this period, and the activities of Soviet agents
among the tribes and among the Iranian army officers stationed
in provinces under Soviet control led, in mid-August, to violent
disturbances in Khorasan and Azerbaijan. The Iranian army put
down the revolt in Khorasan, but was not so successful in
Azerbaijan.[7]

PHASE III₁   *August 26–December 12, 1945*

On August 26, 1945, the Tudeh temporarily took control of
Tabriz, capital of Azerbaijan. The armed partisans

> under the protection of the Russian soldiers . . . first occupied the
> police department, opened the doors of the prison cells and freed
> all the criminals and convicts. Communication between Teheran
> and Azerbaijan was cut. The garrison of Tabriz was kept in its
> barracks by the Red army and the gendarmerie was not allowed to
> leave its headquarters.[8]

Despite Soviet assistance, the Tudeh coup failed to achieve
its goals. One analyst describes the events as follows:

> During the coup d'etat at Tabriz, the Communist force had shown
> confusion, inexperience, incompetence and lack of discipline. When
> they had failed to fulfill their mission, everything had to be con-
> ducted by the Soviet soldiers and officers and this had put the
> Russians in a difficult position.[9]

Within several days, the rebel movement unilaterally relin-
quished the gains it had achieved, evacuated the few buildings it
had seized, reestablished communications with Tehran, and,
officially at least, restored authority to the local governor.

In October 1945 the Tudeh in Azerbaijan was renamed the
Democratic Party of Azerbaijan, with the intention of dissociat-
ing the national Tudeh party from any actions in Azerbaijan.

[6] Lenczowski, op. cit., p. 285.
[7] Ibid., p. 286.   [8] Fatemi, op. cit., p. 265.
[9] Paul E. Weaver: "The Soviet-Iranian Affairs, 1945–1946," master's
thesis, Georgetown University, 1951, pp. 41–2; Fatemi, op. cit., p. 266.

On October 23 several new divisions of the Red Army entered Iran. Meanwhile, the Soviet counsul general in Tabriz was masterminding preparation for the actual rebellion, in which the shortcomings of the abortive August coup would be overcome. He exercised his control through an apparatus of town commandants, military personnel obedient to the political rather than the military command. The rebels were covertly organized and a number of *muhajirs* (refugees) from Soviet Azerbaijan joined them. "On November 15, 1945, the Soviets began the wholesale distribution of arms to the rebels and on the following day a carefully planned revolutionary operation was launched."[1]

The central government sent a relief column north, but it was turned back without a fight by the Soviets on November 20.[2] The Iranian garrison in Tabriz was surrounded by the rebels and eventually surrendered without fighting; the commander of the garrison, who was sent back to Tehran, reported that "the Iranian soldiers, numbering 900, had been surrounded by ten thousand Russian troops and by the Democrats armed with machine guns, who had occupied all the hills around the barracks."[3] General fighting continued for several weeks, until on December 12, 1945, the Autonomous Republic of Azerbaijan was proclaimed in Tabriz.

The Soviets obstructed all movements of the Iranian army or gendarmerie against the rebels, protected all activities of the rebel forces by their own military presence, and intimidated the population by various means.[4] The Soviets also played on Kurdish nationalism and complicated the problem for the Iranians by sponsoring the Kurdish People's Republic of Mahabad.[5] The Republic of Mahabad was geographically contiguous with

---

[1] Rossow, op. cit., p. 18.   [2] Ibid.   [3] Fatemi, op. cit., p. 278.
[4] Lenczowski, op. cit., p. 288.
[5] The People's Republic of Mahabad declared its independence of Tehran in December 1945 and was not reoccupied by the central government until a year later. The Soviets were said to have promised the Kurds planes, tanks, and heavy weapons and to have taken some fifty Kurds to Baku for military and political training; but all that materialized was Soviet pressure on reluctant Kurdish tribesmen to fight for the rebel republic.

the Republic of Azerbaijan and entered an alliance with it, although there was continuous friction between the two rebel regimes.[6]

Altogether, the Iranians directed twenty-four notes of protest to the Soviet embassy in Tehran between May 2 and November 23, 1945. The Soviet ambassador to Iran, however, absented himself from Tehran during the November uprising in Azerbaijan, and the Soviet chargé d'affaires professed complete ignorance of the rebellion.[7]

The question of evacuation of troops was discussed without effect at the London Big Four Foreign Ministers' meeting in September–October 1945. In November, after the rebellion had broken out, the Iranian ambassador in Washington brought the question to President Harry S Truman's attention and publicly accused the Soviet Union of engineering the revolt in Azerbaijan.[8] The United States and Britain sent parallel notes to the Soviet Union proposing the withdrawal of all foreign troops by January 1946. In reply, the Soviet Union denied that it had interfered with the movement of Iranian troops already in Azerbaijan and claimed that the introduction of further Iranian troops would have increased rather than calmed disturbances in the province, thus necessitating the introduction of further Soviet troops.[9]

PHASE IV[1]   *December 12, 1945–December 10, 1946*

Except for minor and transitory episodes, hostilities did not break out again between Iranian and Soviet or Soviet-sponsored rebel forces for almost a year. This year can be divided into several distinct sub-phases.

---

[6] Archie Roosevelt, Jr.: "The Kurdish Republic of Mahabad," *Middle East Journal*, Vol. I, No. 3 (July 1947), pp. 247–69. Roosevelt was U.S. Assistant Military Attaché in Tehran from March 1946 to February 1947.   [7] Weaver, op. cit., p. 93.   [8] Fatemi, op. cit., p. 270.

[9] Raymond Dennett and Robert K. Turner, eds.: *Documents on American Foreign Relations* (Princeton: Princeton University Press; 1948), Vol. VIII (July 1, 1945–December 31, 1946), pp. 851–3.

Sub-Phase A: December 12, 1945–March 2, 1946

This was a period of relatively little military activity, considerable diplomatic activity, and a general hardening of positions. The government of the Autonomous Republic of Azerbaijan consolidated its control over the province, pursuing a dual policy of popular reforms (such as land redistribution and use of the Turkish language in the administration and in schools) and police-state terror methods of control. The new government was composed of men who were strongly linked to the Soviets or directly imported from the Soviet Union.

The Soviets made a serious effort to develop the Azerbaijani army. The Red Army uniform was used, the training of the new army was entrusted to Soviet officers, and the army cadres were heavily infiltrated by Soviet agents.[1] One observer describes the objective as:

a tough little Azerbaijani army, intended to provide a backbone for the mass of Communist irregulars who had pulled off the revolt. . . . The basic weapon was a sub-machine gun of Czech manufacture, and the Russians later added a number of light tanks and artillery. Several hundred officer candidates were taken to military bases in Soviet Azerbaijan . . . for intensive training in artillery, armor, aviation, and chemical warfare. Soviet officers and troops could be seen almost daily in the training grounds just beyond the Tabriz barracks area carrying out joint maneuvers with Azerbaijani forces and training them in the use of Soviet heavy artillery, rocket launchers, and heavy armor.[2]

In December 1945, at the Allied Foreign Ministers' meeting in Moscow, U.S. Secretary of State James Byrnes told Stalin that unless the Tehran Declaration on Iran were honored, Iran would probably place its complaint before the United Nations and that, as a signatory of the Declaration, the United States would feel obliged to support Iran's right to be heard.

In response to this,

[1] Lenczowski, op. cit., p. 290; Fatemi, op. cit., p. 277.
[2] Rossow, op. cit., p. 25.

Stalin outlined what he termed the "pertinent facts" in the matter. The Baku oil fields in the south of Russia lay close to the border and this created a special problem. These fields had to be safeguarded against any possible hostile action by Iran against the Soviet Union, and no confidence could be placed in the Iranian Government. Saboteurs might be sent to the Baku oil fields to set them on fire, he continued. Since the Soviet Union had a right, by treaty, to maintain troops in Iran until March 15 [1946], it did not want to withdraw before that date. At that time, he said, it would be necessary to examine the situation and see whether or not it was possible to evacuate the soldiers. That decision would depend upon the conduct of the Iranian Government. He pointed out that the 1921 treaty with Iran gave the Soviet Union the right to send troops into northern Iran if there was a possible danger from an outside source.[3]

This statement by Stalin is perhaps the best official definition of the Soviet claims. The Soviets relied on the terms of the 1942 tripartite treaty as a basis for refusing to evacuate before March 1946, and on the terms of the 1921 treaty, combined with alleged danger to the Baku oil fields, as a basis for a possible refusal to withdraw after the March deadline.

Despite the failure of the Moscow Foreign Ministers' conference in December 1945, all U.S. troops were withdrawn from Iran by January 1, 1946.[4] The British did not complete their evacuation until the date prescribed by the 1942 treaty, but their remaining forces were not large.

On January 19, 1946, the Iranian government (then under Premier Ebrahim Hakimi) lodged its first complaint with the UN Security Council: "Owing to the interference of the Soviet Union, through the medium of its officials and armed forces, in the internal affairs of Iran, a situation has arisen which may lead to international friction."[5] The Soviet representative at the UN denied the truth of the Iranian complaint and attempted to present the issue as a purely Soviet-Iranian matter, appropri-

---

[3] James F. Byrnes: *Speaking Frankly* (New York: Harper; 1947), p. 119.
[4] Dennett and Turner, op. cit., pp. 851–2. On November 24 the United States announced that the order had been given for complete evacuation by January 1, 1946; there is no evidence that any U.S. forces remained after that date.   [5] Van Wagenen, op. cit., p. 111.

ate for bilateral negotiations rather than international consideration.[6] The United States and Britain, while supporting Iran, were reluctant to take an extreme position, and the Security Council finally passed a resolution calling on the parties to negotiate (but did not drop the complaint from its agenda).[7]

The Soviets kept up their pressure on the Iranian government, including severing all trade between Azerbaijan and the rest of Iran. According to one analyst, "the economic strain thus created was intolerable."[8] In the face of this and other pressure, there was a cabinet crisis in Iran while the Security Council debate was taking place, and Premier Hakimi was replaced by Premier Ahmad Qavam, "known for his flirtation with the Tudeh."[9] Qavam took several steps directed at propitiating the Soviets, such as arresting General Hassan Arfa, who was considered pro-British. Qavam then went to Moscow for negotiations on February 19, 1946. The negotiations were not successful. The Soviets made extreme demands: for instance, that Soviet troops continue to stay in some parts of Iran for an indefinite period and that the Iranians agree to an Iranian-Soviet joint-stock oil company, 51 per cent Soviet-owned.[1] During this period the Iranians received assurances of U.S. and British support.

Sub-Phase B: March 2–25, 1946

This was the peak of the conflict, in terms of the threat to general international peace. It was dominated by military developments, even though no actual fighting took place. The Soviets did not evacuate on March 2 and thus unambiguously violated the 1942 treaty. At this point the other party to the treaty (Britain) and the other parties to the Tehran Declaration (Britain and the United States) were drawn actively into the conflict. The United States and Britain both sent notes of protest.

[6] Ibid., pp. 32, 36; Fatemi, op. cit., p. 276.
[7] Van Wagenen, op. cit., pp. 30–41.   [8] Lenczowski, op. cit., p. 295.
[9] Ibid.   [1] Ibid., p. 296.

After March 2 the U.S. government began receiving reports from Tabriz of a massive Soviet military build-up in the province. According to the U.S. consul in Tabriz,[2] the movements consisted almost entirely of armor and motorized infantry with supporting artillery; at least fifteen armored brigades, composed of some five hundred tanks with appropriate auxiliary forces, were brought in, in a massive, sudden, offensive build-up. According to a report from Tehran dated March 22, a "responsible" source said official estimates of Soviet strength in northern Iran had reached nearly 100,000.[3]

The new troops were divided into three assault forces and one reserve. One assault force was deployed in a manner to menace Tehran, and the other two were directed toward Turkey and Iraq. While introducing this major offensive force into Azerbaijan, the Soviets simultaneously moved another armored force through eastern Bulgaria, deploying it along the frontier of Turkey-in-Europe. They concurrently opened a diplomatic and propaganda offensive against Turkey, while the Kurdish People's Republic of Mahabad proclaimed rights of sovereignty over the Turkish Kurds.[4]

On March 9 the United States sent another protest to the Soviet Union,[5] and in British and American newspapers during the weeks that followed there were daily headlines and front-page reports on the Soviet-Iranian situation. One account speculated:

The seizure of Iranian Azerbaijan and northern Kurdistan and the extraction of various concessions from Iran were the primary Soviet goals. Now it seems clear that these are only subordinate means toward a far larger end—the reduction of Turkey, the main bastion against Soviet advance into the entire Middle East.[6]

As far as can be determined, neither Britain nor the United

[2] Rossow, op. cit., p. 20; Peter Lisagor and Marguerite Higgins: *Overtime in Heaven: Adventures in the Foreign Service* (New York: Doubleday; 1964), pp. 156–8.
[3] *The New York Times,* March 25, 1946.   [4] Rossow, op. cit., p. 21.
[5] *U.S. Department of State Bulletin,* March 17, 1946, p. 435.
[6] Rossow, op. cit., p. 21.

States threatened a direct military response.[7] During March, however, the U.S. battleship *Missouri* was sent to Istanbul with the remains of the Turkish Ambassador Mehmetmunir Ertegon, who died March 7, 1946. According to military analyst Hanson Baldwin, this cruise was a response to the Soviet build-up in Iran; Baldwin also reported that plans to send the entire Eighth (*sic;* there *was* no "Eighth" Fleet) Fleet on a Mediterranean cruise were cancelled at the instigation of the U.S. State Department, which decided that such a sizable force might be interpreted as unnecessarily provocative.[8]

Iranian Premier Qavam returned from negotiations in Moscow shortly before March 14, the last day of the term of the Majles. Since a law had been passed the year before that no new Majles could be elected while foreign troops were still in the country and since Tudeh-sponsored demonstrations prevented a quorum from entering the parliament building until after the date had passed when any action could be taken, Premier Qavam became the virtual dictator[9] and remained so until elections were held the following January.

Premier Qavam remained silent when the Soviets poured in additional offensive forces and when the Soviets on March 16 warned Iran that resistance "might prove calamitous to her existence."[1] A complete Soviet take-over looked imminent. The U.S. ambassador in Tehran told Qavam that if he did not submit the case to the Security Council, the United States would do so itself. "As a result of the American activities in Teheran and the pressure on the part of the Shah on March 17, Qavam decided to refer the Iranian case to the Security Council."[2]

On March 18 the second Iranian complaint was lodged at the

[7] In a news conference in 1952, President Truman referred to an "ultimatum" he had sent Stalin during the Iranian crisis, giving him a "day certain in which they were to get out . . . or we would put some more people in there." *The New York Times,* April 25, 1952. No available evidence makes it possible to confirm or refute the existence of such an ultimatum.   [8] *The New York Times,* March 18, 1946.

[9] Lenczowski, op. cit., p. 297.

[1] Fatemi, op. cit., p. 300.   [2] Ibid., p. 301.

Security Council,[3] and Iran requested that it be put on the agenda of the next regularly scheduled council meeting, March 25. The United States supported the Iranian position. The Soviet Union requested that the meeting be postponed until April 10, on the grounds that negotiations with Iran were continuing. On March 24, the day before the meeting was to take place, Moscow announced that all Soviet troops would be evacuated within six weeks, "if no unforeseen circumstances occur."[4] This announcement marked the end of the most acute period of the conflict.

Sub-Phase C: March 25–May 10, 1946

The Moscow announcement of March 24 was greeted with considerable skepticism. The Security Council met as scheduled and included the Iranian question on its agenda despite Soviet opposition. "In essence this represented more a vote of no confidence in the USSR than any positive knowledge of the actual situation."[5] The council then had to choose between several possible courses of action: delay debate until April 10, as the Soviet Union requested; delay until further information in writing from Iran had been received;[6] or immediately hear the Iranian representative. On March 27 the council rejected a Soviet motion to postpone discussion, whereupon the Soviet delegation, led by Andrei Gromyko, walked out.[7] After continued debate, the council on April 4 deferred further proceedings until May 6, when both Iran and the Soviet Union were requested to report to the council as to whether Soviet troop withdrawal had been completed. The council reserved the right to take up the matter sooner than May 6 should there be any unfavorable developments.

The council resolution of April 4 held that troop withdrawal

[3] Van Wagenen, op. cit., p. 45.   [4] Ibid., pp. 46–7.   [5] Ibid., p. 49.
[6] During this period, Ambassador Hussein Ala of Iran was receiving contradictory instructions from Premier Qavam, who was under intense pressure from the Soviet ambassador in Tehran, and his veracity and authority to represent his government were questioned by the Soviet representatives. There was genuine doubt as to whether an agreement between Tehran and Moscow existed or not.
[7] Van Wagenen, op. cit., pp. 50–4.

should not be contingent on the outcome of other matters under negotiation between Iran and the Soviet Union. But on the same day, Premier Qavam signed an agreement with the Soviet government which stipulated: that the Red Army be evacuated within six weeks after March 24; that a joint-stock Iranian-Soviet oil company be established and ratified by the next Majles; and that the matter of Azerbaijan was an internal Iranian affair to be settled between Tehran and the "government and people of Azerbaijan."[8] Troop withdrawal and oil rights were thus in fact linked in the agreement. Since the oil company agreement depended for ratification on the political composition of the next Majles, it was by no means a certain Soviet gain, but it was at the time widely interpreted as such. Following the signing of the agreement, the Soviet government put even heavier pressure on Iran. It was reported that Soviet troop movements increased without evidence of preparation for withdrawal[9] and that the Azerbaijan government began to move troops in the direction of Tehran.

This threat of renewed hostilities led to further Security Council attempts to obtain Soviet withdrawal, although during the same period the Soviet Union made a concerted effort to get the matter entirely off the council agenda. In view of reports from Iran, the council decided to reopen discussion earlier than May 6. When it met on April 15, however, the council learned that Premier Qavam now also requested that the matter be taken off the agenda. The Iranian request was widely thought to be the result of pressure from the Soviet Union. While the United States and Britain had no desire to see the matter off the agenda, there was a "question of principle dressed in procedural clothing"[1] since both parties had requested that the council not consider the question. After a week's debate on the proper interpretation of the UN Charter in such a situation, the council on April 23 voted against removing the matter from its agenda.

"Suddenly, on April 22, they [the Soviet troops] began

---

[8] Lenczowski, op. cit., p. 300.   [9] Van Wagenen, op. cit., p. 67.
[1] Ibid., p. 69.

coming north in droves. . . . On May 5 Tabriz itself was evacuated to the accompaniment of a brass band."[2] Evacuation of Soviet troops from Iranian territory was completed sometime in early May, probably by May 10.

Sub-Phase D: May 10–October 19, 1946

Despite its withdrawal of troops, the Soviet Union vigorously pursued its objectives in Iran through nonmilitary means. On May 22 the Security Council voted to retain the Iranian question on its agenda indefinitely, in view of conflicting reports concerning Soviet evacuation. But this was the last time the council was to discuss the conflict.

On June 14 Premier Qavam concluded an agreement with the Ja'afar Pishevari regime in Azerbaijan which preserved the nominal authority of Tehran over the province but made concessions to the Azerbaijanis in many important areas—election laws, land distribution, choice of the governor, and ultimate incorporation of Azerbaijan's army and irregular soldiers into the national army and gendarmerie.[3] The Azerbaijanis thus were in a position to infiltrate the Iranian army and to send Tudeh representatives to the next Majles. At the same time, for the immediate future they retained their army and *de facto* control over the province.[4]

The main Soviet effort during this period went into an attempt to gain control of the Iranian government at the cabinet level. On August 2 Qavam reshuffled his cabinet to include three members of the Tudeh; this "popular front" government was formed while violent riots provoked by the Tudeh broke out in Khuzistan.[5] Then the British entered the conflict actively. On August 3, the day after the new cabinet was announced, British troops were moved to Basra in Iraq, near the Iranian border, "to protect British interests."

A tense period followed the British move. Soviet troop concentrations were reported north of the Azerbaijan border, and anti-Tudeh tribal unrest developed. Qavam's arrest, on

[2] Rossow, op. cit., p. 24.   [3] Lenczowski, op. cit., p. 302.
[4] Rossow, op. cit., p. 25.
[5] Lenczowski, op. cit., p. 303; Rossow, op. cit., pp. 26–7.

August 18, of a number of Tudeh leaders did not ease the tension. On September 23 an open tribal rebellion broke out in Fars. The several rebellious tribes demanded the ouster of Tudeh ministers from the cabinet, local self-government for the southern provinces, and an increase in parliamentary representation.[6] According to General Arfa, on October 3 a confederation of western tribes joined the southern tribes in their demands, and the army was "lacking in enthusiasm for a fight on what they considered the Tudeh side." Arfa says that during the period of the tribal uprisings, the Tudeh and the government of Azerbaijan offered to allow the Azerbaijani forces to assume garrison duties in Tehran and other towns in order to allow the regular forces to be sent to the south.[7]

The Soviets accused the British of sponsoring the tribal rebellions; and, in response to Soviet allegations, the Tehran government requested the recall of one British consul. It cannot be definitely established that the British instigated or supported the tribal rebellions, but there is no question that the rebellions were favorable to British policy. In mid-October the central government signed an agreement with the tribes, meeting most of their demands. Following an interview with the Shah, Qavam reformed his government on October 19, eliminating all Tudeh members.

Sub-Phase E: October 19–December 10, 1946

Following the appointment of his new cabinet, Qavam announced on November 21 that elections for the new Majles would begin on December 7. He further stated on November 23 that they would not be held unless the government could supervise them in all areas of the country, including Azerbaijan. On November 24 he announced that central government troops would march into Azerbaijan for that purpose.[8]

The Soviet government informed Iran that it would take a serious view of disturbances in Azerbaijan and advised that the central government troops not be sent. At the same time, in

[6] Lenczowski, op. cit., pp. 304–5.   [7] Arfa, op. cit., pp. 374–5.
[8] He also arrested approximately one hundred Tudeh leaders in Tehran.

Tabriz, the Soviets informed the Azerbaijani regime that it was on its own militarily.[9] At this juncture the U.S. ambassador in Tehran made a public statement in support of Iran's right to send its troops into Azerbaijan. Premier Qavam, thus supported, notified the UN Security Council of the Soviet protest and of the fact that Tehran had not yet established control over Azerbaijan but intended now to do so.[1]

PHASE III₂   *December 10–15, 1946*

On December 10 minor hostilities broke out when forces of the central government entered Azerbaijan. On December 13 the government forces entered Tabriz and arrested several Azerbaijani leaders, although Pishevari and many of his followers had already fled across the border into the Soviet Union. Pishevari's army put up little resistance and the fighting ended with a complete victory for Tehran.[2] On December 15 the government troops also took control of the Kurdish People's Republic of Mahabad.

PHASE IV₂   *December 15, 1946–October 22, 1947*

During this period there were no further hostilities or threatened hostilities, either between Iran and the Soviet Union itself or between Iran and Soviet-supported rebel forces. With the issue of control over Azerbaijan resolved, however, there remained the question of the Soviet-Iranian oil company agreement.

Following the re-establishment of its control over the entire country, the Tehran government took vigorous action against the Tudeh, raiding its Tehran headquarters, arresting 150 of its leaders, and suppressing its newspapers.[3] In the elections held

---

[9] Rossow, op. cit., p. 30.

[1] Lenczowski, op. cit., pp. 307–8; Van Wagenen, op. cit., pp. 84–5.

[2] Rossow, op. cit., p. 30; Lenczowski, op. cit., pp. 308–9; Roosevelt, op. cit., p. 268.

[3] Lenczowski, op. cit., p. 309; Fatemi, op. cit., p. 323.

during January and February 1946 only two Tudeh members were sent to the new Majles.

On October 22, 1947, by a vote of 102 to 2, the Majles passed a bill sponsored by Qavam himself declaring null and void his earlier negotiations with the Soviet Union for an oil agreement. Before the vote, the Soviet ambassador had pressed hard for ratification; the U.S. ambassador had made a public statement to the effect that Iran was free to accept or reject the oil agreement and could count on U.S. support against any Soviet threats or pressure.[4]

SETTLEMENT   *From October 22, 1947*

With the refusal of the Majles to ratify the oil agreement that had been extracted from Qavam while Soviet troops were still in Iran, the conflict passed into Settlement. The *status quo ante* World War II was re-established, insofar as Azerbaijan and Soviet oil interests were concerned. The opposing forces were, however, stabilized at a higher level than before the outbreak of the conflict: the Soviet army was a much more powerful instrument than in pre-World War II days and the Iranian army continued to receive direct and indirect U.S. aid and support.

[4] Lenczowski, op. cit., pp. 310–11.

Phase I *to* Phase II: *The Introduction of a Military Option*

1. Factors Tending to Introduce a Military Option

   a. Larger great-power strategic concerns of World War II led to the introduction of British and Soviet troops into Iran in August 1941. These concerns included: the need to neutralize German influence on the southern flank of the Soviet Union; the need to insure access to Middle Eastern oil; and, subsequently, the need to maintain supply routes for lend-lease materials to the Soviet Union.

   b. Important factions within the Iranian government were pro-German.

2. Factors Tending to Keep the Dispute Nonmilitary

   a. Historic British-Soviet rivalry in the area made each power reluctant to see the introduction of the other's forces. (This factor was weakened by World War II concerns and was in part neutralized by the joint occupation, each state moving its troops into the portion of the country of greatest historic interest to it.)

   b. Iran was suspicious of the intentions of both occupiers and desired to avoid occupation altogether. Its military weakness left it powerless to resist.

Phase II *to* Phase III$_1$: *The Outbreak of Hostilities*

In August 1945 fighting broke out between Soviet-armed Azerbaijani rebels and the Iranian government's garrison forces in Azerbaijan.

1. Factors Tending to Promote the Outbreak of Hostilities

   a. Very early in its occupation of northern Iran, the Soviet Union began to use its military presence to pursue long-range, long-held ideological, political, economic, and strategic interests in the area.

   b. Soviet policy was made easier by sectional and tribal divisions in Iran, notably in the Azerbaijani area occupied by Soviet troops. There was thus a proxy available for Soviet actions.

   c. The military balance in Iran during the occupation favored the Soviet Union vis-à-vis both Iran and Britain.

   d. British weakness reflected both wartime losses and the relatively low priority of Iran in terms of other wartime demands.

Keeping the Dispute Nonmilitary

1. Measures to Offset These Factors

   a. All these concerns would not exist[5] or would have less saliency if great-power conflict has been avoided. Even with World War II, the specific concerns could be met by: neutralization of Iran; the possible development of alternate sources of energy (today, atomic power); and the possible development of long-range air-lift capacity.

   b. Strengthening Iran's internal integrity. Neutralizing Iran.

2. Measures to Reinforce These Factors

   a. Introduction into Iran of troops of states without historic and continued interest in the area.

   b. Strengthening Iran militarily to resist the need for occupation. Occupation by troops neutral in this conflict.

Preventing the Outbreak of Hostilities

1. Measures to Offset These Factors

   a. Strengthening Iran. Occupation by troops neutral in this conflict.

   b. Strengthening Iran internally, both politically and militarily.

   c. Retaining adequate great-power or third-power counterforce in the area. Strengthening Iran.

   d. Avoiding great-power conflict. Occupation by troops neutral in this conflict.

[5] Note that, for simplicity and as an aid to future applications, the

    e. U.S. lack of partiality in the conflict at this stage reflected a preoccupation with wartime goals, an almost equal suspicion of British and Soviet intentions, and prewar perceptions of the nature of the proper U.S. world role.

    f. Wartime strategic requirements also placed a high priority on avoiding a situation in Iran that would interfere with Allied wartime cooperation and lend-lease routes.

    g. In these circumstances, the proximity of the Soviet Union to the conflict area and its overwhelmingly greater power vis-à-vis Iran (quite apart from its occupation forces) had great influence.

    h. Finally, as the end of the war approached, the time was growing short during which the opportunity created by the wartime situation could be exploited.

2. Factors Tending to Inhibit the Outbreak of Hostilities

    a. International agreements existed—to which the United States, Britain, and the Soviet Union were parties—that prohibited intervention in Iranian internal affairs.

    b. While pursuing an active policy in support of the Azerbaijani rebels, the Soviet Union appears to have wished to keep the Soviet role covert and indirect.

    c. Although it was weak, there was countervailing force in the area. In addition to British forces and a small U.S. military contingent, the British controlled the Iraqi and Jordanian armies.

PHASE III₁ to PHASE IV₁: *The Termination of Hostilities*

Fighting between Soviet-backed Azerbaijani rebels and Iranian garrison forces in north Iran ended quickly in victory for the former. The issue was, therefore, to accept the new status quo or to continue hostilities. In the circumstances then prevailing, this latter course would have meant intensifying the hostilities, at a minimum involving direct clashes between Soviet and Iranian forces. It is possible that it would have meant clashes between Soviet and British/ U.S. forces and perhaps involvement of other areas of Iran and the Middle East.

1. Factors Tending to Inhibit the Termination of Hostilities

    a. The factors listed above that had tended to inhibit the outbreak of hostilities tended, once they had broken out, to encourage their continuation and intensification.

authors have used present tenses, present conditionals, and present participles at will throughout the RELEVANT CONTROL MEASURES.

    e. More active, vigorous U.S. counterpressure.

    f. Avoiding great-power conflict. Developing technical alternatives to bases.

    g. Renunciation of concept of spheres of influence.

    h. Time-stretching devices: "Stand Still" agreements, diplomatic delays, etc.

---

2. Measures to Reinforce These Factors

    a. Strengthening nonintervention agreements by provision for inspection, fact-finding, guarantees, sanctions, etc.

    b. Encouraging the Soviet Union to keep its role covert where the alternative is overt intervention.

    c. Creating a military counterforce, or conveying clear intention to do so, by strengthening Iran's forces, adding to U.S. forces, and deploying available third-party forces.

Moderating/Terminating Hostilities

1. Measures to Offset These Factors

    a. Treaty commitments should not be taken seriously or enforced. Third-party force available in the area should not be strong enough to intervene. Soviet involvement should be overt. (Clearly such policies would have disserved U.S.

2. Factors Tending to Promote the Termination of Hostilities

    a. The factors listed above that had favored the outbreak of hostilities favored, once hostilities occurred, their termination.

Within PHASE IV₁: *Restriction of the Scale/Scope of Potential Hostilities and Prevention of the Resumption of Hostilities*

Phase IV$_1$ went through a number of sub-phases in which the hostilities not only threatened to resume but also to expand to involve additional adversaries and a wider geographic area. The factors in these sub-phases that pressed for restricting or for expanding the scale/scope of the conflict and of potential hostilities will be examined here. The following section, Phase IV$_1$ to Phase III$_2$, will deal with the actual resumption of hostilities on a small scale and unexpanded.

Sub-Phase A: Soviet Failure to Withdraw on Date Specified by Treaty

1. Factors Tending to Expand the Scale/Scope of Potential Hostilities

    a. Factors that had earlier tended to lead to the outbreak of hostilities continued to exist.

2. Factors Tending to Restrict the Scale/Scope of Potential Hostilities

    a. At the same time, factors that had tended to prevent the outbreak of hostilities were weakened by the removal of the U.S. military mission and the reduction of British forces.

    b. A new factor in the conflict, brought into operation by the end of the war, was the treaty obligation to withdraw within a specified period.

interests. The question here is, however: If you want to suppress hostilities, what would you do?)

2. Measures to Reinforce These Factors

a. Promoting distracting great-power conflict outside the area of this particular conflict. Weakening Iran politically and militarily (perhaps including formal partition). Keeping great-power and other third-power force out of the conflict area. Introducing additional Soviet troops into the area or strengthening pro-Soviet forces. U.S. noninvolvement. Strengthening and formalizing spheres of influence. Insisting on settlement while the issue is most acute.

Restricting the Scale/Scope of Potential Hostilities and Preventing the Resumption of Hostilities

1. Measures to Offset These Factors

a. Strengthening Iran. Occupation by troops neutral in this conflict. Retaining counterforce. Avoiding great-power conflict. Great-power counterpressure. Renunciation of spheres of influence. Time-stretching devices.

2. Measures to Reinforce These Factors

a. Restriction of the scale/scope of potential conflicts can be achieved by withdrawing counterforce available in the area. (Note, however, that this can be interpreted as a signal that pursuit of expansionist policy objectives—in this case, Soviet designs on Iran—will not be resisted. Should that prove not to be the case—and in Iran it was not—such a policy can generate later pressure toward expanded hostilities.)

b. Strengthening nonintervention agreement. Impartial supervision of adherence to them.

   c. Another new factor arose with Iran's appeal to the United Nations for assistance in obtaining Soviet compliance. Whereas Security Council action was moderate and UN involvement was not major, it focused world attention on the Soviet action in Iran.

   d. The United States publicly endorsed the Iranian case at the United Nations and in bilateral communications with the Soviet Union and Iran.

   e. The Soviet desire to keep its role indirect and covert continued to exist but was made more difficult and perhaps less salient by (b) and (c) above.

Sub-Phase B: Soviet Agreement to Withdraw

1. Factors Tending to Expand the Scale/Scope of Potential Hostilities

   a. The military balance in Iran shifted more markedly in favor of the Soviet Union with the introduction of additional Soviet troops and the completion of British withdrawal.

   b. The deployment of Soviet troops, furthermore, suggested a threat not just to northern Iran or even all of Iran but also to Turkey and Iraq.

   c. Internal political division in Iran had led to the formation of a government ready, if not eager, to accommodate Soviet demands.

   d. The United States made what could have been interpreted as veiled threats to reintroduce its military force into the area. If this had indeed been done, it would have constituted a factor in this category. Similarly, an ultimatum, if actually sent, belongs here.

---

2. Factors Tending to Restrict the Scale/Scope of Potential Hostilities

   a. All the factors mentioned above that threatened to expand the scale/scope of potential hostilities served to deter actions that would make the threat a reality.

   b. Public opinion in the United States and Britain was becoming intensely anti-Soviet, and public attention to events in Iran was high. This conveyed a greater sense of determination to the Soviets but also compelled the United States and Britain to take active steps to counter Soviet actions.

   c. The UN Security Council continued to keep the issue on its

   c. The restricting impact of UN action could be enhanced by stronger UN action—creation of a UN presence in Iran, adoption of more substantive resolutions, etc.

   d. Stronger U.S. pressure.

   e. Encouraging Soviet Union to keep its role covert, where the alternative is to make it overt.

---

1. Measures to Offset These Factors
   a. Creation of counterforce by strengthening Iran or introducing friendly forces. (See, however, the caveats in 2(a) of Sub-Phase A above and 1(d) and 2(a) of Sub-Phase B below.)
   b. Strengthening militarily the other potentially threatened states in the conflict area.
   c. Strengthening Iran.
   d. While great-power counterforce already in the area—or threats to introduce it—can deter expansion of the conflict situation, the action or threat to act must be restrained and limited or it can have the reverse effect.

---

2. Measures to Reinforce These Factors
   a. Threatening to expand the scale/scope of potential hostilities. Threatening great-power involvement. (This set of factors and measures, appearing as it does on both sides of this equation, represents the classic dilemma of deterrence policy where deterrence depends on threatening to create a larger and more costly conflict out of a smaller one. If the deterrent is not successful, the potential hostilities may be much more expanded in scale and scope than might otherwise have been the case.)
   b. Aroused public opinion can increase the effectiveness of control measures; but unless it is also enlightened, it can have the reverse effect.
   c. UN action could be stronger—threats of sanctions, UN

agenda and thus before world attention, despite Soviet objections.

Sub-Phase C: Withdrawal of Soviet Forces

1. Factors Tending to Expand the Scale/Scope of Potential Hostilities

   a. Following its announced intention to withdraw its forces, the Soviet Union introduced additional forces into Iran.

2. Factors Tending to Restrict the Scale/Scope of Potential Hostilities

   a. All the factors listed above in Sub-Phase A, 2(a–e), and in Sub-Phase B, 2(a–c), continued to operate. In addition, the Iranian government yielded to a key Soviet demand for a joint Soviet-Iranian oil company.

   b. Iranian internal weakness, particularly the strength of the Tudeh party, appeared to offer a good prospect of an Iranian government even more amenable to Soviet pressures.

Sub-Phase D: Failure of the "Popular Front" Government in Iran

1. Factors Tending to Expand the Scale/Scope of Potential Hostilities

   a. While Soviet forces were withdrawn from Iran, they were just across the Soviet-Iranian border, and reinforcement of and maneuvers by these forces maintained military pressure on Iran.

   b. British forces landed at Basra in Iraq, just across the Iranian border.

2. Factors Tending to Restrict the Scale/Scope of Potential Hostilities

   a. Counterpressures on the pro-appeasement Iranian government were developing, some indigenous, some perhaps externally inspired. The Iranian army remained largely anti-Tudeh while anti-Tudeh tribal unrest developed, perhaps with British encouragement.

   b. During the period, the United Nations continued to claim a role in the conflict, although it took no action. Its right to continued cognizance of the matter was challenged by both the Soviet Union and the "popular front" government of Iran.

PHASE IV$_1$ *to* PHASE III$_2$: *The Resumption of Hostilities*

With the withdrawal of Soviet troops from Iran and the return to power of an Iranian government prepared to reassert its authority over the rebel Azerbaijani regime, the scene was set for renewed hostilities.

presence in Iran, resolutions on the substance of the
conflict, etc.

1. Measures to Offset These Factors

   a. Strengthening of Iran. Creating great-power counterforce.
   (See, however, the caveats in 2(a) of Sub-Phase A and in
   1(d) and 2(a) of Sub-Phase B above.)

2. Measures to Reinforce These Factors

   a. While in this case complete Iranian concession to Soviet
   pressure would likely expand the scale/scope of potential
   hostilities, limited concessions on nonvital issues, particularly
   ambiguous concessions, facilitate settlement.

   b. The availability of alternatives to military means of obtaining
   political goals.

1. Measures to Offset These Factors

   a. Iranian border patrols, controls. Similar maneuvers by opposing great powers. (But see 2(a) of Sub-Phase A and 1(d) and
   2(a) of Sub-Phase B above.)

   b. Creation of great-power counterforce. (But see 2(a) of
   Sub-Phase A and 1(d) and 2(a) of Sub-Phase B above.)

2. Measures to Reinforce These Factors

   a. Promoting internal unrest against a government whose
   actions are likely to expand the scale/scope of the potential
   hostilities.

   b. Stronger UN action, including border patrols and discussion
   of the substantive issues.

Preventing the Resumption of Hostilities

1. Factors Tending to Promote the Resumption of Hostilities

    a. The outcome of the developments within Phase IV$_1$ was to diminish greatly the credibility of the threat to expand the scale/scope of the conflict to cover a greater part of the Middle East or to involve additional great powers.

    b. The outcome, furthermore, was a unified government in Iran, determined to reassert its control over its entire territory.

    c. With the withdrawal of Soviet troops and the lack of Azerbaijani military strength without them, the Iranian government became the dominant military force in Iran.

    d. U.S. and British perceptions of the intentions of the Soviet Union had been made hostile by Soviet actions in Iran and elsewhere. U.S. and British interests in seeing the Azerbaijani rebellion ended quickly and decisively were high.

2. Factors Tending to Inhibit the Resumption of Hostilities

    a. While the Soviet forces were no longer in Iran, they were just north of the border and constituted the major military force in the area.

    b. UN cognizance of the conflict continued.

PHASE III$_2$ *to* PHASE IV$_2$: *The Termination of Resumed Hostilities*

> *Hostilities ended quickly in a victory for the Iranian government forces. The issue was, therefore, to accept the new status quo or to continue hostilities. In the circumstances then prevailing, the latter course would have meant intensification of hostilities by the reintroduction of Soviet forces, which might also have led to the reintroduction of other great-power forces in opposition.*

1. Factors Tending to Inhibit the Termination of Hostilities

    a. Long-range Soviet interests, proximity, and domination of the regional military balance, factors that had been present throughout the conflict, continued to be valid.

2. Factors Tending to Promote the Termination of Hostilities

    a. The factors that had promoted the outbreak of hostilities favored their termination, once hostilities had resulted in a government victory.

1. Measures to Offset These Factors

   a. To the extent that U.S. deterrence policy during Phase IV$_1$ successfully avoids a potential U.S.-Soviet clash in Iran, it also removes one inhibition on the Iranian government against renewing hostilities against the rebels. Thus mutual great-power deterrence can stimulate lower-level hostilities. The offsetting measure, however—reducing the credibility of mutual deterrence—can stimulate hostilities of expanded scale/scope.

   b. Promoting internal instability, weakness. Discouraging territorial integrity.

   c. Interposing forces (neutral or not) between potential combatants. Strengthening rebel movements militarily.

   d. UN or Soviet pressure on the United States and Britain to refrain from intervening.

---

2. Measures to Reinforce These Factors

   a. Threatening or actual reintroducing of Soviet or pro-Soviet forces.

   b. Strong UN stand against resumed hostilities. Creation of a UN presence.

Moderating/Terminating Resumed Hostilities

1. Measures to Offset These Factors

   a. Creating counterforce. Renouncing spheres of influence. Creating UN presence.

---

2. Measures to Reinforce These Factors

   a. Threatening to intensify the hostilities. Promoting internal weakness. Interposing forces. UN or Soviet pressure.

PHASE IV$_2$ *to* S: *Settlement of the Dispute*

1. Factors Tending Away from Settlement
   a. The factors just mentioned—Soviet interests, proximity, and military strength—continued.
   b. Whereas the Azerbaijani rebellion was crushed following its military defeat, unrest among the Azerbaijani and other tribes continued.
   c. Furthermore, the Azerbaijani rebel leaders fled to the Soviet Union and continued from there to call for Azerbaijani autonomy or independence.

2. Factors Tending Toward Settlement
   a. U.S.-British deterrence policy. Unified government in Iran. Iranian military strength vis-à-vis rebels. U.S.-British hostility to Soviet expansion in Iran and elsewhere.
   b. The Tudeh party was defeated in the Iranian elections, thus removing or weakening one source of internal pressure on the Iranian government.

THE WEAPONS

Very little data have been found on the arms that were available in Iran to the Soviet Union and Iran in the 1940's. The following account presents what few facts have been found in the open literature.

Soviet Forces' Weapons Acquisition

Between 1941 and 1945, while the Soviet army was occupying Iran, there were reported to be about three Soviet divisions in Iran. Their supporting armor consisted of about sixteen Sherman tanks, provided to the Soviet Union by the United States under lend-lease, and four self-propelled guns. During this time, Soviet troops also confiscated some 100,000 rifles and submachine guns from Iranian forces and subsequently handed these weapons over to Communist insurgents in Azerbaijan.

Settling the Dispute

1. Measures to Offset These Factors
   a. Creating counterforce. Renouncing spheres of influence. Creating UN pressure.
   b. Political development. Strengthening internal cohesion.

   c. Enforcement of agreements against hostile acts by exile groups against their home country.

2. Measures to Reinforce These Factors
   a. Threatening to expand the scale/scope of potential hostilities. Promoting internal political and military strength. Containment.
   b. Strengthening Iranian internal integrity. Stronger measures against dissident groups.

Weapons Available to Soviet Forces in Iran in 1946[6]

Weapon	Number	Source
7.92mm ZB Mauser 98/29 } 7.92mm Mauser Gewehr }	100,000 confiscated	Iran
rifle	?	U.S.S.R.
submachine gun	?	Iran
submachine gun	?	U.S.S.R.
light machine gun	?	U.S.S.R.
heavy machine gun	?	U.S.S.R.
light artillery	?	U.S.S.R.
heavy artillery	?	U.S.S.R.
self-propelled gun	large number	U.S.S.R.
Sherman tank	at least 16	U.S.
tank (unidentified)	500	?

[6] Data on the weapons used in a conflict—and on those available but not used—are of great relevance to arms-control policy activities that may help control local conflicts. The task of acquiring such data, even about recent conflicts, is difficult. Historians generally are much

By October 1946 there were reports that several new divisions of the Red Army had entered Iran. The Soviets added a number of light tanks and artillery pieces to the weapons of the Azerbaijani rebel forces. After March 2, 1946, the Soviet Union moved an additional large amount of armor, artillery, and mechanized infantry into Iran. Tanks, for example, are reported to have totaled 500.

Most of the Soviet weapons were produced by Soviet industry, although some are known to have been provided by the United States under lend-lease.

Iranian Government's Weapons Acquisition

During the entire period covered by this conflict, Iran was poorly equipped in relation to the Red Army. Before World War II, the Shah had accepted German aid in building a small-arms factory as part of his program of modernization. This industry produced a number of 7.92mm Mauser rifles and machine guns of German design. Large quantities of rifles and

---

more concerned with the political and diplomatic aspects of conflict and deal inadequately, almost casually, with the military aspects. Sales or transfers of big, expensive, sophisticated weapons systems, such as jet aircraft, are usually well reported. But many of the conflicts we examined were *armor* wars or *artillery* wars or even *rifle* wars—categories of weapons that scarcely attract the attention of the newspaper reporter, let alone the historian.

In short, to develop data on weapons requires a type of research effort very different from that employed in preparing the narrative case studies. The challenge was to build up, from widely scattered bits of information, inventories of all types that were available in each of the conflicts. Several thousands of documentary sources—books, newspapers, military journals, and technical and trade publications—were screened. From this variety of sources, an approximate picture began to emerge of the numbers and types of weapons available to each side in the various conflicts. In general, the completeness and reliability of the data diminished with the size of the weapons. Data on jet aircraft, for example, were found to be nearly complete; data on small arms were fragmentary and occasionally inaccurate. Although the nomenclature of the small arms present in a conflict was usually available, the numbers of weapons present could only be estimated. For all types of weapons, however, it was usually possible to establish the source and circumstances of supply, a topic we consider of paramount importance. The authors wish to acknowledge the assistance of Miss Priscilla A. Clapp and Mr. John H. Hoagland in assembling and evaluating these weapons data.

submachine guns were also bought from Czechoslovakia. During World War II, the Iranian arsenal produced the Czech ZB 7.92mm rifle. The Iranians also began producing the Soviet PPSh submachine gun for the Soviets on a contract basis. After the war, they continued to produce it for their own forces.[7] In addition, Iranian armed forces claimed to have two batteries of artillery, one battalion of light tanks, a squadron of Avro Anson bombers, and some Hurricane fighters.

During the years of occupation, Iran received considerable aid from the United States in reorganizing, training, and equipping its gendarmerie. After occupation, Iran continued to receive military aid from the United States.

Weapons Available to the Iranian Government Forces in 1946

Weapon	Number	Source
7.92mm ZB Mauser 98/29	?	Czechoslovakia
7.92mm Mauser Gewehr	?	German license to Iran
7.62mm PPSh M1941 submachine gun	?	Soviet license to Iran
7.92mm ZB 30 machine gun	?	Czechoslovak license to Iran
machine gun	?	German license to Iran
artillery	2 batteries	?
light tank	1 battalion	?
Hurricane fighter	?	?
Avro Anson bomber	1 squadron	U.K.

SUMMARY OF CONTROL MEASURES

In summary form, the key conflict-control measures in this case might have been the following (an asterisk indicates that the measure was actually taken):

[7] Joseph E. Smith: *Small Arms of the World* (Harrisburg: Stackpole; 1966), p. 463.

KEEPING THE DISPUTE NONMILITARY

Avoidance of great-power war.
Avoidance of presence of foreign troops.
Neutralization of Iran.
Renunciation of spheres of influence.
Development of alternative energy sources.
Long-range air-lift capability.
Strengthening of internal political, social, and economic fabric.
International military presence.

PREVENTING THE OUTBREAK OF HOSTILITIES

Stronger, healthier Iran.
Strong counterforce in area.*
Credible great-power deterrence.
International jurisdiction for:
>   "Stand Still" agreement,
>   Diplomatic delays,
>   Fact-finding,
>   Border watch,
>   Sanctions.

MODERATING/TERMINATING HOSTILITIES

Acceptance of pro-Soviet victory.
Encouragement of country's disunity.
Disregard of treaty commitments.
Reduction of locally available counterforce.

RESTRICTING THE SCALE/SCOPE OF POTENTIAL HOSTILITIES AND PREVENTING THE RESUMPTION OF HOSTILITIES

More specific U.S. deterrence.*
More specific UN actions.
Local arms limitation,
Backed by:
Multilateralized deterrence.
Limited and nonvital concessions.
Ways for interested powers to achieve influence without war.
Secure frontiers.
UN observation and patrol.

MODERATING/TERMINATING RESUMED HOSTILITIES

Stronger national fabric.*
Effective Western deterrence.*

CHAPTER 6

The Bay of Pigs,
1960-1961[1]

THE PHASES OF CONFLICT

PHASE I   *Background of the Conflict*

Ever since the Spanish-American War, Cuba and the United
States had—until 1960—enjoyed close relations both politically
and economically. A large percentage of Cuban business was
U.S.-owned before the coming to power of Castro, and the
United States traditionally exercised great influence over the
island government.

The Bay of Pigs conflict centered around a force of Cuban
exiles, equipped and trained by the U.S. government, who
invaded the island of Cuba in an effort to precipitate the overthrow of Premier Castro and establish a new government
acceptable to the United States. Military action against Castro
was devised by and dependent upon a coalition of the Cuban
exiles and the U.S. government; neither of these forces was in a
position to carry out this action independently.

Out of concern for international opinion, the United States
was apparently unwilling to initiate direct U.S. military action
against Castro.[2] The U.S. government, however, felt that it

---

[1] The authors wish to acknowledge the contribution to this chapter
of Miss Priscilla A. Clapp.
[2] Haynes Johnson: *The Bay of Pigs* (New York: W. W. Norton;
1964), p. 66, adds that, without the proxy of the Cuban exiles, the
United States would have run the risk of a direct confrontation with
the Soviet Union. (Johnson's book is based on information obtained from

could utilize anti-Castro Cuban exiles. The Cuban exiles, for their part, were split into too many factions to organize themselves into an effective counterrevolutionary force. Support and training from the United States provided them with the necessary rallying point from which to attempt perhaps the only objective upon which they could all agree—the overthrow of Castro.

The U.S. government was concerned with Castro's anti-Americanism and his desire to export his increasingly Communist-dominanted revolution to the rest of Latin America. The Cuban exiles desired to return to their homeland and set up a different type of government.

The End of the Batista Regime

When it became obvious that the Batista government had lost its popular support, the United States (both the government and the public) began to see Castro as a possible alternative. During the early days of his insurgency, many of his supplies and arms came from friends in the United States.[3] Within Cuba, those who were later to make up the bulk of the Cuban exile forces were either sympathetic to the Castro cause or actively fighting beside him. The dispute—both between the United States and Castro and between Castro and his former Cuban supporters in exile—developed only after Castro came to power on January

---

Cuban exiles as well as on Washington sources.) There is some reason to doubt the degree to which possible direct Soviet involvement weighed heavily in decisions concerning the Bay of Pigs. Arthur M. Schlesinger, Jr., mentions his own personal concern at Soviet reactions in other parts of the world; Schlesinger: *A Thousand Days: John F. Kennedy in the White House* (Boston: Houghton Mifflin; 1965), pp. 215–97. Theodore C. Sorensen mentions the possibility of a direct U.S.-Soviet clash if a full-scale U.S. invasion had been attempted; Sorensen: *Kennedy* (New York: Harper & Row; 1965), p. 297. Neither of these men, however—the former a participant in the decision-making process, the latter writing on the basis of conversations after the event—places these considerations high on the list of factors influencing U.S. policy.

[3] Earl E. T. Smith: *The Fourth Floor* (New York: Random House; 1962), p. 65; Theodore Draper: *Castro's Revolution* (New York: Praeger; 1962), p. 110. Earl Smith was U.S. Ambassador to Cuba during the last years of the Batista regime.

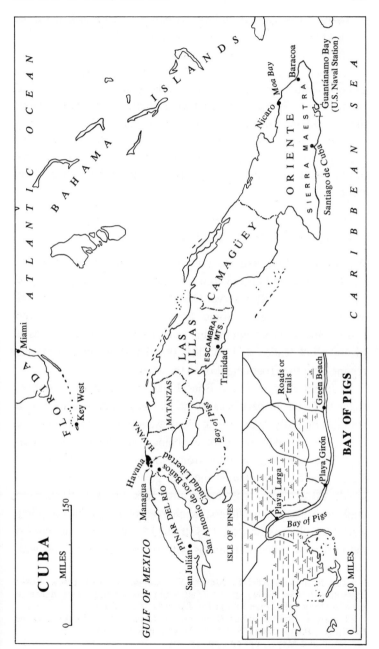

1, 1959; it was caused and aggravated by his progressive steps toward Communism and alliance with the Soviet bloc.

Many previous Cuban governments had forced their opponents into exile, usually to the United States. Castro's did the same. Members of Batista's government and others who had been close to him comprised the first anti-Castro exile group; they began independent military action against Castro shortly after they went into exile. But the bulk of the Bay of Pigs fighting forces were early supporters of Castro who had become disillusioned with him at various points during the course of his reforms.

Castro's First Months in Power: Deteriorating Relations with the United States

When Castro first assumed power, the U.S. government recognized the new Cuban government immediately and greeted the change with friendly reserve. Castro, however, made a point of his anti-Americanism. Some argue that Castro needed the United States as an enemy in order to retain his image as a strong rebel leader and to shift popular discontent from his regime onto the great neighbor to the north.[4]

In January 1959, Philip Bonsal was appointed U.S. Ambassador to Cuba, in part because he was generally identified as a liberal.[5] Friendly overtures to the Castro government from the U.S. government were, however, being compromised by bombing flights over Cuba mounted from Florida by exiled Batistianos. Castro vociferously blamed the U.S. government for the resulting deaths of Cuban citizens because no successful efforts were made to prevent these flights; he charged that some of the pilots were U.S. citizens or were U.S.-trained.[6] Castro also demanded the return of exiled Batistianos with the money they took with

[4] Tad Szulc and Karl E. Meyer: *The Cuban Invasion* (New York: Ballantine Books; 1962), p. 13. Tad Szulc was an important figure in press coverage of Cuban affairs for *The New York Times*.

[5] Robert F. Smith: *What Happened in Cuba?* (New York: Twayne Publishers; 1963), p. 245; Szulc and Meyer, op. cit., p. 20.

[6] Szulc and Meyer, op. cit., pp. 25, 41.

them when they fled.[7] The United States, however, was not prepared to send the exiles to certain execution. The mass political executions that Castro had initiated upon his take-over were by now turning U.S. public opinion against him.

In April 1959 Castro made his first visit to the United States as Cuban Premier. He was accompanied by the moderates in his government,[8] but he received a very cautious welcome. President Dwight D. Eisenhower was on a golfing trip, and Secretary of State Christian Herter received Castro in a hotel room.[9] On this visit, Castro was mild in his approach and asserted that he was not a Communist. After a three-hour talk with the Premier, however, Vice-President Richard Nixon became alarmed that Communist influences were gaining control in Cuba. He reportedly expressed this view to President Eisenhower and suggested that Cuban exiles be trained by the U.S. government to fight Castro.[1]

When Castro returned to Cuba, he resumed his verbal attacks on the United States and, in May 1959, introduced a radical land-reform law.[2] After unsuccessful attempts by Ambassador Bonsal to have the law moderated, relations between the United States and Cuba began to deteriorate.[3]

[7] R. Hart Phillips: *The Cuban Dilemma* (New York: Ivan Obolensky, Inc.; 1962), p. 57, states, however, that "an official [of the U.S. embassy] told me that no formal documented petition had been presented by the Cuban government. It was obvious that Castro did not want to extradite the Batista officials." Phillips was head of the *New York Times* office in Havana during this period.

[8] The fact that they were the Minister of Finance, the Minister of Economy, the head of the National Bank of Cuba, and the managing director of the Cuban Bank of Foreign Trade led U.S. officials to believe that Castro was interested in loans. His aides, however, made no approaches to the State Department, the Development Loan Fund, or the International Cooperation Administration in Washington. *The New York Times,* March 13, 1960.

[9] R. Smith, op. cit., p. 246.

[1] Johnson, op. cit., p. 25, states that Nixon urged a "stronger policy within Administration councils" and "favored a military solution, if necessary." See also Draper, op. cit., p. 62; Schlesinger, op. cit., p. 226.

[2] The Agrarian Reform Law was promulgated on May 17, 1959; under Article 48 of this law, the INRA (National Institute of Agrarian Reform) was established with, among other powers, the authority to seize lands and redistribute them.

[3] R. Smith, op. cit., p. 246.

The Problem of Expropriated Property

The land-reform law helped to confirm suspicions in the United States that Castro's was a Communist revolution. The spectre of a possible Communist political and military base of operations ninety miles from the Florida coast began to take on ominous substance. It was also becoming evident that steps taken by the U.S. government to moderate Castro's policies were producing just the opposite results. Castro began interpreting the actions of the United States as hostile to his revolution and using them as fuel for his "anti-Yankee" campaign.[4] And since the United States had exercised virtually total control over the Cuban economy since the Spanish-American War, Castro was able to persuade many Cubans that the United States was responsible for all the economic and social inequalities present in Cuba.

Following the introduction of the Agrarian Reform Law, great pressure was brought to bear upon the U.S. government by those who had economic interests in Cuba. Just after the law was drafted, Senator George Smathers of Florida, speaking before the Sugar Club of New York, voiced the first public warning to Cuba that its sugar quota would be reduced if it chose to carry out drastic land reform.[5] At that time, five American sugar companies owned or controlled more than two million acres of Cuban land and stood to lose all but 16,650 acres.[6] The U.S. government soon told Cuba officially of its fear that the new land-reform law would not give American investors fair compensation. At the same time, Castro was proposing to sell eight million tons of sugar in the United States in 1961.[7] The regular sugar quota only provided for three million tons, a third of total U.S. consumption; under a reciprocity agreement signed by Cuba and the United States in 1934, Cuba had been guaranteed a U.S. market for three million tons of sugar a year at two cents per pound above prices

[4] Szulc and Meyer, op. cit., p. 18.
[5] *The Wall Street Journal*, June 3, 1959.   [6] Ibid., June 12, 1959.
[7] Ibid., June 16, 1959.

in the world sugar market. During 1959 the U.S. State Department suggested that the premium quota payment be put into an internationally administered fund to compensate American landowners until Cuba agreed to settle their claims.[8]

In October 1959 the Cuban government passed a law that would deprive American owners of most of their mining and petroleum rights on the island.[9] Later, in answer to threats of curtailment of the sugar quota, the Cuban government issued this statement:

It might be interesting to ask the American statesmen and public opinion at large if they believe it possible for a small country like Cuba to bear indefinitely a trade and payment deficit resulting from its relations with its powerful neighbors . . . particularly considering that the international exchange reserve of the Island, with which that deficit was covered, was practically exhausted . . . owing to the fatal policy so unwisely followed by the tyranny [i.e., of Batista].[1]

In reply, Secretary of State Herter offered the alternatives to Cuba of discussing complaints peaceably with the United States or of pursuing anti-American policies and risking loss of the sugar quota.[2]

In January 1960 Ambassador Bonsal attempted new negotiations regarding confiscation of American property. *The New York Times* gave a good summary of his case:

Though several notes have been exchanged between the United States and Cuba since the [agrarian reform] law was promulgated last spring, the Government of Premier Fidel Castro has made no concessions to Washington's demand that, under international law, United States citizens whose land has been expropriated should receive "prompt, adequate and effective" payment. . . . The Cuban Government is apparently willing to let the matter drift. . . . Since the exchange of these notes, the United States has become increasingly concerned over the manner in which the Cuban Government has inplemented the agrarian reform.[3]

---

[8] R. Smith, op. cit., p. 248; Szulc and Meyer, op. cit., pp. 63–4.
[9] *The New York Times,* October 29, 1959.
[1] *Boletín* of the República de Cuba, Ministerio de Estado, No. 92 (December 8, 1959).   [2] *The Wall Street Journal,* December 11, 1959.
[3] *The New York Times,* January 10, 1960.

Despite continued U.S. efforts at negotiation, the Cuban government increased the pace of its seizures of American-owned property in 1960. In February Castro announced the start of his industrialization program with the statement that private foreign investment would be accepted in Cuba only if delivered to the government to be used as it saw fit.[4]

Other Sources of Tension

Although uncompensated confiscation of American property in Cuba seemed to be the main issue at this time, there were other issues that were being debated. Bombing runs over Cuba by exiled Batistianos continued and in early 1960 became more frequent;[5] it was even rumored that Castro had instigated some of the raids himself, because they provided effective propaganda against the United States. In any event, *The New York Times* reported that an

analysis of the available evidence, including eyewitness reports, indicates that many, if not all, of the persons injured received their wounds either from stray rounds of 20 mm. and 40 mm. shell fragments from anti-aircraft fire of the Cuban armed forces or from grenades or bombs thrown from automobiles by terrorists.[6]

As the Batistiano raids increased over sugar fields in an effort to destroy the sugar crop, the Castro government complained bitterly about the refusal of the United States to sell it fighter aircraft and about attempts by the United States to dissuade Britain from exchanging with it several jet Sea Hunters for some obsolete Sea Furies. "For this reason we cannot defend ourselves against the raiders," it claimed.[7] On March 6 a shipload of guns from Belgium blew up in Havana harbor, and there were subsequent charges of U.S. sabotage.[8] This incident pro-

[4] Ibid., February 26, 1960.
[5] Some observers contend that, while some efforts were made to stop flights originating from U.S. territory, they were not pressed very vigorously. Szulc and Meyer, op. cit., pp. 25, 41; *The New York Times*, October 17 and 23, 1959.
[6] *The New York Times*, November 10, 1959.
[7] Boston *Daily Globe*, February 17, 1960.
[8] Szulc and Meyer, op. cit., p. 42.

vided Castro with some of his most effective propaganda against the United States at the time.

As early as the autumn of 1959, Castro was insisting that the United States would invade Cuba in the near future.[9] Likewise, he blamed all the exile activities against his government on U.S. government policy. His refusal to negotiate differences with the United States was further indication of his determination to consolidate his revolution against the United States.

In 1959 U.S. concern over Castro's continued hostility increased as members of the original revolutionary government were gradually replaced by Communists. This trend culminated in February 1960 in a trade and economic agreement between Cuba and the Soviet Union[1] that gave the Soviets a major role in Cuban affairs.

This pro-Soviet trend in Cuba's orientation made more serious another development that had taken place during 1959: Castro's engaging in military forays in Central America and the Caribbean. The U.S. State Department charged that he had "aided or supported armed invasions of Panama, Nicaragua, the Dominican Republic and Haiti. These projects failed and all invited action by the Organization of American States."[2] Efforts to get decisive OAS action failed, however. The strongest language the OAS foreign ministers could agree upon at their Santiago, Chile, meeting in August 1959 was that "the existence of anti-democratic regimes constitutes a violation of the principles [of OAS] . . . and a danger to united and peaceful relations in the hemisphere."[3] Many Latin Americans were at that time sympathetic toward the Castro revolution.

[9] Ibid., p. 26.

[1] On February 14, 1960, Anastas Mikoyan signed a trade agreement in Havana under which the Soviet Union would buy one million tons of sugar a year and extend $100 million of credit to Cuba. Szulc and Meyer, op. cit., p. 42.

[2] U.S. Department of State: *Cuba*, Department of State Publication 7171 (Washington: GPO; April 1961), as referenced in R. Smith, op cit., p. 322.

[3] U.S. Department of State: *Inter-American Efforts to Relieve International Tensions in the Western Hemisphere, 1959–1960*, Department of State Publication 7409 (Washington: GPO; July 1962), p. 70.

Even those who may have shared Washington's concern over the nature of the Castro government were too committed historically to an anti-intervention stance to contemplate decisive OAS action.

Efforts to negotiate differences with Cuba continued, despite mounting U.S. concern over the political orientation of the Castro government and over its active efforts to stimulate similar movements elsewhere in the hemisphere. For example:

As late as January 1960 the United States government made a new effort to reach an understanding using Dr. Julio A. Amoedo, the Argentine ambassador to Havana and a personal friend of Castro's, as an intermediary. There appears to have been still another attempt in March through [Cuban Finance Minister] Rufo Lopez Fresquet. On the morning of March 17, 1960, President [Osvaldo] Dorticós [Torrado] rejected this last United States overture.[4]

Schlesinger reports that "on the same day in Washington President Eisenhower agreed to a recommendation from the CIA to train a force of Cuban exiles for possible use against Castro."[5]

If the various Cuban exile groups were to be united and to make effective contact with the underground that was rising inside Cuba, some external party needed to assume the role of organizer and benefactor to these groups. The fact that the U.S. government decided to organize the potential for military action against Castro did not necessarily mean a commitment to use that force. It seems clear, however, that the U.S. decision to utilize Cuban exiles was a result of both an increased readiness to employ force in the mounting U.S.-Castro crisis and an unwillingness to use U.S. force directly. There were, of course, circumstances that could have changed this decision. During this period, however, Castro appears to have been very cautious not to provide the United States with a clear case for direct

[4] Schlesinger, op. cit., p. 222. When Fresquet told Dorticós that he would resign if no reconciliation were possible with the United States, Dorticós accepted his resignation. According to Phillips, op. cit., p. 178, two other high-ranking Cuban officials also resigned on March 17 in protest against Communist control in Cuba: the Cuban naval attaché and the military and air attaché in the Washington embassy.

[5] Schlesinger, op. cit., p. 222.

military action; for example, he made no move against the Guantánamo Naval Station. Sensitivity to world opinion appears also to have played a large part in determining the extent of U.S. action against Castro; although there were certain to be widespread presumptions of an active U.S. role in the exiles' activities, "the hope existed that it could be plausibly disclaimed by the United States government."[6]

PHASE II   *March 1960–April 1961*

Three main sub-phases can be identified in Phase II. The first extended from the spring to the fall of 1960, when the proposed use of indirect U.S. force through the Cuban exile groups centered around prospects for effective guerrilla opposition within Cuba. The second sub-phase, from the fall of 1960 to early 1961, saw a gradual shift of emphasis from activities designed to support and encourage the guerrilla movements toward plans that involved an invasion by exile forces. The third sub-phase, from early 1961 to the April invasion, saw many modifications and amendments of the proposed Cuban assault, and, more significantly, was the period in which the decision to *use* force—as distinct from having it readily available—was made.

Sub-Phase A: Spring–Fall 1960

In the spring of 1960 the United States made contact through its intelligence system with Cuban exiles here and with underground leaders inside Cuba. These Cubans were reportedly told that wealthy interests in the United States who were sympathetic to their cause were prepared to give them financial and other support.[7] The Cuban exiles and the underground leaders report, however, that they realized from the beginning that their benefactors had the full support of the U.S. government. This support provided the incentive these Cubans needed to embark on a serious campaign against Castro despite problems posed by

[6] Information from an interview with former CIA official Richard M. Bissell, Jr., in the Washington *Star,* July 20, 1965.

[7] Johnson, op. cit., p. 31.

their unreconciled factions; they believed that with the backing
of the United States they could not lose. As one of the Cuban
troops later said, "We thought Uncle Sam was behind us. He
wanted to do this secretly. That was all right because he was
Uncle Sam, and he is strong."[8]

One group of Cubans with professional military experience
was gathered at Miami and sent to a small island in the Caribbean to be tested for officer ability. Twenty-eight were chosen
from this group to train in guerrilla tactics at the U.S. Army
jungle-warfare school in the Panama Canal Zone. On August
22, after seven weeks of training, they were taken to a camp on
the Pacific coast of Guatemala,[9] where they assisted in training
larger numbers of exiles in guerrilla tactics. The Cuban troops in
Guatemala then numbered 160, forty-seven of whom were pilots.
In the middle of September the first weapons arrived,[1] and
shortly after that an additional twenty guerrilla instructors of
various nationalities were brought in to help train the Cubans.[2]

At this time there was no definite commitment by the United
States to use the Cuban exile force, only a decision to train it.
The U.S. intelligence community was executing the mandate it
had been given to carry out the day-to-day routine of military
training. A recommendation to the President on the specific use
to be made of the troops[3] was to be the prerogative of a special
interdepartmental committee in Washington, consisting of top
officials from the State Department, the Pentagon, and the
White House.

Such planning *for actual use of the force* as appears to have
existed when the force was conceived and being gathered was
based on the assumption that existing, isolated guerrilla bands
in Cuba could be effectively coordinated by the creation of
communication networks and that these networks would make
it possible to bring in supplies and men for larger guerrilla
operations. With such developments inside Cuba, the small

---

[8] Ibid., p. 37.   [9] Ibid., pp. 37–9.
[1] Thirteen Springfield rifles, vintage World War I, and a few pistols.
Ibid., p. 48.   [2] Ibid.   [3] Ibid., p. 53.

numbers of exiles then training in Guatemala could be infiltrated to strengthen a guerrilla network sufficiently powerful to
ignite an anti-Castro campaign. Simultaneously with the training of exiles in Guatemala, therefore, efforts were being made to
establish effective liaison with guerrillas inside Cuba.

Meanwhile, Castro continued to warn against impending
invasion from the United States. Because his warnings contained a considerable amount of accurate detail about the
training of exiles, it can be assumed that *his* intelligence network was keeping him well informed. As early as May 1, while
the Guatemalan camps were being readied—but before any
Cubans had arrived—Castro had warned that the United States
was preparing aggression against Cuba with the aid of Guatemala. By July he was stirring up public militancy against
invaders and impressing upon the Cuban populace the idea that
any invasion would be the direct responsibility of its enemy, the
United States.[4]

During the spring and summer of 1960, political relations
between Cuba and the United States deteriorated steadily, and
soon it became impossible for the two countries to communicate
diplomatically.[5] Castro refused to meet with the U.S. ambassador to discuss differences. Instead, he told a CBS correspondent
that Cuban-U.S. relations would be improved if he could meet
privately with President Eisenhower or Secretary of State
Herter. A State Department spokesman answered that Castro
should tell this to Ambassador Bonsal.[6]

Castro's continued expropriation of U.S.-owned land led to
the suggestion in Congress in March 1960 that the Cuban sugar
quota be cut.[7] In May the State Department announced that the
small remaining economic-aid program to Cuba would be ended

[4] Szulc and Meyer, op. cit., p. 47.
[5] Also, the popular support in the United States that Castro had
enjoyed when he first came to power had largely disappeared, weakened
by his mass executions of counterrevolutionists and his apparent repudia-
tion (which he made official on May 1, 1960) of promised elections and
representative democracy.   [6] *The New York Times,* April 18, 1960.
[7] R. Smith, op. cit., p. 277; Szulc and Meyer, op. cit., pp. 60–2.

within six months.[8] By June, as signs in Washington pointed
toward the likelihood of a cut in the sugar quota, Castro warned
that this "economic aggression" by the United States would be
met with the seizure of all remaining American-owned property
and business in Cuba.[9] On July 5, President Eisenhower received authority from Congress to cut the quota; and the next
day he announced that he was reducing the quota sharply,
adding that

The inescapable conclusion is that Cuba has embarked on a course
of action to commit a steadily increasing amount of its sugar crop
to trade with the Communist bloc, thus making its future ability
to fill the sugar needs of the United States ever more uncertain.[1]

Castro seized the U.S. oil refineries on the same day. The
next day, he was given authority by his government to expro-
priate U.S.-owned land with "nothing more than a decision and
a signature."[2] On August 8, in retaliation for "economic aggression" by the United States, Premier Castro began implementation of this authority to nationalize U.S.-owned property
in Cuba.[3]

Since February 1960, Cuba had been drawing closer to the
Soviet Union. Just after the sugar quota was cut, the Soviet
Union promised to buy more Cuban sugar, and Soviet Premier
Khrushchev announced that he would defend Cuba with rockets
if necessary.[4] On July 8, 1960, Castro announced the imminent
arrival of Soviet-bloc arms in Cuba. On July 26 he told the
militia that it was the last time they would have to march
without arms, because Czech rifles had already arrived.[5]

---

[8] *The New York Times,* May 28, 1960.   [9] Ibid., June 27, 1960.
[1] President Eisenhower, Statement on Signing of the Cuban Sugar
Quota Bill, July 6, 1960, as cited in R. Smith, op. cit., p. 278.
[2] *The Wall Street Journal,* July 7, 1960.
[3] *The New York Times,* August 8, 1960. It is interesting to note that
Castro did not begin to use the authority until after Soviet arms had
arrived.   [4] Szulc and Meyer, op. cit., p. 72.
[5] *Revolución,* July 27, 1960, cited in Andrés Suárez: *Cuba: Castroism
and Communism, 1959–1966* (Cambridge: MIT Press; 1967), p. 93.
The U.S. State Department later confirmed the arrival of Soviet arms
in July. *The New York Times,* November 18, 1960.

As U.S.-Cuban economic and political relations rapidly deteriorated over the summer of 1960, the number of incidents in Central and South America which the United States attributed to Castro increased. One later account summarized these as including all the following: Guatemala and Nicaragua were facing rebel movements directly inspired by Castro and armed from his arsenal; many copies of Major Ernesto Guevara's book on guerrilla tactics had been sent into Chile along with supplies for earthquake victims; the Cuban ambassador to Panama, who was endowed with a fine voice, was singing in villages and asking parish priests to lead Friends of Cuba chapters; "Fidelista" rifle groups in Peru were training members in guerrilla tactics; the peasant revolt in northeastern Brazil was becoming "Fidelista"; radical groups in Venezuela were demanding alliance with Cuba and land reform on the Cuban pattern (the "Fidelista" movement centered in Caracas had actually battled with police and soldiers); the Cuban ambassador to Bolivia was sponsoring anti-U.S. demonstrations; and British Guiana had gone to Cuba for a $5 million loan.[6] With a good supply of weapons in Cuba to add force to pro-Cuban movements in other Latin American countries, Castro's threat of exporting his revolution was appearing more real and immediate.

On several occasions in the summer of 1960, the United States registered its growing alarm over Castro's policies with the Inter-American Peace Committee, which in the previous year had been given the responsibility for a general survey of causes of tension in the Caribbean. In August the OAS foreign ministers met again, at San José, Costa Rica, to consider U.S. charges against Cuba. The final resolutions adopted were stronger than those of the previous summer but still fell short of the condemnation Secretary of State Herter is said to have wanted,[7] much less a decision for action that some had thought possible. The Declaration of San José condemned "energetically the intervention or threat of intervention . . . by an extra-

[6] Tad Szulc: "Castro Tries to Export 'Fidelismo,'" *The New York Times,* November 27, 1960. [7] R. Smith, op. cit., p. 277.

continental power in the affairs of the American republics" and said further that "the attempt of the Sino-Soviet powers to make use of the political, economic, or social situation of any American state" could endanger the peace and security of the hemisphere. At the same meeting, however, the ministers also reaffirmed the general OAS prohibition of intervention by one state in the affairs of another.[8]

On September 26, 1960, at the UN General Assembly, Castro reiterated all the charges that he and the Soviet Union had made against the United States. His speech ended with a plea that the United Nations condemn the U.S. government for supporting insurgents in Cuba and for planning an invasion of Cuba in the near future.[9] He also stressed the Soviet pledge of July 9 to defend Cuba with rockets.[1] A month later, however, Khrushchev announced that his pledge to defend Cuba with rockets should be interpreted "really to be symbolic."[2]

On October 19 the United States increased its economic pressure on Castro by imposing an embargo on U.S. exports to Cuba. The U.S. Department of Commerce charged that from the start of the Castro regime a variety of discriminatory taxes and trade regulations had been instituted in an effort to divert trade away from the United States and that, as a result, U.S. exports to Cuba had fallen to less than 50 per cent of the 1958 total. The department also cited Castro's seizure of American-owned properties and claimed that "all efforts on the part of the United States to reach a fair and equitable solution . . . have been rebuffed by the Castro regime."[3] On the same day that the United States announced the embargo Major Ernesto "Che" Guevara, who served as president of the National Bank of

[8] U.S. Department of State: *Inter-American Efforts* . . . , pp. 368–9.
[9] The Cuban complaint was placed on the General Assembly's agenda, but the assembly had not reached the item when the invasion at the Bay of Pigs occurred.
[1] Speech by Fidel Castro to the General Assembly of the United Nations, September 26, 1960, as referenced in R. Smith, op. cit., pp. 284–303.   [2] TASS release, October 30, 1960.
[3] U.S. Embargo on Exports to Cuba, October 19, 1960, as referenced in R. Smith, op. cit., pp. 280–2.

Cuba, was reported to be making plans to leave for the Soviet Union to negotiate a new trade agreement.[4]

During the summer of 1960, while the camps for training Cuban exiles were being developed in Guatemala, Castro was establishing firm control over his militia and the civilian population. He was also carrying on a vigorous campaign against a counterrevolutionary guerrilla group that was operating from the Escambray mountains in central Cuba.

As was noted earlier, contingency plans for the use of trained Cuban exiles were, at this time, based on the development of anti-Castro guerrilla forces within Cuba; this development required, in turn, the improvement of communications both among isolated guerrilla groups and between them and those seeking to supply them by air. But the communication network was proving very difficult to achieve. Failure to develop communications skills adequate enough to guide in supplying aircraft was resulting, by the autumn of 1960, both in Castro's frequent interception of supplies intended for the guerrillas and in greater risk-taking by the guerrilla bands as they were forced to leave secure bases to forage for supplies. The guerrillas were also becoming isolated in small, weak groups vulnerable to attack by the Castro forces. In effect, Castro was succeeding in localizing guerrilla operations against him. The situation seemed bound to worsen as the unsettled autumn weather made air supply even less reliable.

Castro was also strengthening his military forces during the summer of 1960. A State Department release in November 1960, summarizing these developments, stated that Castro had already built a force ten times the size of Batista's and larger than any other Latin American army. When the eight-thousand-man 26th of July Movement had taken power, it had gained, in addition to its own arms, matériel sufficient for 25,000 men. On this base, Castro had, in less than two years, equipped with modern light and heavy arms a militia of over 200,000 and an army of at least 40,000. In 1959 Cuba had bought 100,000

[4] *The New York Times,* October 20, 1960.

rifles in Belgium, and since July 1960 at least 28,000 tons of arms had been shipped in from the Communist bloc. Among these supplies were anti-aircraft and antitank artillery, tanks, helicopters, mortars, other light arms, and ammunition. (See the WEAPONS section of this chapter for details.) The State Department pointed out that arms deliveries from the Soviet bloc had stepped up noticeably since the OAS resolution in August which had disapproved of extra-continental intervention in the American continents.[5] Many observers were alarmed at the speed with which Soviet-bloc arms were arriving. It appeared that within six months Castro's forces would be sufficiently large and well equipped to make effective action by guerrilla forces impossible.

Sometime between August[6] and November 1960, the contingency plans for a small force of exiles designed to augment a guerrilla movement inside Cuba became transformed into plans for a larger force capable of invading the island and establishing and holding a beachhead.[7] This change was more probably the result of an accruing number of small decisions than of one single act of decision. Two lines of development appear to have been central to the transformation. First, the expectations about guerrilla operations inside Cuba had not been fulfilled, so that the force as originally designed had no role to play. Second, worsening U.S.-Cuban relations, particularly Cuba's growing reliance on the Communist bloc, increasing military strength, and expanded intervention in the hemisphere, added urgency to the need to act.

During the months when the decision to build an invasion force was being formed, the United States was in the midst of an election in which Cuba had become a major issue. Presidential candidate John F. Kennedy appeared especially anxious to debate this issue with his opponent. Nixon advocated noninter-

[5] Ibid., November 18, 1960.
[6] One source (Johnson, op. cit., p. 53) places in August the first suggestion that the plans be changed.
[7] Schlesinger, op. cit., p. 229; Johnson, op. cit., p. 54; Sorensen, op. cit., p. 295.

vention in Latin America, saying that U.S. support for Cuban exile forces would be a violation of international law; Kennedy insisted that Castro was an outlaw and that the U.S. government should train and support Cuban exiles. The Vice-President was aware of the contingency preparations underway; the Senator from Massachusetts had not been briefed on the situation.[8]

Perhaps even more significant, however, was the fact that, regardless of its outcome, the election would bring a new President to office. It was the highest executive office—that of the President—that had made the decisions to limit U.S. involvement, thus far, to indirect support of anti-Castro forces. By the time of the election period, the President was finally divorced from the threat of political repercussions that might be produced by exposure of growing U.S. participation in what might become a Cuban invasion. There was, therefore, no strong political voice to present the case *against* invasion.[9]

Sub-Phase B: Fall 1960–Early 1961

In the camps in Guatemala the remaining months of 1960 were spent in training the exile force for its redefined mission. Castro continued to warn that invasion was imminent. For example, in late October he mobilized his militia in anticipation of an invasion from the United States. One newspaper speculated that his mobilization was an answer to the recent landing of 1,450 marines at the U.S. naval base at Guantánamo.[1] By and large, however, the U.S. press expressed bewilderment at Castro's furious preparation for imminent invasion. For example, *The New York Times* called Castro's actions "hysterical" and remarked,

[8] Johnson, op. cit., p. 49.
[9] Haynes Johnson states that factors "in the nature of the Presidency itself and also in Eisenhower's personality . . . created an atmosphere of not bothering the chief, of going ahead in an interim period, in effect of postponing the final collection in the certainty that payment would be made." The final decision would rest with a new administration. Ibid., p. 54.   [1] *The New York Times,* October 31, 1960.

All this would be comic if it were not so tragic. The United States Government has made it clear that it has no intention of invading Cuba. . . . One obvious intent of this Castro maneuver is to inflame his people's passions against this country and build hatred of the United States. . . . Another reason for this paranoid behavior may be to take the Cuban people's minds off their growing difficulties at home. . . . Finally, there is the worst possibility that Castro may be planning some provocation against the United States, at Guantanamo or elsewhere. This is certainly a time for us to guard against any such provocations, should they occur.[2]

Then, in December, Castro began to demobilize the militia. A new President had been elected in the United States and Castro expressed hopes that perhaps this would provide the beginning of a new attitude toward Cuba in Washington.[3] Despite the fact that, during the election campaign, Kennedy had openly advocated that the United States support the overthrow of the Castro regime, Castro appeared to believe that he could reach an accommodation with Kennedy as President.

In early January 1961 Cuba again urged immediate consideration in the United Nations of its charge that the United States was planning an invasion of the island.[4] Subsequently, Castro declared that the U.S. embassy in Havana was the center of counterrevolutionary activities against his regime and ordered that its staff be reduced to 11 within forty-eight hours. Eighty per cent of the 300 officials, he charged, were spies of the Federal Bureau of Investigation and the Pentagon. There were actually only 42 U.S. officials in the embassy at the time and 87 U.S. employees in all.[5] Eisenhower answered Castro's charges as follows:

This unusual action on the part of the Castro Government can have no other purpose than to render impossible the conduct of normal diplomatic relations with that Government.

Accordingly, I have instructed the Secretary of State to deliver a note [which] . . . states that the Government of the United States is hereby formally terminating diplomatic relations with the Government of Cuba. . . .

[2] Ibid., November 1, 1960.
[3] *Christian Science Monitor,* November 28, 1960.
[4] *The New York Times,* January 1, 1961.   [5] Ibid., January 3, 1961.

This calculated action on the part of the Castro Government is only the latest of a long series of harassments, baseless accusations and vilifications. There is a limit to what the United States in self-respect can endure. That limit has been reached.[6]

Cuban representative Raúl Roa then delivered a speech in the United Nations assailing President Eisenhower for breaking diplomatic relations. He remarked that, "although the Central Intelligence Agency has very often changed its plans and postponed them, we have accurate information that we are now facing the final blow." In his speech were details about where Cuba expected the attacks.[7] Apparently still with the belief, however, that the Kennedy administration would pursue significantly different policies from those of its predecessor, Major Guevara appeared on Cuban television to say that "it was important that President-elect John F. Kennedy took no part in the United States' diplomatic break with Cuba."[8]

Guevara had recently returned from Moscow, where he had been promised increased economic trade and aid. This was a multilateral trade agreement, he announced, under which Communist countries would purchase four million tons of Cuban sugar. Other benefits obtained in the treaty included: assistance in resuming operations at the formerly American-owned Nicaro and Moa Bay nickel plants; technical training in Communist nations for 2,400 Cubans; equipment from Poland for a shipyard capable of building ships of up to 10,000 tons, for facilities to produce shoes and electric batteries, and for two slaughterhouses capable of handling three hundred cattle and three hundred pigs daily; equipment from Communist China for twenty-four plants to make such things as automobile parts, paper, dynamite, and rubber, at prices 50 per cent below those "in capitalist countries"; and 40 million pesos of credit from Czechoslovakia to be used to build a plant for producing motor vehicles in Cuba.[9]

[6] President Eisenhower, Statement Announcing the Break in Diplomatic Relations with Cuba, January 3, 1961, as cited in R. Smith, op. cit., p. 282.   [7] *The New York Times,* January 5, 1961.
[8] Ibid., January 7, 1961.   [9] Ibid., January 14, 1961.

During January 1961 Castro again mobilized his militia against an imminent invasion. At the same time, in an intensified drive, an estimated 10,000 to 15,000 militia and regulars were battling from 300 to 1,000 guerrillas in the Escambray mountains.[1] On January 2 Soviet tanks, vehicle-drawn artillery, and four-barrel anti-aircraft guns were displayed in a Havana parade.[2] The fortification of Havana was then stepped up.[3] On January 9 there was a stir in Cuba when a U.S. aircraft carrier sailed into Guantánamo to be incorporated into the forces there.[4] By late January, reports of executions of Escambray insurgents were becoming more frequent. It had also become expensive to maintain the 200,000-man militia supposedly ready to defend Cuba from invaders, and most of it was demobilized. Castro claimed that he had expected the invasion to come before Kennedy's inauguration.[5]

During late 1960, dissension had developed among the exiles. The political voice for the exile forces was a group in Miami called the Frente. It reportedly "represented the center of the exile world at a time when the Right was still unduly prominent."[6] In December 1960, disagreement had developed between the Frente in Miami and the exile leaders in Guatemala over the question of who would make decisions for the Cuban exile forces. Added to this problem was the fact that many of the lately arrived Cuban exiles demanded representation in the Frente for the socialist elements among them. By January 1961 this dissension was being carried into the Guatemala training camp as new recruits arrived from Miami. There was a general strike against the brigade leader,[7] who then resigned his command. U.S. leaders, however, refused to let him step down and

[1] These figures are from several newspaper accounts. It is quite probable that the number of remaining guerrilla troops was exaggerated, because they were completely defeated about three weeks later.

[2] *The New York Times,* January 2, 1961.

[3] This was calculated, most likely, for its propaganda value, since it was improbable that invaders would choose Havana for their attack.

[4] *The New York Times,* January 9, 1961.

[5] Ibid., January 21, 1961.   [6] Draper, op. cit., p. 70.

[7] The official name of the Cuban exile troops was Brigade 2506.

convinced the strikers that they should obey him.[8] This division among the exile troops threatened to force cancellation or delay of the invasion. Another of the problems in maintaining order at the Guatemala camp was that many of the recent arrivals had no military background and were more concerned with their political beliefs than with military discipline.

Sub-Phase C: Early 1961–April 1961

After his inauguration, President Kennedy called for a review of the invasion plan. As it stood at that point, the plan provided for a landing at Trinidad, a city of 20,000 at the base of the Escambray mountains in which there had been an extensive guerrilla force (although it was rapidly dwindling). The idea was that the invaders could link up with what remained of this guerrilla force and gain a foothold in Cuba that would serve as a base for operations against Castro. The Kennedy administration was anxious to conceal its participation in the proposed action and feared that a landing at Trinidad, with its relatively large civilian population, might require additional commitment by the United States. Another drawback to the Trinidad plan was that there was no nearby airfield capable of servicing B-26 bombers that could be easily secured and held. It was regarded as essential that Cuban exile aircraft operate from Cuban soil as soon as possible after the invasion.[9]

President Kennedy is reported to have been particularly concerned with the consequences of unfavorable world opinion regarding U.S. intervention. He stipulated that no U.S. forces whatsoever would be used in the invasion and that the U.S. position remain correct in the United Nations: "The integrity and credibility of Adlai Stevenson constitute one of our great

[8] Johnson, op. cit., pp. 60–3. While available accounts of events in Guatemala at this point suggest that the strike was of serious proportions and arose from political differences among the exiles, the episode may have been exaggerated and may, in any event, have contained large elements of personal rather than political rivalry.

[9] This information is compiled from several sources: Johnson, op. cit., pp. 64–7; Schlesinger, op. cit., pp. 242–3; and Charles J. V. Murphy, "Cuba: The Record Set Straight," *Fortune*, September 1961.

national assets. I don't want anything to be done which might jeopardize that."[1]

In early February the Cuban militia forces battling the Escambray guerrillas were reportedly increased to 40,000.[2] Beginning at this time, several teams of Cuban exiles trained in the United States, Guatemala, and Panama were infiltrated into the island and began efforts to foster popular discontent and upheaval. They reported that Castro had tightened his militia operations to the point where it was impossible for them to receive any of the air-dropped supplies. As Castro had announced earlier in great detail, his troops were intercepting the air drops[3] and had also captured several U.S. citizens who had been fighting against him.[4]

The captured U.S. citizens were executed with much publicity; and Castro declared that if the United States could promote counterrevolution in Cuba, he could promote revolution elsewhere in Latin America.[5] By the end of February the guerrilla uprisings in Cuba had been virtually erased.[6] Reports also circulated that short-range Soviet rockets were in place near Havana.[7]

At the same time, Castro continued to make overtures to Kennedy for negotiation of Cuban-U.S. differences. Since January there had been a marked decline in anti-U.S. harangues from Havana. Castro proclaimed that he was ready to "begin anew with the United States," although he would wait to see what Kennedy would do about the "anti-Castro mercenaries being trained by the United States in Florida and Guatemala."[8] President Kennedy answered that the United States wanted a

[1] Schlesinger, op. cit., p. 271.

[2] The New York Times, February 10, 1961.

[3] Ibid., January 7, 1961. The list of arms captured (from only two air drops) included 67 Garand rifles, 23 machine guns, 61 (unidentified) rifles, 3 bazookas, 2 mortars, hand grenades, and large amounts of ammunition. At this rate, Castro could have accumulated a good arms supply just from intercepted air drops.   [4] Johnson, op. cit., pp. 59–60.

[5] The New York Times, March 15, 1961.

[6] Ibid., February 28, 1961.

[7] New York Herald Tribune, February 20, 1961. These were reportedly 19.6 feet long, but no substantiation of the report can be found.

[8] The New York Times, January 20, 1961.

better life for Latin American people and would welcome progressive governments that promised this. He would not consider a restoration of diplomatic relations with Cuba, however, "as long as he was convinced that the Castro Government was aligned with the Communist bloc."[9] Castro answered that Cuba's economic ties with Communist nations were "totally without political commitments." He suggested that, if President Kennedy were to demonstrate "by deeds" that Washington would not interfere in Cuban internal affairs, Cuba was prepared to "do its part" to reduce tension in the Western Hemisphere. He insisted, however, that the United States would have to end its "economic aggression" against Cuba as a condition of negotiations.[1] In March President Kennedy cut off a large part of the remaining trade between Cuba and the United States.[2] The presence of Soviet military equipment and technicians in Cuba, as well as Castro's clear intention to continue his strong relations with the Communist bloc, made it impossible for Kennedy to accept Castro's professed good intentions.

Meanwhile, arguments among the Cuban exiles had been eased with the dissolution of the Frente and creation of the Cuban Revolutionary Council, which provided representation to those exiles who had socialistic leanings. With this matter settled and a stronger bond established between the council and the camp in Guatemala, recruitment increased rapidly. From three hundred to four hundred men a week began to arrive at the Guatemala camp in February.[3]

At the end of February 1961, it has been reported, an inspection team from the Pentagon was sent to Guatemala to report on the readiness of the troops. When the team returned, with the judgment that morale was high and combat readiness good, the National Security Council met to consider the undertaking.[4]

By the middle of March a new invasion plan had evolved. The landing point had been changed from Trinidad to an area more remote from population centers and one with a suitable

[9] Ibid., January 26, 1961.   [1] Ibid., February 15 and 25, 1961.
[2] Ibid., March 11, 1961.   [3] Johnson, op. cit., p. 63.
[4] Ibid., p. 66.

air strip that could easily be secured. Such an air strip would eliminate the need for long bombing runs from Central America. One other change in strategy called for by the new plan was a night landing, instead of a day landing as had been planned previously. By the time the Revolutionary Council had been formed, the new plan was set for an invasion at the Bay of Pigs on April 5. (The date was subsequently postponed to April 10 and finally to April 17.)[5] The Kennedy administration stressed that under no circumstances would U.S. forces enter the conflict—short of an attack by Castro on Guantánamo.[6]

To improve the chances of the exile landing, it was decided that B-26 bombers manned by Cuban exiles would attack military airports in Cuba before the invasion in an effort to wipe out Cuba's small air force and thus prevent air strikes against the invasion force.[7] The exile air force was to consist of sixteen B-26 bombers, two of which would attack Managua, two San Antonio de los Baños, two Santiago de Cuba, four Ciudad Libertad (the main base), and one San Julián and Baracoa.[8] Castro's air force was regarded as disorganized and lacking experience, and few of its planes were considered to be in combat condition. Two bombing attacks on the Cuban air force before the invasion were calculated as sufficient to destroy it.

Up to this point it appears that, although detailed plans were far advanced for the use of the exile forces, the final commitment to their use had not yet been made. The time was rapidly nearing, however, when some action would have to be taken or the effort dismantled.

The authors of the plan urged its immediate implementation on various grounds. According to current intelligence, by June Cuba would have fliers trained to man the Soviet MiG aircraft that Castro had received, a factor which might make the invasion effort disastrous. The number of Cuban exile troops in Guatemala had increased rapidly, and, it was argued, it would

[5] Ibid., p. 67.
[6] Opinion of Stewart Alsop, as referenced in R. Smith, op. cit., p. 70.
[7] Johnson, op. cit., pp. 67, 70, 88.
[8] Eight more bombers were later added to the sixteen originally planned.

be unwise to return them to Miami in their present frame of mind. Morale was then high among the troops, but it was likely that unrest could break out anew at any time.[9] President Miguel Ydígoras Fuentes of Guatemala was anxious that the troops be removed from his country by June, because their presence was causing political unrest.[1] And despite his repeated assertion that they were his own troops training to defend Guatemala from imminent attack by Castro,[2] it was becoming public knowledge that they were actually Cuban troops training with U.S. aid. Also, the rainy season would start shortly in Guatemala, making further training operations impossible.[3]

On April 3, 1961, the State Department issued a strongly worded White Paper on Cuba that made clear the gravity with which the United States viewed the situation:

> The present situation in Cuba confronts the Western Hemisphere and the inter-American system with a grave and urgent challenge. . . .
> What began as a movement to enlarge Cuban democracy and freedom has been perverted . . . into a mechanism for the destruction of free institutions in Cuba, for the seizure by international communism of a base and bridgehead in the Americas, and for the disruption of the inter-American system.
> It is the considered judgment of the Government of the United States of America that the Castro regime in Cuba offers a clear and present danger to the authentic and autonomous revolution of the Americas—to the whole hope of spreading political liberty, economic development, and social progress through all the republics of the hemisphere.[4]

At a news conference on April 12, President Kennedy said, however, that "there will not be, under any conditions, an intervention in Cuba by the United States Armed Forces." He declared that

> The basic issue in Cuba is not one between the United States and Cuba. It is between the Cubans themselves. I intend to see that

---

[9] Szulc and Meyer, op. cit., p. 104.   [1] Ibid.
[2] *The New York Times,* March 21, 1961.
[3] Schlesinger, op. cit., pp. 239–40.
[4] U.S. Department of State, *Cuba,* as referenced in R. Smith, op. cit., pp. 312–13.

we adhere to that principle, and, as I understand it, this administration's attitude is so understood and shared by the anti-Castro exiles from Cuba in this country.[5]

On April 10 the Cuban exile forces in Guatemala (numbering about 1,400) were moved to Puerto Cabezas, Nicaragua, the embarkation port. On April 14 the bulk of the force left for Cuba on several old cargo ships, which were armed with .50-caliber machine guns.[6]

At the same time, a diversionary action was being attempted between Baracoa and Guantánamo. This plan called for a small landing of Cuban exiles to draw Castro's attention and forces to the lower end of Cuba, away from the actual invasion point. This group of exiles never landed, however, reportedly because they encountered evidence that Castro's militia had anticipated their arrival and set up an ambush.[7]

On April 15 several B-26 aircraft manned by exile pilots trained in Guatemala bombed Castro's air force at various points on the island. Much of the Cuban air force was destroyed in the raid, but four fighters and two bombers survived. As was noted earlier, the invasion plan had called for *two* raids on Cuban air bases prior to the landing. The decision to cancel the second raid, and reportedly to scale down the one that did occur, is one of the more obscure and controversial aspects of the entire Bay of Pigs episode. That the failure to eliminate Castro's air power had serious implications for the invasion will become clear, although no one can say with certainty that the invasion would otherwise have succeeded. Among the explanations offered for the decision to limit the pre-invasion air attacks are: the adverse international reaction to the first raid; pressures within the U.S. government, especially from UN Ambassador Adlai Stevenson; faulty military advice as to the significance of the remaining Cuban aircraft; underestimation of the number of planes remaining and their type; and failure to anticipate the novel use Castro would make of the remaining craft.

[5] U.S. Department of State: *American Foreign Policy: Current Documents, 1961*, Department of State Publication 7808 (Washington: GPO; 1965), p. 288.   [6] Johnson, op. cit., pp. 74–87.
[7] Ibid., pp. 85, 88, 95.

After the air raid and reports of ships off Baracoa, Castro braced himself once again for an invasion. On April 16 the Brigade 2506 paratroop battalion, numbering 176 men, left Puerto Cabezas in five C-47 transports bound for the Bay of Pigs.

PHASE III   *April 17–19, 1961*

The Bay of Pigs invasion was designed to secure a relatively small base. If this could be accomplished, U.S. planners saw two possibilities for subsequent action. The first would be that the establishment of a beachhead would permit bombing of strategic military targets on all parts of the island, leading potentially to the disintegration of the Castro government. A second possibility would be that the two opposing forces might reach an impasse, in which the exiles could neither extend their territory nor be forced off the island; the impasse might result in a negotiated cease-fire and free elections.[8] In either event, the presence of the exile forces in Cuba would provide a rallying point for anti-Castro Cubans.

Initially, only a small area of combat would be involved. There were three major strategic points—Playa Larga, Playa Girón, and San Blas—which formed a triangle. The beach was firm, rocky soil extending inland for three miles, bordered by impassable swamps and accessible only by three highways. This is one of the reasons it was chosen as the invasion point, for the beachhead could be held fairly easily by a small number of troops blocking the access routes. Because the Cuban navy was regarded to be of no consequence[9] and because the air force would presumably have been destroyed by the Brigade's air

[8] Information from an interview with Richard M. Bissell, Jr., Washington *Star,* July 20, 1965.

[9] No account mentions the Cuban navy as a consideration in the invasion plans. Early in April the U.S. government made an agreement with some members of the Cuban navy for them to escape in several Cuban torpedo boats. The plan failed when a private U.S. vessel stationed in the area to fuel the escaping boats was intercepted by a Cuban warship. Szulc and Meyer, op. cit., p. 117.

raids, Castro would, it was assumed, have to depend upon his ground forces.

The Brigade infantry was to land at Playa Larga, Playa Girón, and a point twenty miles east of Playa Girón called Green Beach. From Playa Larga to Green Beach they would extend along forty miles of Cuban coastline. The battalion of paratroopers would land in three places—along each road crossing the swamps—and their commander would then establish his headquarters at San Blas, twenty miles northeast of Playa Girón.[1]

In this way, Castro's counterattack would be confined to very narrow approaches, and the area of battle would be predetermined by the attacking forces. Given sufficient ammunition and the proper weapons, the invading forces would be able to hold their positions despite the superior size of Castro's forces. The invading forces would be brought in by sea and by air. They would, therefore, need the airfield[2] and a protected port. These could easily be secured from ground attack by obstructing the roads; they would, however, be highly vulnerable to enemy air attack.

There were roughly 1,400 men in the invasion force,[3] divided into six regular battalions and one paratroop battalion. Of these, only 135 were professional soldiers; the rest were students, professional men, or peasants. The average age was twenty-nine, but ages ranged from under twenty to over sixty. About half of the men had received less than a month of training or none at all.[4] Their weapons were those readily available in Western markets. (See the WEAPONS section of this chapter for details.) In addition, small arms were being taken along for Cubans who might join the invaders once they had landed.[5] These extra arms were never unloaded in Cuba, and ammunition for the invaders' own arms lasted less than two days. Because those who had been trained were trained well and

[1] Johnson, op. cit., pp. 83-4.   [2] The airfield was near Playa Larga.
[3] This figure is compiled from various accounts, especially those of Schlesinger and Sorensen.   [4] Johnson, op. cit., pp. 98-9.
[5] Ibid., pp. 84-5. It was estimated that 5,000 Cubans might join the brigade voluntarily in the first two days.

used their training to advantage in battle, the invasion force was successful, while ammunition lasted, in holding positions against forces many times its size. The fact that many of the exiles had not received adequate training does not seem to have had a negative effect on their final performance.[6]

Castro's total force prior to the invasion was about 240,000 equipped troops—40,000 regulars and 200,000 militia. (See the WEAPONS section of this chapter for details.) The forces he deployed against the invasion were estimated at 36,000 troops (both militia and regulars) with forty tanks, 122mm artillery, mortars, two bombers, and four fighters (the other aircraft having been destroyed in the April 15 raids). The Cuban troops were not very well trained, and there is evidence that they did not perform well in battle although they were deployed well by their leaders.[7] The invading forces were simply overwhelmed by numbers and disadvantaged by lack of ammunition.

A large portion of Castro's troops were left behind to carry out police duties at the time of the invasion. In Havana alone, 200,000 people were arrested, and such arrests were made all over the island.[8] Very few of the population defected when the invaders landed, and the underground that might have existed was effectively incapacitated by arrests.[9]

The invasion plan hinged on the supposition that it would take Castro enough time to mobilize his forces and reach the beachhead with effective weapons to allow the invaders to land and secure their positions. While it was hoped that the invaders' strength would be increased by defections, the immediate rallying of the Cuban population was not regarded, however, as a prerequisite for success in establishing the beachhead.

The cargo ships carrying the exile force reached the Bay of Pigs before dawn on April 17 and began landing troops under cover of darkness. The first troops ashore encountered some Castro militia guards but overcame them. Castro alerted all his

[6] This comment is derived from Haynes Johnson's description of the battle, pp. 103–72.   [7] Ibid.   [8] Schlesinger, op. cit., p. 274.
[9] Johnson, op. cit., pp. 103–72.

forces in the Bay of Pigs area and mobilized several nearby battalions.[1] His principal objective was to crush the invaders at Playa Larga, the invasion point farthest inland. He also ordered the remainder of his air force to strike the supply ships at dawn.

When the Cuban air force attacked at dawn on April 17, Brigade troops were still coming ashore, their landing having been delayed by reefs that had not been taken into account in planning the operation. The ships were, therefore, forced to leave with most of the supplies and some troops still on board. The command ship, bearing the bulk of the supplies, and the communications ship were sunk by Castro's pilots.

With tanks, heavy mortars, cannon, and bazookas, the invaders had little trouble defending their positions as Castro's troops moved down the highways into the swamps. The exile force did not have enough ammunition to carry on indefinitely, however, and the supply ships did not return that night for fear of further air attacks. During the first day of the invasion, the Brigade troops at Playa Larga faced and defeated ten to fifteen times their own strength in men, arms, and tanks. They retreated to Playa Girón the next morning for lack of ammunition.

Throughout the first day, the paratroop battalion, with headquarters at San Blas, held its positions on the approachways. The ferocity of the battle led Castro's 20,000 troops to believe that they were facing great numbers of men and caused them to delay their attack, thus giving the paratroopers time to retreat to Playa Girón.[2]

On April 18, the second day at Playa Girón, defenses were set up with the hope that the United States might provide direct support rather than see the undertaking fail. When it became

[1] Upon arriving at the Bay of Pigs, Castro received word of another invasion in Pinar del Río Province, and immediately headed there. This was a simulated battle that had been set up with rubber rafts and sound devices to add to Castro's initial confusion. Ibid., p. 110.

[2] A conservative estimate places Castro's losses during the entire battle at 1,250 dead on the battlefield, 400 dead from wounds and lack of medical care, and 2,000 wounded. Ibid., p. 179.

apparent to the Brigade leader that there would be no support from U.S. aircraft, he ordered his troops to disband and destroy their equipment.[3] At this point, U.S. naval destroyers and the Brigade supply ships appeared offshore accompanied by several U.S. fighter aircraft. In the belief that they were planning to attack,[4] Castro halted his forces approaching the beach, and the Brigade survivors escaped possible annihilation.

It had been decided *during* the invasion to make an attempt to bomb the main Cuban air force base at San Antonio de los Baños, but when the Brigade's B-26's had arrived there on April 18, clouds obscured the field and they were forced to turn back without striking. It had also been decided that the B-26's would strike Castro's forces at the battle area under the protective cover of several U.S. fighter aircraft. Due to a miscalculation of time, the B-26's arrived an hour early at the Bay of Pigs on April 18 and were lost to Castro's aircraft. The U.S. fighter aircraft never left their carrier.

For several days after the invasion, U.S. naval forces remained positioned off the coast of Cuba to rescue survivors. They also threatened to attack if Castro should begin to execute his captives.

On April 18 Premier Khrushchev had sent President Kennedy a note defining the position of the Soviet Union: "We will extend to the Cuban people and its Government all the necessary aid for the repulse of the armed attack on Cuba."[5] President Kennedy answered that the United States planned no military intervention in Cuba; but that, should an outside force intervene, the United States would honor its obligations to defend the hemisphere from external aggression.[6]

[3] An alternative plan had been to escape into the Escambray mountains eighty miles away and mount a guerrilla offensive from there, but the Brigade leaders had not been informed of this. It would have been impossible to conduct a guerrilla campaign in the impassable swamps around the Bay of Pigs. Ibid., p. 224.

[4] Earlier in the day, two unmarked F-86 Sabre jets had appeared overhead, and Castro later claimed that they fired on his troops. This has never been proven or disproven. Ibid., p. 148.

[5] U.S. Department of State, *American Foreign Policy* . . ., p. 295.

[6] Ibid., pp. 296–7.

PHASE IV   *From April 19, 1961*

Addressing the American Society of Newspaper Editors on April 20, President Kennedy stated that, while the United States had held to its policy of nonintervention in Cuba, "our restraint is not inexhaustible" and the United States would act to safeguard its security.[7] With this speech, Castro's fear of U.S. intervention increased once again, especially in view of the continued presence of two U.S. task forces in the waters off Cuba.[8]

There was no question of settlement between the United States and Cuba. So the dispute continued, setting the stage for

---

[7] Ibid., pp. 299–302.   [8] Johnson, op. cit., p. 189.

FACTORS BEARING ON TRANSITIONS

PHASE I *to* PHASE II: *The Introduction of a Military Option*

1. Factors Tending to Introduce a Military Option
   a. Historically the United States had dominated the Caribbean and Latin America. This was particularly true of Cuba, whose independence from Spain the United States had directly helped to achieve, on which the United States had a major naval base, and whose economy was U.S.-dominated and closely tied through preferential agreements to the United States; this history colored each adversary's perception of the other. The United States was perhaps even more sensitive to developments in Cuba than in other parts of the region, and anti-Yankeeism had been a favored theme of Cuban and other Caribbean demagogues.
   b. U.S. relations with Batista had been cordial until very late in his regime. Castro was thus able to identify the excesses of Batista with the objectives of U.S. policy and interest in Cuba.
   c. Castro's policies and the political orientation of the men he chose for positions of power created the strong impression

direct confrontation between the United States and the Soviet Union in 1962. The invasion force taken prisoner by Castro was eventually ransomed for a very large quantity of medical supplies; when the exiles returned to the United States, they were still uncompromisingly against the Castro regime.[9] The United States remained for Cuba the imperialist neighbor threatening the Cuban revolution; and the U.S. government continued to see Castro as "no Tito, nor a satellite, nor an immediate military threat, nor simply a minor nuisance, but a persistent source and model for insurgency and terror in the hemisphere."[1]

[9] Ibid., p. 352.

[1] Albert and Roberta Wohlstetter: *Controlling the Risks in Cuba,* Adelphi Paper No. 17 (London: Institute for Strategic Studies; 1964), p. 24.

RELEVANT CONTROL MEASURES

Keeping the Dispute Nonmilitary

1. Measures to Offset These Factors
   a. U.S. initiatives to rectify the consequences of past errors—
      short of reversing history—to remove the events and
      attitudes that adversely colored U.S.-Cuban relations.
      Re-examination of the strategic value of Guantánamo or
      the development of alternate bases or alternate means of
      securing equal strategic value. More U.S. understanding of
      and less sensitivity toward anti-Yankee sentiments.

   b. Re-examination of U.S. relations with unpopular
      dictatorships, in Latin America and elsewhere, in cooperation
      with such organizations as OAS. Active U.S. policies to
      encourage liberal, even if less docile, regimes.
   c. Distinguishing between political/ideological differences
      and security threats. Counteracting latter by other means,

that his regime was Communist-dominated. Broad strategic, political, and ideological concerns of the Cold War were thus injected into the dispute.

d. Support for Castroism in other parts of the Caribbean and active Cuban efforts to foster and support "Fidelista" revolutionaries raised a threat to the stability and security of the whole hemisphere. Increasingly close economic ties between Cuba and the Soviet Union made the development of Cuba as a base for Soviet-sponsored subversion in the hemisphere a distinct possibility.

e. While Soviet support for Cuba was increasing, Cuba's proximity to the United States and distance from the Soviet Union and the overwhelming U.S. military superiority in the Caribbean isolated Cuba from direct Soviet military support in the event of a military showdown, unless— and it appeared unlikely—the Soviet Union were prepared to risk a direct clash with the United States.

f. U.S. public opinion switched dramatically from initial support of Castro to anti-Castroism. This switch was spurred by Castro's growing reliance on Cuban Communists and the Soviet bloc, by excesses in rooting out Cuban liberals as well as Batistianos, and—for specific segments of public opinion—by uncompensated expropriations of American-owned property.

g. Continued opposition within Cuba to Castro was evidenced by the existence of anti-Castro guerrilla bands and a continued outflow of refugees, including increasing numbers of people who had initially supported Castro.

h. The guerrillas and large numbers of Cuban exiles made available a proxy for the achievement of U.S. goals and made it possible for the United States to avoid the undesirable consequences of direct action.

i. The United States had had great success in dealing indirectly with a comparable threat of a Communist-dominated government in Guatemala.

j. The action of the Organization of American States was weak, in terms both of taking effective steps to isolate or counter the threat from Castro and of seeking to limit the range of U.S. responses to that threat.

preferably on a multilateral OAS or UN basis—
"containment" of Castro, strengthening potential Latin
American victims, etc. Ideally, ending the East-West Cold
War.

d. Measures suggested above to contain Cuba and strengthen
potential victims of Castro actions. Direct pressures on
the Soviet Union to desist.

e. Increasing the likelihood of direct Soviet involvement by
Soviet guarantees to Cuba, presence of Soviet forces, etc.
(Note: This would probably have controlled the conflict
at the cost of creating a more dangerous one—e.g., the 1962
missile crisis.)

f. Education of the U.S. public to distinguish between an
irritation and a threat. International instruments and action
on human-rights violations. International agreements, with
international enforcement machinery, to prevent
uncompensated expropriations. U.S. guarantees for private
investors against loss from such expropriations.

g. To the extent that U.S. policies are based[2] on the existence
of an anti-Castro movement in Cuba, more rapid
achievement by Castro of control over dissident Cubans.

h. Enforcement of U.S. laws and international agreements
concerning actions of refugee groups. Dispersal of refugees
both among countries and, within the United States, *away
from* areas proximate to Cuba.

i. Analysis of lessons of past experience, particularly of the
preconditions for success and the chances and consequences
of losses as well as of gains.

j. Strong OAS action to contain Cuba and deal jointly
with its threats to other American states and/or a strong
OAS stand against unilateral U.S. action.

---

[2] Note that, for simplicity and as an aid to future applications, the
authors have used present tenses, present conditionals, and present
participles at will throughout the RELEVANT CONTROL MEASURES.

2. Factors Tending to Keep the Dispute Nonmilitary

   a. The United States was concerned with world reaction to overt U.S. moves against Castro. In the developing countries in general and in Latin America in particular, little distinction was made between Communist subversion and Western imperialism. Credence given to the widespread Latin American suspicion of U.S. motivations and intentions would further weaken the potential of an inter-American system willing and able to maintain peace and stability within and among the American states.

   b. The UN and OAS charters prohibited the threat or use of force among states, and specific inter-American agreements proscribed the training and arming of exiles for action against their homelands and the provision of bases for exiles for this purpose.

   c. For reasons cited above in (a), the United States did not want to intervene overtly against Castro.

   d. Castro avoided direct provocation—such as an attack on the Guantánamo naval base—that might have precipitated a direct U.S. response.

   e. The Cuban refugees were weak and divided over the future of Cuba. They agreed only on the immediate objective of overthrowing Castro. Furthermore, likelihood was great that their ranks were infiltrated by Castro agents.

PHASE II *to* PHASE III: *The Outbreak of Hostilities*

During Phase II, several questions arose concerning the scale/scope of threatened hostilities. In one instance—the shift from a strategy of strengthening anti-Castro guerrilla movements inside Cuba (directly and by infiltration of U.S.-trained exiles) to a strategy for small-scale invasion by exile forces to provide a focus for coalescence of anti-Castro elements there—an expansion of the scale/scope of potential hostilities took place. In at least two other instances, the potential for expansion did not occur: threatened Soviet defense of Cuba with missiles and potential direct involvement of U.S. troops. The invasion plans were twice altered to restrict their scale/scope: cancellation of one pre-invasion air raid and selection of an invasion site far from centers of civilian population. (These shifts will not be analyzed separately.)

2. Measures to Reinforce These Factors

   a. Strengthening the likelihood of adverse reaction to U.S.
      action by the OAS and UN and others. Statements
      opposing unilateral intervention. Public and private
      bilateral pressure on the United States. Creating a UN
      presence in Cuba.

   b. Enforcement machinery for such prohibitions.

   c. UN or other international fact-finding machinery to make
      it more difficult to act covertly. Enhancement of the U.S.
      desire to avoid acting overtly by specific threats of
      counteraction. To raise the political and other costs of action.

   d. Articulation, jointly or reciprocally, of Castro's intentions
      vis-à-vis Guantánamo and clarification of what acts the
      United States would regard as a *casus belli*.

   e. Further weakening the cohesion of exile groups. Dispersion
      of these groups. Legal controls of their activities.

Preventing the Outbreak of Hostilities

1. Factors Tending to Promote the Outbreak of Hostilities

   a. The arrival of Soviet arms in Cuba gave substance to the prospect of Cuba's becoming a base for active Soviet subversion in the hemisphere.

   b. The prospect of such a base for subversion was made more salient by continued activities of Castro to foment and encourage rebellious groups in Latin American and Caribbean countries.

   c. Normal channels of diplomatic communication were disrupted, first by Castro's refusal to use them and subsequently by the formal severance of diplomatic relations by the United States.

   d. OAS took no concrete action either to counter the potential threat of Castro and Castroism or to place obstacles in the path of U.S.-Cuban exile actions.

   e. While it was the scene of heated U.S.-Cuban exchanges, the United Nations took no action either to counter the potential threat of Castro and Castroism or to place obstacles in the path of U.S.-Cuban exile actions.

   f. The Presidential election in the United States heightened public attention to events in Cuba. The widely publicized debates on television saw the advocacy of strong action against Cuba by the candidate who eventually won the election.

   g. The timing of the U.S. election and the Presidential inauguration were such that either an administration about to leave office or one freshly installed was in office when critical decisions were made.

   h. Castro's growing internal military strength, success of his efforts against the guerrillas, the arrival of Soviet arms, and in particular the impending availability of trained pilots to man Soviet-supplied MiG's created a time pressure. Unless action were taken quickly, it was doubted that the exile effort could succeed without U.S. involvement.

   i. While at one point in Phase II the Soviet Union threatened to defend Cuba with missiles, the threat of direct Soviet involvement was discounted. This discounting was given added credence when the Soviet Union later qualified its threat as "symbolic."

   j. As their training progressed, the motivation of the exile forces increased. It was feared that U.S. efforts to halt the

1. Measures to Offset These Factors

   a. Agreement among arms suppliers to avoid introducing additional arms to conflict areas. In this case, such agreement coupled with alternate guarantees of Cuban security by United Nations, Soviet Union, others.

   b. Measures to contain Castro and strengthen capacity of potential victims to resist. Hopefully, UN or OAS action to achieve or supplement these goals. International fact-finding to determine extent of Cuban complicity. UN or OAS sanctions or other strong measures against Cuba, if proven violations persist.

   c. Creation of neutral—UN or other—channels of communication, good offices, mediation.

   d. Stronger OAS action to reduce or counter Castro threat (the above suggestion on fact-finding (b), for example) and to place obstacles in the way of U.S. unilateral action.

   e. UN action to reduce or counter Castro threat and to place obstacles in the way of U.S. unilateral action—fact-finding, UN presence, multilateral assistance to potential victims of Cuban subversion, etc.

   f. Short of altering the U.S governmental system, measures to insulate sensitive foreign-policy issues from partisan election-time politics.

   g. Short of altering the U.S. governmental system, time-stretching devices proposed internationally or taken on U.S. initiative.

   h. Time-stretching devices, which would in this instance include a delay in the delivery of Soviet aircraft and in the return of trained pilots.

   i. Increasing likelihood of Soviet involvement. (See, however, the caveats in 1(e) on p. 129.)

   j. Willingness to control and physically restrain, if necessary, disgruntled exile forces.

            invasion plan would lead to independent action by exiles who would, furthermore, be embittered by a U.S. policy reversal.

  k. Other channels of U.S. influence over Castro and Cuban policy had been tried but had failed. In particular, the leverage of U.S. economic pressure had been weakened by the willingness of the Soviet Union to fill the breaches created by the cut in Cuba's quota of sugar sales to the United States and the U.S. embargo on Cuban trade.

2. Factors Tending to Inhibit the Outbreak of Hostilities

  a. Despite the position taken by Kennedy during pre-election debates, Castro made overtures to the new President for a negotiated *modus vivendi.*

  b. The dissensions among the Cuban exiles increased, spreading at one point from political leaders in Miami and New York to the training camps in Guatemala.

  c. Concern over world reaction was given substance by the international outcry over the first of two planned pre-invasion air strikes. Reputedly partly in response to this reaction, the second strike was cancelled.

PHASE III *to* PHASE IV: *The Termination of Hostilities*

    Hostilities ended quickly with the military victory of Castro's forces over the exiles. The issue for the U.S.-exile side was whether to accept the situation created by the defeat or to continue hostilities. In the circumstances, continuing the hostilities would have required the direct introduction of U.S. forces, thus intensifying hostilities.

1. Factors Tending to Inhibit the Termination of Hostilities

  a. Despite U.S. hopes to keep its role covert, the prime U.S. role in the invasion was widely presumed, and in fact was publicly acknowledged by President Kennedy. There was thus little strength left to the argument that U.S. prestige would not be harmed so long as its role could be successfully denied.

  b. The United States continued to have overwhelming military preponderance in the area.

  c. The United States felt a high sense of responsibility for the fate of the captured exiles.

k. To the extent that Soviet backing removes pressure on Castro
to seek an accommodation with the United States,
maintaining that pressure by reducing Soviet incentives to
replace the United States as Cuba's chief trading partner by
increasing the cost to the Soviets, threatened trade reprisals,
pressure from other producers, etc.

2. Measures to Reinforce These Factors

   a. Increased international pressure on the United States to
   seize the opportunity of a new administration to seek
   negotiations. Enhancement of prestige value of agreement
   to negotiate by offer of prestigious auspices, etc.

   b. Promoting weakness and division among exiles.

   c. Clearer, earlier, and more explicit criticism of U.S. actions.
   UN and OAS articulation of the obligations of the United
   States not to take unilateral action.

Moderating/Terminating Hostilities

1. Measures to Offset These Factors

   a. To the extent that the desire of the United States to keep its
   role covert has served as a restraint on its earlier actions,
   maintaining the pretense might reinforce arguments against
   intensifying hostilities. Conversely, increasing the costs
   in propaganda and influence for actions taken and
   acknowledged would have the same effect.

   b. Creating countervailing force in the area (but see caveats
   in 1(e) on p. 129). Enhancing legal and propaganda
   restraints on use of great-power force.

   c. International (OAS or UN) action to prevent inhumane
   treatment of prisoners.

2. Factors Tending to Promote the Termination of Hostilities
   a. Castro not only defeated the invasion forces but also jailed or otherwise neutralized thousands of potential dissidents when the invasion began. There was thus little chance that internal unrest would be triggered by a continuation of hostilities.
   b. U.S. officials, including President Kennedy, had repeatedly and publicly pledged that no U.S. forces would be used to topple Castro.
   c. Castro heeded U.S. warnings that harsh measures against the captured exile forces would risk direct U.S. action.

PHASE IV

> *The analysis of this conflict ends with the termination of hostilities. The dispute that underlay the U.S.-Cuban conflict in which the Bay of Pigs hostilities occurred has not been settled. While U.S.-Cuban hostilities have not been resumed, Cuban exile forays have continued, at times accompanied by allegations of U.S. involvement. The U.S.-Cuban conflict laid the foundations for the much more serious crisis over Soviet missiles in Cuba in the fall of 1962.*

THE WEAPONS

Cuban Weapons Acquisition

When Fidel Castro took power in Cuba on January 1, 1959, he inherited an assortment of weapons that had been imported by previous governments; many of these arms were of U.S. origin. Rifles, machine guns, perhaps some heavier battlefield weapons, Sherman tanks, B-26 bombers, and a small number of T-33 jet trainers, all supplied under military agreements between the United States and Castro's predecessors, were at the disposal of Castro's armed forces.

During the course of his first year in power, Castro evidently

2. Measures to Reinforce These Factors
   a. Increasing stability of Castro control in Cuba.

   b. Reinforcement of the value of honoring these pledges, e.g.,
      their endorsement by leading world statesmen and public
      figures.
   c. International action to secure humane treatment of prisoners.

---

applied in several quarters (especially Europe) for a further
supply of arms to equip his revolutionary forces. He was
successful in buying a large number of NATO "FAL" automatic rifles and NATO "MAG" machine guns from Fabrique
Nationale of Belgium. The price, however, was high (reportedly
$150 apiece), about twice the usual amount. When these
weapons arrived in Havana harbor in early 1960, one of the
three ships carrying the consignment blew up. Castro blamed
the United States for this, implying that it was attempting to
undermine his revolution by impeding weapons supply to his
forces.[3]

Another well-publicized effort on Castro's part to equip his
military forces was his attempt to replace aging piston-engine

[3] *The New York Times*, March 11, 1960.

Sea Furies with more modern jet Sea Hunters. The United
States is reported to have informed Britain of its disapproval of
any such transaction. The transaction never took place, and
Castro claimed that the United States was directly responsible
for his defenselessness in the face of the aerial raids being made
on Cuba, presumably by Batistiano exiles in Florida.[4]

Cuba's armed forces increased rapidly between 1959 and
1961. When Castro assumed power, there were probably only
about 8,000 armed men, under some sort of loose organization,
whom Castro could have regarded as military forces. By mid-
1960 the Cuban army was estimated at 35,000 armed men; and
a militia of perhaps as many as 200,000 men had been formed,
although these were not trained or adequately armed.[5] During
the next six months, the militia received weapons (mainly
Soviet and Czech), and the regular army increased to between
40,000 and 50,000 men. Thus the number of armed forces
available to Castro at the time of the Bay of Pigs invasion was
about 250,000.[6]

The first significant contacts between Cuba and the Soviet
Union appear to have been made in February 1960, and it was
perhaps at this time that arrangements were made to supply
Cuba with weapons. It can be deduced from statements made
by Castro in mid-1960 that July was the time when the first
shipments of small arms began to arrive in Cuba. These probably consisted of Czech and Soviet rifles, submachine guns, and
machine guns. The quantities shipped during July–October
1960 were sufficient to arm the 200,000-man militia.[7]

It was perhaps between August and October 1960 that larger
Soviet weapons began to appear in Cuba; in November 1960
the U.S. State Department reported that Soviet assault guns,
antitank guns, field guns, howitzers, medium and heavy tanks,
and armored cars had been shipped to Cuba in significant

---

[4] Boston *Daily Globe,* February 17, 1960.
[5] Jack Raymond: "A Military Embargo of Cuba?" *New Republic,*
July 18, 1960, p. 8; *Newsweek,* September 5, 1960, p. 43.
[6] *Newsweek,* April 24, 1961, p. 62.
[7] *The New York Times,* November 18, 1960.

Weapons Available to Castro's Cubans in April 1961

Weapon	Number	Source
.30-cal. M1903 Springfield rifle	?	U.S.
M1 Garand rifle	?	U.S.
7.62mm FN NATO "FAL" rifle	about 65,000	Belgium
Browning machine gun	?	U.S.
7.62mm Model 52 rifle	45,000	Czechoslovakia
.30-cal. ZB R-2 automatic rifle	125,000	Czechoslovakia
9mm Browning automatic pistol	very few	Cuba
.45-cal. Cuban Sten submachine gun	very few	Cuba
9mm Models 23 and 25 submachine gun	10,000	Czechoslovakia
7.62mm FN NATO "MAG" machine gun	200	Belgium
Uzi submachine gun	1,000	Belgium
7.92mm Model 37 machine gun	?	Czechoslovakia
7.62mm AK47 assault rifle	?	U.S.S.R.
7.62mm DP, DT, and DTM machine gun	?	U.S.S.R.
7.62mm SG-43 Goryunov machine gun	?	U.S.S.R.
bazooka	a few	U.S.
flame thrower	about 10	U.S.
Quad 12.7mm AA heavy machine gun DShK M 1938/46		Czechoslovakia
14.5mm KPV heavy machine gun on ZPU4 mount (anti-aircraft)	80	U.S.S.R.
mortar	150	U.S.S.R.
mortar	104	?
assault gun	19	U.S.S.R.
rocket launcher	30	U.S.S.R.
antitank gun	60	U.S.S.R.
76mm field gun	78	U.S.S.R.
122mm field gun (D-74?)	4	U.S.S.R.
howitzer	?	U.S.S.R.
field artillery	?	Italy
Sherman tank	15	U.S.
T-34/85 medium tank	50	U.S.S.R.
JS2 and JS3 heavy tank	50	U.S.S.R.
armored car	60	?
T-33 jet trainer	4 originally, 2 in battle	U.S.
B-26 piston-engine bomber	15 originally, 2 in battle	U.S.

Weapon	Number	Source
Sea Fury piston-engine fighter	10 originally, 2 in battle	U.K.
MiG-15 fighter	8 in crates	U.S.S.R.
patrol vessel (ex-sub chaser)	1	U.S.
coast-guard cutter	10	U.S.
coast-guard cutter	1	Cuba
auxiliary coast-guard cutter	2	Cuba
motor launch (ex-MTB)	3	U.S.
auxiliary patrol craft	12	U.S.
PCE-type patrol escort	2	U.S.
motor torpedo boat	10	E. Germany
cruiser (frigate rated as cruiser)	1	U.S.
PF-type frigate	3	U.S.

quantities.[8] These had, of course, been accompanied by large amounts of ammunition. In addition, it was rumored that Cuban pilots were being trained in Eastern Europe to fly Soviet MiG fighters. And the first MiG-15's were scheduled to arrive in Cuba during the spring of 1961.[9]

Other than about ten fast motor torpedo boats, which had been supplied to Cuba by East Germany, the Cuban navy was still limited in April 1961 almost exclusively to old U.S. equipment. As it was, the motor launches, coast-guard cutters, patrol vessels, and four frigates—which made up the bulk of the Cuban navy—were insignificant during the fighting at the Bay of Pigs.

Cuban Exiles' Weapons Acquisition

The brigade of Cuban exiles that invaded Cuba at the Bay of Pigs in April 1961 was armed exclusively with weapons supplied free of cost by the U.S. government. Some significance can be found in the types of weapons supplied. The early history of military build-up on the part of the Cuban exiles is concerned mainly with organization and training. In March 1960 the decision was taken by the U.S. government to support

[8] Ibid.   [9] Szulc and Meyer, op. cit., p. 104.

anti-Castro forces both inside and outside Cuba.[1] This involved supplying arms and communications equipment to anti-Castro groups in Cuba by means of air drops and selecting and training guerrilla reinforcements from Cuban groups outside Cuba.

The type of training and weapons that the United States gave these Cuban exiles was determined by the mode of battle the planners thought would be most effective against Castro. During the first few months of training, the Cuban exiles were instructed in guerrilla warfare; the limited number of Cubans who received this training were then to train more of their own kind in camps in Guatemala (and eventually in Cuba, if the original plans could have been followed).[2]

During September 1960, as Soviet arms were pouring into Cuba, Castro was breaking the supply lines of the guerrilla groups. Lack of success in creating an effective network of anti-Castro groups in Cuba and the rapid build-up of Soviet arms were probably the two most important factors that led the U.S. planners to change their battle plans from protracted guerrilla warfare against Castro to a conventional beach landing. In response to this decision, the nature and composition of the Cuban forces being trained in Guatemala changed.[3]

By November 1960 the Cuban exile forces were preparing for a beachhead landing. Their numbers increased quite rapidly; by April 1961 there were about 1,500 men in this invasion force—three times as many as in November 1960. Many of these troops had been recruited at the last minute and were trained poorly or not at all. This factor does not seem to have figured heavily, however, in the outcome of the Bay of Pigs invasion.[4]

There seems no doubt that the United States made a careful assessment of the weapons that would be both most effective in the hands of the Cuban invaders and common enough that they could have been bought by the Cuban exiles themselves. In the

[1] Schlesinger, op. cit., p. 222.
[2] Johnson, op. cit., pp. 37–9.
[3] Ibid., pp. 54–5; Szulc and Meyer, op. cit., p. 87.
[4] Johnson, op. cit., pp. 63, 74.

case of the smaller weapons—such as rifles, machine guns, bazookas, and mortars—this double requirement does not seem to have affected the firepower of the invading force, the weapons of this nature available on the market being quite effective by any standards. Similarly, the Sherman tanks provided to the Cuban brigade were quite capable of meeting those

Weapons Available to the Cuban Exiles in April 1961

Weapon	Number	Source
MI Garand rifle	unlimited	U.S.
.50-cal. heavy machine gun (Browning)	?	U.S.
75mm recoilless rifle	?	U.S.
2.36" or 3.5" bazooka	70	U.S.
4.2" mortar 81mm mortar	30	U.S.
antitank gun	18	U.S.
Sherman medium tank	5 or 6	U.S.
armored car	10	U.S.
Douglas B-26 light bomber (piston-engine)	24	U.S.
C-47 transport	a few used for dropping paratroops	U.S.
LCI (W. W. II)	2	U.S.

Castro would send against them. Where the double requirement had a damaging effect was with the aircraft provided to the Cuban exiles. These were limited to old piston-engine aircraft— bombers that could carry the large fuel load needed to fly missions from Nicaragua to Cuba. Unopposed in the air, the B-26's, even with their small bomb loads, might well have been entirely adequate in this case. But the presence of Castro's two small jet trainers proved to be devastating to the B-26 bombers of the Cuban exiles and to their supply ships.[5]

---

[5] Bissell interview, cited above; Johnson, op. cit., pp. 112–14.

SUMMARY OF CONTROL MEASURES

In summary form, the key conflict-control measures in this case might have been the following (an asterisk indicates that the measure was actually taken):

KEEPING THE DISPUTE NONMILITARY

Peaceful liberalizing policy prior to revolution.
Emphasis on political rather than military view of situation.
Containment rather than intervention policy.
Multilateralization of disputes.
Pressure on U.S.S.R. not to intervene.
Prophylactic OAS action:
> Inspection and publicity,
> Believable deterrence,
> Training of internal defense forces.

UN fact-finding machinery.
Internal political, economic, and social health.
Minimizing of external subversion.
Limited U.S. definition of strategic value.
Universal rules against unilateral intervention.
Ban on exile military training and activity.
International human-rights tribunal.
Dispersal of exile groups.
Isolation of remediable issues.
International arbitration, conciliation, good offices, mediation, and
> adjudication.

Guarantee of private investors from expropriation losses.

PREVENTING THE OUTBREAK OF HOSTILITIES

Strong UN measures:
> Fact-finding and publicity,
> Time-stretching delays,
> Channels of communication,
> Good offices and peaceful-settlement procedures.

OAS deterrence of unilateral intervention.
Soviet deterrence of United States.
Restrictions on arms transfers to internal security needs.

MODERATING/TERMINATING HOSTILITIES

U.S. restraint.*
Effective internal control.*
Better intelligence.
Mutual strategic deterrence.*
U.S. marginal strategic superiority (preferably at low levels).*

CHAPTER 7

The Greek Insurgency, 1944–1949

THE PHASES OF CONFLICT

Each of our other case studies begins with a full narrative reconstruction of the events of the conflict in order to develop its complete phase structure. In the analysis of the Greek Insurgency, that procedure will be omitted, and in its stead brief statements of the transitions from phase to phase and of the sub-phases will be substituted. This is possible in the present case because of the existence of a thorough history of the Greek crisis.[1] From it one can identify phases and transitions; we have used it as a basis for an analysis of factors bearing on conflict control.

---

[1] W. C. Chamberlin and J. D. Iams: *Rebellion: The Rise and Fall of the Greek Communist Party* (Foreign Service Institute, Fifth Senior Seminar in Foreign Policy, June 2, 1963 [mimeographed]). There is a large literature on the Greek Insurgency, but this study, with its parallel histories of the Greek Communist Party (KKE) and the military aspects of the Insurgency, seemed especially rich in the kinds of material this analysis required. The only aspects of the conflict for which supplementary material appeared necessary were the role of the United Nations and the details of U.S. and Soviet policy statements. Materials on these have been drawn from David W. Wainhouse et al.: *International Peace Observation: A History and Forecast* (Baltimore: The Johns Hopkins Press in cooperation with The Washington Center of Foreign Policy Research, School for Advanced International Studies, The Johns Hopkins University; 1966), pp. 221–41; and *A Decade of American Foreign Policy: Basic Documents, 1941–49*, U.S. Congress, 81st, 1st Sess., Senate Committee on Foreign Relations, Document No. 123 (Washington: GPO; 1950), pp. 765–82.

GREECE

Transition from PHASE I
to PHASE II   *March 10, 1944*

The decision of the wartime resistance coalition—the National Liberation Front (EAM), which was dominated by the Greek Communist Party (KKE)—to challenge the royalist government-in-exile for the control of postwar Greece led to the creation of the Political Committee of National Liberation (PEEA) on March 10, 1944. This marked the conjunction of the available force—EAM's wartime guerrilla resistance force (the National Popular Liberation Army, or ELAS)—and a political decision to employ it in a struggle for control of

Greece. It signaled, therefore, the introduction of a military option into the long-standing political dispute between the Greek government and KKE.

Transition from PHASE II
to PHASE III₁   *December 3, 1944*

In a bid to seize power in Athens (virtually the only part of Greece not under ELAS control) from the returning Greek government and the British, KKE initiated major hostilities in Athens between ELAS and their forces.

Transition from PHASE III₁
to PHASE IV₁   *February 12, 1945*

Militarily defeated, KKE agreed at Varkiza on February 12, 1945, to cease fire, disband its forces, and surrender its weapons.

Transition from PHASE IV₁
to PHASE III₂   *February 1946*

Since KKE was actively rebuilding its organization and expanding its political base, hostilities eventually broke out in the Greek countryside, particularly in the northern regions near the Yugoslav, Albanian, and Bulgarian borders.

Intensifications within PHASE III₂

Sub-Phase A: February–September 1946

Hostilities during this first part of Phase III₂ took the form of actions between the Greek government gendarmerie and small, isolated, largely uncoordinated bands, not all of them under KKE control. During this sub-phase, guerrillas who had fled to Yugoslavia, Albania, and Bulgaria following the Varkiza Agreement began to re-enter Greece, although they continued to use territory north of the border as a sanctuary.

Sub-Phase B: September 1946–October 1947

After September 1946 the guerrilla bands grew larger and their operations more coordinated. Markos Vafeiadis became military leader of the guerrilla movement. On the government side, the main arm of action shifted from the gendarmerie to the armed forces.

Sub-Phase C: October 1947–July 1949

Until October 1947, KKE continued to function as a legal political party, endorsing the rebels' aims but denying sponsorship of the insurgency. In that month KKE came out in open endorsement of the revolt and assumed open leadership of it. Shortly thereafter, KKE formed a Provisional Democratic Government. Militarily these events signaled the emergence of large, coordinated guerrilla units and a formal military command structure. During this sub-phase, one threatened intensification —the involvement of the cities in the insurgency—failed to materialize.

Sub-Phase D: July–October 1949

In July the closing of the Yugoslav border to the guerrillas and their supplies forced on them a major tactical decision: whether to continue the type of hostilities involving large guerrilla units, while holding the mountain strongholds of Grammos and Vitsi as sanctuaries and depots within Greece, or to revert to the less coordinated tactics pursued in Sub-Phase B. The guerrillas chose the former course.

Transition from PHASE III$_2$
to PHASE IV$_2$ October 1949

In an effort to defend the Grammos and Vitsi strongholds against conventional assault by the Greek National Army, the guerrillas were decisively defeated and their remnants driven into exile in Albania. On October 16, 1949, the Provisional Democratic Government declared that it had, for the moment, put aside its arms.

PHASE I *to* PHASE II: *The Introduction of a Military Option*

1. Factors Tending to Introduce a Military Option

   a. In January 1942, after the German attack on the Soviet Union, ELAS was formed as a resistance force against German, Italian, and Bulgarian occupation forces.

   b. In December 1942 KKE decided to take over control of ELAS. This was quickly accomplished, but ELAS included non-KKE elements. KKE used the issue of antimonarchism to rally to ELAS non-Communist groups that shared that sentiment, one widely held among Greek liberals who equated the monarchy with the prewar Metaxas dictatorship.

   c. ELAS managed, during the wartime period, either to liquidate or to absorb most of the resistance groups that were not KKE-dominated.

   d. The largest non-Communist force that ELAS did not succeed in liquidating was EDES. While initially antimonarchy as well as anti-Communist, EDES was persuaded by the British to support the cause of the monarchist government-in-exile. This helped further to reinforce ELAS's appeal to the entire spectrum of liberal, antimonarchist sentiment in Greece.

   e. Factors related to the strategic requirements of World War II led Britain in particular, and subsequently also the United States, to give support to the resistance forces in money and matériel. As the largest and most effective resistance group, ELAS received the bulk of this aid. Strategic considerations leading to Allied support for ELAS included: the need to disrupt supply lines through Greece to German forces in North Africa, diversion of attention from Sicily as the point of Allied landings in southern Europe, and (later) harassment and delay of German withdrawal from Greece.

   f. In addition to the arms given the resistance by the Allies, ELAS captured or took over large stores of arms and ammunition at the time of the Italian surrender.

2. Factors Tending to Keep the Dispute Nonmilitary

   a. Under the prewar Ioannis Metaxas dictatorship, KKE had been thoroughly infiltrated by Greek security police—so

RELEVANT CONTROL MEASURES

Keeping the Dispute Nonmilitary

1. Measures to Offset These Factors

   a. Avoiding great-power hostilities that create the situations in which resistance forces develop; specifically, in this instance, facilitating the Nazi-Soviet pact's continuation in order to neutralize local Communist groups. Encouraging anti-Communist resistance forces.

   b. Pressure on the Greek government-in-exile to submit the question of the monarchy to popular vote. Liberalization of the political composition of the exile government.

   c. Active assistance to non-Communist resistance groups. Denial of matériel and other aid to Communist-dominated groups.

   d. Major assistance to EDES. Encouraging EDES to follow a popular, liberal policy to give non-Communist liberals a democratic alternative.

   e. Ideally, avoiding World War II. Alternatively, seeking other means to secure strategic objectives. Tighter control on use made by resistance of the assistance given.

   f. Measures to control disposition of arms left over from great-power conflicts.

2. Measures to Reinforce These Factors

   a. Vigorous measures, draconic if necessary, to destroy KKE structure and its leadership.

much so that at one point there were rival Politburos, one made up almost exclusively of Greek police plants. Party leaders were in jail or exile, the party structure destroyed or discredited.

b. Anti-KKE resistance forces existed. The largest was EDES which, although reduced in size and confined to a small part of Greece, was never eliminated by ELAS.

c. The British gave some money and matériel assistance to EDES as well as to ELAS.

PHASE II *to* PHASE III₁ (*the Second Round*): *The Outbreak of Hostilities*

As early as September 1943, KKE decided to create in occupied Greece the nucleus of a political structure that would make Allied reoccupation of Greece militarily and politically unnecessary. This decision culminated in the creation on March 10, 1944, of PEEA, which assumed administrative responsibility in areas under ELAS control. Despite this, ELAS did not contest the landing in Athens in October 1944 of British and Greek government troops. By December, however, this position was reversed, and KKE initiated a battle for Athens. This section will look first at the factors bearing on the potential outbreak of hostilities in October that did not occur—the so-called First Round—and subsequently the Second Round in December 1944, when they did occur.

THE ABORTED FIRST ROUND

1. Factors Tending to Promote the Outbreak of Hostilities

   a. In addition to the arms acquired from the British and Italians, ELAS captured large quantities of arms and ammunition from the retreating German forces.

   b. With the withdrawal of German troops on October 12, 1944, ELAS was in unchallenged control of almost all of Greece.

---

2. Factors Tending to Inhibit the Outbreak of Hostilities

   a. King George of Greece agreed to submit the constitutional question of restoration of the monarchy to a postwar plebiscite.

   b. PEEA had a significant following among exiled Greeks, including members of the Greek Army of the Middle East (the British-trained and -equipped army of the government-in-exile). This sympathy for the antimonarchy cause among exiled political leaders led to the formation of a coalition Government of National Unity in which the KKE-dominated

    b. Large-scale assistance to non-Communist resistance forces.

    c. Restricting matériel assistance only to non-Communist groups. Control over use of assistance given.

Preventing the Outbreak of Hostilities

1. Measures to Offset These Factors
    a. Measures to control disposition of arms left over from great-power conflicts.

    b. Immediate introduction of massive counterforce—Greek government, friendly ally, or neutral.

2. Measures to Reinforce These Factors
    a. Administration of proposed plebiscite under neutral supervision, with guarantees as to its fairness and implementation.
    b. Creation of government reflecting all segments of popular opinion. Enabling all parties, including KKE, to compete in open political forum. Alternatively, strong measures to reduce, eliminate KKE. (Note: While KKE's belief that it could "win" by legitimate political means helped *at this time* to avoid hostilities, KKE was not prepared to abandon its

National Liberation Front (EAM) had a part. Such political successes led KKE to believe that it could gain control through political means.

c. Initially, EAM repudiated the concessions made by its representatives at the meeting that created the Government of National Unity. Reportedly, however, at the urging of the Soviet Union, EAM reversed its position and agreed to participate.

d. Both EDES and ELAS agreed to place their resistance forces under the orders of Lieutenant-General Sir Ronald MacKenzie Scobie, GOC (General Officer Commanding) Allied Forces in Greece.

e. In Moscow on October 9, 1944, the Soviet Union and Britain agreed to respective spheres of influence in the Balkans by which Greece was placed in the sphere of British predominance.

f. ELAS and EAM appear to have underestimated their own military strength and overestimated that of the British and Greek government forces.

THE SECOND ROUND

While the factors identified above combined to abort the threat of hostilities in October 1944 and to permit unopposed landing by British and Greek government forces, the decision not to use force was reversed by KKE between October and early December, when KKE contested British-Greek government control of Athens—regarded by both sides as the key to control of all Greece.

1. Factors Tending to Promote the Outbreak of Hostilities

   a. The factors favoring the outbreak of hostilities listed above still applied. In addition, KKE recalculated the balance of strength and concluded that it favored KKE's chances. In particular, the small size of the British contingent was taken as an indication of a limited British commitment to the Greek government's cause.

   b. U.S. policy at this time appeared to be friendly to EAM's aims or at least generally distrustful of both the British and the Greek government's apparent efforts to force an unpopular, undemocratic government on an unwilling Greek people.

goal of "winning" and later resorted to force when political avenues appeared closed. The measures noted here need to be coupled with preparations to inhibit the temptation to try any but a political course.)

c. Encouragement of Soviet attitude toward KKE. (See, however, note to preceding measure.)

d. Immediate steps to take over and disband ELAS in particular.

e. Strengthening and formalizing agreement that place[2] Greece outside Soviet sphere. (Note: This, however, would have sanctioned a reciprocal strengthening of Soviet control within its sphere).

f. Keeping real strength concealed. More realistically, making balance in reality what EAM thought it was.

---

1. Measures to Offset These Factors

   a. Clarification of British intention both by formal statement and, more importantly, by actual force on the scene.

   b. Clarification of U.S. policy. Greater U.S. understanding of nature of EAM and its objectives. Articulation of U.S. support for liberal aims but rejection of autocratic means.

[2] Note that, for simplicity and as an aid to future applications, the authors have used present tenses, present conditionals, and present participles at will throughout the RELEVANT CONTROL MEASURES.

   c. U.S. public opinion also was generally more sympathetic
      toward EAM than toward the Greek government. U.S. press
      coverage of events in Greece reinforced the view of EAM as
      liberal antimonarchists with a romanticized resistance past
      and of the Greek government as both a tool of British
      imperialists and the heir of the discredited pro-Fascist
      prewar Metaxas dictatorship.

   d. EAM had agreed to demobilize ELAS by December 10.
      Once disbanded, it would have been difficult and
      time-consuming to reorganize.

PHASE III$_1$ *to* PHASE IV$_1$: *The Termination of Hostilities*

> *Hostilities broke out in Athens on December 3, 1944,
> when violence arose out of a prohibited KKE-sponsored
> demonstration. It seems clear from the sequence of events
> that the incident was deliberately provoked and staged by
> KKE. After over a month of fighting in Athens, EAM
> agreed to a cease-fire, which was signed at Varkiza in
> mid-February 1945. From the point of view of conflict
> control, the most interesting question is why, given its virtual
> control of Greece outside Athens, KKE declined to make the
> struggle nationwide and, instead, accepted defeat in Athens
> as terminating the Second Round. The issues to be analyzed
> here, therefore, are "moderation and termination" versus
> "intensification and continuation" of hostilities.*

1. Factors Tending to Inhibit the Termination of Hostilities

   a. The factors favoring outbreak of hostilities listed earlier
      continued to apply.

   b. By resorting to force, KKE had revealed its hand and alerted
      the British and the Greek government to its intention to
      seize power if possible. Some, but by no means all, of
      EAM's non-Communist supporters, in Greece and elsewhere,
      were alienated by this. EAM's pose as a political force not
      dominated by KKE and KKE's posture as a legitimate
      political party were thus already compromised.

---

2. Factors Tending to Promote the Termination of Hostilities

   a. KKE won a further political concession when King George
      agreed not to return to Greece until the promised plebiscite
      on the monarchy had been held.

   b. No matériel assistance to the insurgents was forthcoming
      from either the Soviet Union or its satellites on Greece's
      borders. The Soviet Union was preoccupied with its own
      domestic affairs and with the consolidation of its new East
      European satellite systems. It hoped, furthermore, to solidify

   c. Public education as to the nature of EAM. Greater public information on Greek events, if necessary through neutral fact-finding, in the credibility of which the public has confidence. Vigorous steps by the Greek government to liberalize its policy and disassociate itself from the prewar dictatorship.

   d. Introduction and rapid deployment of force necessary to ensure compliance with demobilization order.

Moderating/Terminating Hostilities

1. Measures to Offset These Factors

   a. Measures listed earlier to control and counteract KKE power.

   b. Vigorous public information campaign about KKE's role and nature, through neutral, believable channels—if possible, by neutral fact-finding.

---

2. Measures to Reinforce These Factors

   a. Neutral auspices to organize and supervise plebiscite, with guarantees as to its fairness and implementation.

   b. Encouraging Soviet disinterest in Greece by observing an equal disinterest in Russia's actions in areas it regarded as being within its sphere of influence.

into a longer-term arrangement the spheres-of-influence agreement with Britain.

c. Many members of KKE and EAM were fearful of Bulgaria's and Yugoslavia's intentions toward Greek Macedonia. Particularly in the case of Yugoslavia, it was feared that the price of Yugoslav aid might be the movement of its forces into Greek Macedonia, under the guise of aid to the insurgents but equally in pursuit of Yugoslavia's hope of uniting all of Macedonia under its control.

PHASE IV$_1$ *to* PHASE III$_2$ (*the Third Round*): *The Resumption of Hostilities*

For nearly a year, relative peace prevailed in Greece while EAM played the role of a political party. There were some small bands operating in the mountains, but these appear to have been independent, local bands.

1. Factors Tending to Promote the Resumption of Hostilities

   a. While ELAS agreed at Varkiza to surrender its arms and, in fact, turned in larger quantities than it was required to, it kept its *best* arms and equipment.

   b. Some elite ELAS forces did not surrender and disband, as agreed at Varkiza, but fled instead to Albania, Yugoslavia, and Bulgaria, where they received training in guerrilla warfare. The main base for this training was in Yugoslavia.

   c. The Greek government, while allowing EAM and KKE to operate openly, punished and harassed former ELAS-EAM members, who were thus driven back into the KKE fold.

   d. The Greek government was unable to control—or, in the view of EAM, made no effort to control—the activities of right-wing terrorist groups. The national guard, which the government created to restore order, operated more vigorously against suspected left-wing than right-wing groups.

   e. Soviet expressions of hostility toward the Greek government increased. British protests over Soviet actions in Romania may have weakened the value to the Soviet Union of the wartime British-Soviet spheres-of-influence agreement for the Balkans.

   f. KKE estimated that, despite government efforts to exclude it, KKE influence in the Greek armed forces and police was high. (In September 1945 KKE estimated this as 15 per cent of the army, 17 per cent of the air force, 5 per cent of the navy, and 2 per cent of the police.) KKE thus felt that the Greek armed forces would be ineffective in engagements with it.

   c. Strengthening historic Balkan linguistic rivalries, which were much older, and perhaps even stronger, than new-found ideological affinities. Strengthening both Greek and Yugoslav chauvinism, revanchism.

Preventing the Resumption of Hostilities

1. Measures to Offset These Factors
   a. Supervision, inspection, and control—by joint groups or neutral authority—of arms surrendered and arms retained.

   b. Border control to prevent guerrilla movements into neighboring territories initially or to keep them from returning. Vigorous steps to deny guerrillas unmolested sanctuary in neighboring states.
   c. Measures by the Greek government to weaken and restrain KKE while appealing to its non-Communist and non-hard-core following (i.e., just the opposite of the policy pursued).
   d. Vigorous, unbiased enforcement of public order.

   e. Strengthening and formalization of spheres of influence.

   f. Improving the political reliability of government forces.

g. The Greek economy had been severely damaged by invasion
and occupation—agricultural production was much below
standard, industry was at a stand-still, and the transportation
system was virtually destroyed. Inflation was out of control
and the measures Greece could take on its own to begin
reconstruction only added to inflation. The occupation period
had displaced thousands of people. All these problems were
exploited by KKE and aggravated both by KKE-inspired
urban unrest and continued low-level rural tension.

h. KKE organized an extensive information and supply net in
the towns and villages—the Self-Defense Forces (MLA).
MLA was not primarily a military force, except for operations
in the immediate vicinity of a home town or village.

2. Factors Tending to Inhibit the Resumption of Hostilities

a. KKE lost much support in Greece as a result of its action,
at the close of the Athens hostilities (Phase III_1), in taking
large numbers of hostages as it withdrew from the city and
in mass killings of alleged "traitors" and "enemies."

b. The Varkiza Agreement that ended Phase III_1 included
further government political concessions—Allied supervision
of the plebiscite on the monarchy and of the purge from
the civil service, police, and gendarmerie of wartime
collaborators and members of the German-sponsored
occupation security force.

c. EAM changed its name (while retaining its initials) to
National Anti-Fascist Front and announced it would act
purely as a political party. It initially instructed its members
to participate in the coming Greek elections. (Subsequently
this position was changed, and EAM, charging the
government with using right-wing terrorists to control the
election, decided to boycott them. The Soviet Union had
urged EAM to participate, but apparently its instruction did
not reach Athens until after the boycott decision had been
announced. In any event, EAM did not reverse its stand to
accord with the Soviet decision.)

d. Britain, which had initially seen its role as a limited one of
helping the government restore itself to Athens, agreed to
assist in organizing, equipping, and training the Greek army
and gendarmerie.

e. KKE leadership was split on a range of personal and policy
issues. Its rapid wartime expansion had seen the rise to
power in ELAS and EAM of many younger men who
challenged the older, prewar leadership for control of the
party. Even more serious was the perennial split on the
Macedonian question. In an earlier period (1920's, 1930's),
KKE endorsement of Macedonian autonomy had almost

   g. Massive economic and financial assistance, bilateral or multilateral.

   h. Vigorous government measures to control KKE operations. Active development and security programs by the government to reduce the appeal and pressure of KKE in towns and villages.

2. Measures to Reinforce These Factors

   a. Public information on KKE excesses. Neutral fact-finding to establish facts.

   b. Government accommodation to legitimate political demands endorsed by but not exclusive to KKE. Creating a liberal, democratic alternative to the reform promised by KKE.

   c. Encouragement to keep the conflict in the political arena by protecting the right of dissenters to engage in legitimate modes of dissent. This coupled with strengthened internal security to close off other alternatives.

   d. External assistance to develop internal security forces.

   e. Strengthening and exploiting divisions within KKE by appealing to Greek nationalism and, at the same time, Macedonian separatism. Accommodation measures by Greek government to legitimate Macedonian demands within framework of Greek Macedonia's remaining a part of the Greek state.

destroyed KKE's following in Greece, where Macedonian autonomy was equated with Bulgarian aggrandizement. Practical considerations of its position in Greece, as well as nationalist sentiments among KKE leaders themselves, therefore counseled against endorsing any separation of Macedonia from Greece. At the same time, Soviet pressures and both Yugoslav and Bulgarian interests in Macedonia, coupled with KKE's need for the support and assistance of its northern neighbors, created pressure on KKE to clarify its position on Macedonia's future. KKE's response was to seek to straddle the issue—a position that led to persisting tensions within KKE and between it and its Communist mentors.

f. The Soviet Union took to the UN Security Council in January 1946 the charge that British forces in Greece represented a potential threat to peace.

PHASE III$_2$ to PHASE IV$_2$: *The Termination of Resumed Hostilities*

Phase III$_2$, the Third Round, lasted from early 1946 until late 1949, when the guerrillas were decisively defeated by the Greek armed forces. (The opening of Phase III$_2$ coincided roughly with KKE-EAM's decision in January–February 1946 to boycott the Greek elections.) During these nearly four years of hostilities, four distinct intensifications *took place. The first three represented deliberate KKE decisions and correspond to the classic three stages of guerrilla warfare—sporadic violence, coordinated larger-scale guerrilla warfare, large-scale guerrilla-conventional operations. The fourth intensification was, in a sense, forced on the guerrillas by the closing of the Yugoslav-Greek frontier to them. (This section will examine these four sub-phases separately.)*

Sub-Phase A: The Period of Increasing but Not Large-Scale Violence

Beginning early in 1946, violence in the mountainous and border regions of Greece increased sharply. More formally organized groups entered Greece from the Yugoslav camps and attacked isolated gendarmerie posts. The units sought to avoid clashes with Greek army units and concentrated, instead, on consolidating their hold on the mountain areas. During this sub-phase, however, EAM and KKE continued to function as open, legal political groups and denied responsibility for the violence, which they blamed on government and right-wing terrorist repression. In this

f. UN fact-finding. Creation of UN presence in Greece.
Replacement of British forces by international force.

Moderating/Terminating Resumed Hostilities

(In the Greek Insurgency, as in some other cases examined,
the conflict-controlling goals of keeping the hostilities
moderate and terminating them were related to each other in
complex and frequently competing ways. In general, the focus
of this analysis will be the *moderation* of hostilities. For this
reason, any factors that tended to intensify hostilities—even
if their rationale were the termination of hostilities—are
regarded as conflict-promoting factors to be countered. A
quite different picture would emerge if the goal of *termination*
were placed at first rank. In the last sub-phase of these
hostilities, termination was the end product of intensification.)

---

sub-phase, the relevant questions concern which factors favored intensification and which favored moderation; either course might have led to termination.

1. Factors Tending to Favor the Intensification of Hostilities

   a. KKE's hope for further political gains was not fulfilled. In the March 1946 elections, which KKE boycotted, the Populist party won handily. KKE estimated its strength, represented by abstentions, as over 50 per cent; the Allied commission that supervised the election put it at less than 10 per cent. Similarly, in the September 1946 plebiscite on the return of the King, nearly 70 per cent voted "yes" although KKE instructed its followers to vote "no."

   b. Preparations required to counter guerrilla activities, as well as those activities themselves, further weakened the economic, social, and financial situation in Greece and, as yet, adequate international assistance had not been found.

   c. Training of guerrillas in Albania, Bulgaria, and Yugoslavia —particularly the last—continued, and bands operating from these areas succeeded in gaining control of the mountainous areas of northern Greece. Greece's military, police, and administrative authority in the border regions was destroyed.

---

2. Factors Tending to Favor the Moderation of Hostilities

   a. The splits within KKE continued, and added to them was a difference over whether to begin large-scale hostilities immediately or to exhaust political avenues first. This latter position prevailed and included among its adherents the head of KKE, Zakhariadis.

   b. In early 1946 the U.S. government loaned Greece $25 million to import reconstruction goods and $10 million to purchase surplus army equipment.

   c. In mid-1946 the government took strong measures to counter insurgent operations and reduce KKE freedom of action— the right to strike was restricted, *habeas corpus* suspended, and permission granted for arrest and search without warrant. Local security committees were created with authority to exile anyone suspected of activities "dangerous to the state." Initially these committees were to be created only in areas of guerrilla operations, but they soon extended to all of Greece.

   d. In August 1946 the Ukranian S.S.R. brought before the UN Security Council a complaint about incidents along the Greek-Albanian border. The United States proposed an

1. Measures to Offset These Factors

   a. Keeping conflict in the political arena while closing off alternative paths—including resort to force—by enhanced government internal-security capability.

   b. Major external assistance in economic reconstruction and in developing internal-security capability.

   c. Pressure on Albania, Bulgaria, and Yugoslavia to refrain from providing refuge and assistance to the Greek insurgents. Threat of sanctions, multilateral or bilateral. Neutral or other third-party border control. Threat to extend hostilities to include the sanctuaries. (Note, however, that if the threat to extend hostilities does not succeed, the result could be a further broadening of the war.)

2. Measures to Reinforce These Factors

   a. Strengthening and exploiting divisions within KKE, especially where the moderates can be strengthened. Making it possible for the moderates' approach to achieve positive goals while taking steps to close off the course advocated by the extremists.

   b. Massive bilateral or multilateral economic and financial assistance to aid Greek reconstruction and development. At this stage, strengthening Greek government forces to inhibit any KKE resort to more intense hostilities.

   c. Strong measures to restrain and, if possible, break up KKE structure. (Note, however, that if such measures are not applied equitably, they can have the effect of driving non-Communist dissidents into the KKE camp.)

   d. Bypassing Security Council and acting through General Assembly. Action by the assembly or by the Secretary-General on his own initiative to create a UN presence in the

investigating commission to look into the whole border
situation, but the Soviet Union vetoed the proposal.

Sub-Phase B: Organized Guerrilla Operations

*In the early fall of 1946 the character of the military
operations on both the guerrilla and government sides
changed. Guerrilla operations were coordinated under the
control of Markos Vafeiadis and took place on a larger
scale. The organization of the guerrilla forces and their
command structure was made more formal. On the
government side, responsibility for internal security was
transferred to the army. The relevant questions here are
which factors favored intensification and which favored
moderation; either course could have led to termination
of hostilities.*

1. Factors Tending to Favor the Intensification of Hostilities

   a. The Greek government armed forces had been rapidly
      expanded to meet the growing guerrilla threat. But in the
      process of such rapid growth, quality and the period of
      training had been sacrificed. Throughout most of this
      sub-phase, the guerrilla forces were better trained, better
      equipped, and better led than the Greek National Army.

   b. Britain, which had been chief source of external support for
      the Greek government, found the continuing and expanding
      financial burden too great to bear, particularly considering
      the war-weakened state of its own economy. It therefore
      announced that it would relinquish its role in Greece. Greece
      officially requested U.S. assistance. The outcome was the
      Truman Doctrine, a program of massive U.S. economic and
      military aid to Greece as well as Turkey.

---

2. Factors Tending to Favor the Moderation of Hostilities

   a. KKE continued to operate as an open political party and to
      deny any connection with the insurgency, although it was
      under increasing government pressure. During this sub-phase,
      its preoccupation was with strengthening its underground
      operations—a fact most observers took to indicate an
      impending worsening of the conflict.

   b. While the United States began large-scale military assistance
      to Greece during this sub-phase, the U.S. role was limited
      to giving matériel aid and assistance in planning for its
      arrival and use. Initially, no U.S. role was seen in providing
      advisers or observers in operations. And no U.S. forces were
      to be committed in actual hostilities.

   c. The military tactics pursued by the Greek government tended
      to restrict the scale/scope of hostilities at that time. A large

area of conflict. Action by the assembly to create a UN observation group, UN force to control borders, etc.

1. Measures to Offset These Factors

   a. Since in this instance the greater strength of the guerrilla forces, as compared with the government forces, encourages the guerrillas to intensify the hostilities, the development of stronger government forces may deter the intensification. At the same time, this course will enable the government forces to intensify their response to the guerrilla attacks.

   b. Expanded U.S. and other economic assistance. Restraint on building up military forces of either adversary. Introduction of neutral force to interpose itself between the adversaries.

2. Measures to Reinforce These Factors

   a. Encouragment to keep conflict in political arena. Alternatively, swift, decisive government action to eliminate KKE.

   b. Assumption of U.S. role by neutral party. Strong stands by the United Nations, Soviet Union, and others against expansion of U.S. role. Threat by others to take reciprocal action in support of guerrillas.

   c. Inadequate counterinsurgency strategy by the government helps keep hostilities moderate; hence, weakening government

push was made to clear the valleys of guerrilla forces and to garrison army units in vulnerable towns and cities. The result was to disperse the government forces and reduce them to a static defensive role, while initiative passed to the guerrillas. (The government created the National Defense Corps, a type of home guard, to free the regular armed forces for combat duty. But during this sub-phase, the move had little effect.)

d. While Yugoslavia and, to a lesser extent, Albania and Bulgaria provided the guerrillas a sanctuary and matériel assistance, their own armed forces did not become involved in the hostilities.

e. Greece took its charge that the three northern neighbors were aiding the guerrillas to the UN Security Council. The Council unanimously agreed to create a Commission of Investigation, composed of all eleven Council members, to conduct an on-the-spot investigation. The Commission visited the respective capitals and heard many witnesses. However, its observations on the border itself were confined almost exclusively to the Greek side because the other states declined to cooperate. The Commission's report corroborated the Greek charges and proposed border conventions and continued UN border observation. In the Security Council the Soviet Union vetoed resolutions designed to put these recommendations into effect. The majority of the Council then voted to remove the item from the agenda, thus opening the way for General Assembly action.

Sub-Phase C: Full-Scale Insurgency

On October 8, 1947, the character of the Greek Insurgency changed dramatically, in both its military and political aspects. On that date, KKE issued an open call for revolt— in contrast to its earlier denials of any connection with the hostilities. What KKE sought to spark was a full-scale civil war, but in this, for reasons noted below, it was unsuccessful. This sub-phase saw large-scale conventional clashes between government forces and the insurgents (who at the same time continued guerrilla operations) as well as altered tactics on the part of the government forces, who were seeking a definitive military victory over the insurgents. In the following analysis, the relevant questions are: Which factors favored intensification (including those factors that tended to make it possible for either side to achieve a military victory)? and Which favored moderation (including those that tended to make it impossible for either side to employ its force effectively in search of victory)?

counterinsurgency doctrine and capabilities. (However, this inadequacy also prolongs hostilities.)

d. Strong measures and pressures to prevent the introduction of military forces of involved neighbors, by threatening reciprocal action in support of the Greek government.

e. Creation of UN force to patrol, control borders. Threat of sanctions against intervening neighbors. Arbitration, good offices.

1. Factors Tending to Favor the Intensification of Hostilities

   a. The scope of the U.S. military mission in Greece expanded from its initial role of logistic support and supply to one of advice on and observation of military operations.

   b. On December 24, 1947, the insurgents declared the creation of a rival government—the Provisional Democratic Government of Greece.

   c. The National Defense Corps, created to relieve the Greek army of garrison duties and increase its flexibility and offensive strength, had some limited success in this mission. During 1948 campaigns, however, the lack of training and low quality of leadership of the Greek forces became evident. While the armed forces succeeded, after a two-month assault, in overrunning the guerrilla bastion in the Grammos area on the Albanian border, the largest part of the refugee force escaped into Albania. The army was unsuccessful in its efforts to storm the guerrilla bastion at Vitsi, at the junction of the Greek, Albanian, and Yugoslav borders. Following the appointment of General Alexander Papagos as commander-in-chief in January 1949 and the granting to him of sweeping authority within the military, hard-fought campaigns in southern and central Greece in the spring and early summer of 1949 succeeded in driving the guerrillas back into the border areas.

   d. During this sub-phase, matériel assistance and sanctuary continued to be offered to the insurgents by Albania, Yugoslavia, and Bulgaria, as well as financial assistance, propaganda, and diplomatic support by the other states of the East European bloc. Committees for Aid to Democratic Greece were formed in all the Soviet satellites and in West European countries with large Communist parties (e.g., France and Italy). There were periodic rumors of volunteer brigades being formed, but, if the rumors had any substance at all, the volunteers were not observed in Greece. Aside from periodic but infrequent clashes between Yugoslav border guards and Greek forces pursuing guerrilla bands, the fighting was confined to Greek fighting Greek—with Soviet-bloc-supplied weapons on one side and Western-supplied weapons on the other.

   e. Following the 1948 campaigns in the Grammos-Vitsi areas, Markos was relieved of all but the title of commander of the guerrilla forces—in January 1949 he was formally discharged. Markos opposed conventional stands such as those the guerrillas waged in that campaign and advocated instead continuation of rural-mountain warfare. (Part of Markos's

1. Measures to Offset These Factors

   a. In this case, expanded great-power involvement enables the Greek government to intensify the hostilities in an effort to terminate them; avoiding intensification means restricting or withdrawing U.S. assistance.

   b. International agreements to withhold recognition from such insurgent government. Pressure on other countries, especially the bloc countries, not to recognize such governments.

   c. In this case, the inadequacies in training, matériel, and leadership in the Greek armed forces help to keep the hostilities moderate; hence, avoiding intensification means keeping the Greek forces weak and their leadership poor.

   d. Threats to extend the hostilities to sanctuaries and/or to introduce third-party forces on the Greek government side. Neutral or third-party border control.

   e. Seeking to strengthen more moderate elements on guerrilla side.

argument was based on the potential loss of the Yugoslav
sanctuary as relations between KKE and Yugoslavia
deteriorated following the Tito-Cominform split. See below.)

2. Factors Tending to Favor the Moderation of Hostilities

   a. The UN General Assembly created the UN Special
   Committee on the Balkans (UNSCOB) with the authority
   formerly exercised by the Security Council's Commission
   of Investigation, which a Soviet veto had prevented being
   made permanent (see above). The Soviet Union and Poland
   did not accept membership on UNSCOB, so it was composed
   of Brazil, China, France, Mexico, the Netherlands, Pakistan,
   Britain, and the United States. With headquarters in
   Thessaloniki and observation posts on the border, UNSCOB
   operated chiefly on the Greek side of the frontier. It was
   able to verify Greek charges that the guerrillas were making
   active use of bases in Albania, Yugoslavia, and Bulgaria
   and that most matériel for the guerrilla forces came over
   these same borders.

   b. In part as a result of UNSCOB's verifications and in part
   as a result of generally altering perceptions of the Soviet
   bloc's postwar policy goals, both public and governmental
   opinion in the West became much more hostile to the
   guerrillas and more sympathetic to the Greek government's
   cause.

   c. In renewing UNSCOB's mandate in November 1948, the
   UN General Assembly openly condemned Yugoslavia,
   Albania, and Bulgaria for interference in Greece's internal
   affairs.

   d. Although there is some evidence that the Soviet Union
   endorsed KKE's plan to set up a rival Provisional Democratic
   Government in Greece, neither the Soviet Union nor any
   satellite, including the three northern neighbors of Greece,
   recognized the new government. UNSCOB issued a sharply
   worded warning to the latter three that such a step could
   lead to a much wider involvement by other states on the
   Greek government's side. The guerrilla forces were never
   able to seize and hold a city or town in Greece worthy of
   becoming their capital city and, throughout this sub-phase,
   the headquarters of the Provisional Democratic Government
   remained in Yugoslavia.

   e. When KKE issued its call for open rebellion, it set in motion
   a network of organizations in the cities of Greece that were
   supposed to embroil them, along with the countryside, in
   the struggle. The plans failed to materialize: KKE
   overestimated its city following and did not realize the extent

2. Measures to Reinforce These Factors

   a. Increasing UNSCOB's authority by expanding its capabilities for border observation, placing a UN force on the borders, etc.

   b. To the extent that this weakens the guerrillas' external support, it tends to moderate the conflict and can be enhanced by further exploitation of the bad press they are receiving. (Note: This same factor also helps to strengthen the determination of the government to intensify and continue hostilities.)

   c. Threat of sanctions against states openly intervening. Threat to extend hostilities to sanctuaries.

   d. International agreements not to recognize insurgent governments before free supervised elections can determine the popular will.

   e. Vigorous government action to deny cities to insurgents and to extend this denial to towns and countryside. Government measures to deny insurgents sources of recruitment, as well as financial and other support.

to which its actions in Phase III$_1$ and subsequently had lost it support; and the Greek security forces had effectively infiltrated the city organizations. The failure of KKE to retain a foothold in the cities cut the guerrillas off from recruits, money, and supplies and freed government forces for operations outside the cities.

f. Despite the relative security of the cities, there was strong political pressure on the government forces to retain garrisons in cities and towns because of potential adverse reaction from frightened city populations. (This and other political interference in the military command structure was largely overcome under the strong leadership of General Papagos.)

g. Ideological splits within KKE continued to polarize around the Macedonian issue. Prior to the Tito-Cominform split, the pressure on KKE was to endorse a position on Macedonia that would, in effect, have led to its detachment from Greece and domination by Yugoslavia. After the split, the issue became more complex because Tito and the Soviet Union and Bulgaria called for Macedonian autonomy and self-determination (which, as far as Greece was concerned, meant secession); but the Yugoslav formula would have united Greek Macedonia with Yugoslav Macedonia under Yugoslav control, while Bulgaria saw it united with Bulgarian Macedonia under Bulgarian control. Neither course was palatable to KKE. But the need for assistance from the north pushed it constantly toward one or another of these solutions. The role of Macedonian nationalists within the guerrilla leadership grew, and their numbers in the guerrilla forces increased.

h. The Tito-Cominform split of July 1948 did not have an immediate impact on the Greek Insurgency, although relations between KKE and Tito began to deteriorate shortly thereafter. The split did, however, accentuate a variety of tensions within KKE—the Macedonian issue just mentioned, as well as the strategic debate about the type of warfare to be waged. The issues became intermixed: on the one hand were those who felt the Yugoslav bases to be indispensable and who wanted to make concessions to Yugoslavia on Macedonia and other issues in order to retain the bases; on the other hand were those who felt that the guerrillas could wage successful conventional warfare without Yugoslav aid and who pressed for a united anti-Tito stand.

i. On several occasions during this sub-phase, the insurgent government—or the Soviet Union on its behalf—indicated a willingness to discuss an end to hostilities; but the Greek

f. Pressing for strategies that minimize the possibility of offensive use of military force.

g. Exploiting and strengthening splits within KKE. Encouraging Macedonian separatism. Encouraging KKE nationalism.

h. Encouraging divisions within the Communist bloc by emphasizing ideological, historical, linguistic rivalries.

i. Seeking a formula that met basic demands of each side regarding preconditions for negotiation—replacement of U.S. forces by neutral, UN force and control of border by

government and its supporters doubted the sincerity of the moves and felt KKE wanted only time to recoup and prepare for a Fourth Round. In May 1948 and again in January 1949 the insurgents announced that they were always ready to explore ways to peace. In April 1949 the Soviet Union proposed withdrawal of all foreign military matériel and personnel, general amnesty for all insurgents, and new elections in Greece in which the insurgents would participate. The United States and the Greek government countered that the key step was to halt assistance from the north. The Soviets supplemented their proposal by saying they would participate in supervising new elections and in a commission to control the frontiers.

Sub-Phase D: The Last Battle

In July 1949 Yugoslavia closed its border to the Greek insurgents, who were thus cut off from their main sanctuaries and supply routes. While Albania and Bulgaria were prepared to continue to assist the insurgency, the isolation of the former from the rest of the bloc and the remoteness of Bulgaria from the parts of Greece where hostilities were being waged made their help inadequate. The choice faced by the guerrillas was to seek a quick victory with the resources at hand or to moderate hostilities and prepare for a long struggle. They chose the former course.

1. Factors Tending to Inhibit the Termination of Hostilities

    a. The insurgents had not achieved their goals and, in the process of trying for them, KKE had revealed its willingness to use force to gain power. The prospects of rebuilding the party in any near future were slim indeed.

2. Factors Tending to Promote the Termination of Hostilities

    a. The Greek government forces, greatly improved in morale, training, and leadership, won a decisive victory over the insurgents, who tried to wage a conventional defense of the Grammos and Vitsi strongholds. The insurgents' defeat was swift and complete, and the scattered survivors fled to Albania.

    b. For practical and political reasons, Albania and Bulgaria were unprepared to intervene on a scale necessary to turn the tide, and the Soviet Union did not—and had not throughout the insurgency—become directly engaged.

PHASE IV₂

This analysis ends with the declaration by the Provisional Democratic Government on October 16, 1949, that it had

this force; UN supervision of new elections; UN and other guarantees of internal and external security; etc.

---

1. Measures to Offset These Factors
   a. More decisive defeat of insurgents or accommodation to their demands.

---

2. Measures to Reinforce These Factors
   a. Pursuit of fleeing insurgents to the complete decimation of their forces. Sealing border to prevent their return.

   b. Threat to extend hostilities to neighboring or other third states seeking to intervene on insurgents' behalf.

---

*temporarily put aside its arms. This action was echoed by
KKE in November, when it formally called off the armed
struggle. Both blamed the Greek government's matériel
superiority and Tito's "treachery" for their decisions.*

THE WEAPONS[3]

The following analysis deals only cursorily with the pre-Varkiza
period.

Greek Guerrilla Forces' Weapons Acquisition

Following its unsuccessful effort to seize power in Athens in
December 1944–January 1945, ELAS agreed to disband and to
surrender its arms. The Varkiza Agreement which terminated
the fighting specified the following numbers and types of arms
that ELAS was to turn in:[4]

>   41,500 rifles
>   650 submachine guns
>   1,050 light machine guns
>   315 heavy machine guns
>   108 light mortars
>   55 heavy mortars
>   32 artillery pieces
>   15 radio sets

In fact, ELAS turned in even more than this number. But it
quickly became clear that not all—perhaps not even most—of
ELAS's arms had been surrendered. Large numbers were se-
creted in mountain caches for possible future use. For example,
in the ten months following the Varkiza Agreement, over
25,700 more arms were discovered, including 166 heavy mor-

---

[3] The data for this section were compiled by Mr. Lewis Frank.
[4] Chamberlin and Iams, op. cit., p. 154.

tars.[5] These arms represented in type and numbers the matériel supplied to the wartime resistance by the Allies (primarily Britain), as well as the matériel captured by ELAS from the Italians at the time of their surrender in 1943 and from the Germans upon their withdrawal from Greece in 1944.

Weapons of these types remained in the insurgents' inventory throughout the insurgency. In addition, the insurgents received large quantities of matériel support from Greece's northern neighbors, Albania, Bulgaria, and primarily Yugoslavia.

It is extremely difficult in any insurgency situation to identify *the actual supplier* with *the original source* of a given type of weapon. Several factors make this doubly difficult in the Greek Insurgency. For one, the Allies had also supplied large numbers of arms to the Tito partisans in Yugoslavia during the war, for the most part the same types supplied to the Greek resistance. For another, the Germans had captured numbers of Soviet arms and frequently German occupation forces were equipped with such arms. The Soviets, in turn, had captured much German equipment, which was made widely available to the Soviet Union's wartime allies—including KKE. The Soviets also had in the Balkans weapons from their own inventories, some of which were also doubtless given to the insurgents.

The numbers of individuals in the insurgent forces also varied over time. In addition to violating the provisions—the spirit if not the letter—of the Varkiza Agreement about the surrender of arms, ELAS disregarded its provision about disbanding. About 3,000 guerrillas preferred to flee to sanctuaries in Albania,

[5] Ibid., p. 157.

Yugoslavia, and Bulgaria rather than disband, as Varkiza specified. These guerrillas, whose numbers were augmented by subsequent arrivals, concentrated in training camps in Yugoslavia.
They constituted the core of the insurgent forces, although
throughout the post-Varkiza period smaller groups continued to
operate in the mountainous area of Greece.

Official Greek General Staff estimates of the numbers of
guerrillas operating in Greece (i.e., exclusive of those in rest
and training areas north of the border) were as follows:

	1946	1947	1949	1948
January		10,820	22,350	23,900
February		14,850	24,110	20,150
March		16,250	26,000	20,020
April		17,050	24,300	19,780
May		16,450	25,600	19,000
June	2,600	16,900	23,300	17,490
July	3,150	16,900	22,090	17,400
August	3,620	16,700	21,100	3,710
September	4,490	17,400	23,700	2,150
October	5,930	18,600	25,480	1,760
November	7,450	18,600	25,450	1,275
December	9,285	20,350	25,000	815

Putting together the accounts of specific engagements, information on the arms captured by the government forces,
arms known to have been available in the area, and the
reported numbers and varying equipment of insurgent groups in
the course of the hostilities, one arrives at the following list of
categories and types, numbers, and likely sources of weapons
available to the insurgents:[6]

[6] The sources used to compile this information were Chamberlin and
Iams, op. cit.; Major Edgar O'Ballance: *The Greek Civil War: 1944–49*
(New York: Praeger; 1966); George B. Johnson and Hans Bert Lock-
hoven: *International Armament*, 2 vols. (Cologne: International Small
Arms Publishers; 1965). See also Colonel J. C. Murray: "The Anti-
Bandit War," *Marine Corps Gazette*, January 1954, pp. 14–23; February
1954, pp. 50–9; March 1954, pp. 48–57; April 1954, pp. 52–60; May
1954, pp. 52–8.

Weapons Available to the Greek Guerrilla Forces During the Insurgency

Weapon	Number	Source
German Mauser 7.63mm automatic pistol		captured
German Luger 9mm automatic pistol		captured
German Walther 9mm automatic pistol	about 700	captured
Canadian/Belgian FN Browning 9mm automatic pistol		U.K. in W. W. II, captured
Soviet Tokarev 7.62mm automatic pistol		sponsor countries (Yugoslavia, Albania, Bulgaria)
German Mauser 98K 7.92mm rifle		Yugoslavia, captured
Männlicher Model 1888 rifle	12,000– 15,000	Yugoslavia
Soviet Moissin-Nagant 7.62mm rifle		sponsor countries
British Sten 9mm SMG	about 1,500	U.K. in W. W. II to Greek and Yugoslav partisans
German MP 40 9mm SMG	about 2,500	Yugoslavia, captured
Soviet PPSh 41/PPs 43 7.62mm SMG	500–1,000	Albania
German MP 43/44 7.92mm automatic carbine	about 100	Yugoslavia, captured
Czech ZB 26/30 7.92mm LMG	about 200	sponsor countries and possibly Romania
Soviet Degtyarev DP 7.62mm LMG	about 200	sponsor countries
German MG-34 7.92mm LMG	about 400	sponsor countries, captured
British Bren (special model) 7.92mm LMG	about 100	U.K. in W. W. II to Greek and Yugoslav partisans
Soviet 12.7mm anti-aircraft MG	over 25	sponsor countries
Soviet Maxim 7.62mm HMG	300–400	sponsor countries
light mortar (probably Soviet or German make)	300–400	sponsor countries

Weapon	Number	Source
medium mortar (probably Soviet or German make)	75–100	sponsor countries
Czech Skoda 75mm field gun	at least 45	sponsor countries
German or Soviet 105mm field gun	at least 15	sponsor countries
German or Soviet rocket launcher	over 140	sponsor countries
antitank gun (possibly Soviet make)	over 20	sponsor countries
anti-aircraft gun (possibly Soviet or Swedish Bofors 37mm used by Soviets)	at least 19	sponsor countries
German or Soviet mines, AT and AP type	several thousand	sponsor countries

There were no combat surface vessels except one ex-Italian pre-World War II submarine, furnished by Albania, which was converted to transport and ferry duty. Its operational capability is doubtful. There were no combat aircraft.

Greek Government's Weapons Acquisition

The Greek government forces also came out of World War II with a force size, structure, training, and equipment determined by their wartime role and experience. Only the Greek Royal Navy (whose role in the Insurgency was to be minor) had escaped the German invasion relatively unscathed; the army and the air force had been virtually destroyed as fighting forces. When Greek forces returned to Greece in late 1944, after the German withdrawal, they included: a navy of approximately 12,000—equipped with ships—returned to Greek control from the British forces, into which they had been integrated during the war, and additional British vessels loaned temporarily to meet current requirements; the Third Brigade of 2,100 officers and men; and the air force Sacred Squadron of 600–800.

The British accepted initial responsibility for training a new Greek military establishment. After the December 1944–January 1945 fighting in Athens, this role was stepped up and expanded. By late 1946, the Greek army had grown to 100,000 men, equipped mostly with British matériel. But the rapid growth, which the insurgents' challenge made essential, had been bought at the expense of inferior training; the resulting defects showed up in the poor performance of the Greek government forces during the first years of the Insurgency.

By late 1946–early 1947, the economic strain on Britain of the greatly enlarged burden in Greece and Britain's own postwar recovery effort led to a much reduced British role in Greece. The major burden of building and supporting Greek military force was assumed by the United States.

During the wartime period and the first two postwar years, the bulk of matériel supplied to the Greek armed forces was British. As the U.S. role became predominant, increasing amounts of U.S. matériel were supplied. Substantial amounts of British equipment, however, continued to be purchased by the United States for the Greek forces, both because of the great expense that would have been involved in totally re-equipping the Greek forces and because some types of British equipment were found more suitable to the special type of warfare being fought. For the most part, the equipment supplied—both British and U.S.—was war surplus. Total U.S. military aid from July 1, 1948, to June 30, 1950, was $476.8 million, while the British component from October 1944 to June 1947 amounted to $152 million.

The expansion of the size of the Greek government forces is shown as follows:

	Army	Air Force	Navy	Gendarmerie and National Defense Force	Total
1946					
	100,000	5,000	12,000	30,000	147,000
1947					
	110,000	5,000	12,000	30,000	157,000
	120,000	6,500	12,000	35,000	173,500

	Army	Air Force	Navy	Gendarmerie and National Defense Force	Total
1948					
	132,000	7,200	13,500	47,500	200,200
1949	132,000	7,200	13,500	50,000	202,700
	160,000	7,200	13,500	50,000	230,700
1950					

The following tabulation of weapons used by the Greek government armed forces during the Insurgency is compiled from information available on weapons supplied and the organization and standard equipment of different military units, as well as from accounts of Greek government military operations:[7]

Weapons Available to the Greek Government Forces During the Insurgency

Weapon	Number	Source
Webley .38-cal. revolver		U.K.
Canadian FN Browning 9mm automatic pistol		U.K.
Colt M1911 .45-cal. pistol	about 3,000	U.S.
German Lugers and Mausers		Allies
.303-cal. Enfield rifle	over 50,000	U.K.
Springfield .30-cal. Model 1903 rifle	about 125,000	U.S.
U.S. M1 Garand rifle	about 10,000	U.S.
Sten 9mm SMG	about 3,000	U.K.
Thompson M1 .45-cal. SMG	about 5,000	U.S.
German Schmeisser 9mm SMG	few	?
Bren .303-cal. LMG	about 1,000	U.K.
U.S. .30-cal. BAR	about 5,000	U.S.
U.S. M1919A4 .30-cal. LMG	about 2,100	U.S.

[7] The sources used were those listed in the preceding note.

Weapon	Number	Source
Vickers .303-cal. MMG	over 300	U.K.
2″ mortar	about 350	U.K.
3″ mortar	81–108	U.K.
4.2″ mortar	1–2 batteries	U.K.
60mm mortar	about 500	U.S.
81mm mortar	about 170	U.S.
3.7″ howitzer	about 8 batteries	U.K.
75mm pack howitzer	about 32	U.S.
2.36″ rocket launcher	over 70	U.S.
75mm recoilless rifle	several	U.S.
25-pounder gun	about 8 batteries	U.K.
5.5″ gun	about 2 batteries	U.K.
Centaur light tank	30–40 in 3 units	U.K.
M4 Sherman medium tank	about 50	U.S.
Supermarine Spitfire IX	about 36	U.K.
U.S. AT-6 Harvard	about 12	U.K.
U.S. C-47 Dakota	about 6	U.K.
U.S. SB2C Curtiss Hell-diver	49	U.S.
destroyer	8	transferred from U.K.
destroyer	2	on loan from U.K.
submarine	6	transferred from U.K.
sub chaser	1	transferred from U.S.
corvette	8	transferred from U.K.
minesweeper	25	U.S.-U.K.
cruiser, light	1	Italy, war prize
motor gunboat	6	transferred from U.S.
landing craft	12	on loan from U.K.

SUMMARY OF CONTROL MEASURES

In summary form, the key conflict-control measures in this case might have been the following (an asterisk indicates that the measure was actually taken):

KEEPING THE DISPUTE NONMILITARY

Avoidance of great-power war.
Avoidance of Communist take-over of legitimate nationalist and patriotic resistance movements.

Efforts not to create postwar conflicts by shortsighted wartime
        policies.
Recognition of and support for popularly based non-Communist
        elements to provide democratic alternative.
Pressure on autocratic governments to liberalize.
Plebiscite on form of government.
Prevention of the acquisition of surplus arms by potential conflict
        makers.

PREVENTING THE OUTBREAK OF HOSTILITIES

Neutral administration of plebiscites with guarantees of fairness.
Support for popular non-Communist reform elements.
Clearly stated intentions on part of deterrers.

MODERATING HOSTILITIES

Discouragement of diplomatic recognition of insurgents.*
Urging of free elections under international supervision.*

TERMINATING HOSTILITIES

Threat of U.S. intervention.

PREVENTING THE RESUMPTION OF HOSTILITIES

International cognizance including investigation, fact-finding,
        reporting.*
Pressure on potential mischief makers not to intervene,
    Backed by:
Meaningful threats.*
Joint or impartial supervision, inspection, and control of arms-
        surrender agreements.
Postwar reconciliation, even-handed justice, and incorporation of
        dissenters into legitimate modes of dissent.
Economic and financial assistance,* preferably multilateral.
Vigorous internal-security operations, with foreign military
        assistance.*
Splitting of Communist opposition, isolation of irreconcilable
        radicals.
Accommodation of legitimate political demands.
Preventive international peacekeeping capability interposed between
        potential adversaries.

The Indonesian War of Independence, 1945–1949[1]

THE PHASES OF CONFLICT

PHASE I   *Background of the Conflict*

The islands of the East Indies archipelago fell under Dutch control in the seventeenth century. Despite stirrings of nationalist sentiment since the early 1900's, the islands achieved their independence only in 1949, after more than four years of intermittent warfare. Our focus here is primarily on developments on the island of Java, for it was there and to a lesser extent on Sumatra that the Republic of Indonesia had effective power. In any event, such political and military movements as developed on other islands were not so significant in determining the large course of the conflict or its eventual outcome.

Geographic and Physical Factors

The physical features of Indonesia had a profound effect on the manner in which the conflict unfolded. In the first place, the centers of power and decision making of the adversaries were separated from each other by nearly half a world. Indonesia lacked resources to carry the war outside its borders, and for the Netherlands to bring its power to bear in an area many thousands of miles away added greatly to the cost of the conflict. The island nature of the Indies isolated the Indonesian

---

[1] The authors wish to acknowledge the contributions to this chapter of Mr. R. Lucas Fischer and Mr. Lewis Frank.

nationalists from easy assistance by potential Asian friends. And, by virtue of Dutch control of the seas in the archipelago, it was difficult for efforts against the Dutch on the several islands to be coordinated or for one group to render effective assistance to another.

The terrain and climate of Java and Sumatra were favorable to guerrilla warfare. The mountainous jungle, extreme heat, and November-to-January rainy season facilitated Republican control of pockets of territory away from the Dutch-controlled roads.

The strategic location of the Indies at the junction of the Indian and Pacific Oceans and their rich wealth in people, oil, and rubber made them valuable assets to the Dutch. The rivalries among the United States, Soviet Union, and Communist China that color current perceptions of the area were not so central at the time of the Indonesian struggle for independence. But even then no great power with colonial, commercial, or security interests in the South Pacific, Oceania, or South and Southeast Asia could be indifferent to developments in the region.

Wartime Experience

For both the Dutch and the Indonesians, World War II brought invasion and occupation by Axis powers. But their experiences were totally different. While Nazi occupation of the Netherlands was brutally repressive and those few who collaborated with the occupying powers were reviled by the vast majority of Dutchmen, Japanese occupation of the Indies removed Dutch power and created an opportunity for the nascent Indonesian nationalism to develop. There were oppressive features to the Japanese occupation, and some Indonesian nationalists led anti-Japanese underground movements. But many of the men who were to become leaders of the postwar independence struggle participated in the Japanese-sponsored administration.

By the end of World War II, a number of Indonesian political parties emerged, many of which had their origins in the prewar period. The largest and most important of these were the

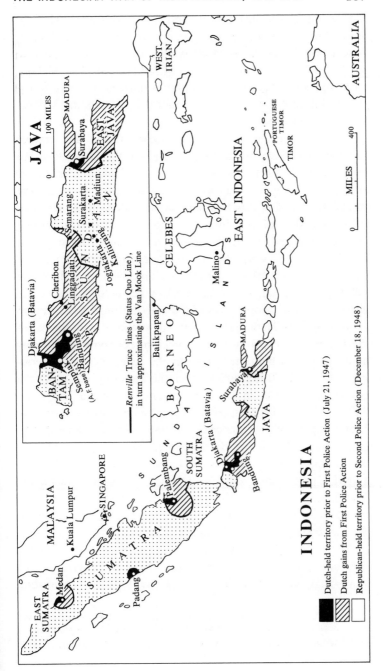

INDONESIA

■ Dutch-held territory prior to First Police Action (July 21, 1947)

▨ Dutch gains from First Police Action

□ Republican-held territory prior to Second Police Action (December 18, 1948)

Indonesian Nationalist party (PNI), the Masjumi (Madjelis Sjuro Mushlimin Indonesia, Council of Indonesian Muslim Associations), the Socialist party, the Indonesian Communist party (PKI), and a strong group of followers of Tan Malaka, an independent Marxist. These parties differed in political and social philosophy, but they were united in demanding Indonesian independence.

During the occupation, the Japanese created and trained Indonesian military forces. The Corps for the Defense of the Fatherland (PETA) included about 35,000 Indonesians trained and equipped by the Japanese as an auxiliary to their own forces. It served as a militia and was intended, in the event of Allied invasion of the Indies, to fight a rear-guard holding operation against the Allies while the Japanese, if necessary, withdrew.[2] There were also a variety of paramilitary organizations, for example labor battalions, that received some degree of military instruction. Other Indonesians acquired experience in guerrilla warfare as members of the anti-Japanese underground.

Although the Netherlands itself was occupied and control of the Indies was seized by Japan, Dutch forces continued to play an active part in both the European and Asian theaters. Operating not only in Dutch units under the authority of the Dutch government-in-exile in London but also integrated into other Allied units, the Dutch received from Britain, Australia, and the United States military matériel and training comparable to that given other Allied forces. In the immediate area of Indonesia in the closing days of the war, a battalion of the Dutch army (KNIL) participated with Australian forces in recapturing the East Indian islands of Tarakan and Balikpapan; and an estimated 10,000 Dutch troops were being trained, at the end of the war, by the British in Singapore.

As the end of the war approached, several events occurred that had profound effects on the subsequent course of the 1945–1949 conflict. Early in 1945 the Japanese occupation

[2] Guy Pauker: "The Role of the Military in Indonesia," *RAND Memorandum RM-2637-PC* (Santa Monica: RAND; September 1, 1960), p. 7.

authorities in Java promised early independence to the Indonesian leaders and in March created a committee of Indonesians
to consider constitutional questions concerning the future independent state. A similar committee but with more restricted
powers was created on Sumatra in July. Political developments
in the other islands had been more restricted by the Japanese
during the occupation, but on August 7, 1945, the Japanese set
up an all-Indonesian preparatory committee to lay the foundations for independence.

On the Allied side, developments concerning the future of
Indonesia were also taking place. The strategy of the war
against Japan had placed relatively low priority on the liberation of the Indies, and only a few of the lesser islands had been
reconquered at the time of the Japanese surrender.

Since 1942 the Indonesian archipelago had been divided
between British and U.S. areas of operational military responsibility. The South East Asia Command (SEAC) under Admiral
Lord Louis Mountbatten included Sumatra and adjacent dependent islands. The rest of Indonesia was part of the South
West Pacific Area (SWPA) under General Douglas MacArthur.[3]
As early as 1944 the British had pressed for the assignment of
more of the Indies to SEAC in order to facilitate operations
against Singapore. After initial resistance from SWPA, the
reassignment was approved in July 1945. The transfer was
reportedly favored by the U.S. State Department, which feared
U.S. involvement in postwar colonial problems in the area.[4] At
Mountbatten's request, the formal transfer of authority was
delayed, pending the collection of adequate intelligence on his
new command.

Phase II   *August 17–Mid-October 1945*

The Japanese surrender on August 15, 1945, found Allied
responsibility for the liberation of the Indies still divided be-

---

[3] Idrus N. Djajadiningrat: *The Beginnings of the Indonesia-Dutch
Negotiations and the Hoge Veluwe Talks* (Ithaca: Cornell Modern Indonesia Project; 1958), p. 8. At the time he wrote this study, the author was
a member of the Indonesian Foreign Office.   [4] Ibid., p. 15 *n.*

tween Britain and the United States, the Indonesian nationalists rapidly consolidating their position, and no Allied force in the major islands of the Indies. Furthermore, there was little or no firsthand information available to SEAC about the situation on the islands. The response of the Allies to the Japanese surrender was to order Mountbatten to assume immediate command of that portion of the Indies that had been under SWPA, thus placing all of the Indies in the British area of operations. The Indonesian nationalists' reaction was to proclaim, on August 17, 1945, the independence of the Indonesian Republic.

The Dutch had not objected to the consolidation of all of the Indies under British command. But Hubertus van Mook, then Lieutenant-Governor of the Netherlands East Indies, and Charles van der Plas, Dutch representative to SEAC, objected vigorously to the proclamation of the Republic and asked that orders be issued to the Japanese to restore the status quo as of the date of their surrender, August 15. Such an order was in fact issued by Mountbatten, but the Japanese commanders in Indonesia refused to accept responsibility for events after August 15. The transfer of the whole of the Indies to British command appears to have been a disappointment to the Indonesians, who felt that the United States was more likely to be sympathetic to the independence movement. Upon learning of the transfer, the Republican authorities communicated to SEAC their determination to resist militarily any Dutch effort to re-establish control in Indonesia.[5]

There were, as was noted earlier, military resources available to the new Republic. Although the Japanese formally disbanded PETA, the organization remained essentially intact and retained the small arms that had been issued by the Japanese. In early October the Indonesian Republican army was formed, drawn primarily from former PETA forces. There were also irregular forces of uncertain numbers growing both out of the paramilitary groups sponsored by the Japanese occupation authorities

[5] Information from a conversation with Colonel Thomas L. Fisher, II, USAF (Ret.), U.S. Army liaison officer with the British 15th Corps in Java, October to December 1945. The message may have been in the form of a radio broadcast.

and the anti-Japanese underground. In addition to the light arms originally provided by the Japanese to some of these groups, they captured, seized, and in some cases were given additional Japanese equipment. (See the WEAPONS section of this chapter for details.)

The first Allied personnel to land in the main Indonesian islands was a small group parachuted into Djakarta on September 8, 1945, to obtain a firsthand assessment of the situation and prepare for a larger Allied military mission. This group found the nationalists organized for recognition as the legitimate civilian authority in Indonesia. Although later developments suggest that the Allied group underestimated the magnitude of the problem, they did recommend to SEAC that the first Allied troops landed in Java be composed largely of British rather than Dutch forces in order to avoid immediate violence. On September 16 the military mission itself landed, and at the end of September the first British force of fewer than one thousand men arrived. Further landings continued thereafter, including in their numbers some small Dutch contingents.[6] These Dutch units were supplemented by liberated Dutch internees and prisoners of war, rearmed possibly with Dutch arms hidden in Java before the Japanese invasion and undiscovered during the occupation.[7] By early October, the Dutch were estimated to number 1,700.[8] No U.S. forces participated in the Allied landings, although a small U.S. liaison mission was with the first forces to arrive.

The situation that had developed in Indonesia posed delicate political problems for the British. The mission of the troops under their command was to accept the surrender of local Japanese forces and prepare them for return to Japan, to liberate Allied prisoners of war and interned civilians, and to prepare to turn the country over to civilian authorities. There were, however, two competing groups claiming to be the legitimate civilian authority to whom power should be transferred.

[6] Djajadiningrat, op. cit., p. 27.
[7] Information from a personal conversation with Colonel Fisher (see earlier footnote).   [8] *Christian Science Monitor,* October 2, 1945.

By the time of the British landings, a tentative policy had evolved. Mountbatten told Van der Plas during meetings on September 27 and 28 that the British forces would not be used to impose Dutch authority on the nationalists.[9] The new commander of the Allied forces in the Netherlands East Indies, General Sir Philip Christison, is reported to have characterized this policy as cooperation with and implicit *de facto* recognition of the Republican government.[1]

The Dutch government found the British policy highly unsatisfactory, charging that it implied recognition of a Japanese-inspired regime headed by collaborators.[2] On the other hand, the Republicans protested the entry of Dutch troops into Java and either threatened or warned the British of violent action by the armed irregular groups. For their part, KNIL troops, liberated and rearmed prisoners of war, and civilians were becoming engaged in provocative shooting incidents.[3]

As a result, the British began to take a more active role, encouraging the Dutch and the Indonesians to negotiate a peaceful settlement of the political question. During meetings on October 10 and 11 in Singapore, Mountbatten reportedly promised Van Mook and Van der Plas additional British forces to speed up the tasks of freeing Allied prisoners and internees and disarming the Japanese if the Dutch would agree to talks with the Republican leaders.[4] Van Mook met with the nationalist leader Sukarno twice in late October, but the meetings were repudiated by the Dutch government.

By late October 1945, clashes involving Indonesian forces, regular and irregular, Dutch and British patrols,[5] and European

[9] Djajadiningrat, op. cit., pp. 24–5.

[1] David Wehl: *The Birth of Indonesia* (London: George Allen and Unwin; 1948), p. 42. The author was reportedly the chief intelligence officer at Mountbatten's headquarters.

[2] Djajadiningrat, op. cit., p. 27.

[3] Frederick E. Crockett: "How the Trouble Began in Java," *Harper's Magazine,* April 1946, p. 281. The author was a U.S. Army liaison officer in Java from September 16 to mid-October 1945.

[4] Djajadiningrat, op. cit., pp. 29–30.

[5] George Kahin: *Nationalism and Revolution in Indonesia* (Ithaca: Cornell University Press; 1952), p. 144. This study is drawn from first-hand observation in Indonesia.

civilians[6] reached the level at which Phase III$_1$ may be said to have begun.

PHASE III$_1$ *Late October 1945–October 14, 1946*

Sub-Phase A: Late October– Mid-November 1945

The first major military clash, the battle of Surabaya, involved British-Indian troops which had landed at Surabaya on October 25. By early November a division and a brigade of the British-Indian troops were engaged in heavy fighting against Indonesian armed youth organizations. The fighting lasted until the end of November, with heavy casualties.

After Surabaya, British operations were cautiously limited to avoid another battle of that scale.[7] Nevertheless, British forces involved in the task of bringing Allied prisoners of war and civilian internees from camps in the hinterland were frequently involved in serious fighting with the Indonesians, who particularly resented the fact that liberated Dutch prisoners and internees were being armed and were involved in actions against the nationalists. These developments delayed the disarming of the Japanese troops, and in several instances the Japanese were used by the British in combat against the Indonesian forces and to guard Allied personnel.[8] Toward the end of October the Allied command announced the suspension of further landing of any Dutch forces in Java and Sumatra.

Until November 1945, Dutch attention in the Indies had focused on Java and Sumatra. At that point in the period during which Allied forces were re-entering Indonesia, Dutch attention turned to the Australian-controlled islands on the northern and

[6] Charles Wolf, Jr.: *The Indonesian Story* (New York: John Day; 1948), p. 22. Wolf was a U.S. vice-consul at Batavia from February 1946 to June 1947.   [7] Djajadiningrat, op. cit., p. 48.
[8] In January 1946 the Ukraine asked the UN Security Council to condemn the actions of British forces in Indonesia, particularly the use of Japanese troops. No action was taken by the council. *The United States and the United Nations: Report by the President to the Congress for the Year 1946*, Department of State Publication 2735 (Washington: GPO; 1947), p. 35.

eastern portions of the archipelago.[9] Republican sentiment was not strong in those areas, and the nationalists exercised almost no control there.

Sub-Phase B: Mid-November 1945–April 24, 1946

Efforts to induce the Dutch and the nationalists to negotiate continued, and in December the U.S. State Department issued a statement expressing the hope that Dutch-Republican talks would take place. Finally, in meetings between British and Dutch officials in London on December 25, 1945, the Dutch government agreed to talks with the Indonesian Republican leaders.

The idea of negotiations was opposed by important groups in both the Netherlands and Indonesia. Dutch conservatives were critical of Van Mook's policy and urged the restoration of prewar Dutch authority.[1] The first postwar elections in the Netherlands were scheduled to be held in May 1946. Dutch governments since liberation had been, for the most part, uneasy coalitions of parties that differed on Dutch policy in the Indies and on many other issues. Both the delicate balance of the successive coalitions and the impending elections made domestic dissent on a major foreign-policy issue a very serious matter. At the time negotiations were undertaken, the Dutch government was headed by the Schermerhorn-Drees cabinet, a Labor government with general Catholic support.[2] In Indonesia, where, in a November governmental reorganization, Soetan Sjahir (a former leader of the anti-Japanese underground) had become Prime Minister, there was an influential element opposed to any negotiations with the Dutch. Tan Malaka was one of the leaders of this group.

---

[9] Mountbatten had responsibility for all the Indies but had turned over to Australia responsibility for the islands north and east of Java, Sumatra, Bali, and Lombok. Djajadiningrat, op. cit., p. 19.   [1] Ibid., pp. 51–3.

[2] Ibid., pp. 91–3. See also Alastair M. Taylor: *Indonesian Independence and the United Nations* (Ithaca: Cornell University Press, 1960), pp. 19–24. Mr. Taylor, a Canadian, was a member of the UN Secretariat's field machinery in Indonesia during the later phases of the revolution and attended the Round Table Conference at The Hague.

Despite opposition, negotiations opened in Djakarta in February 1946 between Van Mook and Sjahir, with the assistance of a prominent British diplomat, Sir Archibald Clark-Kerr. The Dutch proposed an interim period in which the relationship between the Netherlands and Indonesia should be based on "democratic partnership" within the Kingdom of the Netherlands; after this transition period the partners would independently decide on the nature of their relations.[3] The Republic, on the other hand, initially demanded immediate recognition of its sovereignty over the whole of the Netherlands East Indies. By the end of March, the negotiators reached preliminary agreement. The Republic would be recognized as having *de facto* authority in Java and Sumatra and would cooperate in forming an Indonesian federation as a partner with the Netherlands for an interim period. The core of this preliminary agreement—the status of the Republic as a constituent part of an Indonesian federation in union with the Netherlands—was suggested by Van Mook, acting on his own initiative.[4] The negotiators in Djakarta were optimistic about the success of formal negotiations in the Netherlands.

The talks in the Netherlands—the so-called Hoge Veluwe negotiations—failed, however. The Dutch government sought to dilute the formula agreed to in Djakarta and, in particular, to restrict the Republic's *de facto* authority to Java. The Indonesian delegation was unprepared and unauthorized to make concessions that would, in their stated view, reduce the status of the Republic to a provincial administration for Java.[5]

While these futile negotiations were underway, the military situation in the Indies was changing. The scale of hostilities in Java had greatly lessened in early 1946 as the Republic gained greater control over the activities of the various armed organizations. The British contingents were being withdrawn; the last was scheduled to leave by November 30, 1946. The Dutch had been successfully reoccupying the islands other than Java and

[3] Djajadiningrat, op. cit., pp. 51–2.
[4] Taylor, op. cit., pp. 20–1; Djajadiningrat, op. cit., pp. 55–9.
[5] Djajadiningrat, op. cit., p. 68.

Sumatra, thus limiting the Republic's *de facto* authority to those
two islands. Finally, large numbers of Dutch troops were being
landed in Java. By early March 1946, there were an estimated
21,000 Dutch troops in the Indies—10,000 on Java and 11,000
on the remaining islands. A further reserve force of 13,000 was
in Malaya.[6] These numbers were, however, still fewer than the
Indonesian forces, which numbered around 37,500, not including paramilitary groups of from 200,000 to 250,000.

The Indonesian forces had adequate supplies of Japanese
arms and ammunition at this stage of the conflict, although
most of the heavier equipment and artillery had been lost at
Surabaya or abandoned. U.S. matériel supplies to the Dutch
forces had ended with the Japanese surrender, but no shortages
had as yet developed. The Dutch at this stage, however, had to
rely on the British for logistic support and transport. Nevertheless, the World War II–type equipment of the Dutch forces was
more plentiful, diverse, and powerful than that available to the
Indonesians. (See the WEAPONS section of this chapter for
details.)

Sub-Phase C: April 24–October 14, 1946

Following the failure of the Hoge Veluwe negotiations, the
Dutch took another political initiative. The elections in May
had put a Catholic-Labor coalition party in power and, while
conservative opposition to concessions in the Indies persisted,
the new Beel government operated from a more solid base of
support than the pre-election coalitions. In July, Van Mook
convened a conference at Malino on Celebes with representatives from the islands under Dutch control (the so-called Outer
Islands). The conference agenda consisted of the Dutch proposal for a federated United States of Indonesia composed of
Java, Sumatra, Borneo, and the Great East, each with a high
degree of autonomy. The Republic of Indonesia regarded the
conference as a fraud since the participants had been selected
by the Dutch to consider a Dutch proposal.

---

[6] Captain Edwin Klein: "The Dutch Marines and the Indonesian Problem," *Marine Corps Gazette,* August 1946, p. 15.

In September 1946 the Dutch government appointed a high-level commission—including former Prime Minister W. Schermerhorn, Max Van Poll (the head of the Catholic party), and Hubertus J. Van Mook—to prepare a new political structure for the Indies and gave it almost plenary power to negotiate with the Republic. Negotiations began on October 7 under the chairmanship of a British representative. On October 14 the parties concluded a cease-fire agreement, calling for immediate stabilization of existing military positions and limiting the number of Allied forces (Dutch and British) in the Indies to 92,000.[7]

PHASE IV[1]   *October 14, 1946–July 21, 1947*

The Linggadjati Agreement, initialed on November 15, followed and was closely related to the cease-fire negotiations. The principal provisions of the agreement were: recognition of the *de facto* authority of the Republic over Java, Madura, and Sumatra; cooperation of the Netherlands and the Republic in setting up a sovereign federal state, the United States of Indonesia, consisting of the Republic, Borneo, and the Great Eastern State; and cooperation of the Netherlands and the Republic in forming a Netherlands-Indonesian Union composed of two basic units, the Kingdom of the Netherlands (which was made up of the Netherlands, Surinam, and Curaçao) and the United States of Indonesia. The agreement represented Dutch concessions in two important respects: Republican control was recognized as extending to Sumatra as well as Java and the United States of Indonesia would be a sovereign state in partnership with the Kingdom rather than only one part of the Kingdom. Despite considerable opposition from groups in the Netherlands who regarded the agreement as capitulation, it was formally signed on March 25, 1947.

While the Linggadjati Agreement resolved some basic issues, it either did not deal with others or dealt with them ambiguously. These omissions and ambiguities formed the basis for

[7] Wolf, op. cit., p. 25. By this time there were 55,000 Dutch troops in Java, according to Wehl, op. cit., p. 134.

subsequent controversy. For example, the agreement recognized the *de facto* authority of the Republic in Java and Sumatra but did not specify where *de jure* authority lay. Even the nature of the agreement itself was unclear: the Indonesians were later to contend that it was a treaty between sovereign states, while the Dutch regarded it as a statement of principles. The relationship between the Republic and the other states in the United States of Indonesia and the nature of the cooperation called for between the Netherlands and the Republic in forming it were ambiguous. The agreement was silent on the nature of the interim government of the Indies while the United States of Indonesia was being set up; in particular, the Agreement did not deal with the important matter of where responsibility lay for internal order.

Even before the agreement was formally signed, political controversy was renewed. The Dutch created states in East Indonesia in December 1946 and in West Borneo in May 1947. In both cases, important governmental powers continued to be under Dutch control, and in neither case was the Republic allowed to "cooperate," as it claimed the Linggadjati Agreement required. Furthermore, the creation of a state of West Borneo, excluding eastern and southern Borneo where the Republic claimed support, did not follow the Indonesian interpretation of the agreement.

In addition, the Indonesians charged that elements of the Dutch civil service and army fostered a short-lived and highly artificial Sundanese separatist movement in West Java.[8] Also, the Dutch navy refused to allow the Republic to export any goods that could be considered as having originated on European-owned estates before the war; imports of military equipment by the Republic were forbidden as well.

The Dutch maintained that the foreign diplomatic activity of the Republic violated the Linggadjati Agreement. The Dutch held that the agreement had granted only *de facto* recognition to the Republic and that *de jure* recognition as a sovereign state was to be accorded only to the United States of Indonesia. In

[8] Wolf, op. cit., pp. 108–9.

addition, the Dutch accused the Republic of numerous violations of the cease-fire agreement.[9]

In both the Netherlands and the Republic, groups favoring extreme policies gained in strength as the mutual trust and confidence that the Linggadjati Agreement envisioned rapidly moved further away. In the Netherlands, conservative pressure on the Catholic-Labor coalition government was increasing. Indeed, the parliamentary wing of the Catholic party was openly supporting the use of force, and even the Labor party, while still opposing force, wanted a speedy solution to the impasse.[1] There had been no appreciable resumption of trade, especially of Indonesian exports, since the reoccupation. Exports of oil were at a standstill, and exports of rubber were running at less than 15 per cent of the 1940 figure, while maintenance of the Dutch armed forces in the Indies was estimated to be costing roughly $1 million a day.[2]

On May 27, 1947, the Dutch presented a set of proposals to the Republicans with a demand for acceptance that amounted to an ultimatum. The proposals called for an interim federal government to have power until January 1, 1949, when the United States of Indonesia would be established. This interim government would consist of representatives from "the various political entities in Indonesia," as well as a Representative of the Crown who would be "in a special position with power of decision"; the government would form and direct the federal organs and departments that eventually would be part of the United States of Indonesia. The proposals also called for a joint Indonesian-Dutch gendarmerie (not Republican-Dutch) under the interim government, empowered to enforce law and order anywhere in the archipelago. Furthermore, a joint economic administrative council was to be set up under the interim government, with representatives from the Netherlands, the Republic, West Borneo, and East Indonesia, and the president of the Netherlands-owned Java Bank. Decisions of the council were to be arrived at unanimously; if this could not be done, the

[9] Ibid., pp. 113–14.   [1] Ibid., p. 115.   [2] Ibid., p. 117.

interim government was to decide. A reply to the proposals was required from the Republic within fourteen days.[3]

Sjahir responded with concessions and counterproposals, but in so doing he went beyond his weakened support in the Republican legislature and was forced to resign on June 27. On the same day the United States sent an *aide-mémoire* to the Republic and to the Netherlands Indies Administration urging cooperation by the Republic in the formation of an interim government and promising economic aid after such an interim government would be established. The new Prime Minister of the Republic, Amir Sjarifuddin, stood by the concessions that Sjahir had offered, but refused to agree to the joint Indonesian-Dutch gendarmerie.

On July 21 the Dutch government informed the UN Secretary-General that, since the Republic was incapable of maintaining law and order in its territory, the Dutch were impelled to take police measures "of a strictly limited character."[4] The Dutch initiated their first police action on the same day,[5] attacking with three divisions in Java and three brigades in Sumatra. The Dutch land, sea, and air force numbered 109,000 men.[6] Indonesian forces at the time were about 200,000 regular troops[7] and approximately the same number in irregular units.[8] (See the WEAPONS section of this chapter for details.)

PHASE III₂   *July 21, 1947–January 19, 1948*

Sub-Phase A: July 21–August 5, 1947

The Dutch attack met with little resistance. On July 25, for example, Van Mook reported that Dutch casualties were still

---

[3] Ibid., pp. 118–20.

[4] *The United States and the United Nations: Report by the President to the Congress for the Year 1947* (Washington: GPO; 1948), p. 93.

[5] One source reports a statement by Van Mook to the effect that Dutch troops had begun to move on June 24 and that the U.S. *aide-mémoire* caused a hasty postponement of the attack. Louis Fischer: *The Story of Indonesia* (New York: Harper; 1959), pp. 198–9. See also Justus M. Van der Kroef: "The Indonesian Revolution in Retrospect," *World Politics*, April 1951, p. 388.

[6] *Casebook on Insurgency and Revolutionary Warfare: 23 Summary Accounts* (Washington: Special Operations Research Office; 1962), p. 58.

[7] Ibid., p. 58.   [8] Fischer, op. cit., pp. 108–9.

under one hundred and that Indonesian casualties were not much higher. Within two weeks the Dutch had control of most of the cities and major towns of West and East Java, all remaining Republican deepwater ports in Java, and partial control over the roads in these areas. In Sumatra the Dutch concentrated on the rich estate area on the east coast, the oil fields in the south, and the chief ports on the west.[9] They were not, however, able to destroy the Republic's armed forces, which refused to engage in frontal combat and withdrew from the flat country and the roads to hilly and mountainous "pockets." As they withdrew, the Republicans adopted a scorched-earth policy. Guerrilla attacks were launched from the Republican-held areas until the January 1948 truce. But their scale decreased as arms and ammunition shortages developed, both because of losses in the police action and because of the tight Dutch blockade.[1]

India and Australia both brought the conflict to the UN Security Council in July 1947. The Australian submission implied strong condemnation of the Netherlands, for it asked that the matter be handled by the council under Article 39 of the Charter, which dealt with threats to the peace, breaches of the peace, and acts of aggression and which could have led to council consideration of collective measures against the Netherlands. India, on the other hand, invoked the authority of Article 34, under which the council's action, however severe, could only be recommendatory. Also at issue in these distinctions was the question of whether the Republic had been recognized by the Dutch as a state, as the Republic maintained, or not, as the Dutch argued. The council declined to commit itself on these serious issues. On August 1 it adopted a U.S. compromise resolution that, without mentioning the specific Charter article under which action was being taken, called for a cease-fire and settlement of the dispute by arbitration or other peaceful means.

Both the Netherlands and the Republic issued instructions to their forces to carry out the cease-fire at midnight August 4–5.

[9] Kahin, op. cit., p. 213.   [1] Ibid., p. 228.

Sub-Phase B: August 5, 1947–January 19, 1948

The cease-fire was ineffective, however. While generally halting its forward advance,[2] the Dutch army began mopping-up operations in the huge tracts of territory bypassed by its armored columns.

In the UN Security Council, France vetoed creation of a commission to observe and supervise the truce; but a motion was approved to have a Consular Commission made up of governments with consuls at Djakarta report to the council on the situation in Indonesia, including implementation of the cease-fire. The council also created the Good Offices Committee to assist the parties to arrive at a stable cease-fire and to negotiate their differences. The Security Council thus equipped itself with a source of information on events in Indonesia independent of the parties directly involved and made its auspices available on the scene to encourage and hasten a settlement. The Good Offices Committee, of which the United States, Australia, and Belgium were selected members, arrived in Indonesia on October 27.[3]

During the period between the abortive cease-fire and the arrival of the Committee, the Dutch continued their mopping-up operations. On August 29 they unilaterally proclaimed the Van Mook Line, which connected the points of farthest Dutch advance into Republican territory[4] and announced that the areas within the Line were under Dutch control, although in fact they included substantial areas of Republican resistance. The Van

[2] Though territory *beyond* the farthest advance at the time of the cease-fire was captured by the Dutch as late as November 1947—the eastern half of the island of Madura, off the coast of Java.

[3] For a useful summary of UN action on the Indonesian question, see David W. Wainhouse et al.: *International Peace Observation: A History and Forecast* (Baltimore: The Johns Hopkins Press in cooperation with The Washington Center of Foreign Policy Research, School for Advanced International Studies, The Johns Hopkins University; 1966), pp. 293–323.

[4] At best. The Consular Commission found in many areas that the Van Mook Line lay beyond the points of farthest advance reached at the time of the cease-fire. UN Security Council, Document S/586/Rev.1.

Mook Line had the effect of restricting the Republic, especially in Java, to poor agricultural land. In addition, the Dutch threw a nearly absolute economic blockade around the Republic.

During October, debate at the United Nations centered on the demand of the Republic that the Dutch withdraw their forces to the positions of July 20. This demand received support from the Soviet Union and Australia, but was opposed by the United States, Britain, and France as prejudging the issue.

On November 1, a U.S. motion was adopted which called upon the parties to consult with each other directly or through the Good Offices Committee about means to put the cease-fire resolution into effect and advised the parties that an interpretation of the cease-fire that allowed the use of armed forces to extend control over territory not occupied as of August 4 was inconsistent with the original cease-fire resolution. On November 14, special committees of the two parties began preliminary meetings with staff members of the Good Offices Committee.

The Good Offices Committee had its first formal session with Dutch and Republican delegations on December 8, 1947, on the U.S.S. *Renville,* a U.S. naval transport anchored in the harbor of Djakarta to provide a neutral meeting ground. The Committee took an active role in the talks, submitting proposals to the parties for approval. The Dutch, however, refused to give ground on the question of the withdrawal of Dutch forces and the restoration of the Republican civil authority in the territory occupied by the Dutch since the beginning of the police action on July 21.

The Dutch put forth a set of twelve political principles as a basis for negotiation. Their statement accepted the continued participation of the Good Offices Committee in the negotiations. It at no point, however, mentioned the Republic by name, and it hinted that further states might be set up in the newly occupied territory.[5] This hint was, in fact, substantiated while the truce

[5] Wolf, op. cit., p. 187. The significance of the creation of such additional states was that it implied both a permanent diminution of the Republic's territory and also additional units in the projected federated United States of Indonesia, lessening the chances that the Republic would dominate the federation.

negotiations were still in progress—on December 29, Van Mook announced the establishment of East Sumatra in territory captured from the Republic.

The Dutch applied strong pressure for the acceptance of their principles. On January 9, 1948, they submitted an ultimatum demanding the Republic's acceptance of their proposals within three days—later extended to five days. It was made clear that if the proposals were not accepted, the Dutch might resume their freedom of action. The Good Offices Committee attempted to find a solution by suggesting six supplementary principles. The most important of these called for: (a) plebiscites under UN supervision in the various parts of Java and Sumatra "within a period of not less than six months . . . after the signing of this agreement"[6] to determine whether each territory wanted to be part of the Republic or a separate state within the United States of Indonesia; and (b) after the plebiscites, convening of a convention to draft a constitution for the United States of Indonesia, in which states would be given representation proportional to their population. Since the population of Java and Sumatra was a large majority of the total population of the Indies, this meant that if the Republic regained control over all of Java and Sumatra—which it felt plebiscites would ensure—it would have a dominant position in the United States of Indonesia.

The Dutch accepted the additional six principles on condition that the Republic accept all eighteen within the five-day time limit. Under strong pressure from the Good Offices Committee (especially from the U.S. member, Dr. Frank Graham) and with an unofficial Committee interpretation of the meaning of the twelve Dutch principles, the Republic agreed, though not without the opposition of Sjahir, the Masjumi, and PNI. On January 17 and 19, 1948, the Netherlands and the Republic signed the *Renville* Agreement, including a military truce based

[6] The Dutch later interpreted this to mean six months after agreement to a final political settlement, whereas the Indonesians contended that it meant six months from the signing of the *Renville* Agreement. Kahin, op. cit., p. 241.

on the Van Mook Line, the twelve principles of the Dutch, and
the six additional principles of the Good Offices Committee.

PHASE IV₂   *January 19–December 19, 1948*

The *Renville* Agreement did not clarify many of the issues that
had led to the breakdown of the Linggadjati Agreement. The
nature or extent of the Republic's authority prior to the creation
of the United States of Indonesia was not mentioned, nor was
the question of the Republic's relations with foreign states.
While the Netherlands was to create a provisional federal government prior to the establishment of the sovereign United
States of Indonesia, the provisional government's structure and
functions were not defined and the power of the Representative
of the Crown during this period was not specified.[7]

The specifically military aspects of the *Renville* Agreement
were implemented fairly smoothly. The approximately 35,000
Republican troops remaining behind the Van Mook Line—now
called the Status Quo Line—were evacuated to Republican-held
territory.[8] The line itself was delineated, demilitarized zones
were established along the boundary, and prisoners of war were
exchanged.

After the signing of the *Renville* Agreement, the parties and
the Good Offices Committee set up the *Renville* Conference.
The Conference had the immediate tasks of implementing the
military truce and overseeing the resumption of trade and commerce between Republican and Dutch areas. It also faced the
complex of problems related to the construction of the United
States of Indonesia and the definition of the role and powers of
the interim federal government which was to operate prior to
the transfer of sovereignty.

At this time, a new government took power in the Republic.
Because of their opposition to the *Renville* Agreement, the
Masjumi and PNI (the two largest parties of the Republic)
withdrew their support and forced Sjarifuddin to resign. A
cabinet was formed that would be responsible to President

[7] Taylor, op. cit., p. 95.   [8] Ibid., p. 104.

Sukarno rather than to the legislature. The new Prime Minister was Mohammed Hatta, formerly the Republic's Vice-President, and the Masjumi and PNI dominated the cabinet.

Since the Dutch refused to lift their tight blockade, the Republican-controlled areas were short of food, fuel, raw materials, and medicines. Hatta tried to control expenditures and stabilize the economy, for example by reducing the number of people employed in the government and the larger factories and transferring them to the farms and small industrial units.

In part as an economy move, in part as an effort to increase military efficiency, and in part as a consolidation of political control, Prime Minister Hatta also began a reorganization and restructuring of the Indonesian army, which had been renamed the National Indonesian Army in May 1947. Under Hatta's direction, numbers were reduced to 160,000, with the eventual goal to be a force of 57,000.[9] (See the WEAPONS section of this chapter for details.) Only the first stage of the reduction was actually carried out, however, because the reductions brought Hatta growing opposition from the People's Democratic Front (FDR), a coalition including the Labor party, the Communist party, and Sjarifuddin's Socialist party.[1] FDR possessed a strong political base in the army, and the discontent of the demobilized troops proved a fruitful issue for FDR to exploit. Several times in 1948, troops had to be used against units that refused to disband.

Meanwhile, the negotiations between the Netherlands and the Republic were breaking down over conflicting interpretations of the *Renville* Agreement. The Dutch were continuing their policy of creating states in the regions they had occupied. The state of Madura was created on January 21, 1948, on the basis of an unsupervised plebiscite,[2] and the state of West Java was created in late February. The Dutch position was that the states were

[9] Pauker, op. cit., p. 29; Kahin, op. cit., p. 262.
[1] Sjahir had left the Socialist party in protest against its increasingly Marxist tendencies and had formed his own Indonesian Socialist party.
[2] Kahin, op. cit., pp. 235-8.

only provisional and thus not in contravention of the *Renville* Agreement.

In March 1948, Van Mook announced the establishment of an interim federal government, to function until the creation of the United States of Indonesia. The Republic, the Dutch contended, could not participate in the interim government until a final political agreement was signed. In May the Dutch held a conference with the Dutch-created states, now thirteen in number with five on Borneo alone, to consult on various federal matters. Again the Republic was excluded. At the same time, the Dutch protested the Republic's continued expansion of its foreign relations and accused the Republic of being responsible for the small-scale clashes that occurred along the Status Quo Line.

The Dutch encountered some opposition from the Dutch-created states as well as from the Republic. In July 1948 the prime ministers of the states of East Indonesia, Timor, and Pasundan convened a meeting of the Dutch-created states which took the name Federal Consultative Assembly. The members of this assembly, who came to be known as Federalists, wanted more direct control over the interim government than the Dutch had provided for. They proposed that the interim government be composed of Indonesians chosen by representatives of the states and be given full control over the administrative departments. This proposal differed from the interim government the Dutch had created, in which the states were represented by the heads of administrative departments selected by the Dutch rather than elected, and frequently Dutchmen rather than Indonesians. The assembly's plan, furthermore, interposed Indonesian, elected ministers between the administrative departments and the Netherlands government.

In an effort to prevent the breakdown of the *Renville* accord, the U.S. and Australian members of the Good Offices Committee produced the so-called DuBois-Critchley Plan, calling for an indirectly elected constituent assembly representing all Indonesia that would delineate the boundaries of the states of the

United States of Indonesia, elect a President who would in turn
appoint a Prime Minister responsible to the assembly, and have
a large measure of self-government. The plan provided for a
Netherlands High Commissioner with veto powers and the
power to declare an emergency and assume command of the
armed forces. The Republic accepted the proposal, but the
Dutch refused to consider it.

In July 1948 the Netherlands held general elections. The
result was an increase in conservative strength; Labor lost two
of its twenty-nine seats in the parliament. The new government,
with Willem Drees (Labor) replacing Louis J. Beel as Prime
Minister, was a coalition of Catholic, Labor, and VVD (a new
centrist party). Beel of the Catholic party replaced Van Mook
and took the title of High Representative. The Ministry of
Overseas Territories also passed from the Labor party to the
Catholic party's E. M. J. A. Sassen.

In September the Republic went through a severe crisis. The
Communist-dominated FDR[3] denounced the *Renville* Agreement, demanded that negotiations with the Dutch cease until the
Dutch withdrew from Indonesia, and called for nationalization
of Dutch and other foreign properties without compensation. At
the end of August 1948, Labor-party members and the Social-
ists merged with the Communist party; the head of the new
party was Musso, just returned from twelve years in the Soviet
Union and just appointed general secretary and leader of PKI.

In late September 1948 an insurrection was begun in Madiun
and Surakarta by local army officers, members of PKI, who
were under orders from the Republican government to demobilize their units. The revolt was unsuccessful. Musso's calls
for general popular risings had no response, and the area under
the control of the troops supporting Musso was quickly subdued
by some of the Republic's best military units. The last large
rebel military unit was captured October 28, and Musso was
killed in a skirmish three days later.

[3] Sjarifuddin himself later claimed that he had been a secret Communist during this period and during his six months as Prime Minister.
Fischer, op. cit., p. 108.

The extent of Communist-led opposition within the ranks of the Indonesian nationalists became manifest at a time when the United States and other Western powers were becoming increasingly alarmed over the postwar policies of the Soviet bloc. In China, Greece, Western Europe, Malaya, and elsewhere, Communist efforts to exploit the chaos left by the war, and legitimate nationalist and liberal aspirations were causes of grave concern.

In September the new U.S. member of the Good Offices Committee, Merle Cochran, attempted again to break the deadlock in negotiations. The Cochran Plan was similar to the DuBois-Critchley Plan but provided increased safeguards against Republican domination of the United States of Indonesia. The Netherlands agreed to discuss the Cochran Plan but proposed extensive modifications. While the proposal was under consideration, new Dutch Foreign Minister Dirk Stikker arrived in Java to negotiate directly with Hatta.

The Dutch position emphasized that organs of the interim government should be selected rather than elected and that the Representative of the Crown should have ultimate discretionary control in the most important areas of government. The Republic maintained that the Cochran Plan required it to give up control of its armed forces with no safeguards against unilateral use of federal troops against it. The Republic also saw in the proposed Dutch modifications of the Cochran Plan ways in which the Dutch could further increase the number of states in the federation at the expense both of the territorial size of the Republic and of its voice in the federal government.

Despite these problems, the Stikker-Hatta negotiations made some progress. Hatta accepted the principle that the organs of the interim government be selected rather than elected. He also accepted the states that had been formed after the Dutch police action. And he agreed that the High Commissioner should have emergency powers and veto rights in some cases.

A second series of talks began in November 1948, with the Dutch represented by Stikker, Sassen, and a group of members of the parliament. The Dutch put much emphasis on the growing number of truce violations and asked for a binding political commitment from Hatta. Not receiving it, the Dutch informed Cochran that agreement was impossible to reach, that further negotiations were futile, but that the possibility of including Republican areas in the federal system must remain open.[4] There was no longer any suggestion in the Dutch position that the Republic should participate as a government in the federal scheme.

Hatta's position continued to be conciliatory. He stated that the Republic was willing to admit that *de jure* sovereignty rested with the Netherlands, that the Representative of the Crown should be given emergency powers, and even that the Representative should himself be the judge of the propriety of the use of these powers in given circumstances. The Republic asked only that definite standards be laid down for the Representative's decision.

The Dutch reply on December 17 amounted to another ultimatum, demanding complete Republican acceptance of the Dutch plan within eighteen hours. At eleven thirty P.M. on December 18, Cochran was informed that the Dutch were terminating the *Renville* Truce. Cochran was in Djakarta and was refused use of telegraph facilities to notify the rest of the committee, which was at Kaliurang in Republican territory.

PHASE III₃   *December 19, 1948–August 1, 1949*

Early in the morning of December 19, a Dutch parachute force captured the airport at the Republican capital of Jogjakarta. By mid-afternoon, Sukarno, Hatta, and half the cabinet were captured by Dutch marines and KNIL troops brought in by air. Between December 19 and 22, Dutch attacks were begun in other parts of Java and Sumatra.

Militarily the second Dutch police action started off well. The Dutch army of 130,000 raced forward with few casualties and quickly occupied most of the major cities in the Republic's

4 Taylor, op. cit., p. 158.

territory. (See the WEAPONS section of this chapter for details.) An emergency Republican government had begun operating in Sumatra, however, and Republican military units were infiltrating through Dutch lines to reach assigned areas from which guerrilla operations could be begun.[5]

Politically, however, events went differently. On December 20 the Prime Ministers and cabinets of East Indonesia and Pasundan, two of the states that had previously cooperated in large measure with Dutch plans, resigned in protest against the Dutch military action; other states of the Indies followed the same course. The reaction of nations throughout the world was almost unanimous in condemning the Dutch action. On December 22 the United States suspended Marshall Plan aid to the Netherlands East Indies Administration. On December 24 the UN Security Council met in emergency session and called for a cease-fire and the immediate release of Sukarno and other political prisoners.[6] The Dutch informed the council that hostilities on Java would cease by December 31 and shortly thereafter on Sumatra. The Republic's representative said that his government could not respond while its leaders were held captive.[7] On January 10 the Dutch informed the captured political leaders that the Republic was no longer recognized as a political entity with a territory of its own.[8]

Upon learning from the Good Offices Committee that compliance with the December resolution was not satisfactory, the Security Council on January 28 adopted a further resolution. In addition to reaffirming its demand for a cease-fire and prisoner release, the council transformed the Good Offices Committee into the UN Commission for Indonesia (UNCI) with greatly

[5] Abdul H. Nasution: *Fundamentals of Guerrilla Warfare* (New York: Praeger; 1965), pp. 179–80.

[6] The initial draft resolution included a demand that troops be drawn back to the *Renville* Truce lines. *United States Participation in the United Nations: Report by the President to the Congress for the Year 1948* (Washington: GPO, 1949), p. 88. Without this clause, Dutch compliance with the cease-fire would have left the Netherlands in control of substantially more Republican territory than before the police action.

[7] Ibid.   [8] Kahin, op. cit., p. 343.

expanded powers. UNCI was authorized to reach decisions by majority vote (with the effect of placing authority in U.S. and Australian hands, bypassing the Belgian member who tended to be more sympathetic to the Dutch view than were his colleagues), to assist the parties to carry out the Security Council's resolutions, to recommend the extent to which areas should be progressively returned to the Republic, and to recommend to the Security Council the conditions necessary to ensure free and democratic elections under UN observation.[9]

Direct action against the Netherlands was threatened when, on February 7, the Brewster Resolution was introduced in the U.S. Senate urging that all Marshall Plan aid to the Netherlands be stopped until the Dutch ceased hostilities, withdrew their troops, released the Republican leaders, and opened genuine negotiations. This strong U.S. opposition to Dutch policy, evidenced both by its position in UN debates and by its apparent willingness to apply sanctions, created a serious problem for the Dutch cabinet. Negotiations were underway for what was to become NATO, and the Dutch shared the general Western European perception that U.S. power must be brought to bear to prevent a Soviet take-over of all Europe. There were some who would have made an effort to explain the Dutch view to Washington in order to persuade the United States to reverse its policy. Sassen, for example, proposed that the cabinet appeal to the United States for cooperation against UNCI, with the warning that the Dutch would otherwise have to abandon Indonesia. The cabinet refused to take this approach, and Sassen resigned to be replaced by a liberal member of the Catholic party.[1]

---

[9] *United States Participation in the United Nations: Report by the President to the Congress for the Year 1949* (Washington: GPO, 1950), p. 30.

[1] Kahin, op. cit., p. 144. Dutch Communists in the Netherlands parliament were caught in a dilemma. While the Soviet and other Communist parties were assailing the Dutch government for its actions in Indonesia, the Dutch Communists charged that the government was "sacrificing national interest to the Marshall Plan and 'Pax Americana.'" Taylor, op. cit., p. 198.

To the plan of action proposed by the United Nations the Dutch finally offered an alternative which represented a substantial departure from their former position that the Republic had ceased to exist. The plan called for an accelerated transfer of sovereignty to a United States of Indonesia. The transfer would be arranged by a Round Table Conference, to be convened at The Hague, which would at the same time establish the Netherlands-Indonesian Union and an interim government for a brief period. The Republic would participate in the Conference. But the Dutch proposal made no provision for the return of the Republican leaders to Jogjakarta. Sukarno refused to consider the new Dutch proposal for this reason. At first the Federalists approved the proposal and accepted the invitation to the Round Table Conference.[2] Later, they reversed themselves and made acceptance conditional on the restoration of Republican leadership. The United Nations found the proposal acceptable but held that no progress could be made unless the Dutch first restored the Republican government to Jogjakarta.

During this period the Republican guerrilla campaign, which had been carefully prepared and organized, had significant success. By the end of February, one source states, less than half of Pasundan and East Java were under Dutch control and the Republican forces had nearly recaptured Jogjakarta.[3]

At the end of March, Dutch Foreign Minister Stikker visited Washington for talks with Secretary of State Dean Acheson, where it was made clear the U.S. aid would be cut off if the Dutch did not agree to a cease-fire, the return of the Republican leaders and government to Jogjakarta, and the inclusion of the Republic in the projected federal structure.[4] On April 1, Senator Arthur Vandenberg offered an amendment to the economic aid bill, obligating the United States to withdraw assistance from any government against which UN enforcement actions were proceeding. Vandenberg's amendment was adopted on

---

[2] Wolf, op. cit., p. 22.   [3] Kahin, op. cit., pp. 410–12.
[4] This is Kahin's view; other sources are less definite about the detailed requirements.

April 6, instead of a more drastic amendment by Senator Owen Brewster which would have withdrawn aid if the orders and requests of the Security Council were not being carried out.

On April 14 the preliminary conference between Republican and Dutch officials began, with UNCI taking an active part in the negotiations. Progress was made despite the mutual suspicions of the two parties. The Netherlands wanted an early Republican commitment to a cease-fire, saying that continuing guerrilla warfare might force Dutch military responses. The Republicans, on the other hand, insisted on a commitment that the Dutch would not continue their policy of dividing captured territory while the Republic was paralyzed by a cease-fire agreement. After some days of private discussions,[5] the Van Royen–Roem Statements were produced. The Republican government did not formally agree to order a halt to guerrilla warfare, promise to cooperate in restoring peace and maintaining law and order, or promise to participate in the Round Table Conference; but Sukarno and Hatta gave their personal assurances that they favored these steps in conformity with the Security Council resolution of January 28 and would undertake to urge the adoption of such a policy by the Republic as soon as possible after its restoration to Jogjakarta.

For the Dutch, Van Royen announced that, in view of the undertaking of Sukarno and Hatta, the Republican government would be returned to Jogjakarta and freed to govern in that residency; that all Dutch military operations would be discontinued; that the Dutch would refrain from recognizing states on soil controlled by the Republic prior to the second police action; that the Dutch favored the existence of the Republic as a state in the United States of Indonesia, with one third of the total membership in the federal representative body; that, in all areas (outside the Residency of Jogjakarta) where Republican civil, police, and other officials were still operating, these would re-

---

[5] Kahin, op. cit., pp. 421–2, states that Cochran applied heavy pressure on the Republicans to make concessions, promising that the United States would stand behind a transfer of sovereignty by the Dutch.

main in operation; and that the Round Table Conference would discuss accelerating the unconditional transfer of complete sovereignty to the United States of Indonesia.

The Van Royen–Roem Statements were not unanimously endorsed by all groups in the Netherlands or the Republic. Beel resigned from the Dutch cabinet in protest, but the Labor party fully supported the government. In the Republic, opposition centered around Sukarno's and Hatta's apparent acceptance of the states that had been formed by the Dutch between the first and second police actions and the one-third limit on the Republic's representation in the United States of Indonesia. It is also possible, as one source suggests, that the increase of guerrilla activity in June reflected Communist dissatisfaction with the terms.[6]

The Dutch evacuation from the Residency of Jogjakarta began on June 24, 1949, and was completed on June 30; Sukarno and Hatta returned on July 5. On August I final agreement on a cease-fire was reached by the Dutch and the Republicans, to take effect August 11 on Java and August 15 on Sumatra. With that accomplished, Republican and Federalist delegations left for The Hague for the Round Table Conference.

PHASE IV₃   *August 2–December 27, 1949*

The five months following the end of Phase III₃ were not marked by military moves or military preparation. Negotiations were concerned primarily with setting up the Netherlands-Indonesian Union, settling a variety of economic questions (principally that of who would pay the debt of the Netherlands East Indies), and taking up the West Irian (Dutch New Guinea) question. With the settlement of those issues—or agreement to postpone the most intractable—the conflict proceeded to Settlement with the formal transfer of sovereignty to the United States of Indonesia on December 27, 1949.

[6] Taylor, op. cit., p. 221 and *n*.

PHASE I *to* PHASE II: *The Introduction of a Military Option*

1. Factors Tending to Introduce a Military Option

   a. During the Japanese occupation in World War II, many Indonesian nationalists had been able for the first time to organize and to participate in government; the return of the Dutch seemed to the nationalists to threaten a setback to their aspirations.

   b. At the end of World War II, the only political and military force on the major islands was that created by the Japanese; upon their surrender, it was dominated by the nationalists.

   c. For the nearly three and a half years that the Indies were occupied, very little information was available to the West on development there.

   d. The humiliation of defeat, at home and in the Indies, created in the Dutch a strong psychological need to reassert their strength and pride.

   e. The rich Indies were a key element in Dutch commercial and economic strength; indeed, the Dutch feared that without them they would become just another small, third-class power.

2. Factors Tending to Keep the Dispute Nonmilitary

   a. During World War II, the Dutch had promised that after the war they would work toward a future for the Indies as equal partners with the Netherlands in some form of commonwealth.

   b. The Dutch did not have many forces in the area of the Indies immediately after the Japanese surrender.

   c. Such Dutch forces as were in the area were heavily dependent on Britain and the United States for logistic support of all kinds.

   d. In general, the Netherlands just after the war was, and was going to continue to be, heavily dependent on external assistance for economic reconstruction.

RELEVANT CONTROL MEASURES

Keeping the Dispute Nonmilitary

1. Measures to Offset These Factors
   a. Pre-World War II enlightened Dutch colonial policy that has taken[7] responsible Indonesian nationalism into account.

   b. Anticipation by Allies of extent of postwar colonial problems and consequent adjustment of wartime military priorities to take account of objectives beyond the fighting (all this suggesting a thought-out plan for introduction of appropriate Allied forces into the islands).
   c. Adequate wartime intelligence effort focused on the Indies, plus prompt and effective postwar fact-finding machinery—bilateral, third-party, or international organization.
   d. Creation and development of alternative goals for Dutch postwar assertiveness and pride—an imaginative program of European integration, a positive Dutch role in technical assistance to the developing world, etc.
   e. Measures suggested above to create alternate bases of prestige, plus Dutch development of industries placing a high premium on value added by skilled labor.

2. Measures to Reinforce These Factors
   a. More effective articulation of Dutch promises. Communication of these intentions to Indonesian nationalists. Moral pressure on Dutch by wartime allies (especially the United States and Britain) to give substance to their promises.
   b. Policy agreement between the United States and Britain—if necessary, by U.S. pressure on Britain—to keep Dutch forces out of the area.
   c. Withholding of U.S.-British logistic support from any Dutch activities directed against the Indonesians.

   d. Use, especially by the United States, of potential economic assistance as a lever to influence Dutch policy away from concern with recovering the Indies by force.

[7] Note that, for simplicity and as an aid to future applications, the authors have used present tenses, present conditionals, and present participles at will throughout the RELEVANT CONTROL MEASURES.

e. The United States and Britain, perhaps especially the former, did feel generally that stark reimposition of Dutch overlordship in the Indies was wrong.

PHASE II *to* PHASE III₁: *The Outbreak of Hostilities*

The factors that had operated to move the conflict from Phase I to Phase II continued to operate and to contribute toward the movement from Phase II to Phase III₁. The factors covered in this section represent the new elements introduced during Phase II.

1. Factors Tending to Promote the Outbreak of Hostilities

   a. The liberated Dutch internees and prisoners of war were even more hostile toward the Indonesian Republic than was the Netherlands government. Many of them had personal economic stakes in restoration of Dutch sovereignty and thus were frequently the instigators or targets of inflammatory incidents.

   b. On the other side of the coin, the government of the proclaimed Indonesian Republic was able to exercise only limited control over its military and paramilitary forces, who sometimes undertook actions against the British and Dutch that forced the hand of their own government.

   c. Dutch official authority, at home and in the Indies, was divided on the question of how unyielding or moderate to be toward the Republic. Hence, from time to time, Dutch extremists were able to prevail.

   d. The Indonesian nationalists, especially those over whom the Republican government had only limited control, made little distinction between Dutch and British forces, believing that the latter were merely a cover for the return of the former.

---

2. Factors Tending to Inhibit the Outbreak of Hostilities

   a. The British did not want to allow their forces to act as a cover for the reintroduction of Dutch authority into the Indies; in fact, they so informed the Dutch.

PHASE III₁ *to* PHASE IV₁: *The Termination of Hostilities*

The transition from Sub-Phase A to Sub-Phase B (see pp. 193–4) represented a moderation in the hostilities, the

e. As mentioned above, prompt creation of effective fact-finding machinery—bilateral, third-party, or international—to help focus and strengthen U.S. and British commitment to objectives.

Preventing the Outbreak of Hostilities

1. Measures to Offset These Factors
   a. Isolation of liberated internees and prisoners of war. Denying them access to arms.

   b. Enhancement of the internal stability and political authority of the Republic.

   c. Enhancing the political consensus in the Netherlands government, in part by educating it and the Dutch public on the issues at stake and on the costs of prolonged conflict.

   d. More explicit articulation of British stated refusal to use their forces to reinstate the Dutch. Effective communication of the resolve to the Republican government and its forces.

2. Measures to Reinforce These Factors
   a. More rigorous action by the British in their stated principle; specifically, use of British forces to prevent fighting between Dutch and nationalists. Request by British for introduction of other forces—U.S., other third-party, or international—to effect cease-fire between conflict adversaries or to perform other peacekeeping roles.

Moderating/Terminating Hostilities

conventional warfare of Surabaya being followed by guerrilla warfare. Sub-Phase C was not an intensification or moderation of hostilities but rather a shift from an unsuccessful effort at negotiation to one that succeeded in terminating hostilities. (Major operative factors are included below but are not analyzed separately by sub-phase.)

1. Factors Tending to Inhibit the Termination of Hostilities

   a. All of the factors noted above that favored the outbreak of hostilities, plus the following.

   b. From time to time, extremist political elements in both the Netherlands and the Indonesian Republic gained control over policy; also, in the case of the Republic, relatively uncontrollable military and paramilitary units acted rashly on their own initiative.

   c. The British military presence, which had been on the whole a force favoring moderation and peaceful settlement, began to diminish and phase out.

   d. Dutch military strength increased in the Indies, both in absolute numbers and relatively, as the British withdrew.

   e. The Indonesians' resort to guerrilla warfare after their defeat in conventional combat at the battle of Surabaya had the short-run effect of precluding a termination of hostilities through decisive victory by the British-Indian-Dutch forces.

   f. Surabaya actually made the Dutch forces overconfident of eventual military victory, thus encouraging them to continue seeking a military solution.

   g. Soviet diplomatic support of the Indonesian Republic encouraged it to continue the struggle.

2. Factors Tending to Promote the Termination of Hostilities

   a. Despite their victory at Surabaya in November 1945, the British were unwilling to follow it up with an attempt to impose a definitive military solution.

   b. This unwillingness of the British was reinforced by Commonwealth pressure brought to bear on them, particularly by the Indians, whose troops had taken part in the battle of Surabaya.

   c. The Dutch elections in the spring of 1946 indicated that Dutch public opinion favored a negotiated settlement with the Indonesian nationalists.

   d. During the latter part of Phase III_1, the Dutch were achieving

1. Measures to Offset These Factors
   a. All corresponding measures mentioned above.

   b. Improving internal stability and public education. Introducing international pressures to bring about the effecting of those measures.

   c. Continuation of moderating British presence until some other neutral force, preferably institutionally international, could be substituted for it.
   d. U.S./British pressure to keep Dutch forces out. Introduction of international presence, preferably institutionalized, directed toward same end of excluding Dutch military forces.
   e. Vigorous British-Indian-Dutch follow-up of their victory at Surabaya, so as to compel the Republican government to capitulate prior to its being able to organize for effective guerrilla activity.
   f. Encouraging test of respective military strengths to dispel illusory perceptions of adversary's strength; or, at least, providing for sounder assessment of adversary's capabilities.
   g. Discouraging Soviet diplomatic support of Republic, countering it with strong U.S. support of Dutch, or removing the conflict from the arena of nascent East-West rivalry.

2. Measures to Reinforce These Factors
   a. Interposition of British or—preferably—neutral, third-party forces.

   b. Increased, perhaps institutionalized pressures on both adversaries to end the fighting.

   c. Earlier and better reading of Dutch public opinion by the government.

   d. Earlier and more effective communication of this goal of

substantial success in rallying the support of the non-Republican portions of the Indies to their concept of an Indonesian federation in union with the Netherlands.

e. The initial debate in the UN Security Council on the situation in Indonesia provided an opportunity for many states to register their interest in a peaceful settlement.

f. As one result of the initial UN Security Council debate, the Soviet Union emerged as the champion of Asian nationalism and general anticolonialism. This pricked the conscience of the Western powers, especially the United States, and intensified their interest in a peaceful settlement that would recognize Indonesian nationalist aspirations.

g. After the battle of Surabaya, the Indonesian Republicans avoided conventional military engagements and resorted to guerrilla warfare. This was far harder for the British (who were phasing out) and Dutch to cope with and could have suggested an unattractive prospect for long, debilitating hostilities (though, in fact, it may not have done so; see 1(e) on p. 221).

PHASE IV$_1$ *to* PHASE III$_2$: *The Resumption of Hostilities*

1. Factors Tending to Promote the Resumption of Hostilities

a. Differing interpretations of the Linggadjati Agreement of November 1946 led to a deterioration of confidence of each side in the other.

b. The costs of carrying on the war, added to the cost of reconstruction at home, were becoming increasingly onerous to the Dutch, who therefore felt a short-run time pressure to achieve a quick and decisive military victory.

c. Dutch impatience and anticipation of victory were whetted by the large build-up of Dutch military strength during the truce period after the Linggadjati Agreement.

d. The Dutch believed, wrongly, that the Republic was politically and especially militarily weak, regardless of the large numbers in its armed forces.

---

2. Factors Tending to Inhibit the Resumption of Hostilities

a. The very fact that a truce existed constituted a factor disfavoring an onus-creating resumption of hostilities.

b. Negotiations between the adversaries did continue off and on, with varying success.

c. The U.S. note of June 27, 1947, urged the Dutch and

federation to the nationalists. Enhanced Dutch conciliatory approach.

e. More vigorous introduction of early UN interest in and action on the Indonesian situation.

f. More vigorous Soviet championship of emerging nations in order to energize interest of West, especially the United States, in the problem.

g. Earlier nationalist resort to guerrilla warfare, thus hopefully in the longer run discouraging Dutch hopes of decisive victory. (This same factor of nationalist resort to guerrilla warfare could have the short-run effect of tending to prolong hostilities; it is so treated above, as 1(e) on p. 221.)

Preventing the Resumption of Hostilities

1. Measures to Offset These Factors
   a. International or mutually acceptable third-party "umpire" arrangement to rule on interpretations of the Linggadjati Agreement.
   b. Enhancement of Dutch domestic development and other goals, plus impressing upon the Dutch the more serious economic consequences of a prolonged conflict they could not be at all certain of winning. Raising possibility of adverse effects on foreign economic assistance to the Dutch.
   c. Effective joint, third-party, or international supervision of truce so as to prevent the illegal Dutch military build-up.
   d. Clarification, perhaps by fact-finding initiative, of actual military balance between adversaries. Appreciation by the Dutch of unfavorable balance that guerrillas can accept and still win.

---

2. Measures to Reinforce These Factors
   a. Continuation of truce through international or third-party presence as "trip wire" or interposed force.
   b. Strong pressure to keep negotiations going. Good offices, arbitration, threats.
   c. Dispatch of a stronger U.S. note, one that would threaten

Indonesians to continue negotiating and promised economic assistance to the future United States of Indonesia.

d. The Dutch realized that, in the longer run, they could not afford the costs of continuing the conflict.

PHASE III$_2$ *to* PHASE IV$_2$: *The Termination of Resumed Hostilities*

As in Phase III$_1$, the resumed hostilities had two distinct sub-phases (see pp. 200–4): the first was a major conventional police action by the Dutch; the second, a guerrilla response by the Indonesians. The two sub-phases were separated by a cease-fire in early August 1947 that responded to a resolution of the UN Security Council. Its practical influence on the conflict proved slight, however. (The operative factors below are not analyzed by sub-phases.)

1. Factors Tending to Inhibit the Termination of Hostilities

   a. The United Nations made no provision to insure or observe compliance with the cease-fire that followed its resolution in August 1947.

   b. The Dutch continued to believe that they were so militarily superior to the Republican forces that they could end the expensive hostilities with a decisive victory in the field.

   c. The definitive recourse to guerrilla tactics by the nationalists more than compensated by their numerical inferiority to the Dutch.

   d. The UN Security Council's refusal to agree to the Republican demand—that a Dutch withdrawal to positions obtaining before the police action of July 1947 be made a part of the conditions for a resumption of negotiations—meant that different pressures were placed on the two adversaries.

   e. No matter how thoroughly the United Nations or other instrumentalities had tried to police the cease-fire, the nationalists' resort to guerrilla warfare would still have posed new and difficult problems of peacekeeping.

---

2. Factors Tending to Promote the Termination of Hostilities

   a. The UN Security Council resolution of August 1, 1947, resulted in agreement by the conflict adversaries on a cease-fire—which, however, the Dutch promptly began to circumvent.

   b. The UN Security Council later created a consular commission to send it information directly, unfiltered by either adversary,

both parties instead of trying to cajole the party that at the time is in the weaker position.

d. Enhancing Dutch domestic development and other goals. Threatening to suspend or cut back economic assistance to the Dutch.

Moderating/Terminating Resumed Hostilities

1. Measures to Offset These Factors
   a. Creation and operation by the United Nations of adequate truce observation and supervision machinery.

   b. Tests of military strengths. Sounder assessment of relative strengths. Sounder counterinsurgency doctrine.

   c. Measures listed above to increase Dutch understanding of guerrilla warfare, or tricking or forcing the Republicans into accepting conventional engagements they are certain to lose.

   d. Careful formulation of UN cease-fire proposals to insure fairness to both sides.

   e. Recognition and study of special peacekeeping problem in guerrilla-type contests when no "front lines" or "lines of farthest advance" exist.

---

2. Measures to Reinforce These Factors
   a. Earlier and/or stronger UN action focused on the conflict—specifically, provision for UN sanctions against cease-fire violation.

   b. Greater power for GOC.

and also dispatched to the scene a Good Offices Committee (GOC) to facilitate a resumption of negotiations with a view to termination and settlement.

c. The great prestige and influence of the United States were perceived as being committed to settlement because of the presence of a U.S. national on the GOC and because the U.S.S. *Renville* was used in December 1947–January 1948 as the site for Dutch-Indonesian negotiations.

d. Prolongation of the conflict continued to eat up Dutch resources.

Phase IV$_2$ *to* Phase III$_3$: *The Resumption of Hostilities*

1. Factors Tending to Promote the Resumption of Hostilities

   a. Many of the factors that contributed to this resumption of hostilities had been operative in corresponding earlier occasions. The measures cited earlier thus retained appropriateness in the new circumstances. Listed below are the new factors that appeared.

   b. The Dutch economic blockade was partly responsible for a reduction in the size of the Republic's army that added to the feeling of the Dutch that they could now win military victory.

   c. A serious Communist-led insurrection, while successfully suppressed, demonstrated the deep split within the Republican political structure and also added to the feeling of the Dutch that they could now win military victory.

   d. The non-Republican states of the Indies, which had generally supported Dutch policies, were growing impatient for their promised autonomy in the proposed federation; this created more pressure on the Dutch to end the conflict with a decisive victory so that they could get on with organizing the federation.

---

2. Factors Tending to Inhibit the Resumption of Hostilities

   a. Many of the factors that inhibited this resumption of hostilities had been operative earlier, and the measures suggested retained their general appropriateness in the new circumstances. Listed below are the new factors that appeared.

   b. The evacuation of nationalist guerrilla groups from the Dutch side of the truce line and the creation of a demilitarized zone decreased incidents between the two adversaries.

   c. Additional, more explicit ways of indicating U.S. desire that conflict end.

   d. Measures mentioned earlier to increase economic costs and enhance other goals.

Preventing the Resumption of Hostilities

1. Measures to Offset These Factors

   a. All corresponding measures mentioned above.

   b. Measures mentioned earlier to increase Dutch knowledge of guerrilla warfare and produce a more accurate assessment of military balances.

   c. Increasing the stability and internal cohesion of the Republican government. (As an influence on Dutch perceptions, this would inhibit resumption of hostilities, but its actual effect on the political-military balance can be to prolong hostilities.)

   d. All previously mentioned measures for impressing on the Dutch the prohibitive costs of prolonged conflict and the likelihood that conflict will in fact be prolonged, given the nationalists' guerrilla strategy.

---

2. Measures to Reinforce These Factors

   a. All corresponding measures mentioned above.

   b. International or disinterested third-party supervision and patrol of demilitarized zone. Interposition of international or third-power peacekeeping force.

   c. The United States and Britain began to fear that failure to end the conflict quickly might increase the strength of the radicals in the Republic, thus extending Soviet influence into this strategic part of the world.

   d. In Europe, the Netherlands was becoming involved in the mutual-security arrangements of the Marshall Plan and the nascent NATO.

PHASE III$_3$ *to* PHASE IV$_3$: *The Terminating of Resumed Hostilities*

1. Factors Tending to Inhibit the Termination of Hostilities

   a. In both the Dutch and Republican camps, the extremists continued to press for continuation of hostilities until their maximum demands were met.

2. Factors Tending to Promote the Termination of Hostilities

   a. When hostilities resumed, the Republic's guerrilla efforts proved even more effective than they had in the past, thus helping discourage the Dutch from believing they could win a military victory.

   b. The non-Republican states of the Indies began turning against the Dutch, especially when it appeared that the latter really intended to crush the Republic and its leaders.

   c. The United Nations began to assert itself very strongly, transforming its Good Offices Committee into the UN Commission for Indonesia, which virtually assumed the role of neutral arbitrator.

   d. The United States came down hard on the Dutch with serious and meaningful threats to cut off economic assistance from any government against which UN enforcement actions were proceeding (Vandenberg Amendment, April 1949).

PHASE IV$_3$ *to* S: *Settlement of the Dispute*

The resumed negotiations led relatively quickly to the settlement of most of the outstanding issues between the Netherlands and the Republic. One issue—the status of Dutch New Guinea (West Irian)—remained unresolved and became the focus of a new conflict a decade later.

    c. More vigorous Soviet support of the nationalists, so as to intensify U.S. interest in ending the conflict. Also, increasing U.S. perception that time as well as justice was on the side of the nationalists.

    d. More emphasis on focusing Dutch attention on European problems, opportunities, and obligations.

Moderating/Terminating Resumed Hostilities

1. Measures to Offset These Factors

    a. Continued application of all foregoing measures designed to reinforce factors tending to terminate hostilities.

2. Measures to Reinforce These Factors

    a. All measures mentioned above that impress upon the Dutch the futility of continuing to fight.

    b. Encouragement of divisiveness represented by dissatisfaction of non-Republican Indonesians with Dutch policy.

    c. Impressing on both adversaries the strength of world opinion behind the UN action.

    d. U.S. threat to withdraw aid from the Dutch unless orders and requests of UN Security Council are being faithfully carried out (proposed Brewster Amendment, April 1949).

THE WEAPONS

Netherlands Forces' Weapons Acquisition

Build-up: 1940–Fall 1945

After the fall of the Netherlands to Germany in May 1940, the only Dutch army contingent of significant size was stationed in the Netherlands East Indies. In May 1940 the Royal Netherlands Indies Army (KNIL) consisted of 1,345 officers and 37,583 troops, including some German mercenaries, Eurasians, and a few Indonesian officers trained by the Dutch.[8] Their standard squad support and police weapons were the Belgian-made, German-designed Schmeisser (or Schmeisser-Bayard) MP Model 34 9mm parabellum SMG.[9] These were purchased in quantity from Belgium during the mid-1930's. Also used at the infantry-squad level at this time was the Danish Madsen 6.5mm LMG, purchased in 1939.[1] The basic infantry rifle was the Dutch-made Männlicher 6.5mm bolt-action rifle, officially adopted in 1895 by the Dutch military. The loss of many of the Schmeissers and Madsens after the German blitzkrieg resulted in the Dutch purchase from the United States of about 10,000 Johnson .30-cal. to .60-cal. semi-automatic rifles and the Model 1941 Johnson .30-cal. LMG for supply to KNIL.[2]

After the Japanese conquest of the East Indies in early 1942, some KNIL units in the eastern part of the islands managed to escape with some of the above weapons to Australia. These units were reorganized and re-equipped in Australia as a KNIL battalion, which fought alongside Commonwealth troops in May and July 1945 in the recapture of the East Indian islands

---

[8] Pauker, op. cit., p. 5.

[9] George B. Johnson and Hans Bert Lockhoven: *International Armament*, 2 vols. (Cologne: International Small Arms Publishers; 1965). Vol. I, p. 10.   [1] Ibid., Vol. II, pp. 257, 264–5.

[2] Joseph Smith: *Small Arms of the World* (8th edn.; Harrisburg: Stackpole Books; 1966), pp. 520–1.

of Tarakan and Balikpapan.[3] By the end of the war, the British were also assisting and training two Dutch volunteer groups; and by October 1945, one account estimates, about 10,000 Dutch land troops were in training status with the British at Singapore.[4]

There was no significant build-up of Dutch naval strength during World War II, aside from some ex-British patrol vessels. These were later used—like most of the later vessels acquired from Britain, Australia, and the United States—to enforce a blockade against the Indonesian nationalists. Practically all of the Dutch naval build-up in the Netherlands East Indies co-incided with the hostilities that began after the fall of 1945.

By September 1945, a total of 4,848 marines in the Royal Netherlands Marine Corps (NKM) had been trained and equipped by the U.S. Marine Corps and prepared for assignment to the Pacific theater. Patterned on U.S. lines, this unit consisted of: one headquarters and service battalion, three rifle battalions, one artillery battalion, one motor transport battalion, one engineer battalion, one service and supply company, one tank company, one AmTrac company, and one medical company, plus special intelligence units. The war against Japan ended before this unit left the United States. In November 1945, however, over 4,000 members of this regiment sailed for the Netherlands East Indies, the rest returning home.[5]

The weapons provided to NKM were as up to date or as nearly up to date as those used by their counterparts in the United States. Most of the weapons were types still in at least limited-standard use by U.S. forces.

After the fall of the Netherlands in 1940, the major bases for the Dutch air force were located in Canada and in the Netherlands East Indies. At these bases, Dutch pilots were trained to operate the piston-engine Supermarine Spitfire fighters. After

---

[3] Pauker, op. cit., p. 5.
[4] I. Chaudry: *The Indonesian Struggle* (Lahore, 1950), pp. 108, 109.
[5] Lieutenant Colonel H. W. Edwards: "Netherlands Korps Mariniers," *Marine Corps Gazette*, September 1953, p. 52.

the fall of the East Indies to the Japanese in 1942, the remaining Netherlands Army Air Corps units were incorporated into the RAF. On June 12, 1943, a Spitfire squadron was formed in England that was entirely manned by Dutch personnel, most of whom were trained by the RAF in England after 1942. Some units were transferred to the Netherlands East Indies in the summer of 1945 following the end of operations in the European theater.[6]

The United States had supplied most of the equipment and training for the Dutch bomber crews. The original B-25 medium bombers acquired by the Dutch in early 1943 were assigned to Naval Squadron 320 in England, which at the time was using British-trained Dutch army flying personnel who had been serving with the RAF since 1940. Subsequently the B-25's were initially attached to RAF coastal command and then transferred to the Second ATAF (Allied Tactical Air Force), where fully trained Dutch maintenance crews were used on the aircraft for the first time.[7] The bomber crews and ground crews were trained at Jackson Army Air Force Base, Mississippi. By the end of 1943, another medium-bomber squadron had been formed alongside a fighter squadron that was probably equipped with the U.S. P-40 Hawk, which was then phasing out of front-line service. The fighter squadron was transferred for service in Australia, where the aircraft were maintained by Australian ground crews. The Jackson air base served as the temporary wartime headquarters of the Royal Netherlands Military Flying School, directly under the command of the Chief of the Royal Netherlands East Indies Army Air Corps.[8] The P-40 squadron served in the Netherlands East Indies throughout the conflict and was still in NEIAAC inventory in 1949.[9]

In addition to the above aircraft, the NEIAAC was equipped with and trained in Britain, Canada, and the United States in the use of the British-made Avro Anson multipurpose trainer-

[6] *Jane's All the World's Aircraft* (1945–1946 edn.; London: Sampson Low, Marston, and Co.; 1946), p. 56a.
[7] Ibid., pp. 11a, 56a.   [8] Ibid., p. 57a.
[9] Ibid., 1949–1950 edn., p. 14a.

bomber-transport and the U.S.- and Canadian-made AT-6 Harvard advanced trainer.[1] All were capable of conversion to a limited combat role. By the fall of 1945, NEIAAC was being equipped by Britain with the advanced Spitfire IX fighter.[2]

Combat: 1945–1949

Royal Netherlands Indies Army (KNIL)—It has been estimated that by early 1946 the personnel strength of the Dutch army in the Far East totaled about 15,000 fully trained men organized into several infantry battalions along British lines,[3] indicating a rapid build-up in staging bases in Malaya near Singapore. These forces participated in the joint army-marine amphibious landing in Java on March 9, 1946, in which the army used 5,000 troops. Aside from this landing force, the Dutch had 11,000 army regulars stationed on islands other than Java and 13,000 in reserve status in Malaya, including 7,000 partially trained British colonials.[4]

KNIL also engaged in the first police action on Java, from July 21 to August 4, 1947, as part of a land, air, and sea force totalling some 109,000 men.[5] All available weapons were seemingly used in the attack. KNIL units took part in landings on Sumatra and Madura in addition to Java.[6]

The KNIL role in the police action was significant and probably amounted to a force of over 70,000 by July 1947. According to one report, while well trained and equipped, it lacked sufficient reserves, replacements, and, by implication, ammunition to wage a long campaign.[7]

On December 18, 1948, when the Dutch took a second police action, Dutch forces had grown to a total of 130,000, and KNIL probably had no fewer than 100,000 troops in this campaign. Army paratroops, armed with British .303-cal. jungle carbines and Canadian-made FN Browning 9mm automatic pistols, were used in the initial move to capture and secure the

---

[1] Ibid., 1948 edn., p. 15a.   [2] Ibid.   [3] Fischer, op. cit., p. 81.
[4] Klein, op. cit., p. 15.
[5] H. M. Bro: *Indonesia: Land of Challenge* (New York: Harper; 1954), p. 65.   [6] Fischer, op. cit., pp. 98, 102.
[7] *Time*, August 4, 1947, p. 20.

airfield at Jogjakarta for the use of NEIAAC on December 18, 1948.[8] This second police action, again using massed mobility against large numbers of well-dispersed nationalist forces, continued until August 1, 1949. It was the last major use of KNIL in the Netherlands East Indies, and after Indonesian independence in 1950 KNIL was disbanded (June 26, 1950), at a final strength of 65,000.[9]

Many of KNIL's small arms were turned over to the Indonesians, including "considerable quantities" of Dutch 6.5mm Männlicher rifles plus Enfield .303-cal. rifles and carbines.[1] Many of the Johnson .30-cal. semi-automatic rifles and the Johnson .30-cal. LMG's were repatriated to the Netherlands and sold as surplus in 1953.[2]

Royal Netherlands Navy—The main role of the navy was to impose and maintain a sea blockade of all supplies to the Indonesian nationalists that could be of use to them in their war effort. This also meant restricting Indonesian exports, which thus deprived the nationalists of vital foreign exchange. Despite some blockade running with a variety of small craft, the Dutch navy kept the blockade in force throughout the campaign. Among the items subject to seizure were weapons, machinery, surgical instruments, transportation equipment, communications equipment, railway spare parts, oxygen, sulphur, steel, copper wire, medicine, and clothing.[3]

In 1946 the Dutch fleet in the East Indies, including its auxiliary, the Netherlands East Indies Marine (DVS), consisted of: 12 46-ton armed motor launches acquired from Britain in 1946;[4] 8 corvettes of 560 tons each, converted to minesweeping, made in Australia and sold to the Netherlands in 1946; 31 ex-U.S. and ex-British landing craft (LCT/LCM) used in the Java landing in March 1946 and stationed in the Netherlands

---

[8] Fischer, op. cit., p. 119.   [9] Pauker, op. cit., p. 6.

[1] Smith, op. cit., p. 461.

[2] Johnson and Lockhoven, op. cit., Vol. II, p. 184.

[3] Joseph P. Lyford: "The Dutch Take Aim in Java," *New Republic,* February 16, 1948, p. 24.

[4] *Jane's Fighting Ships* (1946–1947 edn.; London: Sampson Low, Marston and Co., 1946), p. 239.

East Indies;[5] and 1 escort carrier on loan from the Royal Navy (ex-H.M.S. *Nairana*). Its complement of several dozen purchased aircraft included the British-made Fairey F.1 Firefly shipboard fighter and the newer Hawker F.B.11 Sea Fury fighter-bomber.[6] The crews were trained in carrier-operating techniques either in England or at Singapore.

Units of the Dutch fleet supported the army-marine landings on Java in March 1946 and the first police action in July 1947.[7] To help support these landings, some one hundred additional landing craft in reserve status were serving with DVS. The number of landing craft available to the Dutch army and marines remained constant throughout the campaign, with about 30 in first-line service.[8]

By 1948, several destroyers joined in enforcing the blockade, including the 1,760-ton *Tjerk Heddes* purchased from Britain in 1941.[9] In April 1948 the Dutch purchased a fleet aircraft carrier, the H.M.S. *Venerable,* from the Royal Navy. The ship, weighing 13,190 tons standard and 18,000 tons fully loaded, carried a normal load of 19 aircraft with a capacity of between 39 and 44 aircraft of the Firefly–Sea Fury type.[1] It was tropicalized and refitted in Britain for active service and on May 28, 1948, was commissioned the *Karel Doorman* in Dutch service. The ship then took up station off Java, replacing the ex-H.M.S. *Nairana,* which returned to Britain after a two-year loan period.[2] During 1948–1949, DVS purchased over one hundred surplus PT-boats from the United States and Britain for patrol duty, and received 8 patrol minesweepers formerly attached to the navy.[3] The navy was used sparingly in the second police action.

By 1949, the Dutch navy was using at least 25 seaward-defense motor launches of both Dutch and British origin. Three

[5] Ibid., pp. 237, 239.
[6] *Jane's All the World's Aircraft,* 1948 edn., p. 15a.
[7] Bro, op. cit., p. 65.
[8] *Jane's Fighting Ships,* 1946–1947 edn., p. 233; Ibid., 1949–1950 edn., p. 238.   [9] Ibid., 1951–1952 edn., p. 265.
[1] Ibid., 1947–1948 edn., p. 225.   [2] Ibid., 1951–1952 edn., p. 298.
[3] Ibid., 1949–1950 edn., p. 238.

of these were converted later in the year to shallow-draught minesweepers at Surabaya.[4] With the end of the conflict, several ships and landing craft were turned over to the newly formed Indonesian navy, including 4 patrol minesweepers formerly serving with DVS,[5] all 25 seaward-defense motor launches,[6] 1 converted shallow-draught minesweeper,[7] 16 landing craft of DVS,[8] and nearly all 100 PT-boats serving with DVS.[9] All of the transfers were made between late December 1949 and early 1951. Total naval and DVS personnel strength was estimated at 5,000 by March 1946,[1] and there is no evidence of any significant increase over this figure during the remainder of the campaign.

Royal Netherlands Marine Corps (NKM)—By January 1946, 2,000 marines were reported in Java, evidently aggressively attempting to engage the nationalist forces. The British, at this time attempting to pacify the island, ordered 1,200 to leave in January 1946,[2] leaving one battalion of 800 NKM on Java. Assisting them were 2,000 British colonial troops. On March 3, 1946, 5,000 marines out of a total landing force of 10,000 invaded Java in the first massive Dutch assault of the campaign and reformed into one battalion after the landing.[3] The NKM brigade participated in the two police actions of 1947 and 1948–1949.

Royal Netherlands Army Air Corps (NEIAAC)—The air corps had maintained unquestioned air superiority throughout the campaign and, by July 1947, had effectively neutralized the ineffective, poorly manned nationalist air force.[4] The U.S.-supplied B-25's and P-40's and the Spitfires supplied by the British were operating primarily from bases at Bandung, Semplak, Padang, Medan, and Semarang from 1946 through the remainder of the campaign.[5] The crews were experienced and well trained and provided effective air cover and ground support, using machine guns, HVAR's, and bombs. In 1946–1947

---

[4] Ibid., 1951–1952 edn., p. 266.   [5] Ibid., p. 265.   [6] Ibid., p. 266.
[7] Ibid., p. 306.   [8] Ibid., p. 308.   [9] Ibid., 1949–1950 edn., p. 238.
[1] Fischer, op. cit., p. 85.   [2] *Time*, January 21, 1946, p. 32.
[3] Klein, op. cit., p. 15.   [4] *Time*, July 28, 1947, p. 19.
[5] *Jane's All The World's Aircraft*, 1950–1951 edn., p. 12a.

Weapons Used by the Netherlands Forces from 1945 to 1949

Weapon	Number	Source
FN Browning 9mm automatic	5,000–7,000	U.K.-Canada
.38-cal. Enfield revolver	15,000	U.K.
pistol	3,000–5,000	U.K.-U.S.-Netherlands
Enfield SMLE .303-cal. rifle and other marks	about 90,000	U.K.-Australia
Johnson .30-cal. SLR	6,000	Netherlands
Springfield 1903 .30/06-cal. rifle	about 2,500	U.S.
U.S. M1 Carbine .30-cal.	1,500	U.S.
Dutch 6.5mm Männlicher rifle	about 4,000	Netherlands
Thompson M1 .45-cal. SMG	500–1,000	U.S.
Sten 9mm SMG	5,000–6,000	U.K.
Bren .303-cal. LMG	2,500–3,000	U.K.
Browning .50-cal. HMG	2,500–3,000	U.S.
machine gun, other types incl. Vickers .303-cal. BAR	1,200–1,500	U.K.-U.S.
25-pounder gun-howitzer	1,600–2,400	U.K.
60mm mortar	8,000	U.S.
4.2″ mortar	6,000	U.S.
75mm howitzer	about 80	U.S.
Sherman M24 tank	400–600	U.S.
armored personnel carrier and other vehicles	400	U.S.-U.K.

the Dutch purchased some war-surplus P-51 Mustang fighter-bombers from the United States, and these were introduced during the July 20, 1947, police action, where they effectively destroyed the remainder of the nationalist air force.[6] At about this time, a quantity of surplus late-model Spitfire XIV's may have been purchased from Britain.[7] Both Spitfires and Mustangs were used in the initial attack of the second police action on December 18, 1948, during which they bombed and strafed a previously nationalist-held air base at Jogjakarta and after which C-47 transports acquired from either the United States or Britain shuttled in 900 army paratroopers to secure the field.[8]

[6] Theodore H. White: "So the Dutch Are at War," *New Republic,* August 4, 1947, p. 8.
[7] *Jane's All The World's Aircraft,* 1948 edn., p. 15a.
[8] Fischer, op. cit., p. 119.

By 1948, the Netherlands had purchased a quantity of British-built Gloster Meteor IV jet fighters, but these were introduced into service too late to be used in the campaign.[9] Very few of the combat types were transferred to Indonesia, most of them remaining in inventory until phase-out in the early 1950's. The inventory of Harvards, C-47's, and Piper Cubs was transferred, however, along with all Dutch air bases (excluding those in West Irian), to the Indonesian air force (AURI).[1]

Indonesian Nationalist Forces' Weapons Acquisition
Build-up: 1943–1945

The core of the Indonesian Republican army (TKR) was the Japanese-organized and equipped PETA. By the time of the Japanese surrender, PETA consisted of sixty-six battalions on Java formed along lines of the Japanese infantry *daidan* of 522 officers and men each.[2] In addition, 1,626 PETA were active on the island of Bali.[3]

A small Indonesian officer corps had been trained by the Japanese advisers,[4] and after the disbandment of the Imperial Army, there were trained officers sufficient to regroup the forces and utilize in battalion strength all Japanese arms below heavy artillery, armor, and combat aircraft with reasonable efficiency.[5] The training received by the Indonesians was especially intended for the waging of rear-guard actions against an invading force.

PETA was formally disbanded following the Japanese surrender, but this organization, along with the Japanese weapons supplied to it, was carried over into TKR after October 1945 and remained the main nationalist armed force opposing the Dutch.[6]

TKR was the best equipped and organized of several Indonesian nationalist groups. When Allied (British, Australian, and

[9] *Jane's All The World's Aircraft,* 1948 edn., p. 15a.
[1] Ibid., 1950–1951 edn., p. 12a.   [2] Pauker, op. cit., p. 7.
[3] Ibid. Another estimate sets this figure at 8,000 but probably includes some paramilitary; Fischer, op. cit., p. 81.   [4] Pauker, op. cit., p. 81.
[5] Ibid., pp. 12–13.   [6] Ibid., p. 12.

Dutch) forces landed on Java in September 1945, in addition to PETA, which was basically military in character, there were several nationalist paramilitary organizations created by the Japanese; these numbered about 230,000. The paramilitary organizations received military drill, but reportedly were given only bamboo spears instead of firearms.[7]

Combat: Fall 1945–December 1949

Prior to the massive Dutch landings in March 1946, TKR had used artillery and tanks as well as small arms against the British at Surabaya (November 1945).[8] Again, in early December 1945, TKR units had massed against the British and used some of the ex-Japanese 75mm howitzers against them.[9] After these battles, much of the heavy equipment was abandoned because TKR lacked road transport for it, and most of it was captured by the British.[1] From then on, TKR used no weapons larger than mortars, and homemade mines sometimes substituted for antitank or antipersonnel weapons. Hand grenades, probably ex-Japanese, were also used to a large extent.[2]

For the most part during the rest of the campaign, TKR fought rear-guard actions and attacked Dutch communications, patrols, and transport, mostly at night.[3] The two Dutch police actions attempted to engage the nationalists in force but did not succeed in breaking their organization. Personnel mounted to upwards of 400,000 by mid-1947, including some paramilitary detachments;[4] however, the fighting core strength totalled slightly over 200,000 from mid-1947 on.[5]

In May 1947 the nationalists added some less experienced, semi-armed paramilitary units to the existing TKR force, and they named this organization the National Indonesian Army (TNI).[6] By July 1947, at the time of the first Dutch police action, TNI had 150,000 rifles, other small arms including

---

[7] Ibid., p. 10.   [8] Fischer, op. cit., p. 84.
[9] *Time,* December 17, 1945, p. 36.   [1] Pauker, op. cit., p. 13.
[2] Bro, op. cit., p. 65.
[3] *Casebook on Insurgency and Revolutionary Warfare* . . . , p. 55.
[4] *Time,* July 28, 1947, p. 19.   [5] Pauker, op. cit., p. 3.
[6] *Casebook on Insurgency and Revolutionary Warfare* . . . , p. 55.

Weapons Available to the Indonesian Nationalist Forces
from 1945 to 1949

Weapon	Number	Source
Nambu 8mm automatic	about 10,000	Japan, captured stocks
Arisaka-type 38 6.5mm rifle	about 100,000	Japan, captured stocks
Arisaka-type 99 7.7mm rifle	about 40,000	Japan, captured stocks
Dutch Männlicher 6.5mm rifle	about 10,000	Japan, captured stocks
Japanese-type BE 7.63mm SMG	35,000	Japan, captured stocks
MP 18	few	Japan, captured stocks
Japanese-type 96 6.5mm LMG	18,000–20,000[7]	Japan, captured stocks
70mm howitzer	about 50[7]	Japan, captured stocks
75mm field gun	about 50[7]	Japan, captured stocks
light 50mm grenade/all-purpose launcher	30,000–50,000	Japan, captured stocks
combat aircraft including Nakagima-Kawasaki fighters and Mitsubishi bombers	40[8]	Japan, captured stocks
patrol craft and armed motor launch	fewer than 100	left over from Dutch and Japanese

machine guns, and many homemade land mines and hand grenades.[9] The diminutive AURI, poorly trained and randomly equipped, was neutralized on the ground by Dutch air strikes in the first police action.[1]

The nationalist navy during the campaign was confined to running munitions and arms through the Dutch blockade in order to set up caches in mountain areas in anticipation of

[7] These weapons were mostly abandoned in early stages of the conflict.
[8] These aircraft were mostly destroyed on the ground by the Dutch air force.
[9] Bro, op. cit., p. 65.   [1] *Time*, July 28, 1947, p. 19.

greater Dutch military action.[2] Since there were no alternative sources of arms available to the nationalists at that time, it is possible that TNI was reinforced on Java by reallocating current weapons stocks from the other islands and shipping them by sea to Java. The nationalists also used many small wooden vessels as blockade runners to and from Singapore, exchanging produce for imports, and possibly black-market arms.

After the *Renville* Agreement of early 1948, the Republican government considered a force reduction to consolidate its existing weaponry and provide more firepower and mobility. This reorganization plan of February 1948, called the Hatta Plan, consisted of restructuring regular and irregular units of TNI and scaling down force levels to about 160,000 during the first stage, out of which a further reduction would be made to a planned level of 57,000.

SUMMARY OF CONTROL MEASURES

In summary form, the key conflict-control measures in this case might have been the following (an asterisk indicates that the measure was actually taken):

KEEPING THE DISPUTE NONMILITARY
Avoidance of colonialism.
Constructive outlets (e.g., regionalism) for colonialist impulses.
Third-party fact-finding.
Restricted availability of surplus arms.
Tightened controls on use of military assistance.
Equity tribunal for peaceful change.

PREVENTING THE OUTBREAK OF HOSTILITIES
Governmental cohesion and stability.
Preventive interposition by neutral or third-party forces.
International fact-finding.
Diplomatic recognition as legitimation and stabilization of
        de facto situation.
Time-stretching diplomatic devices.
Quarantine of arms importation into crisis areas.

[2] Lyford, op. cit., p. 24.

Local arms balances at relatively low levels, guaranteed by
        potential sanctions.
UN publication of arms inventories and trade.

MODERATING HOSTILITIES

Multilateral machinery on ground.*
Influential great-power involvement.*

TERMINATING HOSTILITIES

UN peacekeeping capability.
Peaceful-change mechanism.*
Arbitration of alleged violations.*
Stern economic pressures.
Superior cooperation.

PREVENTING THE RESUMPTION OF HOSTILITIES

Truce supervisory machinery geared to guerrilla tactics.
Involvement of great power,*
    Supporting:
UN peacekeeping.
Superpower cooperation.

CHAPTER 9

Conflict in the
Middle East, 1956–1967[1]

THE PHASES OF CONFLICT

We shall examine in this chapter two threads of conflict that sprang from diverse backgrounds but, at a critical juncture, converged to spark the Suez crisis of 1956. One thread of conflict—the dominant and persistent one—is the clash between Israel and its Arab neighbors. That conflict entered Phase II even before there was a state of Israel, as millions of Jews fleeing Nazi extermination sought refuge in the homeland Britain had promised them—land occupied by Arabs. The Arab-Israeli Conflict went through Phase III_1 in 1948–1949 and was, at the time this analysis begins, in Phase IV_1. The second conflict was that between Britain and France on the one hand and Egypt on the other; we might call it the British-French-Egyptian Conflict, or Suez Conflict. Dispute and conflict among the three had existed at times since the early nineteenth century, but it acquired renewed virulence in the mid-1950's.

In mid-1956, the two conflicts converged. The Suez war of 1956 is common to both. After the end of that brief war, the British-French-Egyptian Conflict quickly moved through Phase IV to Phase V. The Arab-Israeli Conflict, by contrast, remained in an increasingly tense Phase IV_2, until June 1967 when with increased intensity fighting was renewed.

---

[1] The authors wish to acknowledge the contributions to this chapter of Mrs. Irirangi C. Bloomfield, Miss Patricia A. Clapp, and Mr. Philip M. Raup.

We shall examine here, first, the convergent conflicts—in 1956—and then the continued Arab-Israeli Conflict (1957–1967).

The Converging Conflicts

The Arab-Israeli Conflict,
PHASE IV₁   *1949–October 29, 1956*
Sub-Phase A: 1949–July 1956

The Arab-Israeli Conflict arose from the establishment of the Jewish national state on the territory of Palestine. The war that resulted in 1948 (Phase III$_1$) reached a stalemate in 1949, and UN mediation produced a series of armistice agreements (Phase IV$_1$) that set the Israeli borders that persisted until mid-1967.

For the first several years after the 1949 armistice, Israeli-Egyptian relations were relatively peaceful. Then gradually the conciliatory climate deteriorated. Efforts at negotiation broke down as impasses were encountered on major substantive issues. For example, Israel, while willing to consider granting land-access rights across the southern Negev between Egypt and Jordan, balked at what it regarded as excessive and suspicious demands for a broad corridor.[2] And Egypt refused to consider lifting the ban it had maintained since 1948 on use of the Suez Canal by Israeli ships. In fact, in 1953 the ban was extended to all cargo to and from Israel, regardless of whose ships carried it. In addition, Egypt blockaded Israeli ships from using the Strait of Tiran at the mouth of the Gulf of Aqaba, which linked the Israeli port of Elath with the Red Sea.

During this time, in response to prolonged Egyptian pressures (and the urgings of the United States), Britain began negotiations for the evacuation of its Suez base.[3] Initially, Israel had

---

[2] Earl Berger: *The Covenant and the Sword: Arab-Israeli Relations, 1948–56* (London: Routledge and Kegan Paul; 1965), pp. 172–3.

[3] Kennett Love asserts (in an unpublished manuscript, "The Politics of Force at Suez," p. 3) that Israel began contemplating war when these negotiations opened.

ISRAEL AND NEIGHBORING STATES

Areas under Israeli control at
cessation of hostilities, June 1967

0   MILES   70

*MEDITERRANEAN
SEA*

Beirut

Damascus

L. Huleh
Eshed Kinrot
Acre *S. of Galilee* Qnaitra
Haifa HEIGHTS
Nazareth

LEBANON
SYRIAN

ISRAEL

Jenin
Tel Aviv Nablus
Jaffa
Ramallah Amman
Jericho
Jerusalem MT. SCOPUS

Gaza Hebron DEAD
GAZA STRIP Es Samu SEA
El Arish Rafah Khan Yunis
Dimona
N E G E V
Damietta
Port Said Abu Ageila El Auja
Port Fuad
Suez El Quseima
Ismailia Bir Hama
El Cap *Canal* Bir Gafgafa △ GEBEL LIBNI
Cairo
Port Suez MITLA PASS
Nakhl
U. A. R. SINAI PENINSULA
Elath Aqaba
(E G Y P T)

Nile River

GULF OF SUEZ GULF OF AQABA

S A U D I

A R A B I A

TIRAN
Strait of Tiran
Sharm el Sheikh

J O R D A N

RED SEA

endorsed Egypt's efforts to see Britain evacuate the canal zone. But in the cooling climate of Israeli-Egyptian relations, the prospect of Britain's withdrawal looked more dangerous to Israeli leaders, who felt that the presence of British soldiers in a band separating the Sinai Peninsula from the rest of Egypt was a deterrent to Egyptian attack on Israel. Even any minimal Egyptian move to send large numbers of troops and matériel past the British would be readily observed and the information supplied to Israel. British control of the canal area had not prevented Egypt from stationing some 60,000 troops in the Sinai Peninsula. Still, the British presence may well have acted as a brake on aggressive Egyptian tendencies.[4] Most importantly, Israeli officials believed it so acted.[5]

Soon after the agreement for British departure from the canal area was initialed (July 27, 1954), an organized campaign of terrorism against Israel was launched, the so-called *fedayin* (self-sacrificers) raids. These came primarily from the Gaza Strip, with its heavy concentration of refugees from the 1948–1949 war. During the following eight months the scale of incidents increased and saboteurs penetrated deep into Israel, killing military personnel and civilians and blowing up key installations, notably water pipes. In December 1954, a high Egyptian offical stated that the ruling military junta did not intend then to make peace with Israel and never would.

Israeli activists became united in their demands for an end to the terrorism, and David Ben Gurion, who had never agreed with the attempts at reconciliation with Egypt, returned to the Israeli government in charge of the defense ministry. Soon after, on February 28, 1955, the Israeli army penetrated the Gaza Strip, killing thirty-eight and blowing up key military installations. If Israel took its cue from the growing aggressiveness of Arab propaganda and the expanded scale of sabotage and terrorism, Egypt took its cue from the Gaza raid in February. And

[4] Erskine B. Childers: *The Road to Suez* (London: MacGibbon and Kee; 1962), pp. 286 *ff*.

[5] Jon and David Kimche: *Both Sides of the Hill* (London: Secker and Warburg; 1960), pp. 267–72.

as a result of spiraling events, both countries returned to a state of merely suspended war.[6]

Both Egypt and Israel took their cases to the UN Security Council—the former asking that Israel be punished for the Gaza raid and the latter asking the council to condemn Egypt's sponsorship of the *fedayin* attacks. The pattern of small Arab incursions and massive Israeli reprisal raids was—and remains —a common one along the armistice lines between Israel and its Arab neighbors. In this instance—as had been and by and large continues to be the case—the Security Council's response was to condemn Israel's reprisal action without dealing substantively with the Arab actions in any but the most general terms. The Council, however, urged both adversaries to cooperate in implementing some of the measures proposed by the head of the UN Truce Supervisory Organization (UNTSO) to make border violations by either side more difficult to carry out and easier to detect—barbed wire, joint patrols, etc.

During the months that followed the Gaza raid, the scale of *fedayin* attacks increased, and terrorists penetrated as far as the suburbs of Tel Aviv. In response, the Israeli army raided the Gaza town of Khan Yunis on August 31, 1955, killing thirty-six. At the same time, Israeli military units, organized as agricultural settlements, were being established at the important Negev crossroads of El Auja; and Israel resisted attempts, including pressures from UN Secretary-General Dag Hammarskjöld, to remove them from that demilitarized zone.

Then, on September 27, 1955, Colonel Nasser announced that the Egyptian government would buy important quantities of Soviet-bloc arms from Czechoslovakia.[7] The imminent arrival of Soviet arms in Egypt would clearly affect the military balance between Israel and Egypt. Hence, Israel began an

[6] Love, op. cit., pp. 173–4, 178–80.

[7] In *Arming the Third World: Case Studies in Soviet Foreign Policy* (Cambridge: MIT Press; forthcoming 1969), Professor Uri Ra'anan of MIT and the Fletcher School of Law and Diplomacy cites substantial evidence for a much earlier date. It appears that the preliminary arrangements for the arms deal date back to the opening months of 1955. In any event, some Soviet-bloc arms had arrived in Egypt as early as July 1955.

urgent search for additional arms, in particular for more modern tanks, artillery, and jet fighters. (See the WEAPONS section of this chapter for details on the Israeli and Egyptian inventories prior to the Czech deal and on Israel's response to its announcement.) Israel was ultimately successful in purchasing these things from France.

Israel also sought security guarantees from the West, but its reception was disappointing. British Prime Minister Anthony Eden issued a statement in November 1955 calling for peace in the Middle East and urging Israel to seek a compromise with Egypt on borders somewhere between the existing truce lines and the original UN partition-plan boundaries. Israel refused, since this would involve surrender of some of its territory. Also, in late 1955, rumors circulated about discussions between Britain and Iraq that suggested the division of Jordan between Iraq and Israel; this would have brought a military power instead of a weak, British-dominated state to Israel's eastern border.[8]

While the U.S. government did not adopt a hostile attitude toward Israel during this period, the pronounced neutrality of the Eisenhower administration was viewed by Israelis with disquiet because of their great dependence on U.S. aid. In response to the Czech arms deal, President Eisenhower asserted that the United States would not contribute to an arms race in the Middle East.[9] Secretary of State Dulles later made more explicit the interpretation of this policy to mean no additional arms shipments to Israel. Furthermore, he emphasized, Israel should look for protection not to the United States but to the United Nations.[1] Britain shared this stand, which reaffirmed the position on arms shipments to the Middle East that the two states and France had followed since 1950.[2]

[8] Ibid., pp. 194–6.

[9] U.S. Department of State: *American Foreign Policy: Current Documents, 1950–1955*, Department of State Publication 6446 (Washington: GPO; 1957), p. 2238.

[1] U.S. Department of State: *American Foreign Policy: Current Documents, 1956*, Department of State Publication 6811 (Washington: GPO; 1959), pp. 581–4.   [2] Ibid., *1950–1955*, p. 2239.

Egyptian actions also contributed to growing Israeli unease. In September 1955 the Egyptian government expanded its blockade of Israel, banning flights of Israeli planes, which were generally on a commercial run to Africa, over the Strait of Tiran.[3] While the magnitude of these Egyptian actions was relatively small compared to existing limitations on Israel's trade, the actions were taken as an indication of future efforts to isolate totally the Jewish state.

In Israel, as a consequence of domestic uneasiness over the deepening crisis, moderate Premier Moshe Sharett was replaced in November 1955 by Ben Gurion. Sharett retained the Ministry of Foreign Affairs until June 1956, when he was replaced by another activist, Mrs. Golda Meir.

Finally, during the period March–June 1956, the number of border skirmishes, sabotage incidents, and killings by *fedayin* increased dramatically. In response to these provocations, the Israelis shelled the market place in Gaza, killing more than sixty Arabs. In the first ten months of 1956, some two hundred Arab deaths resulted from Israeli actions, as compared to fifty-eight Israelis killed by Arabs. The impact of the violence was greater, however, in Israel than in Egypt since the Israelis felt that their whole country was threatened.[4]

The British-French-Egyptian Conflict, PHASE I   *Background of the Conflict*

Egypt lies at the meeting point of the Indian Ocean (through its extension, the Red Sea) and the Mediterranean; and since the seventeenth century, Britain has had important military and economic commitments in the Middle East. The importance of Egypt in British strategic and economic calculations increased enormously in the late nineteenth century when the Suez Canal

[3] Moshe Dayan: *Diary of the Suez Campaign* (New York: Harper and Row; 1966), pp. 10–12. Major-General Dayan was Chief of Staff of the Israel Defense Force.

[4] Ibid., p. 207. Unlike the surrounding Arab states, Israel does not have buffer zones between its main centers of population and borders. Israel could be quickly divided in two or more parts and overrun in a matter of hours, if surprised and unprepared.

was completed—on territory nominally under the sovereignty of Egypt but in reality controlled for most of the history of the canal by Britain.

Prior to World War II, the canal (and, as a consequence, Egypt) was more than just one in a long chain of staging points in the Middle East; it was the linchpin, the key to Britain's position in the whole Middle East and the vast lands "east of Suez." These strong British interests in the canal had led on three occasions to British occupation of Egypt to ensure the stability of the canal area and the security of this vital waterway.

Following World War II, and particularly as the Cold War deepened, Egypt, the Suez Canal, and the Middle East generally acquired an added significance in Western strategic thinking. As part of the series of military-alliance systems being developed under U.S. leadership to contain Soviet expansionism, Britain and the United States attempted to build an alliance structure in the Middle East around a Western pact with Egypt—the so-called Middle East Command. When this was rejected by Egypt in late 1951, the West turned to the concept of a defense arrangement with the "northern tier" states bordering the Soviet Union. Out of this grew the Baghdad Pact, which later became the Central Treaty Organization (CENTO) and which linked Turkey, Iraq, Pakistan, and Britain in a mutual-defense system for the region; in this, the United States, though not a member, played a large role. Two consequences of this development are important here. First, CENTO reduced, at least for the moment, the strategic importance of Egypt in Cold War terms.[5] Second, the injection of the Cold War into the Middle East challenged growing neutralist-nationalist sentiment there and also strengthened Iraq, Egypt's chief rival in the Arab world.

While the strategic and military importance of Egypt and the Suez Canal to the West in general and to Britain in particular was changing, the economic importance of the area to Western Europe was increasing. At the base of this change was Euro-

[5] John C. Campbell: *Defense of the Middle East* (rev. edn.; New York: Harper; 1960), pp. 42–6.

pean reliance on Middle Eastern oil, which assumed growing importance as Europe recovered from the war and modernized and expanded its economy. It was estimated that, by 1956, 15 per cent of British energy requirements and 17 per cent of those of Western Europe were supplied by oil. Some 75 per cent of Western Europe's oil came from the Middle East, and fully 50 per cent of it was shipped through the Suez Canal, much of the remaining 25 per cent reaching non-Egyptian Mediterranean ports via pipeline.[6]

Also substantial were British investments in the region. British companies held a 50-per-cent interest in Kuwaiti oil production, a 40-per-cent interest in oil production in Iran, and a 23-per-cent interest in Iraq and the Persian Gulf shiekdoms.[7]

France and the United States also had economic interests in the area that, though large, tended to be dominated by other considerations. For the United States, the strategic concerns of the Cold War have already been mentioned; a parallel and at times conflicting concern was a genuine sympathy with nationalist revolutions and a desire not to be identified, in the Middle East or elsewhere, with those who sought to preserve overlong the prerequisites of empire.

Arab nationalism had been waxing since the end of World War II. But it found its leader only with the rise to power in Egypt of Colonel Nasser. In many ways, Arab nationalism, particularly under Nasser's leadership, appeared to be a threat to the many Western interests.

Economically, Nasserism appeared to endanger the security of Europe's vital oil supply. Politically, the appeal of Nasserism throughout the Middle East threatened to remove from European influence—mainly British—such footholds of Western influence as Jordan, where local Nasser supporters forced the removal of Sir John Glubb as commander of the Arab Legion in April 1956. In terms of global politics, Nasser's acceptance of

[6] Herman Finer: *Dulles over Suez* (Chicago: Quadrangle Books; 1964), pp. 12–13.

[7] Royal Institute of International Affairs: *British Interests in the Mediterranean and Middle East* (London: Oxford University Press; 1958), p. 27.

Soviet-bloc arms enabled the Soviet Union to leap over the "northern tier" and establish its influence in the heart of the strategic Middle East.

Nasser's open and direct support of the Algerian rebellion against France encouraged France to see Nasser's brand of Arab nationalism as a direct threat to French interests. Initially, the government of Premier Guy Mollet attempted to negotiate with Nasser. But when, in April 1956, Foreign Minister Christian Pineau failed to obtain Nasser's agreement to halt aid to the Algerian rebels, French policy became openly hostile toward Egypt.

For both Britain and Egypt the Suez Canal quickly became the focus of dispute. To most Egyptians, British occupation of the canal zone and operation of the canal by an entirely foreign-owned company were visible symbols of foreign domination. After a period of terrorist activities against British forces, and with strong U.S. urging, Britain agreed in 1954 to withdraw its forces. The withdrawal took place gradually over a period of some months and was finally completed in June 1956. While the withdrawal was in progress, Nasser announced that he wished to revise the agreements with the Suez Canal company regarding income from the canal's operations,[8] of which Egypt had received a share only since 1936.

At the same time, Egypt was engaged in negotiations for international assistance in building the Aswan High Dam, which would cost a total of $1.24 billion. Of this amount, $760 million would be labor and materials supplied by Egypt; the balance had to be obtained from external sources. A formula was worked out with Western governments and the International Bank for Reconstruction and Development that would provide $70 million in grants and $480 million in loans over a period of fifteen years.

During the early loan negotiations, the Egyptian government rejected Western conditions that would give the lenders supervision of Egyptian finances. By the time the Egyptian position

[8] Terrence Robertson: *Crisis: The Inside Story of the Suez Conspiracy* (New York: Atheneum; 1965), p. 6.

was softening on this point, U.S. policy began to harden. Secretary of State Dulles was reportedly angered by, among other things, Nasser's recognition of Communist China and hints that he might accept Soviet help for the dam if Western aid were not forthcoming.[9] Such tactics smacked of crude blackmail.

Thus, when Egypt announced its acceptance of the U.S.-British-International Bank offers in July 1956, the U.S. portion of the offer was withdrawn. The Department of State reported that "it is not feasible in present circumstances to participate in the project."[1] Not surprisingly, Nasser was angered by the rejection and by what he regarded as insulting reference to Egyptian ability to repay. In immediate reaction, he announced in a violently anti-Western speech the nationalization of the canal company. The move was partly in retaliation and partly because the canal company was a profitable property that could contribute toward the costs of constructing the Aswan Dam, the canal company having earned more than $56 million in profits in 1955.[2]

The Arab-Israeli Conflict,
PHASE IV$_1$ *Sub-Phase B*
The British-French-Egyptian
Conflict, PHASE II

July–October 1956

Nasser's nationalization of the canal thus precipitated Britain's and France's growing quarrel with Egypt into a conflict at the same time that Israeli-Egyptian relations were approaching a crisis point. The Suez Canal became for Britain and France the visible symbol of their conflict with Nasser, just as it had been the symbol of foreign domination for Egypt. For Israel, the British-French-Egyptian Conflict presented an opportunity for the support it felt it needed to counter Egypt's growing military strength and aggressiveness and rapidly increasing predominance in the Arab world.

[9] Finer, op. cit., pp. 40–2.
[1] U.S. Department of State: *American Foreign Policy: Current Documents, 1956,* pp. 603–4.   [2] Childers, op. cit., p. 165.

Nasser asserted that he had no intention of interfering with canal operations beyond continuing to bar Israeli ships and cargoes, a policy to which the old canal company had never objected. But the possibility of other interference with the smooth functioning of the canal was a particularly serious threat to Europe. As was noted earlier, a high proportion of Europe's oil came through the canal; substituting Venezuelan, Canadian, or American oil or shipping Middle Eastern oil via the Cape of Good Hope would cost Britain and France an estimated additional $500 million in 1956 alone.[3] On the other hand, experience during World War II had demonstrated that use of the Cape route, though costly, was possible.[4]

The Western governments all condemned the nationalization. But while the U.S. expressed concern over the "far-reaching implications" of the act,[5] Britain and France reacted with strongly worded protests and concrete acts. Terming the nationalization totally unjustifiable, British Prime Minister Eden froze all Egyptian assets in Britain. French Premier Mollet denounced Nasser as another Hitler. Other European countries did not take the British and French view. What interested them was assurance from Egypt of their right to unhindered canal passage. Similarly, American oil companies indicated that they were prepared to cooperate with the Egyptian authorities.

Toward the end of July, both British and French cabinets instructed their defense ministers to prepare contingency plans in the event military action against Egypt was decided upon.[6] The larger historic terms in which the British and French saw the issue were clearly set forth in a telegram to President Eisenhower from Prime Minister Eden, who was determined neither to repeat the errors of appeasement nor to yield British primacy:

[3] Finer, op. cit., p. 245.
[4] Royal Institute of International Affairs, op. cit., p. 126.
[5] *U.S. Department of State Bulletin,* August 6, 1956, p. 221.
[6] Childers, op. cit., p. 62; *The New York Times,* July 29 and 31, 1956.

If we do not [take a firm stand], our influence and yours throughout the Middle East will . . . be finally destroyed.

The immediate threat is to the oil supplies of Western Europe, a great part of which flows through the Canal. . . . It is, however, the outlook for the longer term which is more threatening. . . .

We should not allow ourselves to become involved in legal quibbles about the rights of the Egyptian government to nationalize what is technically an Egyptian company. . . . I feel sure that we should take issue with Nasser on the broader international grounds.

As we see it we are unlikely to attain our objectives by economic pressures alone. . . . My colleagues and I believe we must be ready, in the last resort, to use force to bring Nasser to his senses.[7]

Meeting with Eden in July, Secretary of State Dulles reportedly asked the British Prime Minister if the British and French had weighed carefully the risks of using force. "He said—and [Foreign Minister] Selwyn Lloyd repeated it often—they'd rather risk a world war than sink to the level of a third-rate power with a depleted economy."[8]

It is difficult to determine the date on which Israel became set on a policy of preventive war. It seems clear that the decision was not made earlier than November 1955 (when Ben Gurion resumed leadership of the Israeli government) and not later than July 1956 (when the possibility of substantial British and French support became apparent). The first serious discussions with French officials regarding military assistance are reported to have been held in the fall of 1955, when Israel began its urgent search for arms to counterbalance the Soviet-bloc arms just promised Nasser. By January 1956, this contact was expanded to the point where secret talks were reportedly held in Paris, including, on the French side, Foreign Minister Pineau.

One source states that it was at that meeting that France agreed to meet Israeli arms requests to the extent possible, to coordinate military planning, and to continue talks between military officials.[9] Until July 1956, however, no concrete co-

[7] Sir Anthony Eden: *Full Circle* (Boston: Houghton Mifflin; 1960), p. 476.   [8] Robertson, op. cit., p. 81.   [9] Ibid., p. 49.

ordinated military moves were considered seriously. The French were militarily tied down in Algeria and in NATO commitments and were not in a position to carry out a major military action against Egypt unilaterally. Another analyst argues that the key date for the Israeli decision was April 1956; after that time the only important considerations were tactical.[1] Israeli Chief of Staff Moshe Dayan suggests a number of interim decisions leading to a decision to act in July 1956. He notes a speech by Prime Minister Ben Gurion to the Knesset on November 2, 1955, in which the government's intention to halt terrorism and remove the blockade of Tiran was made clear.[2] Dayan also notes that the need for preventive action was brought about by the fear of Egyptian attack: "The decisive intimation to Israel of approaching Egyptian attack was the arms deal concluded between Czechoslovakia and Egypt in September 1955."[3] Finally, he notes the importance of British and French support: "If it were not for the Anglo-French operation, it is doubtful whether Israel would have launched her campaign; and if she had, its character, both military and political, would have been different."[4]

Thus, Britain, France, and Israel each came separately to consider a military solution to its conflict with Egypt. Israel, concerned particularly with a lack of air and naval cover, did not begin serious planning for action until French aid was assured. And France, lacking landing equipment and heavy bombers, did not move until Britain indicated willingness to cooperate.

As has been noted, British and French military leaders had been instructed immediately after the nationalization to prepare plans for possible military action. French Defense Minister Maurice Bourgès-Maunoury reported that it would take at least one month for France to prepare if acting alone, or six weeks if in coordination with the British. The most important needs were for landing craft, the training of paratroops, and the use of the

---

[1] Berger, op. cit., p. 206.   [2] Dayan, op. cit., pp. 12–13.
[3] Ibid., p. 4. See, however, p. 247, note 7, on the date of this agreement.
[4] Ibid., p. 3.

British base in Cyprus for the short-range Mystère fighter squadrons.[5] The British Defense Minister, the Rt. Hon. Sir Walter Monckton, reported that British forces were quite unprepared. There were no landing craft in Cyprus (they would have to come from England and Malta); the paratroop units needed retraining; the nearest supporting artillery units were under NATO command in Germany; and large numbers of troops would be required.[6]

In consultation, the British and French defense ministries prepared an initial contingency plan calling for 50,000 British and 30,000 French troops, a combined British-French naval fleet, bombing of Egyptian airfields by British Canberra bombers, and a target date for invasion of September 15. It was reported that the landing would be first at Alexandria, later proceeding to Cairo, and only afterward moving to the canal zone.[7] A joint command structure was elaborated under British Minister of War Antony Head, with headquarters in London. Throughout the structure, British officers were in command, with French deputies.

While these developments were taking place, Foreign Ministers Pineau and Lloyd conferred in London with U.S. Under Secretary of State Robert Murphy. When Murphy reported the extent of British and French concern and their pressure for immediate action,[8] Dulles joined the discussion to demonstrate the high priority the United States placed on restraining its allies from hasty and violent action. With some reluctance, Britain agreed to Dulles's proposal for a conference of the signatories to the 1888 convention, under which the canal had been operated, and the present canal users; France went along with this in order to retain British support.

U.S. diplomacy in the events that unfolded was determined first by British and French expectations at the outset that Washington would support them,[9] then by growing disillusionment on their part at what they construed as U.S. betrayal, and finally

[5] Robertson, op. cit., pp. 75–6.   [6] Ibid., pp. 76–7.
[7] Ibid., pp. 77–8.   [8] Finer, op. cit., p. 68.
[9] For example, see Love, op. cit., p. 60.

by increasing irritation and concern in Washington at what seemed ill-conceived, archaic, and potentially dangerous illusions in the minds of its closest allies when it came to Egyptian policy. London and Paris were paving the way for war, whereas Washington was seeking to de-fuse the crisis.

At the mid-August canal users' conference in London, the United States proposed an international operating authority for Suez in which Egypt would participate but over which it would not have sole control. Britain and France agreed to go along with the attempt to obtain Egypt's agreement to the plan. Important elements in Britain, including the entire Labour party, had demanded that all peaceful methods of settlement be attempted before resorting to force. In any case, as the defense ministers had made clear, no military action was possible before mid-September. Scandinavian states at the conference were not enthusiastic in their support of the resolution, feeling that an accommodation with Nasser might be possible if the issue were limited to the right of free passage. The non-Western powers opposed the U.S. resolution.[1]

In early September, the Western proposals were taken in person to Cairo by a mission headed by Australian Prime Minister Robert Menzies. Not surprisingly, since they would have repealed nationalization, Nasser declined to accept them. One factor that may have been partially responsible for Egyptian rejection was the statement by President Eisenhower that "We are committed to a peaceful settlement of this dispute, nothing else."[2] Britain believed that this statement virtually eliminated what little bargaining power the Western states may have had to wrest concessions from Nasser.

It is also possible, however, that concrete results might have been obtained if the mission had been freer to negotiate. Nasser had already indicated a willingness to make concessions to allay the fears of the world community, proposing a new international treaty to replace that of 1888, which would reaffirm the right of free passage and authorize UN arbitration in case of

[1] Ibid., pp. 85–92.   [2] Finer, op. cit., p. 189.

disputes.[3] This was, however, unacceptable to Britain and France.

The British and French adopted a policy of noncooperation with the new Egyptian canal authority in the hope, some observers contend, that this might lead to a breakdown of canal operations and provide an excuse for intervention. British and French ships refused to pay tolls to Egypt, depositing them instead in the canal company's accounts in Paris and London. In mid-September 1956 the canal company instructed its pilots to leave, and it was widely believed in some Western circles that this would demonstrate the dependence of Egypt on skilled Westerners. Egyptian authorities were able to recruit foreign pilots, however, to supplement the Egyptian pilots who remained. As a result, canal operation continued smoothly, and it was reported in late September that Egypt was collecting more tolls than before nationalization (the Egyptian authorities did not refuse passage to British and French ships that did not pay tolls).[4]

With Nasser's rejection of the plan of the first canal users' conference, Britain and France continued their military preparations. The Soviet Union added to the uncertainty by veiled threats of intervention. A Soviet diplomat, for example, was quoted as saying in London that "if war broke out over Suez the Arabs would not stand alone; 'It will be a just war for the Arabs, and there will be volunteers.' "[5] Nevertheless, British and French military preparations proceeded, and by mid-September the units on Cyprus were ready for action.

Concerned about the possibility of hostilities, Dulles tried yet another tactic that would keep the conflict at the conference table, if only temporarily. This took the form of a proposal to form a Suez Canal Users' Association (SCUA). Because of continuing concern over the danger of U.S.-British disunity in foreign policy, Eden agreed to try this device. France again agreed to cooperate in order to retain British support for the

[3] Ibid., pp. 126–9.   [4] Ibid., pp. 178–9.
[5] *Times* (London), August 28, 1956, as cited in Finer, op. cit., p. 179.

military action it considered might be necessary. The Suez Canal Users' Association plan was announced on September 13. It stated that the association would employ pilots to take ships through the canal and that if Egypt refused, then "other appropriate" action would be taken. At this point Eden suggested that the "other appropriate" action would be force; Dulles, however, reportedly stated that U.S. ships would sail by way of the Cape of Good Hope. Once again the United States seemed to Britain to be undermining Western bargaining power, weakening Western efforts to make Nasser "disgorge his spoils."[6]

On October 5, as a result of the growing British and French disillusionment with U.S. delaying tactics, London and Paris took the matter to the UN Security Council. This step had reportedly been opposed by the United States since it seemed likely that the Soviet Union would veto any action that would satisfy the British and French. However, Eden and Mollet wanted to be able to argue that they had exhausted the possibilities for peaceful settlement before they resorted to force. There were also domestic political reasons that induced the British, at least, to go to the United Nations. Both Defense Minister Monckton and Deputy Prime Minister R. A. Butler opposed the use of force except after failure of UN mediation, as did the majority of the Labour party and substantial segments of British public opinion.[7]

The Security Council was asked by Britain and France to consider the "situation created by the unilateral action of the Egyptian Government in bringing to an end the system of international operation of the Suez Canal." Simultaneously, Egypt, referring to the British-French military build-up in the eastern Mediterranean, asked the council to consider "actions against

[6] Finer, op. cit., p. 234.
[7] Robertson, op. cit., pp. 130–3. In the left wing of the Labour party, sentiments were strongly anti-imperialist, frequently pacifist, and, on occasion, pro-Soviet. There were a few members of the Labour party, however, who felt that it had been hurt by its postwar identification with the break-up of the empire and should adopt a strong line against Egypt.

Egypt by some powers, particularly France and the United Kingdom, which constitute a danger to international peace and security."[8]

The foreign ministers of France, Britain, Israel, and Egypt attended the UN Security Council sessions. After the public debates, private meetings were held in the office of UN Secretary-General Hammarskjöld during the second week in October. In these meetings, a strong possibility seemed to be developing that some compromise might be arranged.[9] Egyptian Minister of Foreign Affairs, Mahmoud Fawzi agreed to pledge a certain percentage of canal income to canal improvements, to fix tolls for a number of years, to recognize a users' association, and to negotiate a new treaty reaffirming rights of free passage. This preliminary agreement was announced in the form of six vaguely worded principles that all parties understood to represent the more concrete items mentioned above. Thus, when the Security Council meetings ended on October 14, it was generally expected that further negotiations would be held around October 30.[1] The Secretary-General did, in fact, pursue the discussions with the Egyptian foreign minister and achieved a broad area of agreement; but, when Israeli operations against Egypt began, the discussions were suspended.[2]

While the United Nations was dealing with the problem, final plans were being made for the joint French-Israeli action and for possible British-French operations. There are differences of opinion as to the degree to which British officials were fully

[8] *The United States and the United Nations: Report by the President to the Congress for the Year 1956* (Washington: GPO; 1957), p. 43.

[9] Robertson (op. cit., p. 129) quotes French Foreign Minister Pineau as saying: "I felt that if we did not do something [to counter Nasser's nationalization of the Suez Canal company] we would put ourselves in an inferior position in Algeria, that we would give the FLN rebels a major trump." At the same time, the socialist Foreign Minister stated that his government was embarrassed to be acting apparently on behalf of the private Compagnie Universelle du Canal Maritime de Suez, which had its seat of operations in Paris, and several thousand French stockholders.   [1] Finer, op. cit., pp. 308–15.

[2] *Report by the President to the Congress for the Year 1956*, p. 47.

informed of French-Israeli plans; in any event they seem to have been aware that some consultation was taking place.[3]

On September 23, the Israeli officials in charge of coordinating plans with France arrived secretly in Paris to talk with French and British officials.[4] By September 26, a plan was elaborated by the British-French joint command calling for an attack through Port Said to the canal zone. In deference to British military opinion, French arguments for a paratroop action were dropped, and a massive seaborne assault combined with heavy air support was agreed upon. On September 29, Moshe Dayan visited Paris, and during the next four days the details of a three-power coordinated operation were worked out.[5]

Under the revised plan, the Israeli attack would come between October 29 and November 5, a time picked primarily because it would coincide with U.S. presidential elections. It was hoped that the elections would make decisive U.S. action more difficult, in case Eisenhower actively opposed the invasion.

On October 10, Israel made a heavy reprisal raid against Jordan. Britain announced the next day that it would honor its obligations to defend Jordan and warned Israel against future raids. According to one source, the Israeli raid was a feint designed to create the impression that Israeli mobilization was aimed at Jordan rather than Egypt.[6] Another source contends that the British had been previously informed by the French of the possibility of such a raid and had seized upon it as an opportunity to demonstrate the pro-Arab bias of British foreign policy.[7]

By October 16, the French were becoming worried that the proposed operation was slowing down, and Eden and Lloyd

---

[3] Merry and Serge Bromberger: *Secrets of Suez* (London: Pan Books; 1957), p. 42.   [4] Dayan, op. cit., pp. 24–5; Robertson, op. cit., p. 134.

[5] Dayan, op. cit., pp. 29–31.

[6] Childers, op. cit., pp. 231–2. Pro-Nasser groups won the Jordanian elections in October, and there was an immediate realignment of Jordanian foreign policy to support Nasser.

[7] Robertson, op. cit., pp. 129–30.

flew to Paris two days earlier than planned in order to finish arrangements. Earlier, Eden had taken control of the defense ministry from Monckton, who was opposed to intervention; subsequently, Antony Head was placed in charge of the whole defense ministry (in addition to the joint British-French command that he had formed). During the October 16 meetings, decisions were made on the timing and circumstances of British-French intervention.

The Arab-Israeli Conflict, PHASE III₂ *The British-French-Egyptian Conflict,* PHASE III	*October 29– November 7, 1956*

The Arab-Israeli Conflict,
PHASE III$_2$
The British-French-Egyptian
Conflict, PHASE III

October 29–
November 7, 1956

Sub-Phase A: October 29–31, 1956

Hostilities broke out when Israeli forces launched an attack into the Sinai Peninsula which was aimed at the two southern and the middle sectors of the Suez Canal and at Egyptian fortifications dominating the Strait of Tiran.

On October 29, Israel dropped a paratroop battalion at the strategic Mitla Pass, near the southern end of the canal. The unit took up position and awaited supporting troops, which, because of transportation difficulties, did not arrive until late on October 30. With the advantage of effective air cover, Israeli troops secured the Mitla Pass despite heavy opposition and some strafing by Egyptian planes, but they did not proceed to the heavily fortified canal area.[8]

In the second area of Israeli attack, the central region of the Sinai Peninsula (near El Quseima), one Israeli brigade moved north to probe the heavily fortified positions around Abu Ageila. On October 31, another brigade attempted to take the Abu Ageila fortifications from the west but was stopped by heavy fire.[9]

After consultation with France and Britain as parties to the

---

[8] S. L. A. Marshall: *Sinai Victory* (New York: William Morrow; 1958), pp. 65–93.   [9] Ibid., pp. 94–127; Dayan, op. cit., pp. 101–6.

Tripartite Declaration of 1950, the United States requested an immediate meeting of the Security Council. The council met on October 30 and heard from the chief of staff of the UN Truce Supervisory Organization, who reported that the Israelis had attacked and had ignored his call for a cease-fire and troop withdrawal. The United States offered a resolution calling on Israel to withdraw and on all UN members to refrain from the use of force or from giving assistance of any kind to Israel.[1]

The British delegate announced that his government and that of France had that day (October 30) presented an ultimatum to both Israel and Egypt to cease hostilities and to withdraw to within ten miles of the Suez Canal.[2] Also, in order to separate the belligerents and guarantee free transit through the canal, Egypt had been asked to permit British and French forces to move temporarily into Port Said, Ismailia, and Port Suez. Both Israel and Egypt had been given twelve hours to respond, after which British and French forces would intervene in whatever strength necessary to ensure compliance.

When the U.S. resolution was put to the vote, it was vetoed by Britain and France. The council then adopted, over British and French objections, a procedural resolution asking that the General Assembly be called into emergency session under the Uniting for Peace Resolution of 1950.[3]

Sub-Phase B: October 31–November 5, 1956

Hostilities in the opening days were confined to Israeli and Egyptian forces. But they intensified dramatically on October 31 when Britain and France, nominally following up their ultimatum but in reality as a result of preplanning with the Israelis,[4] committed their air power and, in the case of France, some naval

[1] UN Document S/3170, October 30, 1956.

[2] Israeli forces were not that close to the Suez Canal at the time.

[3] *Report by the President to the Congress for the Year 1956*, pp. 47–9.

[4] The British government has consistently denied all accusations of collusion with Israel, and Prime Minister Eden, in his memoirs, claimed that British actions from October 29 only responded to Israeli moves. The contrary case, however, has now been amply demonstrated. See, in particular, Anthony Nutting: *No End of a Lesson: The Story of Suez* (London: Constable; 1967).

units. The uses made of British-French air power, in any event, were hardly calculated to apply force equally to Egypt and Israel. The primary British targets were Egyptian airfields, and the primary French role was in providing tactical support for Israeli ground operations and air cover for Israel.

While Egypt's inventory of modern jet aircraft exceeded that of Israel (see the WEAPONS section of this chapter), the Egyptian air force was operationally weaker. In large measure this was a consequence of the lack of an adequate number of trained Egyptian pilots for the sophisticated planes received from the Soviet bloc. The combined French-Israeli air operations over Sinai led Nasser to ground most of his fighters. And the British bombing led him to evacuate many of them to bases in Syria and Saudi Arabia.[5]

On the ground, the key item of military equipment in the fighting was the tank. (See the WEAPONS section of this chapter for details on Israeli and Egyptian tank inventories at this stage.) Studies of the hostilities make it plain that effective Israeli use of Sherman tanks and the fast French-built AMX light tanks was the key to the defeat of the several important positions fortified by the Egyptians. The Israeli tanks were never seriously challenged by Egyptian tanks during the fighting.

Concerning manpower, one report that was based on Egyptian sources states that Egypt's normal force in Sinai was 60,000 men, but that at the time of the Israeli attack only 30,000 were in position (the others having been withdrawn to the canal zone in August). Against this force, Israel reportedly deployed approximately 45,000 troops. Moreover, some two thirds of the Egyptian force were support, rather than combat, troops, compared to half or less of the Israeli forces intended for that purpose.[6] On the other hand, accounts of the war based on Israeli sources give the impression of small, highly mobile and well-equipped Israeli units defeating very large Egyptian

[5] Leo Heiman: "Moscow's Export Arsenal: The Soviet Bloc and the Middle Eastern Arms Race," *East Europe*, Vol. 13, No. 5 (May 1964), p. 9.   [6] Childers, op. cit., p. 282.

troop concentrations centered on fortifications and fixed artillery.[7]

The air strikes that began on October 31 against the fortified Egyptian elevations were coordinated with heavy attacks by tanks and with the shelling of Egyptian defenses by French naval vessels.[8] Egyptian positions in the northern area around Rafah were overrun between three and nine a.m. on November 1. By the evening of November 1, all Egyptian armor was withdrawing rapidly toward the canal area. Hundreds of military vehicles clogged the roads, offering targets for bombing and strafing by Israeli and French planes. On November 2, Egyptian forces in the Gaza Strip, acting under orders, surrendered after minor skirmishes.[9] In the central area, Egyptian troops from Abu Ageila left their positions, all armor retreated to the canal, and the air bases at Bir Hama and Bir Gafgafa were deserted.[1]

Subsequently, from November 3 to 5 the Israeli southern forces and a brigade proceeding from Elath advanced upon and took Sharm el Sheikh at the southern tip of Sinai, a post that controlled the Strait of Tiran at the entrance to the Gulf of Aqaba. In the southern thrust, as in the central area, the French contributed to Israeli success by flying supplies from Cyprus aboard Noratlas transports.[2]

The First Special Emergency Session of the UN General Assembly met on November 1. U.S. Secretary of State Dulles characterized "the violent armed attack by three of our members upon a fourth" as "a grave error." He offered a resolution

---

[7] See, for example, Dayan, op. cit.

[8] Dayan (op. cit., p. 132) notes the shelling of the Rafah positions but does not indicate who was responsible for it. Also, in contrast to Marshall, who notes the contributions of air attacks in the taking of the Rafah fortifications, Dayan discounts their effectiveness as well as that of the naval bombardments. Marshall does not mention naval bombardments at all. Merry and Serge Bromberger (op. cit., p. 24) stress the significance of the French navy in neutralizing the Egyptian navy. (See the WEAPONS section of this chapter for a comparison of Israeli and Egyptian naval strengths and equipment.)

[9] Marshall, op. cit., pp. 189–91.   [1] Childers, op. cit., p. 292.

[2] Ibid., p. 288; Marshall, op. cit., p. 69. Marshall does not indicate the nationality of the planes.

for a cease-fire that was adopted in the early hours of November 2 with the Soviet Union concurring.[3]

This conjunction of U.S. and Soviet policy in the Middle East took place against the counterpoint of the Hungarian rebellion and its suppression. At this particular moment, however, it appeared that Soviet armor was withdrawing from Budapest following an October 30 announcement of Soviet readiness to negotiate the stationing of its troops in Hungary with the members of the Warsaw Pact. The Hungarian situation was therefore outwardly headed toward a peaceful resolution.[4]

The UN General Assembly met again during the night of November 3 against a background of deepening crisis. Disregarding the November 2 call for a cease-fire, the British and French continued to bomb Port Said and the Israelis to decimate whatever Egyptian forces they could catch in Sinai. The canal had been closed by sunken shipping, and oil pipelines in the Middle East had been cut. Hanging over the UN proceedings was the clear threat of further intensification of hostilities, involving British and French invasion of the canal zone with unknown implications of spiraling interventions on opposing sides by other great powers.

The Canadian delegation under Lester Pearson had been working on the notion of a UN peace force that would separate Israeli and Egyptian forces. Since the declared purpose of any British-French landing was also to separate these combatants, such a UN force would serve to make the presence of other landing forces unnecessary.[5] The Secretary-General was able to

[3] *Report by the President to the Congress for the Year 1956,* p. 50.

[4] Ibid., p. 84. The Security Council, however, was called into session again on November 2 on receipt of news of large-scale Soviet troop movements into Hungary. The council met again on November 3 and at three a.m. on Sunday, November 4, as the scale of Soviet military intervention became apparent. The council's attempted call for withdrawal of Soviet forces was vetoed by the Soviet Union, and the matter was referred, again under the Uniting for Peace Resolution, to a special emergency session of the General Assembly; ibid., pp. 84–6. There were thus two special General Assembly sessions meeting in New York, each dealing with an outwardly separate conflict but with the tensions of one reinforcing the tensions of the other.

[5] William R. Frye: *A United Nations Peace Force* (New York: Oceana Publications; 1957), pp. 6–21.

inform the General Assembly on November 3 that Britain and France had agreed to halt their military action if, among other conditions, both Egyptian and Israeli governments would accept a UN force to maintain the peace until an Arab-Israeli settlement and a Suez Canal settlement were reached. The proposal was strongly supported by the United States and approved, by a vote of 57 to 0 with 19 abstentions, just after midnight on November 4.[6]

Sub-Phase C: November 4/5–7, 1956

Despite strong pressure from the United Nations, the United States, and many others, British and French land operations in the Suez Canal area commenced even as the General Assembly acted. The British and French had been bombing prelanding targets in Egypt (including the Cairo airport) around the clock. After several delays—the force itself took longer than expected to assemble, and the highly selective prelanding bombings of the area had been protracted in order to cut later ground casualties to a minimum—the British-French airborne assault on Port Fuad began on the night of November 4/5, and the city surrendered by that afternoon. There was heavy fighting in Port Said, and the local Egyptian commander initiated discussions for a surrender. At the same time, British and French forces moved south from the two ports, up the canal. Surrender negotiations in Port Said were broken off, and on November 6 the seaborne troops pressing toward the occupation of the Suez Canal area encountered considerable Egyptian resistance, including that of an armed civilian population. By midnight of November 6, the allied forces had reached El Cap, only twenty-three miles from Port Said.

At this point, when Egypt's military plight was becoming extremely grave, strong diplomatic support was received from the Soviet Union and, indirectly, from the United States. The Soviet Union on November 5 sent a series of diplomatic notes: To the United States it was proposed that Soviet and U.S. troops

[6] *Report by the President to the Congress for the Year 1956*, pp. 52–3.

"crush the aggressors and restore peace."[7] To Britain and France there were references, imprecise but ominous, to "countries [that] could have used" rocket weapons against London and Paris.[8]

The Soviet Union also on November 5 requested an urgent meeting of the Security Council to consider a draft resolution calling on all member states, in particular the United States and the Soviet Union, to give military and other assistance to Egypt if an immediate cease-fire and withdrawal of troops were not effected. The Security Council refused to inscribe the Soviet item. The U.S. representative commented on Soviet "cynicism" in making such a request on top of the "butchery which Moscow was in process of carrying out against the people of Hungary under cover of so-called 'negotiations.' "[9]

Domestic pressure for a cease-fire was pressing heavily on the British government during this period. The November 5 debate in the House of Commons reflected the fact that the Suez hostilities were highly unpopular with the majority of the Labour party and many other British subjects. A large number of Conservative Members of Parliament had indicated that they were giving serious consideration to refusing support for the government policy in Suez.[1] British oil interests feared disruption of their supply; some British feared the continuation of stress within the Atlantic alliance; others were disturbed by the fact that Canada was clearly opposed to the Suez action, as were African and Asian members of the Commonwealth; it was clear that world opinion was almost unanimously unfavorable to British actions. And Soviet pronouncements raised fears of a world conflagration growing out of continued hostilities.

In addition, the British financial situation was deteriorating

[7] Frye, op. cit., p. 10. The U.S. rejected this "unthinkable suggestion." *U.S. Department of State Bulletin,* November 19, 1956, pp. 795–6.

[8] Frye, op. cit., p. 10. The next day there were reports of Soviet jets over Turkey and of Soviet surface craft and submarines passing through the Dardanelles. For details, see Finer, op. cit., pp. 420–1. There continues to be controversy over whether, in fact, such maneuvers took place.

[9] *Report by the President to the Congress for the Year 1956,* pp. 54–5.

[1] Finer, op. cit., p. 427.

rapidly, as other countries converted their sterling holdings. Estimating that $1 billion were required to offset the run on sterling aggravated by continuing British involvement in the Suez campaign, Britain on November 6 asked the United States for financial support. The support was promised on the condition that Britain declare a cease-fire by the end of the same day.[2]

By the early hours of November 6, the UN Secretary-General had produced plans for implementing the November 4 General Assembly resolution for an international peace force. The proposed force would not be used to exert political pressure on Egypt; the great powers would not participate; political control was to be placed almost entirely in the Secretary-General's hands.[3]

The proposed UN peace force offered the British a face-saving way to withdraw from an increasingly untenable position. To the neutralists and Egypt, the peace force offered a means for getting rid of the British and French. While they might have hoped for a more unequivocal solution, it was considered to be the strongest measure the United States would support, as well as the only way to avoid long, drawn-out fighting. To the United States it was a way of keeping a direct Soviet presence out of the Middle East. The French preference was to carry the operation through to its end, toppling Nasser or, at a minimum, regaining control of the canal; the French government, however, recognized the impossibility of continuing without British support. Israel, on the other hand, had already achieved its immediate goals—destruction of Egyptian positions in Sinai, capture of war matériel, the opening of the port of Elath, and a dramatic blow to Arab prestige—and had been willing to accept the cease-fire even before the beginning of the British-French landings.[4] Israel, however, made it clear that a UN force would not be permitted on Israeli territory.

---

[2] Ibid., pp. 428–9.   [3] Frye, op. cit., pp. 10–12.
[4] *The New York Times*, July 9, 1966. See also Dayan, op. cit., pp. 180–2; Robertson, op. cit., p. 237. In the confusion of the moment, the Israeli delegate at the United Nations had announced acceptance of the November 2 cease-fire resolution soon after it was adopted, only to

Britain and France accepted the cease-fire called for by the General Assembly on November 2; Egyptian and Israeli acceptance had already been received. The cease-fire went into effect at midnight on November 6.

The British-French-Egyptian Conflict, PHASE IV   *November 7– December 23, 1956*

With the conclusion of the cease-fire, there remained the task of obtaining agreement on the withdrawal of British, French, and Israeli forces. Two resolutions were adopted by the General Assembly on November 7: the first completed the groundwork for the establishment of the UN Emergency Force (UNEF); the second, sponsored by nineteen African-Asian members, called for immediate withdrawal of the invading forces. Britain refused to withdraw forces prior to the positioning of UN troops, alleging that the separation of the parties would break down and hostilities be resumed.

UNEF observers were admitted immediately into the area of military operations. The movement of UNEF troops to Egypt began on November 10. Four days later the first UNEF contingent arrived in Egypt. By November 22, 869 UNEF troops were in Egypt, at which time final agreement was reached with the Egyptian government on the presence and functioning of the force. No British withdrawals had yet taken place, but about one third of the French forces deployed on November 7 had been withdrawn. Some pullback of Israeli forces had occurred along the entire battle line.

On November 24, the assembly voted by 63 votes (including the United States) to 5, with 10 abstentions, a resolution regretting that withdrawals had been so limited. Thereafter, however, the phased take-over by UNEF proceeded steadily, and by December 22, 1956, British and French troops completed their withdrawal.

---

withdraw it the next day with the claim that there had been a misunderstanding.

The Continuing Arab-Israeli Conflict

The net effect of the 1956 Suez hostilities was to remove the element of force from the calculations of Britain and France in reference to settlement of their differences with Egypt. These differences, defined in the narrow terms of the control of the Suez Canal, vanished very quickly. The broader issues took a longer time to disappear. The Arab-Israeli Conflict has proved more intractable.

The Arab-Israeli Conflict,   *December 23, 1956–*
PHASE IV₂   *June 5, 1967*

Sub-Phase A: December 23, 1956–March 1957

While British and French forces evacuated Egyptian territory with relative dispatch, Israeli forces pulled back very slowly— no more than fifteen miles a week. By the year's end, Sinai was almost cleared, but Israeli troops still occupied the Gaza Strip and were deployed along a belt to the west of the Israeli- Egyptian demarcation line and at Sharm el Sheikh. Israel said that it would agree to clear these areas only if steps were taken to prevent a renewal of the blockade of the Gulf of Aqaba and to ensure that Gaza could not again be used as a base for raids against Israeli territory.

Israel held firmly to this policy despite strong UN pressure culminating in two General Assembly resolutions of February 2, 1957, deploring the failure of Israel to withdraw and authoriz- ing the placement of UNEF troops on the Egyptian side of the armistice line. Israel continued to insist on guarantees. The United States promised that, while the United Nations had no authority to require a modification of the armistice agreement which gave Egypt the right to administer Gaza, the United States would use its best efforts to assure that UNEF did move into the area as contemplated by the UN resolution. As to

Aqaba, ". . . In the absence of some overriding decision to the contrary, as by the International Court of Justice, the United States, on behalf of vessels of United States registry, is prepared to exercise the right of free and innocent passage and to join with others to secure general recognition of this right."[5]

On March 1, Israeli forces began to withdraw. On the same day, the U.S. Representative at the United Nations formally endorsed a statement by the UN Secretary-General regarding the procedures under which UNEF might be withdrawn, namely ". . . an indicated procedure would be for the Secretary-General to inform the Advisory Committee on the United Nations Emergency Force, which would determine whether the matter should be brought to the attention of the Assembly."[6] At a subsequent news conference Secretary Dulles asserted that no private assurances going beyond these statements had been made.[7]

Sub-Phase B: March 1957–1964

With the withdrawal of Israeli forces and the emplacement of UNEF along the Egyptian side of the Israeli-Egyptian border— and in addition at Sharm el Sheikh—the causes of the 1956 war were at least temporarily shelved. With the clearance of the Suez Canal in 1957, normal traffic through that vital waterway resumed, although Israeli shipping was still barred.[8] But although immediate irritants had been effectively controlled, the underlying Arab enmity to Israel remained. If anything, the events of 1956, notwithstanding the strong U.S. action against the Israeli-British-French aggression, had reinforced Egypt's view of Israel as the tool of alien Western imperialism. The

---

[5] *U.S. Department of State Bulletin,* March 11, 1957, pp. 392–3, as referenced in *A Select Chronology and Background Documents Relating to the Middle East,* Committee on Foreign Relations, U.S. Senate, 90th Cong., 1st Sess., p. 90.

[6] *A Select Chronology . . . ,* p. 100.   [7] Ibid., p. 103.

[8] When the canal was first cleared, some Israeli cargoes were quietly allowed through in non-Israeli ships, but Egypt put an end to that in 1959.

Soviet Union, by contrast, had emerged as the champion of radical Arab nationalism.[9]

The shattering of British and French influence among the Arab states and the activist policy of the Soviets led to grave U.S. concerns that the Soviet Union, riding a crest of rabid Arab nationalism, would come to dominate the strategic Middle East. Initial U.S. reaction was not to enter into direct competition with the Soviets for radical Arab favor.[1] It was rather to try to win the support of more moderate Arabs while isolating Nasser.

This policy found expression in the so-called Eisenhower Doctrine by which the President on January 5, 1957, pledged U.S. economic and military help, including troops, to any Middle Eastern country seeking protection "against overt armed aggression from any nation controlled by International Communism."[2] On March 9, Congress endorsed the President's pledge and authorized $200 million in aid.[3]

Nasser sought, in turn, to bring the Arab states firmly under his influence. He persuaded Jordan, Saudi Arabia, and Syria to join him in an Arab Solidarity Agreement. Jordan was to be supplied with money and arms to replace the British subsidy. All were to oppose the Eisenhower Doctrine. By June of 1957, the Arab League Economic Council had endorsed Nasser's plan to proclaim a total boycott on Israeli trade. Not only was all

[9] *Sources of Conflict in the Middle East,* Adelphi Paper No. 26 (London: Institute for Strategic Studies; March 1966), p. 14.

[1] For example, the Soviets sent Egypt prompt shipments of wheat and of medical supplies for victims of British-French bombing, both of which the United States had declined to provide. And the United States refused to release blocked Egyptian funds.

[2] President Eisenhower, Special Message to the Congress on the Situation in the Middle East, January 5, 1957, as cited in *A Select Chronology* . . ., p. 81.

One commentary on the diplomacy of this era calls the specific language in the doctrine "a label, it would be charitable to assume, intended rather to placate a suspicious Congress than to indicate the State Department's true assessment of the Middle East situation." Michael Howard and Robert Hunter: *Israel and the Arab World: The Crisis of 1967,* Adelphi Paper No. 41 (London: Institute for Strategic Studies; October 1967), p. 9.

[3] *A Select Chronology* . . ., pp. 83–4.

trade forbidden between Israel and the Arab world, but also all foreign firms and ships doing business with Israel were to be blacklisted by the Arabs.

However, the longstanding rivalries for leadership within the Arab world soon enabled the United States to breach the united Arab front Nasser had sought to build. Within three weeks of the Arab Solidarity Agreement, Washington had successfully persuaded King Ibn Saud of Saudi Arabia—coincidental with a grant of $50 million in aid—to praise publicly the Eisenhower Doctrine.[4] The U.S. policy also found support in Iraq, Lebanon, and Jordan.

To the other Arabs, however, the enemy was Israel, not Communism. They appeared to have no desire to become partisans in the Cold War and resented being asked to choose.[5] Cairo Radio was able successfully to portray the doctrine "as a nefarious new imperialism with all the old tactics—gunboats, bribes, and puppet regimes—and the same old aim 'divide and rule.' "[6]

Jordan provided the first test of the doctrine. In April 1957, King Hussein (Ibn Talal) accused his elected but pro-Nasser government of a Communist plot supported by Egypt. He promptly received assurances of U.S. support and $10 million in aid. To give emphasis to the extent of U.S. concern, the Sixth Fleet was dispatched to the eastern Mediterranean. That summer a Syrian crisis developed out of rumors of a planned pro-American coup. The upshot, after American troop movements along the Turkish border countered by strong Soviet warnings against U.S. aggression, was to send the Syrian leaders to Nasser in search of union to counter rising Soviet prestige and influence in Syria. The United Arab Republic, a federation of Egypt and Syria, thus emerged on February 2, 1958.

The last test of the Eisenhower Doctrine occurred when President Camille Chamoun of Lebanon interpreted a domestic

[4] Richard H. Nolte: "United States Policy in the Middle East," in Georgiana G. Stevens, ed.: *The United States and the Middle East* (Englewood Cliffs: Prentice-Hall; 1964), p. 165.
[5] Secretary of State Dulles, it will be recalled, was unsympathetic to the notion of nonalignment.   [6] Nolte, op. cit., p. 166.

political crisis as being instigated by Egypt and called on the United Nations to intervene. UN observers found little evidence of intervention, but at that point a coup in Iraq overthrew the monarchy and with it Nuri es-Said, the West's firmest friend in the Middle East. Fearing an opportunity for Soviet penetration and an upheaval that would eventually sweep away the pro-Western Chamoun government in Lebanon, the United States responded promptly when the latter appealed for troops. Britain responded to a similar request from Jordan. A full-scale crisis resulted, replete with Soviet threats and war scares—a crisis defused eventually by the early withdrawal of foreign troops in compliance with UN requests.

By the end of the summer of 1958, U.S. policy as defined by the Eisenhower Doctrine had proved ineffective. Soviet prestige was everywhere evident—in arms supplies and cultural exchanges, and even in economic aid including an agreement to help with the Aswan Dam, symbol of Nasser's humiliation by the United States. Yet the Soviet government had been unable to prevent either the continuing interventions by Western powers or the banning of local Communist parties in every Middle Eastern country except Israel. In general, nonalignment had proved more attractive to the Arabs than any consistent support of Soviet policy.

Lebanon had in the wake of the U.S. withdrawal acquired a neutral government. Iraq had signed a mutual-defense agreement with the U.A.R., of which Yemen had also become a member. The two monarchies, Jordan and Saudi Arabia, alone remained in any sense either pro-Western or anti-Nasser. As for the Arabs themselves, moreover, no leader had emerged capable of challenging Nasser's leadership.

Out of the wreckage of U.S. Arab policy emerged two convictions: first, that the best buffers against Soviet influence in the Middle East and penetration into Africa were strong, independent governments; second, that the greatest threat to peace in the area would be a military imbalance between the Arabs and Israel. In 1959 technical assistance was proffered to the U.A.R.

for the first time since the Suez crisis. After 1960, Egypt became the largest single recipient of U.S. aid in the Middle East, excluding Turkey and Iran.[5] The United States refused to enter a mutual-defense pact with Israel but did permit arms sales if and when a specific weapon was required to match a U.A.R. breakthrough.[6]

The possession of military weapons became in this period the intense concern of all parties to the continuing conflict. Militancy toward Israel was the only slogan that commanded wide allegiance in the Arab world. Every ruler felt driven to compete with his neighbor in the ardor with which he expressed this feeling. The degree of hostility toward Israel came to be judged in terms of the size and sophistication of the military establishment each ruler could display. The willingness of the Soviet Union to supply arms to the more militant Arab states and of the United States to arm the more moderate fostered the competitiveness between them and contributed to a spiraling demand for arms that Israel, for its own security, felt constrained to match.[7]

In the absence of the unifying effect of direct great-power intervention and with Arab-Israeli tensions in temporary abeyance, Arab politics fell into "natural disarray."[8] Old rivalries resurfaced. The historic antipathy between Iraq and Egypt proved stronger then the revolutionary brotherhood of Abdul Karim Kessim and Nasser.[9] "Arab socialism" came to be viewed with increasing alarm by a conservative military group in Syria, which in 1961 overthrew the government and withdrew Syria from the U.A.R. This only increased Nasser's own revolu-

[5] Harry B. Ellis: "The Arab-Israeli Conflict Today," in Stevens, op. cit., p. 118. Prior to 1959 Israel had received more U.S. economic aid than all Arab countries combined. The Israelis protested that the United States' supplying massive aid to Egypt ($200 million in 1963 compared with $80 million to Israel) released Egyptian funds for new arms purchases from the Soviet Union; therefore, efforts to limit the arms race were being exerted only against Israel.

[6] Ibid., p. 117.   [7] *Sources of Conflict in the Middle East*, p. 41.

[8] Howard and Hunter, op. cit., p. 9.

[9] Ibid. See also, J. C. Hurewitz: "Regional and International Politics in the Middle East," in Stevens, op. cit., p. 83.

tionary zeal and militancy against "reactionary" Arab governments,[1] and the forces of imperialism, reaction, and Zionism.
One ruler after another was blasted by Nasser and the masses
exhorted to rise. In 1962 he found allies in Ahmad Ben Bella of
newly liberated Algeria, in the republican faction in Yemen
whom Nasser supported with troops, and shortly in Iraq and
Syria following pro-socialist coups. Ben Bella, however, soon
became diverted by his own role in Africa and particularly the
Maghreb; the Yemen conflict was not resolved; and Nasser and
the remaining two allies failed in attempts to agree on the form
of a federation that was to unite them.[2]

Sub-Phase C: 1964–November 1966

In 1964, the issue of the use of the Jordan waters aroused a new
spirit of unity among the Arab militants. The Jordan is formed
from streams rising in Lebanon, Israel, and Syria which merge
in the Huleh basin to become a single river whose riparian
rights are shared by the same three countries. A joint diversion
and irrigation plan which was worked out in 1954 by Eric
Johnston, President Eisenhower's personal envoy, had been
approved by Arab and Israeli engineers but had failed to obtain
political approval.

Israel needed water from the Jordan River to irrigate the
Negev desert region for new settlers. It therefore went ahead
with its own diversion plans, and by 1964 the Eshed Kinrot
pumping station was ready to begin operations. An Arab summit conference adopted plans to divert the Jordan headwaters
and thus head off the diversion of water by Israel. An Arab
Unified Command was agreed on to deter anticipated Israeli
reprisals. States not directly confronting Israel pledged funds for
those who did, and, finally, the Palestine refugees were enlisted
in the struggle.

The refugee issue[3] had continued to fester over the years,

---

[1] Hurewitz, op. cit., pp. 96–7.   [2] *A Select Chronology* . . . , p. 15.
[3] In 1961, Dr. Joseph E. Johnson had undertaken a study of the problem for the UN Palestine Conciliation Commission. His solution—free
choice, under UN auspices, of repatriation or compensation; guarantees

although UNEF's presence had helped to keep the number of incidents low. The 700,000 who fled in 1948 had become some 1,200,000, comprising two thirds of the population of the Gaza Strip and over half the population of Jordan.

The refugees had remained passive until 1964. Then, at a succession of Arab summit conferences, the decision was made to form the Palestine Liberation Organization (PLO) and a Liberation Army. By such means the conflict could be presented to the world as a struggle between a native people seeking to drive out the alien invaders.[4] Ahmed Shukeiry, head of the new organization, added new fire to Arab militancy but actually received little practical help.

Despite these ominous developments, the whole area was reasonably stable for an additional two years. Arab leaders meeting in Casablanca in 1965, for example, concluded that, while war with Israel was inevitable, it would not come for five or ten years. Arab socialism was played down. Nasser was increasingly diverted by his inconclusive intervention in Yemen. The new Arab Unified Command was frustrated by the unwillingness of Lebanon, Syria, and Jordan to accept Egyptian troops on their soil. Even Egyptian differences with Saudi Arabia over Yemen seemed susceptible of solution.

In the competition between East and West for influence, economic aid—being relatively interchangeable—can be an unreliable guide to alignments. In the crucial area of military aid, the Soviet Union had the advantage in the U.A.R., Syria, and Iraq. Elsewhere arms were being supplied by the West.

The West retained its concern for the unimpeded flow of oil to Western Europe and Japan. But the threat of a cut-off did not invoke nearly such tremors as at the time of the 1956 Suez

---

for Israel; and financial assistance—was rejected by both Israel and the Arabs. Ellis, op. cit., pp. 143–4.

[4] Howard and Hunter, op. cit., p. 11. This was designed to appeal particularly to the developing areas of the world. Israel had very early established diplomatic and commercial relationships among the new African states. At the founding of the Organization of African Unity in 1963, Nasser had thus been warned not to try for an anti-Israeli statement such as he had won at Bandung in 1955; Ellis, op. cit., p. 113.

crisis, thanks largely to new suppliers and larger and faster tankers.

As for Israel, the government of Premier Levi Eshkol, which had taken over from Ben Gurion in June 1963, was regarded as moderate and in fact was under some criticism at home for its lack of vigor. Eshkol headed an uneasy coalition which was very sensitive to shifts in public opinion. His major concerns appeared to be Israel's worsening economic situation and a desire to retain the good will of the United States without antagonizing the Soviet Union.

Two events contributed to the reversal of this relatively placid situation. One was the coming to power in Syria of the leftist wing of the Ba'ath party, which ousted a more moderate, rightist group. This was, however, to be a difference only in degrees of radicalism; even the previous regime, for example, had not considered the formation of the PLO a substitute for unilateral action on its own part. In 1965 the El Fatah (Conquest) organization was formed; it bore many similarities to the *fedayin* of earlier years. Now frequent commando raids across the border began to provoke strong Israeli reprisals wherever El Fatah units were suspected of operating, including the Lebanese and Jordanian border areas.[5]

Another crucial event was a call by King Feisal (Ibn Abdel Aziz Al Saud) of Saudi Arabia for an Islamic summit conference. King Feisal had succeeded Ibn Saud in 1964 and had proceeded to court Iran and Jordan and to buy Western arms. His plan of an Islamic summit was a direct challenge to Nasser's leadership, and he became thereafter the rallying point for all the Arab forces who disliked and distrusted the social and political policies of Nasserism.[6] Feisal also seemed in a good position to fill the political and military vacuum being created by the withdrawal of British power from Aden and the

---

[5] In May 1966, Israel asked the United Nations to list all the incidents that had occurred since the establishment of the Mixed Armistice Commissions in 1949. The Secretary-General declined, claiming such a report would be too long and unusable. The number was reported to have exceeded 100,000. *A Select Chronology* . . . , pp. 12–13.

[6] Howard and Hunter, op. cit., p. 12.

Persian Gulf—a role that Nasser regarded as properly his. After Feisal's endorsement of an Islamic summit, Syria immediately demanded a countersummit. Syrian pressure and Nasser's own interests eventually led Nasser to bring the Arab rift into the open once more by denouncing Feisal—eventually Hussein of Jordan and Bourguiba of Tunisia as well—as having sold out to the forces of imperialism.[7] Arab unity was again in shreds.

Sub-Phase D: November 1966–June 5, 1967

In November 1966 two events occurred that in retrospect appear to have triggered the rapid rise in tensions that lead to a renewed outbreak of war. The first was the signing of a defense pact between the U.A.R. and Syria, almost certainly with Soviet encouragement. The second event was an Israeli reprisal attack on the village of Es Samu in Jordan on November 13. The Es Samu attack followed Israeli failure to get satisfaction after complaining to the Security Council about mines laid on Israeli territory by El Fatah units operating from Syria. More mines were laid near the Jordanian border. Israel responded on a scale hitherto unknown—with armor, aircraft, and infantry, and in daylight. The Security Council condemned Israel, but not the Syrian provocateurs. Erstwhile sympathetic opinion was shocked by the scale of the reprisal; and there were demonstrations in Jordan which threatened the stability of the regime. Despite strong criticism of its action, Israel remained firm. "The action at Samu," said the Israeli Minister of Labor Yigal Allon, "demonstrated to the Powers that Israel is not willing to submit its security to diplomatic bargaining."[8]

A further serious incident on the Israeli-Syrian armistice line in April 1967 arose out of Israeli attempts to cultivate land in the demilitarized zone. An exchange of small-arms fire quickly led to an engagement involving artillery, tanks, and finally Israeli aircraft which silenced the Syrian artillery and then flew

[7] Ibid. In March 1965, Habib Bourguiba had appealed for moderation and reason in order to solve the Palestine problem. The reaction among Arab radicals was one of outrage: The U.A.R. withdrew its ambassador from Tunis, and Egyptian mobs ransacked the Tunisian embassy in Cairo.

[8] Ibid., p. 13.

over Damascus in a victory celebration. Syria and Jordan taunted Egypt for hiding behind UNEF and failing to help them.[9] Premier Eshkol said in an interview that the U.S. Sixth Fleet would support Israel,[1] an assertion Arab leaders appear to have assumed was a firm U.S. commitment. Again, on May 11, Eshkol warned that Israel would take retaliatory measures if sabotage did not cease. He also criticized the United Nations for failing to place blame for the incidents on Syria.[2] On the same day, the UN Secretary-General did, however, publicly deplore the increase in El Fatah incidents.[3]

The increasing militancy on Israel's part may have been designed to quiet public opinion in Israel, but it was accompanied by private warnings that the use of retaliatory force might be the only way to curtail the increasing terrorism.[4] It is possible that these warnings, rather than serving to moderate the terrorist attacks, had the effect of convincing Syria, Egypt, and the Soviet Union that a major strike against Syria was imminent.

On May 13, Eshkol announced Israel's determination to stop all Arab attempts at sabotage, to keep the Gulf of Aqaba open, and to resist all efforts to divert the Jordan waters. Israel, he said, would choose the time, the place, and the means of countering the aggression.[5] At the same time General Itzhak Rabin, Israeli Chief of Staff, was quoted as having told a military audience that, as long as the current Syrian government continued in power in Damascus, the El Fatah raids could be expected to continue. This statement was interpreted by the Arab press as a threat to overthrow the Syrian government by force.[6] Whatever the intent of both statements,[7] the effect on

---

[9] Ibid., p. 14.

[1] *A Select Chronology* . . . , p. 22.

In 1964 he had told the Knesset that President Lyndon Johnson's commitment to defend Israel against Arab aggression was a "firm political decision with all that involves." Ibid., p. 17.   [2] Ibid., p. 22.

[3] Charles W. Yost: "The Arab-Israeli War: How It Began," *Foreign Affairs*, Vol. 46, No. 2 (January 1968), p. 307.   [4] Ibid., p. 308.

[5] Howard and Hunter, op. cit., p. 14; *A Select Chronology* . . . , p. 22.

[6] Howard and Hunter, op. cit., p. 14.

[7] Ibid., p. 15. The authors contend that Eshkol was under great do-

the Arab world was electric, and the possibility of war between states backed by the rival superpowers became more real.

This increase in tension between Israel and the Arab states in the early part of May appears to have been fostered to some degree by Moscow.[8] During this period the Soviet ambassador in Tel Aviv reported that Israeli forces were mobilized on the Syrian border, but he declined two invitations from the Israeli government to inspect the border.[9] On May 19, the UN Secretary-General, commenting to the Security Council on the alleged troop movements, reported that UNTSO (United Nations Truce Supervision Organization) observers had no evidence of troop concentrations on either side of the line. In a later speech (on May 22), however, Nasser recalled: "On May 13 we received accurate information that Israel was concentrating on the Syrian border huge armed forces of about 11 to 13 brigades."[1]

The effect of Soviet charges that Syria was about to be invaded increased pressure on Nasser to make a strong demonstration of support for Syria. On May 16 a state of emergency was declared for the Egyptian armed forces.[2] Egyptian troops were moved up to the Sinai border, and the Egyptian chief of staff requested the UNEF commander to withdraw from points along the eastern border.

On receiving this news from the commander, the Secretary-General informed the U.A.R. representative to the United Nations that such a request could be made only by the U.A.R. government to the Secretary-General, that a temporary or partial withdrawal was unacceptable because UNEF could not be

---

mestic pressure, having made too many concessions to the letter of the armistice agreements in planning the annual national day being held for the first time in six years in Jerusalem.

[8] Benjamin Shwadron: "Soviet Posture in the Middle East," *Current History,* December 1967, p. 331, maintains that "the crisis was and still is in reality a struggle between the Soviet Union and the United States for positions in the Middle East."

[9] Ibid., p. 331. This sequence of events is described also by Yost, op. cit., pp. 308–9, and by Howard and Hunter, op. cit., p. 16.

[1] *A Select Chronology . . . ,* p. 132.

[2] Howard and Hunter, op. cit., p. 16.

asked to stand aside to enable the two sides to resume fighting, that the U.A.R. had the right to withdraw its consent for the presence of the force; and that a request for temporary or partial withdrawal would be considered tantamount to a request for the complete withdrawal of UNEF from Gaza and Sinai.

On the following day, May 17, Egyptian troops began to move into and beyond some UNEF positions. The Secretary-General consulted with the seven countries providing UNEF contingents,[3] two of which, India and Yugoslavia, insisted that Egypt's request must be respected promptly. On May 18, the Secretary-General received the formal Egyptian request for withdrawal and referred it to the UNEF Advisory Committee. Yugoslavia and India again urged prompt withdrawal; others wanted to play for time. None apparently suggested requesting a meeting of the General Assembly.[4] The Secretary-General, having raised with Israel the possibility of stationing the force on Israeli territory and having been rebuffed, complied with the U.A.R. request and began pulling UNEF units back.

The Secretary-General's action in rapidly withdrawing UNEF from Gaza, the Israeli-Egyptian border, and Sharm el Sheikh has been and probably will continue to be a matter of controversy. Few challenge the basic legal principle that UNEF was on Egyptian territory with Egyptian consent—and only so long as Egypt consented. The issue is rather whether there were not delaying devices the Secretary-General could have used to allow time for local passions to cool. Many of those most critical of U Thant's actions argue that, at a minimum, he should have consulted the General Assembly (as had been anticipated when UNEF was established[5]) or the Security Council. Even if these bodies had endorsed the Secretary-General's view, the reasoning goes, some few precious days might have been gained. Against this view some practical arguments have been advanced—primarily the Yugoslav and Indian determination to withdraw their units anyway—perhaps even before a General Assembly or Security Council determina-

---

[3] Brazil, Canada, Denmark, India, Norway, Sweden, and Yugoslavia.
[4] Howard and Hunter, op. cit., p. 19.   [5] See above, p. 273.

tion could have been made. Also it is argued that the action of Egyptian commanders in virtually expelling UNEF from some of its posts gave U Thant no real alternative.[6]

The issue is complicated by differences over what Nasser's real intentions and expectations were. Former U.S. Ambassador to the UN Charles W. Yost argues that the actions taken by Egyptian commanders, which forced U Thant's hand, were not authorized by Cairo. He further suggests that Nasser may not have intended the UNEF units at Sharm el Sheikh to be withdrawn, but only those along the Israeli-Egyptian front.[7]

Regardless of what version of intentions and expectations is accurate, the withdrawal of UNEF left Israeli and Egyptian forces face to face in Sinai for the first time in ten years. It also placed Egyptian forces at Sharm el Sheikh, in a position to reimpose the blockade of the Gulf of Aqaba. Egypt was under considerable pressure to take this step, particularly from its radical Arab allies, notably Syria, who had consistently advocated militant action against Israel and seized every opportunity to taunt Nasser for not being as vigorous in anti-Zionist action as he was in words.

On May 22, following limited mobilization of reserves by Israel and Egypt, Nasser declared the Gulf of Aqaba once again closed to all Israeli goods and ships. Israel had, as noted earlier, consistently asserted that it would regard such a step as intolerable. The Israeli port of Elath had become more important commercially to Israel since 1956, and, perhaps more important, the future industrial development of the Negev depended on this outlet. There can be little question, therefore, that Nasser knew his action would be regarded as a grave challenge.

The reaction in the Arab world was immediate. Nasser regained the stature he had lost by his earlier failure to take vigorous action after Israeli raids against Jordan and Syria. Iraq, Algeria, Kuwait, and Sudan pledged troops for the coming showdown. Overnight, intra-Arab quarrels were submerged.

---

[6] This is argued in Howard and Hunter, op. cit., pp. 18–19.
[7] Yost, op. cit., pp. 313–14.

Yet, on June 2, Nasser was telling foreign diplomats he had no intentions of initiating war.[8]

It is not clear what role the Soviet Union played in these events. Some analysts regard it as probable that the Soviets were consulted about troop deployments and UNEF withdrawal but not about the blockade.[9] Others contend that the Soviets not only expected the blockade but also expected the United States to prevail on Israel to acquiesce in it.[1] The Soviet Union warned on May 23 that any aggression in the Middle East would be met with strong opposition from the Soviet Union[2] and on May 24 opposed convening the UN Security Council.

The crucial questions now were how much support the United States would give Israel and how much it could, in any event, restrain Israeli activists. It will be recalled that in 1957 the United States had made quite explicit assurances on the freedom of passage through the strait; Eshkol now publicly demanded that these obligations be honored. He also made clear that, unless the Western powers acted, Israel would.[3]

The United States, mired in Vietnam, and Britain, whose shaky economy could not readily withstand a withdrawal of Arab sterling balances and interruption of oil supplies,[4] cast about for support from other maritime powers to resolve the issue of the strait. Not only was support lacking, but the notion of concerted action by the maritime powers triggered a strong emotional reaction to "Western imperialism" among the Arabs.

By the end of May, it was clear that any forceful action to remove the blockade would have to be taken by Israel alone. But the United States had warned that U.S. support was dependent on Israel not taking initiative on its own.[5] To accept the *fait accompli,* however, would undermine the whole philosophy

[8] Ibid., p. 317.

[9] Ibid., p. 315. The author quotes "reliable Soviet sources" to this effect. The Soviet Union had never endorsed Egypt's legal arguments concerning the Gulf of Aqaba because of its own reliance on narrow exits from the Baltic and Black Seas; Howard and Hunter, op. cit., pp. 19–20.

[1] Shwadron, op. cit., p. 333.   [2] *A Select Chronology* . . . , p. 23.
[3] Howard and Hunter, op. cit., p. 21.   [4] Ibid.   [5] Ibid., p. 26.

of Israeli security. Meanwhile, seven Egyptian divisions were moving into Sinai. Even more significant, on May 30, King Hussein of Jordan appeared in Cairo to sign a defense pact with Nasser. This immediately raised the prospect of Egyptian or Iraqi troops being stationed among the volatile Palestinians in Jordan's West Bank, an event the Israeli high command had long judged to be as serious a threat as the closing of the Strait of Tiran.[6]

Domestically, confidence in the Eshkol government sank rapidly as the Egyptian build-up continued. On June 1, General Moshe Dayan, a hero of the Suez war, and two opposition leaders joined the cabinet. The Dayan appointment to the defense ministry was received warmly at home and widely interpreted abroad as a sign the government had resolved on war.[7] By June 4, U.S. displeasure should Israel be the first to resort to force was the only deterrent left.[8]

The Arab-Israeli Conflict, PHASE III₃   *June 5–10, 1967*

At eight forty-five a.m. Cairo time on June 5, 1967, the Israeli air force struck Egypt's major air bases, destroying in minutes the powerful air arm with which the Soviet Union had equipped Nasser. As soon as planes were freed from their assignment in Egypt, similar raids effectively took out the Iraqi and Syrian air forces (also largely Soviet-supplied) and the air force of Jordan (largely British-supplied, with U.S. endorsement). Israel claimed, in figures widely regarded as accurate, to have destroyed "for certain 286 Egyptian, 52 Syrian, 27 Jordanian, and nine Iraqi aircraft and claimed a further 34 probabilities."[9]

The air attack against Egypt was followed immediately by an

---

[6] Ibid., p. 25.   [7] Ibid., p. 26.   [8] Ibid., p. 27.

[9] Howard and Hunter, op. cit., p. 31. It is assumed that these figures represent mainly combat aircraft, because there were no subsequent offensive air strikes by the Arabs against Israel. In the case of Egypt, it is likely that only a little over three hundred of the jet combat aircraft were operational, and of these the Israelis concentrated their early attacks on the Tu-16's, Il-28's, MiG-21's, and MiG-19's.

armored attack on Egyptian forces in the Sinai Peninsula. Here, Israel had set three main tasks: to destroy the fighting force of the Egyptian army; to establish Israeli forces at Sharm el Sheikh; and to ensure this position by occupying the Sinai Peninsula.

As soon as news of the fighting reached the rest of the world, Premier Alexei Kosygin in Moscow employed the "hot line" to assure President Johnson in Washington that the Soviet Union did not intend to commit its forces in the Middle East, and that it was in the interest of international peace that a cease-fire be reached as quickly as possible. This means of direct communication between Moscow and Washington was used several times in the course of the week to convey assurances of military neutrality.[1]

The United Nations Security Council met in an emergency session. While there was unanimous desire for a cease-fire, there was no agreement on the conditions under which it should take place. The Soviet Union and India demanded that Israel withdraw to its original position of June 4, while the United States and Britain called for an unconditional in-place cease-fire. The major powers in the Security Council failed to compromise these opposing views at the June 5 meeting.

The Arab countries greeted the start of the war with exhortations to the public to seek the long-awaited revenge on Israel. Their governments were quick to declare war; after the U.A.R., Lebanon, Syria, Jordan, Iraq, Yemen, Kuwait, Sudan, and Algeria followed suit. Lebanon apparently sent a flight of three jet fighters along the Israeli border, but quickly withdrew when one of them was shot down.

Soon after the ground attack on Egypt was launched, Israel's Prime Minister, through the chief of staff of UNTSO, sent assurances to King Hussein of Jordan that Israel did not intend

[1] *Christian Science Monitor,* June 12, 1967. Another occasion during the fighting when the "hot line" was employed, this time on U.S. initiative, was when Israeli aircraft attacked the U.S.S. *Liberty,* a communications ship with the U.S. Sixth Fleet. Washington wanted to reassure Moscow that U.S. air and naval activity was directed toward relieving the *Liberty* and not toward involvement in the fighting.

to make any land advances on Jordan so long as Jordan refrained from any serious military action against Israel. Jordan, however, began shelling targets in Israel within a few hours of the initial Israeli attack on Egypt.

There was further evidence of Israeli reluctance to open battle with Jordan on June 5. The chief of staff of UNTSO called for a cease-fire for twelve o'clock local time, to which both Jordan and Israel agreed. Sporadic fire, however, continued from Jordan after the deadline; a second cease-fire was proposed for one thirty and again accepted by both sides. Jordanian artillery fire increased over Jerusalem, Mt. Scopus, and Tel Aviv, with no retaliation from Israeli forces. At one thirty, Jordanian troops occupied Government House (UNTSO headquarters in Jerusalem), and, soon after, Israeli and Jordanian troops began to exchange fire.[2]

At two thirty local time on Monday afternoon, Israeli ground forces were ordered to attack Jordan. During the afternoon and the night, two Israeli brigades fought their way around Jerusalem to the south and to the north, while an armored force advanced north to Ramallah. By the next morning, June 6, Jordan's main defenses on the West Bank had crumbled.

Meanwhile in Sinai, three Israeli divisional groups[3] had fought through the night to break the first line of Egyptian defenses in the Gaza Strip, at El Arish, Abu Ageila, and Gebel Libni. Tuesday, June 6, was spent largely in mopping up and regrouping for the assault on the second line of Egyptian defenses in Sinai.

On June 6, Nasser and Hussein accused the United States and Britain of lending air support to Israel. The charges were promptly denied by both Washington and London—and subsequently rescinded by Hussein—but reaction in the Arab world was sharp. Nasser broke diplomatic relations with the United States[4] and other Arab states followed suit. Oil flow and de-

[2] *The New York Times*, June 6, 1967, p. 17.

[3] Numerically weaker than the Egyptians, but with an equal amount of armor. Howard and Hunter, op. cit., p. 35.

[4] Relations with the United Kingdom had been broken earlier over the Rhodesian issue.

liveries were interrupted. And, despite the falseness of the charges, the certainty is likely to persist in many Arabs' minds.[5]

On Tuesday, June 6, the Soviet Union abandoned its insistence on withdrawal of Israeli forces as a condition for a cease-fire and the Security Council quickly called for an unconditional cease-fire. As the magnitude of the Israeli victory became more obvious, it was clearly more in the Arabs' interests to stop the Israeli advances as rapidly as possible, before the situation deteriorated even further.[6]

Israel agreed to comply with the cease-fire resolution if other parties also complied. Syria, whose forces had as yet confined themselves to shelling Israeli border settlements, rejected the request, as did Iraq. Egypt did not reply. Only Jordan, aware of its impending defeat on the West Bank, accepted the appeal from the Security Council. Israel, apparently reluctant to end the fighting with Jordan before certain objectives had been achieved,[7] noted that such an agreement with Jordan would have doubtful validity because Jordanian forces were under the nominal command of Egypt.

It seems clear that Israel built its military plans around the political assumption that world opinion, acting through the United Nations, would try to bring the fighting to a stop as rapidly as possible. Every major power stood to lose by continued instability in this volatile area. And, despite the cautious approach both the Soviet Union and the United States were taking in the hostilities, the danger always existed that events would get out of hand and drag them both in. One account—the

[5] The Soviet Union, which was undoubtedly tracking U.S. and British air and sea activity in the area, never joined in the Arab charges on this score.

[6] Howard and Hunter, op. cit., p. 31. These authors go on to suggest that Israel deliberately delayed release of information about its successes in order to accomplish just this delay.

[7] Howard and Hunter, op. cit., p. 38. King Hussein apparently had similar misgivings about Israel's intentions, for he told the United Nations later: "I should like to state here for the record that Jordan complied immediately with the United Nations request for a cease-fire, but it was forced to continue the fight because Israel, although it had agreed to the cease-fire, obeyed it only when it had accomplished its predetermined objectives." *The New York Times*, June 27, 1967.

best analysis yet to appear on the 1967 war—sums up the picture this way:

> Although the sympathy of the Western world had not, on the whole, been forfeited by Israel's apparent action in striking the first blow, it was not likely to extend to any blatant violation of a cease-fire resolution by the United Nations. Support from public opinion in the United States, so long as no American involvement was required, was overwhelmingly strong—so strong that Mr. Dean Rusk felt it necessary to soften the statement of one of his officials that the United States was "neutral in thought, word, and deed" by explaining that neutrality was a concept in international law which did not imply indifference. But for Britain, much as she sympathized with the Israeli cause, the prospect of prolonged conflict in the Middle East, with all that this implied for her relations with the Arab world, was intensely disagreeable. The French Government, to the fury of most articulate French public opinion, reaffirmed its position of glacial neutrality; while the Soviet Union could only view the humiliation of her clients in the Arab world with alarm and despondency.[8]

The Egyptian government, while beginning to realize the full magnitude of the defeat of its armed forces, continued to report to its people devastating U.A.R. victories over Israel's forces. Charges of British and U.S. collusion with Israel were continued.[9] The Egyptian diplomatic offensive became more agitated with each new Israeli advance. British consulates were burned, oil supplies were cut off, diplomatic relations were broken, and the harangues against Israel by Arab supporters in the United Nations became more and more heated.

On Wednesday, June 7, the Soviet Union sponsored a stronger motion in the Security Council, *demanding* that the "governments concerned should as a first step cease fire and discontinue all military activities at 20.00 hours GMT [Greenwich Mean Time] on 7 June 1967"; the motion received unanimous support.[1] Apparently this was the signal to Israel that it must now act with all remaining strength to gain its

8 Howard and Hunter, op. cit., p. 37.
9 Randolph S. and Winston S. Churchill: *The Six-Day War* (London: Heinemann; 1967), pp. 159–61.
1 Howard and Hunter, op. cit., p. 38.

desired military objectives. In Jordan, Israeli forces were told to take the Old City of Jerusalem, with the warning that: "We are already being pressed for a cease-fire. . . . don't let the Old City remain an enclave."[2] By Wednesday evening, Jerusalem and the entire West Bank of the Jordan River had been taken by Israel, and the war with Jordan was over.

On the Sinai front, Egyptian forces bowed to defeat in the north. As they retreated southwest toward the Suez Canal, they were ambushed by Israeli armor at Nakhl, Gafgafa, and the Mitla Pass. Meanwhile, on Wednesday Egyptian forces had abandoned Sharm el Sheikh; the Israeli paratroop and naval-assault force that landed there two hours later met with no resistance.[3]

On Thursday afternoon and evening (June 8), Egyptian forces in Sinai suffered their final defeats. Nasser finally accepted the UN demand for a cease-fire on Thursday evening. By the time the cease-fire went into effect on Friday morning, Israeli forces were on the eastern side of the Suez Canal.

For the first three days of the war—after the initial Israeli attacks on the Syrian and other air forces—land action had been confined to the Egyptian and Jordanian fronts. Syrian artillery had shelled Israeli territory from the outset, but Israeli responses had only been defensive. An imminent change was signaled when, on Thursday morning, June 8, Israel launched a heavy air attack on Syrian emplacements in the hills along the border.

There is said to have been "great pressure" to launch an assault against Syria on June 8, "before the Syrians could take advantage of the United Nations' demand for a cease-fire."[4] And, indeed, the Syrian government did accept the cease-fire.

[2] Churchill and Churchill, op. cit., p. 139.
There seems to be general agreement on this point. "By the morning of Wednesday the 7th the two Israeli pincers had almost closed round the Old City, and General Dayan ordered them to seize it before the cease-fire agreement reached at the United Nations the previous evening could come into effect." Howard and Hunter, op. cit., pp. 33–5.
[3] Churchill and Churchill, op. cit., p. 165.
[4] Howard and Hunter, op. cit., p. 39.

At the appointed hour there may have been a lull in Syrian artillery fire and in Israeli air raids, but neither side appears to have been amenable to the idea of the cease-fire.

Who broke the cease-fire is impossible to say. Undoubtedly the Israelis were itching to get at the Syrians and would have regarded it as a most unsatisfactory end to the campaign if they had been stopped by the bell, since it was the Syrians who were in a large measure responsible for the situation which had led to the outbreak of war. Equally the Syrian Army, still feeling secure in its lines of bunkers and gun emplacements, saw no reason why it should obey the call for a cease-fire from New York or even from its own Government in Damascus.[5]

At eleven thirty a.m. on June 9, Israeli ground forces began their assault on the Syrian Heights, which, before bombardment by the Israeli air force, had been fortified with 265 guns, including the latest in Soviet artillery, and some 200 anti-aircraft guns. For years the Syrians had been building underground bunkers and emplacements, impervious even to 500- and 1,000-pound bombs. These defenses extended in from the Israeli-Syrian border for more than ten miles. The Israelis suffered heavy casualties in taking the first line of these defenses on Friday.

At the United Nations, the Syrian representative endeavored through Saturday morning (June 10) to convince the Security Council that Israel should be forced to accept the cease-fire. It may have been to reinforce their plea in the UN that Damascus Radio announced early Saturday morning that Qnaitra, headquarters of the Syrian army and the only major town between the border and Damascus, had fallen. With this, the Syrian troops holding out against the Israeli forces collapsed and fled.[6] It is likely that, had the Syrian army not disintegrated on Saturday morning, it could have taken weeks for Israel to break through the defenses in the Syrian Heights.[7] Qnaitra actually

[5] Churchill and Churchill, op. cit., p. 185.
[6] The Israeli air force also claims some responsibility for the Syrian exodus on Saturday morning. Israeli aircraft had been pounding the Syrian bunkers nonstop, every ten minutes, for two days.
[7] Howard and Hunter, op. cit., p. 39.

did fall on Saturday afternoon when the first Israeli forces arrived at two thirty. The cease-fire came into effect within hours, on Saturday afternoon, June 10.

Thus, in a single morning's air strikes, Israel had eliminated the air forces of its chief local adversaries: Egypt, Jordan, Syria, and Iraq. With full control of the air ensured, in four days it had routed Egypt's forces from Sinai and reached the Suez Canal; in one and a half days of heavy fighting it had defeated Jordanian forces in Jerusalem and the West Bank; and, after a day's aerial bombardment, in two days it had scaled the heavily defended Syrian Heights.

FACTORS BEARING ON TRANSITIONS

(The format of this section will vary from the pattern followed with other cases in order to handle the two conflicts separately from the mid-1950's until July 1956, jointly from July 1956 until December 1956, and separately again after December 1956.)

The Arab-Israeli Conflict, Within PHASE IV$_1$: *Movement Away from Settlement*

For a brief period after the overthrow of the monarchy in Egypt, cautious movements were made by both adversaries toward ending their conflict; these collapsed in late 1953. This section will examine the factors between late 1953 and July 1956 that were pressing the conflict closer to resumed hostilities and those pressing toward Settlement.

1. Factors Tending to Promote the Resumption of Hostilities

   a. Despite the armistice agreements that had been signed between Israel and its Arab neighbors in 1949, basic political problems remained unsettled: permanent borders, return or resettlement of refugees and compensation of their losses, etc.

   b. Egypt continued to deny passage through the Suez Canal to Israeli ships and extended this ban to all goods to and from Israel. Despite UN urgings, Egypt refused to lift the ban.

The Arab-Israeli Conflict, PHASE IV₃

From June 10, 1967

Israel's military defeat of Egypt, Jordan, and Syria left it in occupation of vast areas of Arab land—including, in Gaza and the West Bank—thousands of Arabs, many of them refugees from earlier rounds of fighting. Militarily, the new geographic shape of the country gives it a more readily defensible position. It remains to be seen whether a new and lasting peace can be constructed after the June 1967 war—peace that eluded the Middle East after the 1948 and 1956 wars.

RELEVANT CONTROL MEASURES

Settling the Dispute/Preventing the Resumption of Hostilities

1. Measures to Offset These Factors
   a. Stronger pressure on all parties to resolve these problems bilaterally or accept compulsory third-party settlement. Reinforcement of this pressure by external suppliers of economic and military aid, trade partners, etc., with threat of sanction for noncompliance.

   b. Refusal by all canal users to tolerate the situation. Economic reprisal. Challenges by major powers. UN insistence. Exploration of alternate canal routes (through the Negev?).

   c. Egypt blocked the Strait of Tiran at the Gulf of Aqaba, thus
denying Israel access to the Red Sea. Coupled with the Suez
Canal restriction, this barred Israel from the Indian Ocean
and the Pacific except around Africa or through the Panama
Canal.

   d. The withdrawal of British troops from the Suez Canal zone,
in accordance with British-Egyptian agreement, removed a
potential third-power force from the area and a form of
early-warning system for Israel.

   e. Terrorist raids (the *fedayin* raids) were carried out in Israel
with what Israel claimed was official Egyptian sanction and
encouragement but by what Egypt claimed were discontented
Palestinian refugees from Gaza.

   f. Israeli military forces carried out several large-scale incursions
into Egyptian territory, mainly in Gaza, aimed—Israel
contended—at bases from which the *fedayin* operated, in
order to deter further *fedayin* raids.

   g. Official and quasi-official sources in Egypt made threats of
eventual annihilation of Israel.

   h. Egypt announced that the Soviet bloc had agreed to supply
Egypt with modern military equipment. This threatened to
upset the military balance that had existed between Egypt
and Israel.

   i. Egypt banned Israeli commercial flights over the Strait of
Tiran.

   j. Pressure on the Israeli government mounted from those
favoring a stronger policy toward Egypt. The moderates
were forced out of office and the groups favoring more
extreme policies returned.

2. Factors Tending to Inhibit the Resumption of Hostilities

   a. As part of the agreements ending Phase III_1 hostilities in
1949, UNTSO existed and was responsible for investigating
alleged truce violations and recommending measures to
prevent them.

   b. The UN Security Council explicitly condemned Israel for its
military forays into Gaza and called on the adversaries to
avoid actions likely to disturb the peace of the region.

   c. UNTSO proposed and the UN Security Council
recommended to the adversaries measures to tighten the
armistice line: barbed wire, joint patrols, etc.

c. Insistence by maritime powers on open access to international waters.

d. Substitution of neutral-force presence. Alternate technical-surveillance systems for early warning. (Note that this same factor, here seen as conflict-producing, was conflict-controlling in the British-French-Egyptian conflict; see 2(a) on p. 301.)

e. Fact-finding to determine responsibility. Joint or third-party border control (such as that proposed by the head of UNTSO but rejected by the adversaries). Strong sanctions against infiltration and sabotage.

f. Border-control measures mentioned in (e) above. Third-party border patrol. Strong sanctions against armed incursions.

g. Bilateral agreement to temper propaganda campaign. Development of positive set of goals around which to rally Egyptian and Arab nationalism and aspirations. (See also 1(c) on p. 299.)

h. Agreement among arms suppliers to restrict sale of arms to states engaged in conflicts.

i. Clarification and enforcement of international agreements on peaceful uses of national air space. Reprisals against Egypt by other commercial airlines.

j. Strengthening Israeli moderates and weakening the extremists.

---

2. Measures to Reinforce These Factors

a. Enhanced powers for UNTSO: increased numbers, technical capability, authority.

b. Threat of UN sanctions.

c. Insistence by the United Nations and other third powers that states comply with UNTSO recommendations, with threat of economic and political reprisals against adversary refusing cooperation.

   d. Nasser had a high interest in Egypt's economic development
      and needed time for these programs, as well as to consolidate
      his regime.

   e. Britain urged Israel and Egypt to compromise on a permanent
      border somewhere between the UN partition-plan lines
      Egypt wanted and the armistice line Israel claimed.

   f. The United States and Britain refused to supply arms to
      Israel following Egypt's acquisition of Soviet-bloc arms.

The British-French-Egyptian Conflict, PHASE I *to* PHASE II: *The Introduction of a Military Option*

> *During roughly the same period discussed above, disputes
> developed between Britain and Egypt and France and Egypt.
> Factors described here bear on the transition of those
> disputes into a conflict that aligned Britain and France on
> one side and Egypt on the other.*

1. Factors Tending to Introduce a Military Option

   a. The Middle East generally and the Suez Canal in particular
      had been for centuries of great strategic and economic
      importance to Europe. Britain in particular relied on the
      canal to tie together its dispersed empire. Europe's reliance
      on Middle Eastern oil (much of it shipped through the
      canal) was growing.

   b. Cold War considerations led to the CENTO (Central Treaty
      Organization) security arrangement, which Nasser regarded
      as a barrier to his brand of Arab nationalism and a
      strengthening of his chief rival, Iraq.

   c. In his search for support in the Arab world, Nasser exploited
      the theme of anti-Westernism (as well as that of anti-
      Zionism). Britain thus saw Nasserism as a threat to its
      political position in the Middle East.

   d. Nasser's acceptance of Soviet-bloc arms was seen by the
      West as being fully as much anti-Western as anti-Israeli. The
      move diminished the value of CENTO as a barrier to Soviet
      influence in the Middle East and potentially opened the way
      to the establishment of Soviet military power in the eastern
      Mediterranean as well.

   e. Nasser openly gave matériel and other support to the
      Algerian rebels in their struggle for independence from
      France.

   d. Enhancing value of internal-development goals as rallying point for state and regime.

   e. Other third parties displaying a willingness to incur international and domestic criticism by insisting both adversaries make concessions toward settlement.

   f. Preferably, agreement among all suppliers to restrict arms to conflict areas. Refusal to become engaged in competitive local arms races. Substitution of workable credible guarantees for added arms shipments.

Keeping the Dispute Nonmilitary

1. Measures to Offset These Factors

   a. Development of long-range air-lift capability for both military and commercial purposes. Investigation of alternate canal routes. Development of alternate energy sources. International ownership of vital waterways.

   b. Ideally, ending the Cold War. Alternatively, building stable countries on the Soviet periphery to resist subversion. Guarantees against Soviet aggression. Sea-based missile and air alternatives to land bases.

   c. Developing a positive set of goals and aspirations for Arab nationalists. (See also 1(g) on p. 297.)

   d. Agreement among arms suppliers not to send arms to conflict areas. Strong measures to deter Soviets from attempting to establish bases in area.

   e. Either, measures to cut off and halt Egyptian aid to Algeria; or, acceptance by France of Algerian independence or, alternatively, of the internal Algerian genesis of the independence movement so that Nasser would not appear to be the *cause* of French difficulties.

    f. After long negotiations for international financial support for the Aswan High Dam, Nasser agreed to conditions laid down by the United States, Britain, and the International Bank. The United States abruptly and publicly withdrew its offer.

2. Factors Tending to Keep the Dispute Nonmilitary

    a. Britain agreed, in the face of mounting Egyptian terrorism and strong U.S. pressure, to evacuate its forces from the Suez Canal area.

    b. Britain declined Israel's request for arms following Egypt's agreement to acquire Soviet-bloc arms. In general, Britain sought to pursue a neutral policy on the issues of the Arab-Israeli conflict.

    c. Nasser was concerned with Egypt's economic development and needed and was prepared to accept substantial Western aid for this purpose. The symbol of the growth of modern Egypt was to be the Aswan High Dam.

The Arab-Israeli Conflict, PHASE IV$_1$ *to* PHASE III$_2$:
The Resumption of Hostilities

The British-French-Egyptian Conflict, PHASE II *to* PHASE III:
The Outbreak of Hostilities

1. Factors Tending to Promote the Resumption/Outbreak of Hostilities

    a. British and French leaders saw the situation in the Middle East as analogous to Europe in the late 1930's and felt that now, as then, appeasement of dictators would only whet their appetites and precipitate larger hostilities eventually.

    b. The existence of the British-French-Egyptian Conflict opened for Israel a chance for more major action against Egypt than it could undertake alone. The existence of the Arab-Israeli Conflict, and particularly the state of Israeli-Egyptian relations, gave Britain and France an opportunity to develop a cover story for their military intervention. First, France and Israel and France and Britain discussed bilateral action; subsequently, these discussions developed into trilateral planning.

    c. Britain and France saw little hope for a negotiated settlement with Nasser and felt that the U.S. reiteration of its unwillingness to endorse the use of force undermined what little bargaining power they had.

    f. Disbursement of economic assistance through nonpolitical international agencies. Greater awareness of high emotional value placed on major symbols of progress. Greater finesse in handling delicate diplomatic problems.

2. Measures to Reinforce These Factors

    a. Earlier, more amicable British-Egyptian agreement. (Note: This was a conflict-producing and not a conflict-controlling factor in the context of the Arab-Israeli Conflict; see 1(d) on p. 297.)

    b. Pursuing a more pro-Egyptian policy (which may, however, generate[8] a different conflict). Unilateral British or joint British-U.S. guarantees to victim of aggression.

    c. Enhancing value and symbolism of internal development goals. Extensive economic aid.

Preventing the Resumption/Outbreak of Hostilities

1. Measures to Offset These Factors

    a. Learning all the lessons of history, which include both the dangers of appeasement and the dangers of refusal to accommodate to what others see as their vital interests and needs.

    b. The elimination of one or another of the conflicts. (Note: Either conflict alone might have led to hostilities, but the nature of each would certainly have been different, and probably the timing.)

    c. Articulation of U.S. position as not just nonendorsement of the use of force in these conflicts but determination to react

[8] Note that, for simplicity and for an aid to future applications, the authors have used present tenses, present conditionals, and present participles at will throughout the RELEVANT CONTROL MEASURES.

  d. The availability of the British base in Cyprus made British-
     French military action in the Middle East easier to carry
     out quickly.
  e. The coming U.S. election was probably calculated to make
     rapid U.S. decision making on Suez-Sinai difficult.

2. Factors Tending to Inhibit the Resumption/Outbreak of Hostilities
  a. Nasser offered assurance that he would keep the canal open.
     He offered to negotiate a new treaty guaranteeing this, fixing
     rates, guaranteeing maintenance, etc.
  b. Despite the fears expressed by Britain and France, the canal
     continued to function smoothly under Egyptian control.

  c. The United States exerted strong diplomatic pressure on
     Britain and France not to resort to force in their conflict
     with Egypt. The United States refused to agree that force was
     required if Nasser rejected the various alternate arrangements
     for canal management being considered.
  d. The United States initiated two major efforts to devise a new
     system for operating the canal, both of which involved
     lengthy negotiation. These were designed both to be
     responsive to the expressed concerns of Britain and France
     and to keep Britain and France at the conference table.
  e. The Soviet Union uttered thinly veiled threats to intervene
     on Egypt's behalf, with "volunteers," if Britain and France
     opened hostilities.
  f. The Hungarian crisis, occurring simultaneously, distracted
     Soviet attention but it also raised the likelihood, U.S.
     officials in particular feared, of hasty Soviet reactions in the
     Middle East.
  g. Private negotiations under the auspices of the UN
     Secretary-General appeared to be making progress toward a
     negotiated settlement of the expressed substance of the
     conflict.
  h. Domestic pressure was mounting, in Britain in particular,
     against the use of force against Egypt except as a last resort.

vigorously against those, including its closest allies, who did use force.

d. Elimination of Britain's Cyprus base. International air and sea blockade of it to prevent its use as a staging area against Egypt.

e. Insulation of major foreign-policy issues from election politics. Bipartisan statement of U.S. position.

2. Measures to Reinforce These Factors

a. U.S. and UN endorsement of Nasser proposals. Offer of good offices for negotiations. Guarantee of resulting agreements.

b. Clear intention of other users of the canal not to tolerate British-French use of force so long as the canal operates smoothly and without politically inspired disruptions by Nasser.

c. Equally firm U.S. statement of its position if force is nonetheless resorted to. (Note: The conclusions the British and French drew from the U.S. position were conflict-producing; see 1(c) on p. 301.)

d. Additional time-buying devices. Pressure on Britain and France to continue efforts to negotiate a solution. Pressure on Egypt to seek a negotiated compromise.

e. Threatening to intensify potential hostilities with highly credible threats.

f. Threats of uncontrolled, accidental intensification into global nuclear war.

g. U.S. and other pressure not to countenance force while negotiations are in progress.

h. Strengthening opposition in Britain. Undermining British government in office. Seeking to oust Anthony Eden.

The Arab-Israeli Conflict, Within PHASE III₂

The British-French-Egyptian Conflict, Within PHASE III

The hostilities in the combined conflicts, while brief, included two specific intensifications. These will be analyzed in the following sections.

Sub-Phase A: Israel Invades Sinai

In this sub-phase, only Israeli and Egyptian forces were engaged and hostilities were confined to the Sinai Peninsula. The threatened intensification was the commitment of British and French forces to the hostilities and their extension to the Suez Canal area. Although the British-French ultimatum was phrased as an effort to terminate hostilities, its effect—and probably intent—was to intensify them.

1. Factors Tending to Inhibit the Termination of Hostilities

   a. All the factors outlined above as promoting the resumption/ outbreak of hostilities continued to operate.

   b. Britain and France sent an ultimatum to Israel and to Egypt demanding a cease-fire and a pull-back ten miles from the canal; the demand was further made of Egypt that it admit British and French troops to separate the belligerents and guarantee free transit.

2. Factors Tending to Promote the Termination of Hostilities

   a. Although Britain and France vetoed the resolution in the UN Security Council that would have called for an immediate cease-fire and for all members of the United Nations to refrain from assisting either belligerent, the debate showed united opposition to the Israeli action and to the British-French ultimatum from Britain's and France's European allies, from most of the Commonwealth, from the neutralists, and from both the United States and Soviet Union.

   b. To the extent that the fictions of French and British action independent of Israel were important, the fact that fighting had not reached the canal area when the ultimatum was delivered, and that this was generally known to the various governments involved, may have served as a moderating force.

Moderating/Terminating (Resumed) Hostilities

1. Measures to Offset These Factors
   a. Measures suggested above to offset factors promoting hostilities and reinforce those inhibiting hostilities.
   b. Counterultimatum to Britain and France from the United States, the Soviet Union, and others threatening to block attempted intervention. U.S. articulation of intended response to intervention. Pressure on Israel and Egypt to comply with terms of ultimatum by neutral or UN force instead of British-French force interposed along the canal.

2. Measures to Reinforce These Factors
   a. Increased pressure from allies, trading partners, and Cold War adversaries.

   b. Increasing British and French public opposition to their governments' actions by giving wide publicity to the gaps between the facts and British-French allegations. (Note, however, that accepting in particular Britain's public statement of objectives at face value probably provided a key to early termination of hostilities by making a face-saving retreat possible.)

    c. The procedures of the Uniting for Peace Resolution enabled the Special Emergency Session of the UN General Assembly to be convened in very short order. UN pressure was thus maintained.

    d. The United States was especially fearful that the Suez-Sinai conflicts would grow into a much wider war. The United States brought strong diplomatic pressure to bear on Britain and France.

Sub-Phase B: The Commitment of British-French Air Power

Despite multilateral and bilateral pressures, the British and French, at the expiration of the ultimatum, began to bomb Egyptian airfields and potential invasion points, and French air power directly supported the Israeli land operations in Sinai. The threatened further intensification was the actual landing of British and French ground forces in Egypt.

1. Factors Tending to Inhibit the Termination of Hostilities

    a. The British and French were publicly committed to the terms of their ultimatum.

    b. The one area in which Soviet-bloc arms had most significantly increased Egypt's strength vis-à-vis Israel was in air power (although in terms of pilot training, maintenance, etc., this was only potential power at this time). Israel was anxious to eliminate as much of this potential threat as possible.

---

2. Factors Tending to Promote the Termination of Hostilities

    a. Israel had achieved its primary goals: defeating Egypt in Sinai, capturing or destroying the recently acquired Soviet-bloc equipment, humiliating Nasser, and opening the Strait of Tiran.

    b. A strongly worded resolution calling for an end to hostilities and British-French intervention was adopted by the General Assembly—again with Soviet-U.S. concurrence.

    c. The General Assembly also decided to authorize the creation of a UN force to perform the task for which Britain and France claimed their intervention had been undertaken— separating Israeli and Egyptian forces and protecting the canal.

Sub-Phase C: Termination of Hostilities

Despite the factors noted above, British and French airborne and seaborne forces landed in Egypt and began to fight their way up the canal. Hostilities in Sinai had virtually ceased.

    c. Preserving the UN Charter's evolving flexibility, while exploring techniques to enhance it still further.

    d. Increasing threat of Soviet involvement and intensification of the conflict.

1. Measures to Offset These Factors
    a. Increased opposition to announced policy, especially in Britain, to make the cost of being consistent higher than the cost of reversing policy.
    b. Restraint by arms suppliers in shipping arms to conflict areas. Provision of anti-aircraft defenses to Israel.

2. Measures to Reinforce These Factors
    a. Seeking to separate the two conflicts by seeking to persuade Israel to agree to cease-fire.

    b. Coupling UN condemnation with threat of sanctions.

    c. Prior General Assembly creation of such a peacekeeping force or studies of the organization of one.

1. Factors Tending to Inhibit the Termination of Hostilities

   a. Egyptian resistance in Sinai had collapsed—in part as a consequence of defeat by Israeli military action and in part as a consequence of the British-French threat. In the canal area, Egyptian resistance was steadily weakening.

   b. Strong Soviet diplomatic support for Egypt's position led Egypt to break off local surrender negotiations and continue fighting. Arms were distributed to civilians in preparation for possible guerrilla warfare.

2. Factors Tending to Promote the Termination of Hostilities

   a. The Soviet Union threatened or proposed a variety of kinds of intervention: direct unilateral in Egypt; joint with the United States; missile attacks on Britain and France.

   b. The United States refused to assure Britain and France that it would regard itself obliged to come to their assistance if the Soviet Union attacked their forces in Egypt.

   c. Heavy domestic pressure was being generated in Britain to cease hostilities. Not only members of the opposition Labour party but also important segments of the majority Tory party opposed the Eden government's policies. This opposition was magnified by fears generated by Soviet threats.

   d. A serious run on the pound sterling developed. The United States agreed to help stabilize the situation only if Britain agreed to an immediate cease-fire and withdrew.

   e. France was not prepared to proceed alone (without British assistance).

   f. The plans for the UN force—UNEF (United Nations Emergency Force)—were elaborated and contingents committed.

The British-French-Egyptian Conflict, PHASE IV to S: Settlement of the Dispute

> *With the termination of hostilities, it remained to obtain the withdrawal of British and French forces. The portion of the Arab-Israeli Conflict that overlaps with the period of British-French withdrawal belongs in this general section dealing with the converged conflicts. However, since Israeli*

1. Measures to Offset These Factors

    a. More effective British-French action to complete their military mission. (Note: Rapid British-French "victory" would have terminated hostilities but may have been found intolerable by the United States, Soviet Union, United Nations, etc. The opposite course toward rapid termination—deterring or defeating the intervention attempt—would seem more likely to have achieved conflict control.)

    b. U.S. counterpressure on Soviet Union not to encourage Egyptian resistance. Actions to reduce credibility of Soviet threat to intervene.

2. Measures to Reinforce These Factors

    a. Active U.S. expressions of interest in Soviet proposals (if objective is termination by Britain-France). Active steps to counter and reduce credibility of Soviet threats (if aim is to induce Egypt to give in).

    b. Explicit statement that the United States will not bail out Britain and France in Egypt so long as Soviet action is confined to scene of hostilities and kept to conventional arms.

    c. Strengthening internal opposition in Britain. Seeking to topple British government. Seeking to oust Eden.

    d. Increasing and stimulating the economic costs of hostilities.

    e. Seeking to break up the coalition acting against Egypt. (Note: This clearly was being done, for most U.S. and UN pressure fell upon Britain.)

    f. Either a standing UN peace force or developed contingency-planning for one.

Settling the Dispute

withdrawal was delayed three months longer than British-French withdrawal, and since the issues that delayed it were related solely to the Arab-Israeli Conflict, it is treated as a whole in a following section.

1. Factors Tending Away from Settlement

   a. None of the stated or unstated objectives of the British-French intervention had been accomplished.

   b. UNEF was a novel instrument and had to be assembled piecemeal. While in the circumstances the speed of its arrival was astounding, it was some weeks before it was fully operational.

2. Factors Tending Toward Settlement

   a. UNEF's eventual arrival allowed the British and French to withdraw with some saving of face and without what otherwise might have been dangerous clashes with the armed Egyptian populace.

   b. The United Nations repeated its demand for a speedy withdrawal of intervening forces.

The Arab-Israeli Conflict, PHASE IV₂ Sub-Phase A to Sub-Phase B: The Withdrawal of Israeli Forces

With British-French withdrawal, only Israeli troops remained on Egyptian soil.

1. Factors Tending Away from Settlement

   a. Whereas Israeli forces had accomplished their military objectives, the failure of the British-French intervention meant that these gains could not be regarded as secured. Before agreeing to withdraw, Israel demanded assurances that the blockade at Aqaba would not be reimposed and that Gaza would not again become a base for *fedayin* raids.

2. Factors Tending Toward Lowered Tensions

   a. Strong U.S. and UN pressure for withdrawal continued.

   b. The implied risk of a clash between Israeli forces and UNEF existed in the General Assembly's instruction to the latter to proceed to take up positions on the Egyptian side of the armistice line.

   c. The major maritime powers undertook to give assurances that the Strait of Tiran would remain open to Israeli shipping.

1. Measures to Offset These Factors

   a. Stronger indications, if such are possible, of the high cost, and unlikely prospect, of achieving British-French goals.

   b. Standing UN peacekeeping force. Developed contingency plans for rapid development and deployment of such a force.

---

2. Measures to Reinforce These Factors

   a. Avoiding creation of a situation in which national pride and prestige are committed to a conflict-producing course *by leaving open a face-saving line of retreat*. Accepting an avowed purpose as genuine even in the face of evidence that it is not. Avoiding the cornering of either adversary.

   b. More rapid deployment of UNEF. Potential UN force to compel compliance (not to be confused with UNEF type of peacekeeping force).

---

1. Measures to Offset These Factors

   a. Recognition that, even though aggression is condemned, the aggressor may have legitimate grievances which, while not being a justification of its actions, need to be accommodated in the interests of future conflict control and settlement.

---

2. Measures to Reinforce These Factors

   a. Threat of military/economic sanctions.

   b. Backing up peacekeeping forces with potent political support, deterrence, etc.

   c. Accommodation of legitimate grievances, even of the condemned aggressor. Formal international agreement on right of passage, including enforcement provisions.

d. The United Nations gave assurance that UNEF would maintain the full responsibility for the Gaza area until a peace settlement had been reached.

The Arab-Israeli Conflict, PHASE IV$_2$ Sub-Phase B to Sub-Phase C: From Inter-War to Pre-War

1. **Factors Tending to Promote the Resumption of Hostilities**

   a. The memory of the 1956 war and the humiliating defeat suffered by the Egyptian forces deepened Arab hatred of Zionism and determination ultimately to see it eliminated from the Middle East.

   b. The 1956 events also destroyed whatever restraining influence Britain and France had over events in the area. Their acts had given credence to Arab convictions that Israel was an outpost for a new, more subtle, more dangerous Western imperialism.

   c. The Soviet position with the Arab states had, by contrast, been strengthened by the 1956 events. Its bellicose threats of missiles and volunteers, while not producing any active material support during the fighting, did help convince the Arabs that the Soviets were their only friends. The Soviet Union followed up this advantage with aid, both economic and military.

   d. The removal of British and French influence was seen by the United States as creating a power vacuum into which the Soviet Union was rushing. The United States also distrusted Nasser and other Arab radicals. The result was the Eisenhower Doctrine—an effort to contain both Soviet and radical Arab influence (which the U.S. government tended at this time to equate) by strengthening Arab moderates (Jordan, Saudi Arabia, Iraq, and Lebanon).

   e. The combination of Soviet and U.S. policies thus led each of them to perceive the conflict in Cold War terms, with each loss by one an automatic gain for the other. Thus, the loss of Iraq to Western influence was seen as a Soviet gain; and U.S. and British successful intervention in Jordan and Lebanon to counter Arab radical elements was viewed as a Soviet loss.

   f. The one issue on which all Arabs were united—hatred of Zionism—impelled even more moderate Arabs to be verbally bellicose toward Israel. Competition among the Arabs increasingly took the form of claims to doctrinal purity on this issue and allegations of "softness on Zionism" toward rivals.

d. Accommodation of legitimate grievances, even of the condemned aggressor.

---

1. Measures to Offset These Factors
   a. Full "justice" in the Arab view, which would have involved undoing Middle Eastern history since Balfour. Failing that, "relative justice" particularly in compensating and readmitting refugees. Enhancing—and facilitating—other Arab goals.
   b. An even-handed, nonpartial Western approach to Middle Eastern issues. Israeli nonalignment. Multiracial justice inside Israel and Arab countries alike.

   c. Again, an impartial Soviet policy. Keeping Cold War issues out of local-conflict areas. Multilateral or joint offers of aid and assistance.

   d. U.S. impartiality among intra-Arab contestants. Appreciation of and support for genuine nonalignment. Keeping Cold War issues out of local-conflict areas. Distinguishing between local radicals and nationalists and Moscow-manipulated puppets.

   e. The measures listed above to remove Cold War perceptions from local issues. Clearer understanding of local issues so they do not become obscured by global issues.

   f. Greater appreciation of the psychological importance of even this negative issue. Keeping sense of proportion in interpreting local outbursts. External support and encouragement of other bases for Arab unity, with positive support for the achievement of this goal.

g. One manifestation of this intra-Arab competition was in arms acquisitions, as each Arab nation sought to strengthen its position vis-à-vis its rivals by building up its arms levels. The Soviet Union armed its clients—Egypt, Iraq, and Syria—while the West armed Jordan, Saudi Arabia, and, to a lesser extent, Lebanon.

h. This intra-Arab arms race in turn served as a stimulus to the over-all Arab-Israeli arms competition. The West found itself arming Israel to defend Israel against the Arab states, some of which the West also armed.

i. The substantive issues that had marred pre-1956 Arab-Israeli relations were not resolved—aside from the blockade of the Gulf of Aqaba. The Suez Canal remained closed to Israeli shipping, and the Arab economic boycott of Israel was extended to any outside company, airline, or shipper that did business with Israel. The refugees from the 1948–1949 war continued to sit in Gaza and the West Bank of Jordan.

j. The refugee question was exploited by the Arabs both as a propaganda device and as a direct threat against Israel. The creation by the Arabs of the Palestine Liberation Army in Gaza and the West Bank and by Syria of the El Fatah terrorist organization stimulated renewed terrorist activity inside Israel (particularly by the El Fatah).

k. Another long-simmering issue became acute as Israel proceeded with unilateral plans to tap the waters of the Jordan River for irrigation projects in the Negev; the Arabs countered with their own plans to draw off the same waters for Arab irrigation schemes.

l. The moderate Eshkol government sought to devote maximum public attention to internal Israeli problems, particularly the serious economic problems. The Israeli public grew increasingly uneasy about what it regarded as a dangerously weak policy vis-à-vis the security threat from the Arabs.

2. Factors Tending to Inhibit the Resumption of Hostilities

a. UNEF units along the Israeli-Egyptian front kept that frontier relatively peaceful. UNEF units at Sharm el Sheikh kept the Gulf of Aqaba open to Israeli shipping.

b. The Suez Canal, once cleared of the wreckage of the 1956 war, functioned normally under Egyptian management. Furthermore, the exploitation of oil discoveries in North Africa and the development of large tankers decreased Europe's dependence on the canal and Middle Eastern oil.

c. Intra-Arab feuding consistently thwarted efforts at Arab unity. Thus, the disparity in size and strength between Israel and the Arab world as a whole was offset. (However,

g. Agreements among arms suppliers to keep low the level and lethality of arms in conflict areas.

h. The same measure as mentioned above. Also, avoiding introducing arms within the context of one rivalry that stimulates arms acquisitions by third parties.

i. Strenuous bilateral and multilateral efforts to resolve substantive issues. Barring this, measures to reduce the impact of these issues on the conflict—alternatives to the Suez route, steps to counteract the impact of the boycott, physical control of borders near which large refugee populations live, etc.

j. Resettlement, readmission, and/or compensation of refugees. Barring this, physical barriers to refugee-inspired raids by border controls, patrols, barbed wire, a McNamara-type "electronic barrier," etc.

k. Patient but determined pressures for agreement on joint use of Jordan waters. Barring this, development of alternate sources of water supply—e.g., desalination.

l. Measures to strengthen moderates within Israel.

---

2. Measures to Reinforce These Factors

   a. Retention of UNEF-type units. Improvement of their capabilities by reconnaissance aircraft, greater mobility, etc.

   b. International agreements containing reassurances on continued canal operations. Alternate sources of energy.

   c. Keeping Arabs disunited and quarreling among themselves. Isolating Arab radicals. (Note, however, that this policy, which was the one the great powers pursued, generated many

as noted above, the temptation to seek to rally Arab support by playing on anti-Zionist sentiments was strong as a consequence).

d. U.S. policy toward the Arab radicals—Nasser in particular—became more subtle as efforts to isolate him were increasingly shown to be ineffective. Economic aid and technical assistance were resumed to Egypt.

e. While prepared to accept Soviet aid and diplomatic support, the Arab radicals were hard on their own domestic Communists. In fact, the only legal Communist party in the region was in Israel.

f. The leading radical Arab states became embroiled in other foreign problems—Egypt in Yemen and Algeria with its conflict with Morocco. The former conflict, in particular, dragged on inconclusively and tied up substantial elements of the Egyptian armed forces.

g. The crises in Lebanon and Jordan demonstrated the U.S. and British willingness—and capability—of rapidly deploying their military strength in the Middle East.

h. Some efforts were made to deal with the most acute substantive issues between Israel and the Arab states—Jordan waters, the refugees, and the Suez Canal. None of these succeeded, but continuing international cognizance was demonstrated.

i. Repeated Arab statements about the longer-term timetable for action against Israel suggested that rational judgments had been made about relative present military capabilities.

The Arab-Israeli Conflict, PHASE IV₂ Sub-Phase C to Sub-Phase D (PHASE III₃): The Resumption of Hostilities

1. Factors Tending to Promote the Resumption of Hostilities

    a. As the scale of terrorist attacks against Israel mounted (particularly attacks by the Syrian-sponsored El Fatah across the Jordanian border), Israel reverted to its pre-1956 tactic of staging massive retaliatory raids in reprisal. Large-scale raids were carried out against Jordan and Syria in particular.

    b. The United Nations, while condemning Israeli reprisals, took no action against the terrorist incursions into Israel.

    c. Israeli reprisals led to increased pressure on Nasser to take some action. Syria, his ally, and Jordan, his enemy one day and ally the next, taunted him with "hiding behind UNEF" and being unwilling or unable to act against Israel.

of the factors listed above which worsened the conflict.)

   d. Recognition of the value of true nonalignment. Distinguishing between local nationalists and Moscow agents.

   e. Measures mentioned above to isolate receipt of Soviet aid from Soviet domination. Avoiding reliance on a single major supplier of economic and military aid.

   f. Encouraging distracting Arab conflicts elsewhere.

   g. Maintenance of U.S. willingness and ability to intervene— and credibility that it will use that capacity.

   h. Strenuous pursuit of these efforts. But, failing them, measures to reduce the impact of these substantive issues on the conflict (border controls, desalination, and other measures suggested above).

   i. Assisting Arab leaders in realistically appraising the relative military balance.

---

1. Measures to Offset These Factors
   a. Strong international action to prevent such Israeli reprisals. Extension of UNEF-type operations to Jordanian and Syrian borders. Strong sanctions by United States and other supporters of Israel.

   b. Equally strong condemnation of Arab-sponsored terrorists. Border controls.

   c. Measures mentioned above to prevent Israeli reprisals and the terrorist raids that provoke them. Failing this, measures mentioned above to condemn and punish such acts. Failing this, strong pressures on Syria, Jordan, and Egypt to resist extremist pressures, including time-buying measures.

d. Arab unity—the dream of the Arabs and the nightmare of Israel—appeared nearer than it had for years. Egypt and Syria signed a mutual-defense pact and later Jordan, too. Jordan's action enabled Iraqi units to be moved into that country, which militarily was most menacing to Israeli security and survival.

e. Public reaction in Israel against the moderate Eshkol regime was increasingly harsh. To the security-conscious Israelis, only military strength, exercised pre-emptively, held any hope of survival. Yielding to this pressure, Eshkol brought into his government the military heroes of the 1948 and 1956 wars.

f. The most active sector of the Arab-Israeli border, in terms of action from both sides, was that between Israel and Syria. Rumors persisted of extensive Israeli preparations for action against Syria and were given credibility by thinly veiled Israeli threats to topple the radical Syrian regime. Apparently assurances of an actual Israeli concentration on the Syrian front were given to Nasser by the Soviet Union (which had declined Israeli offers for on-site investigation of the charges).

g. UNEF units were precipitately withdrawn from their positions along the Israeli-Egyptian frontier and from Sharm el Sheikh. Controversy surrounds Egypt's intentions and the speed of the UN Secretary-General's compliance with the withdrawal request. One element seems clear: India and Yugoslavia, whose forces occupied key sectors, were unprepared to delay their withdrawal.

h. The withdrawal of UNEF put Egyptian and Israeli units face to face on the frontier and, perhaps more significant, put Egyptian forces back at Sharm el Sheikh. Nasser immediately reimposed the blockade of the Strait of Tiran—an act Israel had long asserted it would not tolerate.

i. The U.S. and other maritime powers had given assurances, in 1957, of their intentions to keep the strait open to all shipping. Yet, in the face of the blockade, the U.S. and Britain were unable to organize support for multilateral action and were unwilling to act alone.

j. The Soviet Union and the Arab states appear to have assumed that intensive U.S. efforts would be made to persuade Israel to acquiesce peacefully to the new blockade. More importantly, they appear to have overestimated the degree of influence the United States had over Israel.

2. Factors Tending to Inhibit the Resumption of Hostilities

a. While the UN failed to deal effectively with renewed terrorist raids against Israel, it condemned Israeli reprisal

   d. Guarantees to Israel of assistance in the event of Arab
      attack. Encouraging Arab disunity (but see 2(c) on p. 315
      on the limitations and hazards of such a policy).

   e. Guarantees mentioned above, including perhaps maneuvers
      and demonstrations (for benefit of Israelis and Arabs) of
      capacity and will to honor the commitment.

   f. International fact-finding. Better national intelligence on the
      part of Egypt in particular. Time-buying measures.

   g. Measures to buy time by delaying UNEF withdrawal.
      Appeal of the issue to Security Council or General Assembly
      for this purpose even if the outcome is likely to favor
      withdrawal. Use of influence with contributors of UN
      contingents not to insist on hasty withdrawal. In the long
      run, standing UN forces not dependent on political will of a
      particular contributor.
   h. Time-buying devices mentioned above. Efforts to delay
      deployment of Egyptian forces. Strong Soviet pressure
      toward these ends. More credible U.S. assurances about
      keeping the strait open.

   i. Honoring commitments, multilaterally if possible, unilaterally
      if necessary.

   j. Clarification of limits of U.S. influence. Alternatively, strong
      and—if necessary—unfriendly pressure by the United States
      to gain the influence it was thought to have.

---

2. Measures to Reinforce These Factors
   a. Measures mentioned above both to deal equitably with both
      the reprisals and their provocation and to back up verbal

raids. The scale of the reprisal against Jordan, in particular, caused widespread criticism of Israeli policy.

b. The United States, deeply committed in Vietnam and under domestic pressure to avoid any steps that might possibly lead to comparable commitments elsewhere, urged caution and restraint on Israel. In particular, the United States tried to mobilize a diplomatic response to the reimposition of the Aqaba blockade and to head off a unilateral Israeli effort to reopen the waterway by force.

c. While the Soviet Union appears to have urged Syria and Egypt on in some of their actions during this period, the Soviets appear not to have wanted to provoke hostilities. There is some evidence that they were not aware of, and in fact disapproved of, the reclosing of the Gulf of Aqaba.

The Arab-Israeli Conflict, PHASE III₃ *to* PHASE IV₃: *The Termination of Resumed Hostilities*

The hostilities that broke out in the early morning hours of June 5, 1967, were brief but intense, opening with the devastating surprise Israeli air attacks on Egyptian, Syrian, Jordanian, and Iraqi air bases and featuring successive land engagements between Israel and Egypt, Jordan, and Syria. We shall not look here at the military factors that led to Israel's rapid victories. Rather, we shall look, first, at factors that helped to dictate the initial intensity of the fighting and the subsequent spread of the land war, and, second, at factors bearing on the termination of hostilities.

1. Factors Tending to Favor the Intensification of Hostilities

   a. Israel's military plans were based on the assumption that the great powers, acting through the United Nations, would cooperate in seeking an early cease-fire. The campaign had, therefore, to be quick and conclusive.

   b. The major form the Arab-Israeli arms race had taken was in aircraft procurement. The Soviets had given Egypt, Iraq, and Syria—and the West had given Jordan—aircraft that could hit Israeli cities and interfere with Israeli land attacks. Hence, the priority objective of Israeli military planners had to be to neutralize that air power.

   c. Jordan declined an Israeli offer to avoid a land battle. Jordan chose to honor its defense commitment to Egypt and—given the temper of its people and military at the time—probably had no other choice. After continued Jordanian firing, Israel launched a land attack on the Jordanian part of Jerusalem and the West Bank.

condemnation with strong actions.

b. Matching commitments to available means and willingness to back them up. On the Strait of Tiran issue, willingness noted above to act unilaterally if necessary.

c. More complete Soviet control over use made by Egypt of Soviet-supplied arms. Better yet, keeping such capabilities out of the area in the first place.

Moderating/Terminating Resumed Hostilities

1. Measures to Offset These Factors

   a. A slower UN response might, in theory, have moderated the intensity of hostilities.

   b. Keeping arms balances at the lowest possible level. In particular, keeping destabilizing weapons systems out of the conflict areas.

   c. Urging Jordan not to honor its commitments. Deterring Israeli attack by introducing U.S., British, or UN units into Jordan.

   d. Israel reserved a special animosity toward Syria, whom Israel held particularly responsible for the succession of events that led to the June 1967 war. Furthermore, shelling of Israel settlements in the border area had been a constant source of Israeli resentment.

2. Factors Tending to Favor the Moderation of Hostilities

   a. Potential direct involvement by the United States and/or Soviet Union based on a misperception of each other's role was avoided by direct assurances via the "hot line."

3. Factors Tending to Favor the Continuation of Hostilities

   a. Having early achieved air superiority and having, in terms of training, morale, and leadership, more effective military force, Israel won quick military victories and was under no military pressure to end the fighting until its goals were achieved. (Note: There would soon have been military restraints on Israel had its goals not been geographically limited.)

   b. Lack of information on the magnitude of the Arab defeats led the Arab's international supporters—notably the Soviet Union—to adopt tactics in the UN Security Council that delayed passage of a cease-fire resolution.

4. Factors Tending to Favor the Termination of Hostilities

   a. Israel had limited military goals. Once it had accomplished these, it had no interest in pressing its military advantage.

   b. All the great powers were unanimous in their desire to end the fighting as quickly as possible. Despite the "hot line," the possibility was always present that they could become directly if inadvertently involved. Thus, they ultimately achieved unanimity in the Security Council on a cease-fire resolution and on repeated efforts to get it accepted and observed.

THE WEAPONS

This section will examine only the arms available to Egypt and to Israel in the hostilities of 1956 and 1967.

  d. Preferably, to avoid or prevent the past series of incidents. Failing this, introduction of foreign (e.g., Soviet) forces to deter Israeli attack. Efforts to moderate Syrian regime. Expansion of demilitarized buffer strip between hostile forces.

---

2. Measures to Reinforce These Factors
  a. Rapid, secure communications between superpowers. Preferably, to clarify intentions *before* rather than *after* the event.

---

3. Measures to Offset These Factors
  a. If rapid termination is the goal, quick military victory by one party.

  b. Better sources of information on developments in the conflict area—by the United Nations and other interested parties.

---

4. Measures to Reinforce These Factors
  a. Clarification and articulation of Israeli war aims. Pressures to keep Israeli goals limited.
  b. Increasing the risk of great-power involvement (or at least increasing appreciation of the danger).

ARMS ACQUISITION PRIOR TO THE SINAI CAMPAIGN OF 1956

Egyptian Weapons Acquisition

Egypt's arms before the Sinai campaign were acquired in three fairly distinct phases. The first phase ended in 1951–1952, when the British placed a ban on arms exports to Egypt; the second began in 1954–1955, when British and French arms shipments to Egypt resumed with the signing of the agreement to evacuate British forces from the canal zone; the third began in 1955 with the signing of the first agreement for Soviet-bloc arms.

Before 1947, when the British military mission left Egypt, enough .303-cal. Lee Enfield rifles had been supplied for probably as many as 100,000 troops.[9] The British had also provided the Egyptian army with a variety of other battlefield weapons, although details are lacking as to their types.[1] Spitfire fighters, Halifax bombers, and Lancaster bombers were among the aircraft supplied to the Egyptian air force by Britain. Although the British military mission ended its training program in Egypt in 1947, free-lance British pilots were finding training positions with the Egyptian air force up to the time of the Suez attack in late 1956.

It appears that Egypt bought a considerable amount of British and French equipment in 1954 and 1955. The heavier battlefield weapons from Britain included 50 to 60 Valentine Archers with 17-pounder guns, a number of Valentine tanks without the 17-pounder guns, about 120 25-pounder howitzers, and at least 30 Centurion Mk.3 tanks; from France, some 155mm howitzers, a few AMX-13 light tanks, and perhaps 150 to 200 reconditioned Sherman tanks[2] About 70 Meteor jet fighters went to the Egyptian air force from Britain.[3] Sizable shipments of French and British weapons still went to Egypt in late 1955 during the influx of Soviet and Czech arms.[4]

Before the beginning of Soviet aid in 1955, there was a large

[9] The Egyptian national guard was equipped with Lee Enfield rifles by 1956. Alan Barker: *Suez: The Seven Day War* (New York: Praeger; 1964), pp. 61–4.

[1] Major Edgar O'Ballance: "The Egyptian Army," *Royal United Service Institution Journal*, February 1958, pp. 82–8.

[2] Captain Stuart Beckley: "Operation Kadesh—Mobility Masterpiece," *Armor*, March–April 1962, pp. 6–7; Commander H. B. Seim: "Middle East Powder Keg," *Marine Corps Gazette*, July 1956, p. 47.

[3] Barker, op. cit., pp. 59–60.

[4] Benjamin Kagan: *The Secret Battle for Israel* (Cleveland: World Publishing; 1966), pp. 217–19.

assortment of foreign hardware in Egypt. Some 50,000 7.92mm FN rifles had been purchased in Belgium before the end of the Egyptian monarchy,[5] and 7.92mm Alfa heavy machine guns were purchased in Spain.[6] Three anti-aircraft brigades were equipped with Swedish Bofors 40mm light anti-aircraft guns and 30mm Hispano Suiza guns.[7] About 30 Vampire fighters, built by Macchi/Fiat in Italy under license to De Havilland of England, were purchased through Syria after 1951.

At one point, plants were set up in Egypt to manufacture the Swedish Model 42 Ljungman 7.92mm rifle (or modifications thereof) and the Swedish Model 45 9mm submachine gun.[8] It was announced in August 1956 that Egypt had achieved self-sufficiency in small-arms production and was beginning production of heavier arms. The factories were said to have begun rifle production in 1952. This appears to have been the extent of Egypt's success in domestic arms production before 1957, and it is probable that the number of arms being produced in Egypt was small.

The Egyptian army, having been trained, supplied, and maintained by the British until 1947, probably found it increasingly difficult during the next eight years to maintain an acceptable level of readiness. There can be little doubt that Egyptian military equipment deteriorated during the period when France and Britain were banning military exports to the Middle East.

During 1955, Egypt negotiated with the United States for military aid, including some piston-engine fighters, small artillery pieces, and automatic weapons. The United States, it is reported, insisted that Egypt accept conditions that would give the United States some control over the use of the arms and that payment for them would be in dollars.[9] These negotiations ended abruptly in September 1955, when the Egyptian-Czech agreement was announced.

The agreement for Soviet-bloc aid, announced in September

[5] W. H. B. Smith and Joseph E. Smith: *The Book of Rifles* (Harrisburg: Stackpole Books; 1963), p. 117.

[6] Joseph E. Smith: *Small Arms of the World* (Harrisburg: Stackpole Books; 1966), p. 613.   [7] Barker, op. cit., pp. 61–4.

[8] Smith, op. cit., p. 613.   [9] Finer, op. cit., p. 26.

1955, was probably signed much earlier.[1] During the year following announcement of the agreement, there was a rapid build-up in the might of the Egyptian armed forces. The Egyptian regular army was re-equipped with 7.62mm Soviet weapons, and older Egyptian weapons were supplemented with 82mm recoilless rifles, 57mm antitank guns, 122mm and 152mm artillery, SU-100 self-propelled guns, T-34 medium tanks, JS-2 heavy tanks, BTR-152 armored personnel carriers, and Czech antitank guns, anti-aircraft guns, and 122mm field guns. The prestige of the Egyptian air force was greatly enhanced by the 150 MiG-15 and MiG-17 fighters and the 40 to 50 Il-28 bombers that the Soviet Union had supplied by late 1956.[2]

In 1956 the Egyptian army, at an estimated strength of 100,000 with another 100,000 in the national guard, was said to have been composed of eight infantry brigades, one reconnaissance and two armored battalions, five artillery battalions, two antitank battalions, and one coastal-defense and three anti-aircraft brigades.[3]

The rapid build-up of Soviet-bloc equipment was also reflected in the Egyptian navy. The British motor torpedo boats, corvettes, and frigates that show up in the 1956 inventory had all been built during World War II and transferred to Egypt between 1948 and 1951. There were, at the time of the Sinai battle, two ex-British destroyers being refitted and modernized in Britain for the Egyptian navy. In 1956, Soviet aid provided twelve motor torpedo boats, four fleet minesweepers, and two destroyers. Furthermore, there were reports in mid-1956 that two Soviet submarines were sailing from Poland, bound for Egypt. Yugoslavia also contributed six motor torpedo boats to the Egyptian navy in 1956.[4]

[1] As stated earlier, note 7, p. 247, the actual agreement was probably concluded much earlier.
[2] Barker, op. cit., pp. 61–4; Bernard B. Fall: "Two Sides of the Sinai Campaign," *Military Review,* July 1957, pp. 4–23; Dayan, op. cit., p. 101.
[3] Seim, op. cit., p. 47.
[4] *Jane's Fighting Ships* (1965–1966 edn.; London: Sampson Low, Marston and Co.; 1965), pp. 71–3.

There is no information available on the terms under which British weapons were supplied to Egypt. Weapons obtained between 1951 and 1954 by circumvention of the ban on military exports to the Middle East were, of course, purchased outright, and probably for a high price. When the Soviet bloc signed its first military-aid agreement with Egypt, the terms of payment are believed to have been for barter over a period of ten to twelve years, probably with very favorable prices.[5] As far as can be determined, these terms in themselves had no appreciable effect on Egypt in the short period of time that ensued before the Sinai campaign. Similarly, maintenance and resupply do not seem to have presented problems to Egypt. Undoubtedly, Soviet technicians accompanied the weapons to Egypt to maintain them; but lack of operational training must have been an obstacle to effective use of the Soviet weapons by Egyptian forces. This is most evident in the case of the MiG fighters and Il-28 bombers in the Suez crisis. There were no Egyptian pilots who were willing or able to fly the MiG fighters to attack or escape, and the Il-28 bombers were apparently flown to safety by Soviet or Czech pilots. It is most likely that no Soviet controls over the use of the weapons supplied to Egypt were included in the contract. If control were to have been attempted through the supply of spare parts and ammunition, this would only have been effective in a conflict extending over a longer period of time than the Sinai campaign.

Weapons Available to Egypt in 1956

Weapon	Number	Source
.303-cal. No. 1 Lee Enfield rifle	?	U.K.
7.92mm FN Model 1949 semi-automatic rifle	50,000	Belgium
7.62mm rifle	?	Czechoslovakia/ U.S.S.R.
7.92mm Model 42 Ljungman rifle (Hakim)	?	Egypt, license from Sweden
9mm Model 45 submachine gun (Port Said)	?	Egypt, license from Sweden

[5] David Wood: *The Armed Forces of African States,* Adelphi Paper No. 27 (London: Institute for Strategic Studies; April 1966), p. 25.

Weapon	Number	Source
7.92mm Type D automatic rifle	?	Belgium
9mm Beretta submachine gun	?	Italy
9mm Sten submachine gun	?	U.K.
Lewis machine gun	?	U.K.
Bren machine gun	?	U.K.
Vickers machine gun	?	U.K.
7.92mm Alfa heavy machine gun	?	Spain
.82mm recoilless rifle	?	Czechoslovakia
85mm bazooka	?	U.S.S.R.
120mm coastal-defense gun	?	U.S.S.R.
120mm heavy mortar	12 batteries	?
6-pounder antitank gun	about 100	U.K.
antitank mortar	30 platoons	?
57mm antitank gun	140–150	U.S.S.R.
17-pounder antitank gun mounted on Valentine/Archer	50–60	U.K.
122mm gun	about 30	Czechoslovakia
152mm gun	?	U.S.S.R.
25-pounder howitzer	about 120	U.K.
155mm howitzer	about 30	U.S.S.R.
.40mm Bofors anti-aircraft gun	?	Sweden
.30mm Hispano Suiza anti-aircraft gun	?	?
flame thrower mounted on "Wasp"	?	U.K.
rocket launcher	?	U.S.S.R.
Bren carrier	over 300	U.K.
SU-100 self-propelled artillery	100	U.S.S.R.
M4 Sherman tank (modernized)	150–200	U.S.
T-34 medium tank	200–250	U.S.S.R.
JS-2 tank with 122mm gun	50–60	U.S.S.R.
Valentine tank without 17-pounder gun	?	U.K.
Charioteer tank	?	U.K.
Centurion Mk.3 tank	30	U.K.
BTR-152 six-wheel troop carrier	100–200	U.S.S.R.
AMX-13 light tank	a few	France
Spitfire fighter aircraft	more than 20	U.K.
Meteor fighter aircraft	60–70	U.K.
Vampire fighter aircraft (Mk.5)	20–30	Italy-Syria
MiG-15 fighter	?	U.S.S.R.
MiG-17 fighter	150–200	U.S.S.R.
Halifax bomber	30	U.K.
Lancaster bomber	?	U.K.

Weapon	Number	Source
Il-28 bomber	40–50	U.S.S.R.
corvette	2	U.K.
motor torpedo boat	2	U.K.
motor torpedo boat	12	U.S.S.R.
motor torpedo boat	6	Yugoslavia
coastal minesweeper	6	U.S.
fleet minesweeper	4	U.S.S.R.
frigate	7	U.K.
destroyer	4	U.S.S.R.
destroyer	2 (on order)	U.K.

Israeli Weapons Acquisition

When the state of Israel was established in 1948, its forces were armed with a wide assortment of old weapons, many presumably left behind by the British. With the aid of Czechoslovakia, Panama, Yugoslavia, and pilots of various nationalities, the Israelis had purchased a number of small arms and aircraft in 1947–1948. A secret Israeli transport command, perhaps an adjunct of the Israeli air force but composed of U.S., British, South African, and Israeli pilots, operated throughout the world acquiring arms for Israel.[6] Among other things, this command has been credited with: transporting to Israel quantities of small arms, presumably Czech-built Mausers and ZB-37 heavy machine guns, all the foregoing purchased in Czechoslovakia in mid-1948; causing the disappearance from Britain of a number of aircraft, including fighters, bombers, and transports, without export licenses and delivering them to Israel; operating LAPSA, a Panamanian airlines which was ostensibly surveying a route across the South Atlantic; and purchasing a number of aircraft for Israel, including Boeing B-17 bombers, Vickers Spitfire fighters, Avro Lancaster bombers, North American Harvard attack trainers, Bristol Beaufighters, and Czech-built Messerschmitt ME-109 fighters.

By October 1948, the inventory of the Israeli air force was

[6] Kagan, op. cit., provides a detailed account of this operation.

said to include: six C-46 transports; a handful of Harvards; P-51 Mustangs; Beaufighters; DC-3's; Rapides; twelve Messerschmitts; three B-17's; two Mosquitoes; two Norsemen; and a DC-4. At this time, Israeli mechanics were quite adept at repairing and rebuilding these assorted aircraft.[7]

Between 1948 and 1951, Israel bought a large number of Sherman Mark 3 tanks from war-surplus dealers in Europe and reconditioned them, equipping them with larger guns, wider tracks, or whatever modification Israel's needs required. Some 500 war-surplus half-tracks were secured from the United States in 1948.[8] There were also a number of old British Cromwell tanks in Israel.

Most of Israel's artillery also seems to have been acquired early in the nation's existence. British 25-pounders and some 105mm and 155mm guns, along with Czech mortars and artillery, made up a total of about 400 artillery weapons by 1956. Israel began to develop its own design and production facilities for a family of mortars ranging from 61mm to 120mm; and, by 1956, Israeli forces were amply equipped with these weapons.[9] Israel also had a smaller number of 6-pounder and 17-pounder antitank guns.

The wide variety of Israeli small arms during the early days of independence must have created problems with ammunition supply. After 1948, however, Israel tried to standardize on the 7.92mm cartridge for rifles and machine guns and the 9mm cartridge for pistols and submachine guns. A large number of 8mm M40 Mausers were bought from Sweden and rebarreled. Israel had purchased the machinery from Switzerland to manufacture the 7.92 Mauser, but the decision was later taken to standardize on the 7.62 NATO cartridge. No Mausers were ever produced in Israel, though there was an Israeli ammunition factory producing the 7.92 Mauser cartridge. An Israeli general developed the Uzi submachine gun, suited to the needs of the

[7] Lawrence Lader: "From Junk Heap to Air Might," *New Republic*, November 8, 1948, pp. 10–12; Robert H. Luttrell: "I Flew for Israel," *Flying*, May 1949, pp. 23, 58, 60; Rabbi Samuel Burstein: "Israel Aviation," *Flying*, February 1962, p. 44.

[8] Beckley, op. cit., p. 9.   [9] Ibid.

Israeli forces, and it went into production in Israel. Fabrique Nationale of Belgium began to supply 7.62mm NATO automatic rifles and light machine guns to the Israeli forces before 1956.[1]

In the early 1950's, France appears to have become a supplier of more modern arms to Israel. By September 1956, Israel was in possession of some 100 AMX-13 light tanks with 75mm high-velocity guns,[2] Nord SS-10 antitank missiles,[3] some 30 Ouragan jet fighter aircraft,[4] and about 24 Mystère IVA jet fighters.[5] It has been reported that, when Israel was drawing up its plans for the Sinai attack, a request was made to the French government for "100 tanks (Super Shermans), 300 half-track vehicles, 50 tank-transporters, 300 trucks with four-wheel drive, 1,000 bazookas, and a squadron of transport planes."[6] Of this number, 200 half-tracks, 100 Super Shermans, 20 tank-transporters, and 300 trucks were supplied by France in October 1956.[7] In addition, there were as many as 36 Mystère IV aircraft flown into Israel on the eve of the Sinai attack; but it is unlikely that there would have been enough Israeli pilots to fly all of them, because the Israeli air force had found it difficult to train the necessary pilots for the 37 Mystère IV fighters that General Dayan claims were available to the Israelis when they attacked.[8] Thus, by late October 1956, the Israeli air force had available for combat about 64 piston-engine aircraft, mostly of World War II vintage, and 79 jet fighters.[9]

It is estimated that in 1956 Israel was maintaining a standing army of about 50,000 that could be expanded within forty-eight hours to as many as 125,000. According to General Dayan, ten brigades were committed to fighting in Sinai: six infantry, three armored, and one airborne. Since the Israeli brigade is composed of 5,000 to 6,000 men, then 50,000 to 60,000 would have been engaged in Sinai. Apparently, the total Israeli

[1] Smith and Smith, op. cit., p. 296; Smith, op. cit., pp. 264–7.

[2] Beckley, op. cit., p. 9.

[3] Richard Ogorkiewicz: "Missiles Against Armor," *Marine Corps Gazette,* January 1959, pp. 53–4.   [4] Fall, op. cit., p. 10.

[5] *U.S. News and World Report,* October 26, 1956, p. 104.

[6] Dayan, op. cit., p. 30.   [7] Ibid., p. 34.   [8] Ibid., p. 80.   [9] Ibid.

armored strength was used, because there was only enough armor for three brigades.[1]

It appears that, before 1956, Israel paid outright for imported weapons. Various funds, contributed to by Jewish sympathizers all over the world, went far toward making this possible.[2]

It is clear from the history of Israeli arms acquisition before 1956 that no supplier (except possibly France) could have held any control over the use of the weapons by Israel. France does not seem to have been concerned with limiting their use and was in fact aware that French-supplied weapons would be used by Israel against Egypt.[3]

Weapons Available to Israel in 1956

Weapon	Number	Source
.303-cal. No. 1 and No. 4 Lee Enfield rifle	?	U.K.
7.92mm Kar 98K Mauser	?	Czechoslovakia
8.0mm M40 Mauser	?	Sweden
7.62mm FN automatic rifle	?	Belgium
7.62mm FN light machine gun	?	Belgium
0.5-cal. Browning	?	?
9mm Sten submachine gun	?	U.K.
9mm Uzi submachine gun	?	Israel
7.92mm ZB-37 heavy machine gun	?	Czechoslovakia
Beza medium machine gun	?	U.K.
106mm recoilless rifle	?	?
50mm (2″) mortar	?	U.K.
61mm platoon mortar	?	Israel
81mm mortar	?	Israel
82mm mortar	?	Czechoslovakia
120mm heavy mortar	?	Israel, license from Finland
120mm M1951 Roanne mortar	?	France
multiple-rocket launcher	?	?

[1] Beckley, op. cit., pp. 7–9.
[2] John C. Ross: "Air War in Palestine," *Flying,* October 1948, p. 74.
[3] Dayan, op. cit., pp. 30, 34.

Weapon	Number	Source
120mm mortar	?	Czechoslovakia
6-pounder antitank artillery	}	U.K.
17-pounder antitank artillery	}	U.K.
25-pounder field gun	} 400	U.K.
105mm self-propelled field gun	}	?
155mm field gun	}	?
88mm M36 German AA gun	?	Czechoslovakia (?)
Cromwell tank	perhaps up to 50	U.K.
Sherman Mk3 tank	perhaps 100–150	U.S. war surplus
Super Sherman	100	France
AMX-13 tank with 75mm gun	100	France
armored half-track	up to 500	U.S.
armored half-track	200	France
SS-10 antitank missile	a few	France
Mosquito fighter-bomber aircraft	13	France
P-51 Mustang fighter	25	Sweden
Spitfire fighter	some for training	Italy
Meteor jet fighter	12	U.K.
Mystère IVA fighter	37 (only 16 operational)	France
Ouragan fighter-bomber	30	France
B-17 bomber	2	U.S. or Canada
Harvard bomber	21	U.S.
landing craft	several	U.S.
patrol vessel (sub chaser)	1	U.S.
motor torpedo boat	3	U.K.
motor torpedo boat	6	France
coast-guard cutter	1	W. Germany
destroyer	2	U.K.

ARMS ACQUISITION, 1956–1967

Egyptian Weapons Acquisition

Egypt suffered severe losses of equipment in 1956. In the Sinai campaign about 7,600 small arms, 290 pieces of artillery and heavy mortars, and 200 tanks and self-propelled guns (of these, the majority were U.S. and British models) were claimed by the Israelis to have been captured.[4] An estimated 50 per cent of the Egyptian aircraft inventory was lost in the British-French attack.[5]

The Soviet Union responded quickly with new arms supplies to Egypt, reportedly resuming the shipments as early as February 1957. The build-up was most readily noticeable in the Egyptian air force. Within six months after Suez, the Soviet Union sent 100 MiG-17 fighters to Egypt and enough Il-28 bombers to make a total of 60 by late 1958. In 1961 and 1962, 80 to 110 MiG-19 fighters were delivered.[6] Israel claims that a new Soviet-Egyptian agreement was reached in 1960 providing for the supply of MiG-21 fighters and Tu-16 medium bombers.[7] After 1962, about 130 MiG-21's, including 40 to 50 MiG-21D all-weather fighters, were supplied to Egypt.[8] The arrival in 1962 of the Tu-16 bomber, capable of carrying a 10,000-pound bomb load over a range of about 3,000 miles, marked a radical departure from customary export procedures of the main supplier countries.[9] The Egyptians began deploying Soviet-supplied SA-2 surface-to-air missiles in 1963, but it was not until 1966 that they became, with the force of MiG-21's, integrated into a complete air-defense system on permanent sites and with the necessary radar and computer support.[1] The first Egyptian squadron of about a dozen Soviet Su-7 supersonic fighters became operational in early 1967, but it was still listed as a reserve element in June 1967.[2]

---

[4] Dayan, op. cit., pp. 227–8.

[5] John H. Hoagland, Jr., and John B. Teeple: "Regional Stability and Weapons Transfer: The Middle Eastern Case," *Orbis,* Vol. IX, No. 3 (Fall 1965), p. 716.

[6] Major Edgar O'Ballance: "Middle East Arms Race," *United Service Quarterly,* Vol. 18, No. 3 (January–April 1965), pp. 11–12.

[7] Ibid., p. 10.

[8] *The Military Balance: 1966–67* (London: Institute for Strategic Studies; 1966), p. 41; *The New York Times,* July 24, 1966.

[9] The only other reported case of Soviet transfers of the Tu-16 to the developing world was to Indonesia. No transfers of systems of comparable performance have been made by the United States.

[1] *Flying Review,* April 1967, p. 487.   [2] Ibid., August 1967, p. 769.

In armor, the Soviets supplied immediately after the 1956 war additional T-34/85 tanks, JS-2 heavy tanks, SU-100 self-propelled guns, and contracted in 1960 to supply up to 500 T-54 tanks.[3] The first T-55 tank, with infrared lights and radar, was displayed by Egypt in 1966. Soviet military shipments to the U.A.R. also included the SU-152 self-propelled gun and the ZSU-57-2 self-propelled anti-aircraft gun. By June 1967, Egyptian forces possessed substantial numbers of Soviet heavy howitzers and long-range, rapid-fire field guns of recent design. Israeli Foreign Minister Abba Eban claimed that, between 1955 and 1967, the Soviets supplied Egypt with more than 1000 tanks and 2200 field guns, mortars, anti-aircraft guns, and antitank guns.[4]

Egyptian ground forces were supported by a number of Soviet and Czech rocket launchers, ranging from 130mm to 240mm and capable of firing up to thirty-two rockets at a time. The Soviet AT-1 antitank wire-guided missile mounted on the GAZ-69 was also deployed in the Egyptian army by June 1967.[5]

Egyptian forces were presumably equally well equipped with small arms. Soviet weapons became standard in the Egyptian army after 1956; it is likely that the Soviet and Czech rifles and submachine guns that were included in early shipments are being replaced by the superior AK-47. This latter was captured in large quantities by the Israelis in June 1967.[6] The Egyptian small-arms industry has modified the design of the Swedish models being produced before 1956 to the point where they can now be regarded as Egyptian models. Ammunition for all Egyptian service weapons is produced in the U.A.R.[7]

The missile and aircraft programs in Egypt, which began in 1960, employ German and Austrian technicians. Having been initially developed in Spain, the HA-300 supersonic-fighter

[3] *U.S. News and World Report,* November 7, 1958, p. 67.

[4] Ibid., July 3, 1967, p. 20.

[5] *Interavia: International Defense Review,* Vol. XXIII, No. 11 (November 1967), pp. 1635–6.   [6] Smith, op. cit., p. 613.   [7] Ibid.

project was transferred to Egypt in 1960, where it was continued under the direction of Ferdinand Brandner, an Austrian
engineer. By 1965, two HA-300 aircraft were flying in Egypt
under the power of the subsonic Orpheus 703 engine. India
recently joined Egypt in this program, hoping to combine the
Egyptian E-300 engine with the Indian HF-24 airframe. It has
been reported, however, that serious problems have been encountered in this E-300/HF-24 program. The first test flight in
1966 was disappointing.[8]

The Egyptian missile-development program has been actively
pressed. In 1962 the first two Egyptian missiles, Al Kahir (325-
mile range) and Al Zafir (200-mile range), were displayed in
Cairo. The next year, another Egyptian missile appeared, the Al
Ared, with about a 500-mile range.[9] No Egyptian missiles were
fired in the June war, suggesting that they do not yet constitute
a significant weapons system.

The Egyptian navy has received the majority of its equipment
from the Soviet Union. Its inventory in 1966 included 18
missile patrol boats, 10 minesweepers, 6 escort vessels, 11
submarines, and 6 destroyers—all provided with Soviet aid; 2
additional ex-British destroyers were operational, and some
recent purchases had been made in Britain. Egypt announced in
1966 the successful completion of tests on an Egyptian-built
submarine and an Egyptian-built motor torpedo boat, although
no details were given on these projects.[1]

The main trend in Egyptian military acquisition since 1956
has been toward complete dependence on Soviet supplies. Many
Egyptian pilots and officers have been trained in the Soviet bloc,
and Soviet military advisers and technicians have accompanied
Soviet arms to Egypt.

In May 1967 the strength of the Egyptian forces, including
reservists, was 180,000 men.

[8] *Flying Review,* September 1967, p. 833.
[9] Hoagland and Teeple, op. cit., p. 218.
[1] *Jane's Fighting Ships,* 1965–1966 edn., pp. 71–3.

Weapons Available to Egypt on June 1, 1967

Small Arms	Number	Source
7.92mm Hakim rifle	?	Egypt
7.62mm Rashid rifle	?	Egypt
7.92mm FN rifle	?	Belgium
7.92mm Type D automatic rifle	?	Belgium
7.62mm SKS carbine		U.S.S.R.
7.62mm M52 rifle	100,000–200,000	Czechoslovakia
7.62mm AK assault rifle		U.S.S.R.
9mm Port Said submachine gun	?	Egypt
9mm Beretta submachine gun	?	Italy
9mm Sten submachine gun	?	U.K.
7.62mm submachine gun (U.S.S.R.)		U.S.S.R.
7.62mm submachine gun (Czech)	100,000–200,000	Czechoslovakia
7.62mm submachine gun (China)		China
7.92mm Alpha machine gun		Spain
7.62mm Model 52 machine gun		Czechoslovakia
7.62mm SG and SGM 43-cal. machine gun	3,000–5,000	U.S.S.R.
7.62mm RPD machine gun		U.S.S.R.
12.7mm DShK heavy machine gun	up to 2,000	U.S.S.R.
14.5mm ZPU-2 and ZPU-4 heavy anti-aircraft machine gun	200–300	U.S.S.R.

Medium and Heavy Weapons

	Number	Source
45mm bazooka (rocket launcher) P-27		U.S.S.R.
82mm bazooka (AT rocket launcher) SPG 62	200–400	U.S.S.R.
RPG-2 antitank rocket launcher		U.S.S.R.
57mm antitank gun M-43		U.S.S.R.
85mm antitank gun M-45	650	U.S.S.R.
100mm antitank field gun M-44		U.S.S.R.

Medium and Heavy Weapons	Number	Source
37mm automatic anti-aircraft gun M-39		U.S.S.R.
57mm anti-aircraft gun S-60	700	U.S.S.R.
85mm anti-aircraft gun M-44		Czechoslovakia
100mm anti-aircraft gun KS-19		U.S.S.R.
82mm recoilless rifle T-21 (Czech)	?	Czechoslovakia
82mm recoilless rifle B-10	?	U.S.S.R.
107mm recoilless rifle B-11	?	U.S.S.R.
82mm mortar M-37		U.S.S.R.
120mm mortar M-43	400–500	U.S.S.R.
160mm mortar M-53		U.S.S.R.
85mm field gun D-44		U.S.S.R.
105mm howitzer		U.S.S.R.
122mm corps gun	540	U.S.S.R.
122mm howitzer M-38		U.S.S.R.
122mm howitzer D-30 (M-63)		U.S.S.R.
130mm cannon M-76 (long-range)	?	U.S.S.R.
152mm howitzer M-37	?	U.S.S.R.
130mm coastal-defense gun	?	U.S.S.R.
132mm BM-13 multiple-rocket launcher		U.S.S.R.
130mm M-51 multiple-rocket launcher	175	U.S.S.R./ Czecho- slovakia
240mm BM-24 multiple-rocket launcher		U.S.S.R.
AT-1 antitank guided missile "Snapper" (on GAZ-69)	?	U.S.S.R.

Self-Propelled Artillery

ZSU-57-2 anti-aircraft gun	50	U.S.S.R.
SU-100 assault gun	150	U.S.S.R.
JSU-152 assault gun	50	U.S.S.R.

Tanks[2]

PT-76 light amphibious tank	50	U.S.S.R.
T-34 (85) medium tank	800	U.S.S.R.
T-54/55 medium tank		U.S.S.R.
JS-2 heavy tank	50–60	U.S.S.R.
Centurion Mk.3	less than 30	U.K.

[2] AMX-13's may still be in use with the reserves.

Armored Personnel Carriers	Number	Source
B40	?	U.S.S.R.
B152	?	U.S.S.R.
BTR-50	?	U.S.S.R.

Combat Aircraft		
MiG-15	50	U.S.S.R./ Czechoslovakia
MiG-17	100	U.S.S.R./ Czechoslovakia
MiG-19	40	U.S.S.R.
MiG-21	130–60	U.S.S.R.
Su-7	15–20	U.S.S.R.
Il-28	40–60	U.S.S.R./ Czechoslovakia
Tu-16	30	U.S.S.R.

Missiles		
Safir surface-to-surface missile	?	U.S.S.R.
Spoka 2 surface-to-surface missile	?	U.S.S.R.
Luna-1 surface-to-surface missile	?	U.S.S.R.
SA-2 surface-to-air missile	120 launchers	U.S.S.R.
Al Kahir surface-to-surface missile	about 100	Egypt
Al Ared surface-to-surface missile		Egypt
Al Zafir surface-to-surface missile		Egypt

Israeli Weapons Acquisition

Having achieved relative success in the Sinai campaign,[3] Israel spent the next decade maintaining military parity with Egypt, not so much by acquiring equal amounts of military equipment

[3] That is: Having achieved the objectives of ending Egyptian *fedayin* terrorism, neutralizing the immediate threat of an Egyptian-Syrian-Jordanian attack on Israel, and breaking the shipping blockade in the Gulf of Aqaba . . .

as by concentrating on fewer numbers of men and arms backed
by adequate training and maintained in a high state of operational readiness. Israel made an effort to equal Egypt's offensive
and defensive capabilities qualitatively.

Israel's supplies continued to come from a variety of sources,
but France stood out as the major one. After 1956, France
sold Mystère subsonic fighters, Mirage III supersonic fighters
(armed with Matra air-to-air missiles), Ouragan fighter-
bombers, and Vautour II fighter-bombers to the Israeli air
force.[4] French-Israeli cooperation in the missile field became
well established. The Nord SS-10 antitank missiles, which are
said to have proven themselves well in the Sinai campaign, were
superseded by SS-11 antitank missiles.[5] Early in 1966 it was
confirmed that French aerospace companies were cooperating
with Israel in research that might lead to the development of a
medium-range, two-stage missile based on the French SEREB
Topaze test vehicle. There were indications that the project was
military in nature.[6] An earlier report that France had sold
surface-to-surface missiles to Israel was denied by both the
French and the Israelis, but the evidence does suggest that
France was prepared to support Israeli MRBM procurement.[7]

In 1962 the United States became of growing importance to
Israel as an arms supplier. The 1962 agreement for the transfer
of Hawk surface-to-air missiles from the United States to Israel
was an important factor in the Middle Eastern arms race. This
apparently followed a Soviet military-assistance agreement with
Egypt that included the provision of MiG-19's and MiG-21's.[8]
In 1965 about 200 M-48 Patton tanks were acquired by Israel
from West Germany under U.S. agreement.[9] In early 1966 the
United States agreed to supply Israel with a number (possibly

---

[4] William Green: *The World's Fighting Planes* (New York: Doubleday; 1965), pp. 18, 21, 24.   [5] *The Military Balance: 1966–67*, p. 38.
[6] *Aviation Week and Space Technology*, January 19, 1966, p. 27. It
is not clear what impact the French post-1967 embargo on arms ship-
ment to Israel has had on this program.
[7] *Missiles and Rockets*, January 17, 1966, p. 13.
[8] Harold A. Hovey: *United States Military Assistance* (New York:
Praeger; 1965), p. 45.   [9] *Time*, February 25, 1966, p. 39.

18 to 24) of A-4 Skyhawk light attack bombers. The agreement, however, is said to have been accompanied by strict controls on future Israeli arms acquisitions.[1]

Britain's contributions to Israeli military power after 1956 were Centurion tanks and two submarines.[2] West Germany signed an agreement with Israel, presumably in 1964 and with the approval of the United States, for the supply of large quantities of military equipment[3] as part of Germany's reparation to the Jewish people. Before delivery could be completed, Egypt was successful in pressuring West Germany to discontinue supplying Israel with arms. However, 70 to 80 per cent of the original consignment is reported to have arrived in Israel, including 200 M-48 Patton tanks, five motor torpedo boats, several fighter-bombers, and a number of antitank guns.[4]

In small arms and certain battlefield weapons, Israel appears to have achieved relative self-sufficiency. Belgium, in particular Fabrique Nationale, played a large role in this process; by 1961, Fabrique Nationale had been contracted by Israel to manufacture the Uzi submachine gun, and Israel in return had licensing agreements for the production of parts for the 7.62mm FN automatic rifle.[5] It is now reported that Israel is licensed by Fabrique Nationale for the entire production of the 7.62mm FN automatic rifle for Israeli troops.[6] In addition, Israel is known to produce its own LTH flame throwers and Metol 82mm bazookas, which play an antitank role in Israeli strategy in place of medium artillery.[7] Israel produces a whole range of mortars, up to 160mm, the largest of which are mounted on half-tracks. In the case of tanks, the AMX was combined with the Sherman M4 to produce light and medium tanks with high-

---

[1] *Aviation Week and Space Technology*, May 30, 1966. The first of these aircraft were not delivered until December 1967.
[2] J. C. Hurewitz: "The Role of the Military in Israel," in *The Military in the Middle East* (Columbus: Ohio State University Press; 1963), p. 97.
[3] *The New York Times*, January 31, 1965.
[4] Manchester *Guardian*, February 13, 1965.
[5] *Times* (London), December 1, 1961.
[6] Leo Heiman: "Israeli Infantry," *Infantry*, May–June 1964, p. 46.
[7] Ibid., pp. 46–7.

velocity 75mm guns and good maneuverability.[8] Also, 155mm howitzers were placed on Sherman chassis and 105mm on AMX chassis to produce at least 250 self-propelled guns.[9] The Israeli aircraft industry has developed a great capacity for supplying aircraft with spare parts, thus maintaining a high operational percentage.[1] Under license to Potez of France, it also manufactures the Fouga Magister jet trainer and has begun exporting this aircraft.[2]

Israel's navy, though small, has received considerable amounts of new equipment. Motor patrol boats have been acquired from France and Italy, coast-guard cutters from West Germany, and submarines from Britain.[3]

In June 1967 the total number of regulars in the Israeli armed forces was 71,000, but, as was demonstrated, this could be expanded to about 275,000 in two to four days.[4]

In recent years there were recurrent indications that Israel, through the construction and operation of its power reactor at Dimona in the Negev desert, had procured the option to produce nuclear weapons. It is not clear to what extent the Dimona reactor is viewed in this manner by Israel. In any event, there is still no evidence that Israel has launched on a program to build on this option.

Weapons Available to Israel on June 1, 1967

Small Arms	Number	Source
7.62mm FN "FAL" rifle	100,000–200,000	Israel
9mm Uzi submachine gun	100,000–200,000	Israel
7.62mm Kar 98K (rebarreled)		Czechoslovakia
.303-cal. Lee Enfield rifle	with home defense forces	U.K.
.303-cal. Bren and Vickers machine guns		U.K./Czechoslovakia
9mm Sten submachine gun		U.K.
7.92mm MG34		Czechoslovakia

[8] *Armor*, May–June 1962, p. 41.
[9] *The Military Balance: 1966–67*, p. 37.
[1] In particular, Dassault licensed the production of spare parts in Israel.
[2] *Economist*, March 21, 1964, p. 1139.
[3] *Jane's Fighting Ships*, 1965–1966 edn., pp. 137–8.
[4] *The Military Balance: 1966–67*, p. 37.

Small Arms	Number	Source
7.62mm FN "MAG" machine gun	about 10,000?	Belgium
.30-cal. Browning machine gun	on armored vehicles	U.S.
.50-cal. Browning machine gun		U.S.
7.92mm Besa machine gun		U.K.

Medium and Heavy Weapons

	Number	Source
LTH flame thrower	?	Israel
82mm Metol bazooka	?	Israel
61mm platoon mortar	?	Israel
81mm Soltam mortar	?	Israel
120mm mortar on armored half-track	?	Israel
160mm mortar on armored half-track	?	Israel
106mm jeep-mounted recoilless rifle	?	?
L-70 mobile anti-aircraft gun (three 40mm Bofors on each)	?	Sweden
SS-10 and SS-11 on weapons carriers	?	France
105mm self-propelled gun (on AMX chassis)	250	Israeli adaptations
155mm self-propelled gun (on Sherman chassis)		
AMX-13	140	France
Super Sherman with 105mm gun	175	France
Centurion with 105mm gun	250	U.K.
M-48 Patton	225	U.S./W. Germany
armored bulldozer	?	?
armored half-track	up to 500	U.S.
armored half-track	less than 200	France
armored reconnaissance car w/90mm gun		France

Combat Aircraft

	Number	Source
Ouragan	50	France
Vautour IIA	25	France
Mirage III CJ	72	France
Mystère IVA	45	France
Super Mystère	20	France
Magister	60	Israel

Missiles	Number	Source
Hawk surface-to-air missile	2 battalions	U.S.
Navy		
landing craft	several	U.S.
motor torpedo boat	5	W. Germany
patrol vessel	1	U.S.
motor torpedo boat	3	U.K.
motor torpedo boat	6	France
motor torpedo boat	3	Italy
coast-guard cutter	2	W. Germany
frigate	1	Egypt
destroyer	2	U.K.
submarine ("S" class)	2	U.K.

A Special Problem of Control

One feature of Israeli and Egyptian arms acquisition that has special implications is that both, while still very much arms importers, have become arms *suppliers* in their own right. Israel has licensed the production of the Uzi submachine gun to Fabrique Nationale of Belgium and has sold small arms to other countries. It has also supplied to Uganda the Magister trainer aircraft, which was produced in Israel under license to Potez of France. Egypt's arms exports have mostly been Soviet weapons, although a few have been other types of obsolete weapons in the Egyptian arsenal. When the Soviet Union agreed to supply Egypt with MiG-21 fighters, Egypt began to sell its MiG-17 aircraft to help pay for the MiG-21's.

SUMMARY OF CONTROL MEASURES

In summary form, the key conflict-control measures in these cases might have been the following (an asterisk indicates that the measure was actually taken):

The Arab-Israeli Conflict

PREVENTING THE RESUMPTION OF HOSTILITIES IN 1956

Settlement of the underlying disputes on borders, refugees, waters, etc.,
With help of:
Unified pressures by the United Nations, great powers, and other external suppliers.
Readmission by Israel of symbolic numbers of refugees and compensation of others with international financial help.
Resettlement of refugees with international help.
Threat of unified Suez Canal boycott by users.
Threat of military action by maritime and air powers to reinforce rights.*
Retention of third-party troops for deterrence and intelligence,
Or:
Expanded international presence.
More effective identification, verification, and condemnation of raids and reprisals.
Joint or third-party border patrols backed by strong international support and sanctions.
Physical sealing of the Israeli border, with permission only to admit the United Nations.
Condemnation of propaganda warfare,
Accompanied by:
Increase in flow of UN broadcasts,
With aid of:
Strengthened UN information activity with satellite facilities.
Agreements among suppliers to restrict sale of arms to states likely to be engaged in conflict.
Enforcement of border guarantees.
Manipulation of and involvement in internal affairs.

PREVENTING THE RESUMPTION OF HOSTILITIES IN 1967

As before:

Settlement of the underlying dispute; above all, acceptance of Israel's right as state to exist, also the substantive issues of waterways, borders, refugees, Jordan waters, etc.
Readmission by Israel of symbolic numbers of refugees and compensation of others with international financial help.
Resettlement of refugees with international help.
Retention of third-party (UN) troops for deterrence and intelligence.*

Threat of military action by maritime powers to reinforce rights.
More effective international identification, verification, and condemnation of raids and reprisals.*
Agreements among suppliers to restrict sale of arms to states likely
to be engaged in conflict.
Internally, Israeli multiracial policy; and Arab search for other
bases for unity than hatred of Israel.

In addition:

Pressure on Soviets to abandon influence-seeking policies in area.
U.S. willingness to abandon partialty for Israel,
And:
U.S. impartiality among Arab factions,
Necessitating:
Distinguishing better between nationalist and Communist forces.
Credible U.S. willingness to intervene to back its commitments,
preferably through UN but unilaterally if necessary.
Extension of UN forces to other (i.e., Syrian and Jordanian) borders.
Overcoming Security Council veto in order to apply even-handed
justice to complaints from both sides; i.e., recourse to
General Assembly before war.
Reiteration of previous UN resolutions about free use of Suez
Canal and Gulf of Aqaba.
Further development of technological and other substitutes for
Middle Eastern oil* and river waters—nuclear-energy
and desalination plants, etc.
Distractions of Egyptian army.*
Assistance to Egypt particularly in national-defense planning and
improved intelligence.
A courageous and inventive UN Secretary-General.

TERMINATING RESUMED HOSTILITIES IN 1967

Maintenance of local military balance at lowest possible level,
keeping destabilizing weapons out of area,
Or:
Overwhelming advantage to one side.*
Threat of great-power involvement.
Absence of nihilistic goals, or international pressure to keep them
limited.
"Hot line" equivalents between local adversaries—through neutral
embassy, press service, etc.

The British-French-Egyptian (Suez) Conflict

KEEPING THE DISPUTE NONMILITARY

Development of strategic substitutes for oil and land bases:
Nuclear energy,

       Long-range air-lift capabilities,

       Sea-based and land-based missile alternatives,

       Relocation of canal routes.

International regime for vital waterways.

Recognition of sense of regional identity and independence.

Support of popular regimes.

Encouragement of constructive internal and regional developmental
       goals.*

Strengthening of internal political, social, and economic fabric.

Multilateralizing of significant aspects of economic assistance.

Agreement by third parties to abstain from special privileges or
       exacerbation of local quarrels.

PREVENTING THE OUTBREAK OF HOSTILITIES

Encouragement of internal opposition to warmakers.

Candid explanation of parties' aims and limits of their intentions.

Compromise, good offices, negotiations—all accompanied by guar-
       antees.

Abandonment of overseas colonies.

Elimination of foreign bases.

MODERATING/TERMINATING HOSTILITIES

Early and credible superpower and UN deterrent threats.*

Balancing of arms in region.

Restraining agreements among external arms suppliers.

U.S.-Soviet convergence of interests.*

Stand-by UN peacekeeping force,*
    With:

Contingency plans for rapid recruitment and deployment.

Lessons for Conflict Control from the Five Conflicts

In Chapter 3, in describing our research on fourteen of the fifty-four post-World War II conflicts, we dealt with total numbers of control measures that we found applicable; these measures were interesting in the way they distributed themselves along the dynamic course of conflict and among different types of policy actions. *How these measures could actually have been applied* was, however, partly obscure. Let us make this "How" more concrete by looking at what our five illustrative local-conflict cases in this volume may have to suggest to *today's* policy makers.

The five cases illustrate some widely different kinds of conflict-control issues that have confronted the United States and equally varied U.S. responses to them. In Iran in the 1940's, for example, the Soviet Union fomented a conflict in which U.S. interest grew as its perceptions of Soviet policy changed. But in those opening days of the Cold War, the U.S. role was indirect and low-key. Toward Cuba two decades later, on the other hand, the United States cast itself in the role of conflict fomenter, seeking to oust a regime in Cuba that seemed to have come increasingly under Soviet domination.

Toward Greece in the late 1940's, against a background of deepening Cold War, the United States became heavily committed to the struggle against an insurgency that was ultimately dominated by Greek Communists and exploited by neighboring Communist states for their own national and ideological purposes. The parallels with Vietnam in recent years are striking, but with the very important distinction that U.S. forces were not directly committed to the fighting in Greece.

The Indonesian War of Independence illustrated a fast-vanishing variety of conflicts—war against a colonial power. But it was not of only historic interest. Many of the features of this four-year war are found in conflicts fought for other goals. And, more important, although colonialism in its nineteenth-century manifestation may be nearing extinction, other, less overt forms of domination still persist. Moreover, moves toward expansion continue to occur—sometimes with the victims of past colonial domination now acting the role of "imperialist." The U.S. stance during the largest part of the Indonesian conflict was that of the neutral good-officer. In the end, however, the U.S. brought to bear its powerful political and economic influence on one of the parties—the Dutch—and moved the conflict rapidly from bloodshed to Settlement.

Both the U.S. and Soviets have taken ambivalent postures in the cluster of conflicts that have racked the Middle East for twenty years. The area is a rich prize in the superpower competition for influence; each has developed implicit commitments to local adversaries over whom it nonetheless has little control once local passions are loosed. Each has actively contributed to the deepening of the total conflict. But, in large part because of this deep involvement, each becomes an active peacemaker if fighting starts—until the guns are silenced and partial, competitive interests once again prevail. In the 1956 Suez part of the tragedy, the United States found its interests further imperiled when its closest allies, Britain and France, became active participants in a brief but dangerous Middle Eastern war.

The remainder of this chapter consists of the general policy inferences our method enabled us to elicit from each of the five cases analyzed.

THE SOVIET-IRANIAN CONFLICT: LESSONS FOR CONFLICT CONTROL[1]

"CONTROLLING" THE CONFLICT

Once portions of Iran were occupied by Soviet troops during World War II the time for preventive measures had been passed. Under the circumstances, "controlling" the hostilities that broke out in 1945 would have meant, in the first instance, keeping the dispute nonmilitary, and then, in subsequent stages, preventing the Tudeh party from offering tempting prospects for Moscow, deterring the Soviets from directly intervening, and ending the fighting quickly once it broke out.

Keeping the Dispute Nonmilitary

The first transition in 1941 from dispute to conflict was brought about by the creation of a foreign military presence in Iran that became the prime cause of the later outbreak of hostilities. To have prevented this precondition for 1945–1946 would have required that there be no such presence in the first place. More fundamentally, if there had been no World War II, and therefore no strategic need for foreign military presence, no pressures making the dispute military in nature would have been created.

The above seems obvious and even trite. Yet once the larger pressures are set in motion—World War II, Cold War, thermonuclear arms race, imperialist drive, or whatever—powerful forces are at work to generate local conflicts. It goes without saying that most contemporary conflicts have to be dealt with within the framework supplied by the larger strategic scene. But, whether anyone feels they are beyond change or not, it is

[1] See Chapter 5 for the analysis from which these lessons were drawn.

wholesome to keep in mind that a list of conflict-control measures, to be comprehensive, must begin by addressing itself to these larger causative factors.

Even accepting World War II, the move into Iran by Soviet troops might still have been avoided by a policy measure of neutralization of Iran, which would have required an international agreement. This kind of policy is possible and may be increasingly valuable. In modern times an international agreement in 1955 neutralized Austria. It may turn out to be important to neutralize the Indo-Chinese peninsula. Agreements to forego spheres of influence for the benefits of lessened conflict may appeal increasingly to the Soviet Union, and the United States should give high priority to seeking agreements for what might be called "spheres of abstention."

If nuclear-fueled power had been available in 1941, the pressure for oil access would have been lessened. The same would have been true later in Iran in the Mossadegh crisis, and in the Suez war of 1956. Technical developments such as alternative energy sources might help to remove major areas of the Middle East from great-power contention. Similarly, as demonstrated later in Europe, long range air-lift capability, had it been available, could have obviated the need to station ground forces on Iranian soil. Perhaps this capacity will lighten the future U.S. load in Asia. At any rate, alternative energy sources and long-range air-lift capability illustrate the conflict-control pay-offs that come from technology.

If local weakness creates—as it did in Iran—a dangerous vacuum tempting others to intervene, the relevant conflict-prevention activities call for strengthening the internal social, political, and security fabric of the country. If, nevertheless, outside help is required to restore law and order, etc., troops from relatively disinterested countries are obviously preferable to those with direct interests; the UN Congo operation in 1960–1964 rested on this eminently sound principle. For the future, this suggests a most important continuing reason to favor multilateral rather than unilateral military presences when such action is required.

Preventing the Outbreak of Hostilities

Accepting the fact of foreign (Soviet) military presence in Iran during World War II, the next question will be: What actions would have been relevant to avoiding what in fact happened? If one wished, for whatever reason (fear of intensification, pre-occupation elsewhere, etc.), to prevent such a potential conflict situation from exploding into violence, what would have been required?

Apart from the central requirement of a stronger and healthier Iran, relevant counterpressures would have included, first, a potent countervailing force that by presence and believed intention would have deterred a power such as the Soviet Union from believing that its take-over attempt could be pursued with impunity. In this case, U.S. and British power in the area, backing up clearly-expressed Allied opposition, would have fitted the need.

Second, international jurisdiction of the issue could have introduced the whole array of pacific-settlement modalities, many of which were in fact involved later. International (and later UN) cognizance would have spotlighted the Soviet role and bought time by "Stand Still" agreements and diplomatic delays. Above all, it could have reinforced existing nonintervention agreements concerning Iran by providing for fact-finding, inspection, border-watching, guarantees, and, conceivably, sanctions. A combination of U.S. and UN pressures might have encouraged Moscow even further to minimize and conceal its role.

Moderating/Terminating Hostilities

Special problems arise when one considers the implications of a determined conflict-suppression policy after the fighting broke out in Azerbaijan. To have stopped the fighting at that point, given the relative position of the sides at that moment, clearly would have meant victory for the pro-Soviet faction. To have avoided such victory would have meant the necessity of enhancing the pressures for intensification of the conflict or for at least its continuation. Put differently, the factors that the United States would presumably have favored in the pre-hostilities phase would, once fighting started, all have tended to keep it going and intensify it, since the anti-Soviet side would then have seen to it that Moscow's puppets did not bring off a quick victory.

For analytical purposes let us assume, however, that an ending of hostilities was favored *despite* Soviet advantages that would come from this. The following policy measures would by this logic have been involved in the suppression of the conflict: assuring the rebels' clear-cut military superiority on the ground; introducing third-party (Soviet) backing with armed forces on the ground; keeping the country disunited; not taking treaty commitments seriously; reducing the availability of a counter-force in the area. (Clearly, if the result were to be Communist penetration or take-over, the United States would be unlikely to favor policy activities aimed at this kind of conflict suppression. An exception might be made if profound danger of superpower intensification were involved.)

It will be noticed that the measures cited are precisely those the United States would favor (and has favored), *mutatis mutandis,* in a situation where U.S. interest is focused on "our" winning a conflict or on overturning a hostile regime. The above list reads plausibly if one imagines it for Cuba in 1961 instead of for Iran in 1945. The factors needed to ensure local victory of pro-Soviet factions in Iran were precisely those necessary to the victory of pro-Western factions in Cuba. It is currently absurd to think of taking such actions in any purposeful way in the name of conflict control, but, analytically, they represent the policy activities that might have been needed to fulfill the theoretical requirement of *terminating hostilities quickly.*

Preventing the Resumption of Hostilities

Following the termination of the first hostilities phase of the Iranian conflict, the external and internal situations both began to change, and some of the policy activities that were needed—and lacking—earlier came into play. With the end of World War II, U.S. and British policy began to run explicitly counter to Moscow. And Iran took its case to the United Nations. The strongest offsets to renewed hostilities in Iran lay in making U.S. contingent threats more explicit and upgrading the specificity of UN actions in terms of more substantive resolutions, a UN presence, the threat of sanctions, etc.

It should be understood that actions which were taken to deter Soviet intrusion during the first Phase IV by raising the stakes and the potential cost to Moscow would also by definition have had the effect of making it a bigger war if it broke out again. Of course, the expectation would be that such a threat would serve as a deterrent to resumption of hostilities. This relationship is a tricky one, but very important to keeping the peace. The threat of fearful consequences is supposed to deter. But if deterrence fails, the results can be worse than if a lesser deterrent had been used in the first place. Moreover, it could be that the Soviets had no intention of resuming hostilities even if the deterrent had been lessened. If the level of future hostilities had been limited in advance by local-arms limitations or reductions, this would not have necessarily promoted the resumption of hostilities.

Can the conflict controller have it both ways—limiting possible renewed hostilities by cutting down arms, while deterring possible resumption of hostilities by raising the stakes (increasing arms to Iran, pressures on the Soviet Union, etc.)? It would seem that trying to inhibit the resumption of hostilities by threatening heightened retaliation cannot easily be accompanied by arms-control measures. The only way to reconcile this anomaly would be to have the deterrent threat center on strong international machinery, or in any event on some type of collective-security action, thus not being wholly dependent on local-arms levels. This would then be consistent with local and even international arms limitations.

In the sub-phases of Phase IV, when the issue was whether hostilities would resume and if so at what scale, or whether the dispute would be settled, the success of a conflict-inhibiting policy would have perhaps been advanced by further limited and nonvital Iranian concessions to the Soviet Union, along with ways for Moscow to believe it might achieve influence without fighting.

The latter is an extremely dicey game, and many play it badly (although Nasser and Tito at times have done it well). To be too soft invites unexpected responses from a third party (e.g., the United States in Laos in 1960 and 1961) with sudden unpleasant prospects for intensification. Thus, conflict control cannot always mean *any* action designed to avoid conflict, but must take into account the critical limits of policies of appeasement, coalition, concession, and even disarmament, beyond which a backlash is set up leading to potentially worse intensifications.

During the period (Phase IV_1 Sub-Phase D) of the Iranian conflict when Soviet troops had withdrawn just across the borders, more could have been done to secure the Iranian frontiers, including UN observation and patrol activities.

Moderating/Terminating Hostilities

When the second round of fighting began, it was in part caused by the success of the Iranian government in establishing its writ. (Earlier it had been Tehran's weakness that created conflict out of the Tudeh party's relative strength). In fact, this was not a conflict the United States would have wished to control by freezing the positions of government and rebels in order to inhibit the resumption of hostilities. The danger of future conflict may be far greater if a rebel movement is left untouched than if it is defeated; obvious examples, each illustrating a different side of the point, are Katanga province in the Congo and the Kurds in Iraq.

Once hostilities were resumed in Iran, however, their continuation might have led to serious intensification in the form of re-introduced Soviet troops. They were, in fact, quickly terminated, due to policy measures not applied earlier, such as making Iran stronger, and the abstention from the conflict by the Soviets.

Settling the Dispute

To enhance settlement of a dispute such as this one, the key once more is in a strong and cohesive polity for the country in question. In this case the strengthened Iranian government discouraged further Soviet adventurism. But, as a general rule, it may not always be true that measures directed against dissident groups at home will necessarily minimize the chances of violence. Internal health is one thing. But repressive policies, unless accompanied by total social controls as in Communist countries, lead often to new and more widespread political revolution (cf. 1776, 1789, 1848, not to mention more contemporary instances such as those in Cuba, the Dominican Republic, and Ghana).

THE BAY OF PIGS: LESSONS FOR CONFLICT CONTROL[2]

In many ways the Bay of Pigs was a mirror image of the situation in Iran in 1946. In the background was a wider conflict of which this case was merely one sector or front. The invariant factor of proximity to a superpower was paramount in both cases, and nothing could be done to change it. (Neighboring great powers and superpowers do not *have* to intervene in the frequently irritating local politics of lesser states, however: India [if we consider it a weaker power] is certainly a case in point, where massive intervention might not have been surprising but has not been attempted, any more than it has been attempted in recent years by China in Outer Mongolia or by the United States in Mexico during its periods of turbulence.)

In the cases of both Iran and the Bay of Pigs, the neighboring

[2] See Chapter 6 for the analysis from which these lessons were drawn.

superpower fomented internal conflict through subversive guerrilla forces inside, besides training and introducing additional indigenous subversives from without. In both cases, justification for intervention was found in historic precedents and frameworks—spheres-of-influence treaties in Iran, the Monroe Doctrine in Cuba. In both instances, current international law, including the UN Charter, expressly forbade the policies pursued by the superpowers. And in both instances the superpowers were unsuccessful in their aim of overthrowing the neighboring regime.

"CONTROLLING" THE CONFLICT

Prevention, here as elsewhere, would have been the ideal form of conflict control. In this case, prevention would have meant never permitting things in Cuba to reach a point where social, political, and economic revolution could be readily capitalized on—and completed—by Communist extremists.

This had to mean, in retrospect, action during the rule of the Batista regime to encourage peaceful internal change in Cuba—and elsewhere in Latin America—toward greater liberalization. In Cuba this would admittedly have meant painful preventive policy activities: economically painful steps involving U.S. sugar policy, socially painful steps involving changing American attitudes toward darker-skinned neighbors, and politically painful steps involving roiling the smooth and comfortable diplomatic waters of prolonged U.S. coexistence with tyranny and reaction. None of this was really done in Cuba, and the conflict was not prevented.

Later, "controlling" would in fact have meant: not permitting the U.S.-Castro dispute to become viewed in predominantly military terms by the United States, discouraging ourselves from actually exercising a military option, and, once the invasion began, quickly ending the fighting. Of the three, only the last was done, thanks largely to U.S. mismanagement rather than to anything else.

Keeping the Dispute Nonmilitary

To avoid what in fact happened, the United States would have had to keep its general view of the Cuban situation political and defensive rather than military and offensive. Following a containment policy rather than an intervention policy—as the United States now does toward Cuba—would have satisfied this criterion. This policy is today part of the larger issue as to whether both the U.S. and Communists will accept continued stalemate or whether they will go over to the offensive. The answer is, generally speaking, up to the Communists. But U.S. response will often determine what *kind* of conflict it is to be.

In this age, the undesirably sharp edge of unilateral interventionist policy is often dulled when other powers are brought in, i.e., when a direct head-butting contest is "multilateralized." In anything but a direct military-security threat (as existed when Soviet missiles were secretly emplaced in Cuba in 1962), conflict is more likely to be controlled if, as a virtually automatic policy, unilateral quarrels are made multilateral. The Organization of American States and the United Nations are generally thought of as useful only to the extent that they support our side in such quarrels, but their principal value in 1961 might have been, *per contra,* to stay the U.S. hand. If after such multilateral "action" Castro's propaganda were not then validated by U.S. military intervention, such a policy might have done far more to undermine his regime than what in fact happened. The accompaniment of U.S. abstinence would have had to be similar restraint by Moscow, toward which end the United States ought to have applied direct pressure.

OAS might have played a role that, while short of intervention, sufficiently appeared to be "policing" the region to obviate unilateral U.S. invasion plans. This might have taken the form of prophylactic action against Castro's external subversion attempts by means of inspection and publicity, backed by believable deterrence plans plus some responsibility for training internal defense forces in the target countries. All of this would have increased the likelihood of adverse reactions to unilateral U.S. intervention, as would have UN fact-finding machinery.

The irony of Cuba, and other places where anti-U.S. regimes govern, is that general rules apply there as well as elsewhere. In Communist countries, to the extent there is internal political, economic, and social health, opportunities for externally sponsored subversion are minimized, along with temptations to overthrow the government by force. (In fact, Cuba had greater internal cohesion than U.S. intelligence estimated.) Happily, the same rule holds in the far greater number of places where non-Communist nations are struggling, often with U.S. help, for cohesion and strength. But in these places too it will assist in averting conflict if the United States carefully limits its definition of strategic values while displaying less sensitivity to anti-Yankee sentiment.

Wholehearted and rigorous application of universal rules against unilateral intervention would be, in fact, greatly to the benefit of free nations and moreover would be supported by the growing majority of states that cherish their independence from intervention. Strengthening international organizations such as the UN and OAS would tend to reinforce this rule.

It was the U.S. decision to arm Cuban exiles that signaled the implementation of a significant military option; a generally accepted ban on the clandestine training of exile forces for reinvasion of their homeland might have gone a long way toward conflict control. The United States has at various times considered itself disadvantaged if unable to train "freedom fighters" to liberate Eastern Europe, Nationalist Chinese with the same mission toward the Chinese mainland, or Cuban exiles in Guatemala in 1960–1961. In the event, none of these proved useful: the conflicts in Hungary in 1956 and Czechoslovakia in 1968 showed that the United States was in fact unwilling to risk World War III by fomenting revolution in Eastern Europe; Chiang Kai-shek's forces have been leashed since 1950; and the Bay of Pigs turned out to be a self-defeating adventure, its net result to confirm Communist propaganda and unify Cuban opinion.

A practical conflict-control policy today would be one of U.S. or international discouragement of the practice of subversion through exiles. With the whole experience of Communist-inspired subversion in hand, it seems self-evident that the United States—and the cause of conflict control—would benefit from more universal application of rules against this kind of activity. In 1966 and in earlier years, the UN General Assembly passed Soviet-sponsored resolutions against intervention, modified later by other resolutions to condemn the very kind of intervention that Communists practice. Rather than being considered purely hypocritical by Moscow and purely rhetorical by the U.S., these resolutions might be usefully implemented with international machinery. Furthermore, an international human-rights tribunal could hear grievances by individuals and groups that otherwise might have no outlet. A fact-finding agency could add pressure on "host countries" to permit inspection by challenge and invitation in order to refute charges of preparations to intervene with exile forces. Most important, the spotlight of publicity would help keep the potential intervener off balance— as the United States was in the Bay of Pigs, the British and French were in Suez, and the Soviets have been on several occasions in Eastern Europe.

Along these same lines, the handling of refugees and émigrés often has much to do with later conflict patterns. Three prime examples of such refugees are the Germans from the so-called "lost territories" to the East, the Palestine refugees in the Gaza Strip and the West Bank of the Jordan, and the Cubans in Miami. Sound preventive policy calls for encouraging wider dispersal of such groups.

Even though grave and ideologically unbridgeable problems existed between Cuba and the United States at the beginning of the 1960's, some issues—such as that of expropriation—might nevertheless have been fit subjects for international procedures of arbitration, conciliation, good offices, mediation, adjudication, etc. (In the issue of expropriation, U.S. guarantees to private investors against losses due to expropriation might have been appropriate.) It would seem today that only countries enjoying fundamentally good relations tend to employ these procedures. This is absurd, since their value lies in isolating remediable issues from a context of potentially dangerous hostility. Unfortunately it appears "soft" to do so, which is undoubtedly why Britain and France would not hear of going to the International Court of Justice in 1956 on the issue of compensation for the nationalization of the Suez Canal—and why the United States did not seriously think in these terms before the Bay of Pigs.

Preventing the Outbreak of Hostilities

The absence or failure of conflict-control policies in the first phase often has a cumulative effect, and it had one in this case. As the United States became more firmly committed, events could probably only have been diverted with strong and influential measures by the United Nations in the form of fact-finding, publicity, time-stretching diplomatic delays, channels of communications, good offices, and peaceful-settlement proceedings; by OAS in action also deterring unilateral U.S. action; and by the Soviet Union in the form of effective deterrence. Even at a late stage in the pre-hostilities phase, some dramatic change in the situation might have altered the conflict. Guatemala might have refused to serve as a base, particularly if determined efforts were made for more cohesion in OAS. Great-power agreement about arms transfers could have promised to make the Cuban situation less open-ended and thus blunted the U.S. thrust—instead, MiG's and pilots were to arrive imminently. And the U.S. government would have had to be willing to reverse its covert policy and restrain the exile forces in training.

One vital factor making the conflict difficult to abort, once in motion, was the increasingly close Cuban tie to Moscow. This took a chiefly economic form but included arms assistance. Soviet assistance was less than that to Egypt, but this time it was going to a country ninety miles off the coast of Florida. For the United States, what was tolerable in Egypt became a potential *casus belli* in Cuba. Restrictions on arms transfers would today remove some of the inevitability from this kind of situation, since a foothold acquired by a great power all too frequently signals the beginning of an effort to arm the client state with sophisticated weapons that create new tensions in the client's regional neighborhood. The Soviet Union has practiced this mischievous policy in the Middle East, the Horn of Africa, Indonesia, and Cuba. The United States, Britain, and France have created lesser local imbalances and instabilities (often in the name of stability) in Latin America and South Asia and have contributed to local arms races in the Middle East and elsewhere. An alternative to a universally agreed regime of restricting arms transfers to those arms needed for internal security[3] would be a U.S.-Soviet-British-French agreement. Of course, the same thing can sometimes be accomplished by direct and unlimited pressure to desist, exerted by one power on the other. In 1962 the United States applied such pressure on Moscow in Cuba. Perhaps the United States would have been deterred by an all-out threat from Moscow the year before.

Terminating Hostilities

The key policy involved in ending the fighting in Cuba was U.S. restraint in withholding its direct power even when "its" forces were losing. A policy of victory could have been carried through, undoubtedly with local success (though with incalculable consequences for the U.S. reputation in Latin America and elsewhere). Ironically, what caused the U.S. reversal was the degree of effective internal control in Cuba, which, if realized before, might have discouraged even the attempt made at the Bay of Pigs.

"Peace" is currently preserved by a deeply rooted policy of restraint by both Washington and Moscow. This in turn stems

---

[3] *Regional Arms Control Arrangements for Developing Areas,* Report for the U.S. Arms Control and Disarmament Agency (Cambridge: MIT Center for International Studies; September 1964), pp. ix–27.

from a now mutual general strategic deterrence. Clearly a fundamental conflict-control policy is to continue at all costs a situation of deterrence, specifically a secure second-strike retaliatory capability under all conditions, unless and until it can be substituted for by a workable and just structure of disarmament and world order. At the same time, the relative numbers and sizes of U.S. and Soviet strategic forces could be substantially reduced and still maintain the deterrent situation with both its global and local benefits.

THE GREEK INSURGENCY: LESSONS FOR CONFLICT CONTROL[4]

"CONTROLLING" THE CONFLICT

"Controlling" the Greek conflict—like that in Vietnam—would have meant: not allowing a Communist-led movement to dominate wartime resistance; not permitting civil war to break out, and also sealing off the country from external intervention through international-organization mechanisms; and bringing hostilities to an early end, through a combination of firm counterinsurgency measures and political, economic, and social reforms, particularly in the countryside, that would win popular support for moderate non-Communist rule (alternatively, the aim of early termination of hostilities could have been obtained by ensuring a rapid Communist victory—something we would hardly recommend).

Keeping the Dispute Nonmilitary

Like so many other postwar conflicts, the Greek Insurgency had its roots in great-power war and Communist organizing skill that enabled the party to take over control of wartime resistance movements. Short of avoiding great-power war, later political-

[4] See Chapter 7 for the analysis from which these lessons were drawn.

ideological conflict may be averted by preventing Communist take-over of legitimate nationalist and patriotic resistance movements. This in turn implies the need for effective non-Communist organizations that can compete with an ELAS (*or a* Vietminh or Vietcong) for popular support in the "sea" in which, in Maoist terms, insurgent "fish" swim.

The difficulties with this prescription—so important to U.S. policy in the postwar era—are both obvious and chronic. The chief difficulty is ideological: the tendency for the non-Communist left to share many Marxist ideas and thus alienate powerful supporters of anti-Communism, such as the United States, and the tendency of the anti-Communist right to represent unpopular forces of wealth, corruption, landlordism, militarism, and, as in wartime Greece, monarchism. Given this common polarization of the political extremes, a strategy for the United States that could be both conflict controlling and "winning" is recognition and support for popularly based non-Communist elements which work for stability and democratic reform, with eschewal of both blind support for unpopular status-quo powers and the romanticizing of what are in effect Communist take-over movements.

In wartime Greece this meant the desirability of active support of non-Communist resistance groups, notably EDES, plus pressure on the Greek government-in-exile to liberalize its composition, submit the question of monarchy to a popular vote, and generally appeal to popular sentiments while providing a democratic alternative. Strategic considerations that led to all-out Allied support for ELAS should have given equally high priority to avoiding the strengthening of political enemies and the creation of new postwar conflicts by shortsighted "purely military" wartime policies.

As in so many wartime situations, stores of surplus arms (such as those from the Italian surrender as well as those from retreating Germans later) should be prevented from falling into the hands of potential conflict-makers (such as ELAS in Greece).

Preventing the Outbreak of Hostilities

Impulses toward reform in an atmosphere of suspicion and conflict (such as the Greek King's agreement to a postwar plebiscite on constitutional questions—or elections in Vietnam) can benefit by being implemented in ways that lend them maximum confidence, i.e., through neutral (UN, etc.) administration or supervision providing guarantees of fairness.

It is essential to convince radical take-over movements of two things: (1) that they will not be permitted to succeed in their ends through violence and (2) that there is a legitimate role they can play in the political process. Experience with Communist coalition governments is an unhappy one, particularly when the Communists remain convinced of the usefulness of violence and also when they are allowed to appear to retain a monopoly on popular issues of economic and social reform. Given this, the third essential ingredient for the success of political moderation is, of course, that described above: (3) support for popular non-Communist elements of genuine reform. These three factors are central to a successful strategy of internal conflict control. Today Vietnam and much of Latin America bespeak their relevance.

The element of deterrence and discouragement of radical-minority take-over requires clearly stated intentions on the part of the deterrer (which the British did not do at first in Greece), plus the will and strength to carry them out. But that will is, of course, sapped when the action seems entirely repressive and antidemocratic. Thus—and the lesson is still not well learned by the hawks of the world—military power is only useful in counterinsurgency when harnessed to reform and popular consent, except in deceptively short-run terms.

Moderating/Terminating Hostilities

In the Athens round of fighting, Communist forces might have been more deterred by the threat of U.S. intervention, as well as by diverting their attention to traditional Balkan rivalries such as that between Yugoslavia and Greece over Macedonia. (These, like all deterrents, are two-edged swords; as in the later full-scale insurgency, a greatly expanded U.S. presence might have tended to intensify hostilities, and an outbreak of interstate hostilities over Macedonia would have been no improvement.)

Acceleration of insurgent guerrilla action might be avoided by discouraging diplomatic recognition of the insurgents and urging free elections under international supervision.

In Greece, as in many other contemporary cases, conflict control in the sense of violence-minimizing might have been achieved either by moderating hostilities—which might have allowed them to drag on—or by intensifying them with a view to a rapid end to the fighting. This trade-off represented one of the central dilemmas of Vietnam and has no easy answer. The crucial variables are probably the perceived danger of intensification vs. the pressures of public opinion—both able to act in either direction.

Preventing the Resumption of Hostilities

Strong measures are required in an age of competitive intervention to keep internal wars from spreading across national frontiers. The provision of sanctuary and guerrilla training in Greece's northern neighbors of Albania, Yugoslavia, and Bulgaria was countered by some international cognizance, investigation, fact-finding, and reporting. This international spotlight function was of great value in Greece (and in Korea) and might have played a deterrent role in Vietnam if the value of international-organization assistance had been recognized earlier, notably by the United States. The role of U.S. and allied power in backing such multilateral action should include pressure on potential external mischief makers not to intervene, backed by meaningful threats from the responsible powers.

Following the first round of fighting, further hostilities might have been inhibited in Greece by joint or impartial supervision, inspection, and control of the agreement by which ELAS was to disband, for ELAS in fact violated both the letter and spirit of the agreement by sending its hard-core cadres to the northern countries with a substantial number of arms.

As Abraham Lincoln and Winston Churchill so clearly recognized, a policy of reconciliation, even-handed justice, and incorporation of dissenters into legitimate modes of dissent is the only sound one to follow after victory in a bitter war, particularly a war between brothers. Conflict-control strategy at Versailles in 1919 might have avoided a conflict-breeding punitive treaty. The Greek government of 1945, like other right-wing governments, tended to drive non-Communist leftists back into the Communist fold.

The economic distress that Greece was experiencing in late 1945 resembled that existing in such other conflict-prone situations as that of Germany in the early 1930's. Given the political-strategic-ideological position of Greece in 1945 (as of Korea in 1953, and of, say, Brazil or Indonesia in the late 1960's), conflict control indicated economic and financial assistance on a substantial scale. (In the contemporary cases, perhaps multilateral means would be politically preferable.)

Vigorous internal-security operations to preserve law and order, particularly in villages and hamlets, are essential to conflict control; foreign military assistance is frequently needed to this end. Tactics designed to split Communist opposition and isolate the irreconcilable radicals are advisable, but these are made effective only if popular consent can be won through accommodations of legitimate political demands—or opposition suppressed with totalitarian measures. Moreover, repression should only follow efforts to encourage all political elements to employ the political process to pursue their program.

There is no necessary reason why bilateral military assistance should preclude an international presence. Before major insurgency developed in Greece—as during the whole 1946–1949 period—a preventive international peacekeeping capability should have been introduced, going beyond fact-finding and,

ideally, replacing British and later U.S. forces with an international force interposed between adversaries and along the
border.

   One lesson of both Greece and Vietnam is that splits within
the Communist world diminish the capacity of Communist
movements to take over on the basis of unified external support.
At the same time, the Sino-Soviet competition can mean rivalry
to champion the indigenous Communists in various parts of the
world. This particular point remains moot.

THE INDONESIAN WAR OF INDEPENDENCE: LESSONS FOR CONFLICT CONTROL[5]

"CONTROLLING" THE CONFLICT

"Controlling" the Indonesian War of Independence—i.e.,
avoiding or minimizing violence in the archipelago—in simple-
minded terms would have meant preventing World War II,
which provided the preconditions for it, or avoiding the even-
earlier Dutch colonialism and the subsequent independence
impulse. This is obviously unrealistic, but it illustrates how
fundamental were the roots of this conflict. In more realistic
terms, controlling the conflict meant: first, discouraging the
Dutch from believing they could in fact take over again after
having been evicted by the Japanese; second, enabling the
Indonesians to win their independence quickly once fighting
broke out or, alternately, enabling the Dutch to carry out a
quick and successful police action—in any event, stopping the
fighting once it started; and, finally, keeping the parties from
fighting again through diplomatic and military means of pressure. At all stages, genuinely controlling this particular conflict
meant making clear to all sides, but particularly to the Dutch,

---

[5] See Chapter 8 for the analysis from which these lessons were drawn.

the eventual grounds for settling the dispute, namely, independence for the former Netherlands East Indies.

Keeping the Dispute Nonmilitary

The key element in the Indonesian war lay in colonialism and its obverse—anticolonialism. In our vocabulary, a dispute was inevitable. But the transition from dispute to conflict might have been avoided if the approaching end of European colonialism had been more visible in 1945 than it was. With adequate foresight, conflict-preventive policy measures might have afforded constructive outlets for Dutch status-seeking impulses, finding surrogates for the Netherlands' dying empire. In the late 1960's a widespread understanding exists about the inevitability of decolonization. But there is still a need for economic and spiritual alternatives to the colonialist and imperialist impulse. Ironically, in the years ahead the chief would-be imperialists may be found outside the white Western world. One has already had glimpses of an imperialist urge, however impotent, in contemporary China, North Vietnam, Indonesia, Ghana, and the U.A.R. Remedial policy prescriptions might take such forms as: first, deterrence and the courage to stop expansionism; second, the encouragement of regional associations, common-market schemes, and cooperation in economic and social development, in a kind of neo-William Jamesian substitute for neo-empire. Unbridled nationalism is still—as it was—the prime enemy. As for such "imperialism" as is found in some investment and trade policies of developed countries, answers may be found in enlightened governmental aid and trade philosophies, plus support for more rational mechanisms to resolve fundamental problems of foreign investment, commodity marketing, and balance of payments. Seemingly remote from conflict control, these are in fact central to it.

The most operational conflict-control lesson to be derived from the Indonesian war turns on the problem of serious misconceptions that may lead parties to blunder into conflict. In the Indonesian case, the need was for reliable information about the situation to be conveyed to both parties. Given the dispute, a third-party presence able to undertake this sort of fact-finding could have been of great value, above all preventively if brought in before fighting broke out.

Part of any postwar planning ought to deal with the matter of collecting arms suddenly found to be in surplus. The presence and availability of arms in large quantities may have made the difference in turning the Indonesian dispute into a militarily-flavored conflict situation. In this case, Japanese arms were available in quantity to the Indonesian nationalists. (Note also that the Chinese Communists took over Japanese arms left in Manchuria in 1945, with epochal results.) And the other side of the coin was the use by returning Dutch colonial masters of Allied-supplied military matériel originally intended for use against the Japanese. The history of military-assistance programs has often been one of undesirable use of arms by metropolitan countries against their colonies and by neighbors against each other. The United States should continually re-examine its military assistance program in the light of what use has, in fact, been made of the arms supplied.

Above all else, machinery for peaceful change should have played a crucial role in this case. One still important form of peaceful change involves the relatively bloodless and equitable alteration of the legal and political status of territories.[6] In the postwar years the former Italian colonies, some French, British, Australian, and New Zealand colonies, Trieste, West New Guinea, and Austria represent the only major examples of peaceful change. The Palestine experience was a mixed one; and there has been no real effort to deal with Kashmir equitably. It might be helpful, as suggested by a number of observers, for an equity tribunal to deal in a semijuridical fashion —yet within the context of the UN political machinery—with thorny territorial issues.

[6] Lincoln P. Bloomfield: *Evolution or Revolution? The United Nations and the Problem of Peaceful Territorial Change* (Cambridge: Harvard University Press; 1957).

Preventing the Outbreak of Hostilities

Here, as in other cases, internal cohesion and stability on the part of governmental authorities were preconditions for asserting sufficient control over a local situation to prevent the actual outbreak of hostilities in a tense period. Historically, it would only have postponed inevitable conflict if the Dutch had been adequately strong; the realistic conflict-controlling need was for a strong *Indonesian* authority. But whether Dutch or Indonesian, such an authority was necessary if the conflict were to be kept isolated and dissident groups disarmed. This point has been since underscored by the widely varying experiences of newly independent governments; the Congo in 1960 was an extreme example of insufficiency on the part of such a government.

History is full of situations in which a legitimate authority seeks to apply or restore its writ in a territory and encounters serious opposition. Consequences arise out of efforts by the authority to suppress such opposition or out of efforts by outsiders to help either the government or the rebels. Examples are: 1945—Iran, Indonesia; 1950–1954—the Nationalist Chinese in Burma; 1960—the Congo; 1961—the Bay of Pigs; and 1965—the Dominican Republic. The best policy instrument to keep such an explosive situation from producing open hostilities takes the form of preventive interposition by neutral or third-party forces between the parties. This has, in fact, never been done preventively but only after some bloodshed and the threat of major military action. Next best would be pre-hostilities fact-finding on the spot; it is sobering to consider what political and even strategic value a more viable international presence of this sort in Vietnam, reporting to the entire world community, might have had during the early years of infiltration from the north. The essential element for this sort of pacificatory strategy is of course neutrality between the parties. In the Indonesian situation, the mediatory instruments and agents introduced into the scene were not always perceived as completely neutral. (A parallel of this in more recent times is found in the behavior of the members of the then Casablanca bloc of African states who put troops in the UN Congo operation but then acted disruptively and non-neutrally.)

Once fighting is terminated, to prevent it from breaking out again the cease-fire that has been achieved must be made firm, with guarantees that it will not be easily breached. Diplomatic recognition as a form of legitimization and stabilization of the *de facto* situation can be a useful means toward this end, particularly if accompanied with time-stretching diplomatic devices. A buffer force similar to the 1956–1967 UN Emergency Force in Egypt, put on the ground to monitor a cease-fire, could have been very helpful in Indonesia, along with continuous pressures to negotiate. *Per contra,* unsupervised truces can be positive sources of tension by creating incidents that can lead to resumed hostilities. One of the most serious problems of the times is the stubborn refusal of the Communists in Laos, Vietnam, and Korea to accept adequate truce supervision on their territories. The same thing can be said of Israel.

During a pause in longstanding conflict situations (such as in Kashmir on two occasions and in the Middle East on three), the parties often use the time to replenish their military stocks in order to arm for the next round. There is room in such a pause for redressing military imbalances, either through arming and training of the weaker side, or through mutual arms-control agreements. The effect of arming the weaker side can be either conflict controlling or not, depending on such factors as the rate of arming, the possibility of surprise attack, or the availability of "breakthrough" weapons.

This represents a complex problem. For deterrence purposes, arms balances are desirable. If hostilities *do* break out in balanced situations, however, they may be prolonged to the extent that neither side can win a quick victory. Another defect of the parity policy is that if it does not rest on agreement among suppliers, it can lead to the introduction of major sophisticated weapons systems. Such systems will raise the level of violence and risk of intensification if deterrence fails. In addition to keeping the local balance at low levels, external guarantees with sanctions are needed to reinsure deterrence in seeing that the arms are not in fact used. The ideal would be a general agreement keeping arms levels substantially low. As long as this is not possible, one might consider imposing quarantines against the importation of destabilizing arms into the general area of a given conflict when it is acute in order to insulate it from possible exacerbation. (Paragraph 3 of the Suez cease-fire resolution of 1956[7] aimed at precisely this.) In this general connection, the very notion of mutual deterrence means that information about the arms balance is in many ways as important as the arms themselves, perhaps more important. This is another major reason why the United Nations should be required to publish information on world-wide military establishments and inventories, arms transfers, and arms trade.[8]

Moderating/Terminating Hostilities

It was only after the fighting broke out again in Indonesia, in July 1947, that UN pressure began to become positively strong, vigorously backed by the United States. Two very important instruments for both moderating and eventually terminating the conflict were adequate machinery on the ground and influential great-power involvement carrying the implied threat of meaningful sanction. It hardly seems necessary to reiterate the need to strengthen the United Nations' capacity to back up its peacekeeping capabilities with peaceful-change mechanisms, emphasis on arbitration measures regarding alleged violations, and the threat of sanctions. These were by no means perfect in 1947, for a third round of fighting was yet to break out. They seem if anything less perfect today.

[7] UN General Assembly Resolution 997 (ES-1).
[8] As recommended in *Regional Arms Control Arrangements for Developing Areas,* pp. ix–28.

The pressures for terminating the fighting might have been reinforced with sterner economic measures on the part of external powers in a position so to influence matters.

The Indonesian second round particularly suggested the desirability of having available specialized truce-supervision machinery for situations of guerrilla warfare. This problem has never been thoroughly analyzed, but Vietnam could be a crucial customer for this sort of capability, as might also parts of the Arab-Israeli confrontation. This special problem surely belongs on the agenda of needed operational research in the realm of peacekeeping.

The involvement of U.S. citizens in the peacemaking machinery that was available during the Indonesian fighting implied the involvement of the prestige of the United States and its implicit commitment to control of the conflict. Moscow was similarly involved in late 1965 in the Kashmir Conflict. This involvement can only be healthy, since international-organization machinery itself is meaningful only with substantial great-power support. The argument is not for the presence of superpower military units in multilateral peacekeeping exercises (although changing U.S.-Soviet relations may make that contingency less undesirable), but for the lending of their prestige to peacemaking efforts through their service as guarantors and influential brokers.

It should not escape notice that if the superpower standoff tends to allow lesser conflicts to flourish, a brooding Cold War or other global-level threat can have the reverse effect of suppressing local conflict. Ironically, it can be speculated that an even more aggressive Soviet foreign policy in December 1948 might have stayed the Dutch hand from the second round in Indonesia by requiring it to focus on Europe. Similarly, it might have intensified the desire of the Allies to see early control of a dangerous situation where the great powers might potentially become entangled. The interaction between superpower relations and local conflicts represents one of the major sets of trade-offs in conflict control. But while the last argument is a serious one, an optimum conflict-control policy would call for superpower *cooperation* above all other policy considerations. Not only would this bring maximum pressure for settlement on local parties, control the flow of arms to both sides, and ensure the mobilization of UN machinery; but also, above all, it would remove that which makes failure in conflict control so potentially disastrous—the possibility of intensification to the great-power nuclear arena.

CONFLICT IN THE MIDDLE EAST: LESSONS FOR CONFLICT CONTROL[9]

"CONTROLLING" THE CONFLICT

The Suez-Sinai war of 1956 represented a convergence of two otherwise distinct conflicts—the protracted Arab-Israeli cold war and the British-French quarrel with Nasser. To "control" the first would have meant, realistically, to seal off a highly inflammable and volatile substance and keep it from bursting into flame, or, alternatively, to break a deadly ten-year cycle of wars. To "control" the second would have meant lessening the strategic importance of the Suez Canal, arbitrating the canal issue after its seizure, maintaining sufficient rationality in London and Paris to preclude a punitive-war policy and deterring their action up to the moment it took place.

The Arab-Israeli Conflict

Preventing the Resumption of Hostilities

It goes without saying that movement toward the settlement of the underlying dispute would have been the best means of preventing resumed hostilities. In theory, this would have involved action on fundamental substantive issues such as borders, resettlement of refugees, and their compensation. Toward this end one could, again theoretically, envisage unified

[9] See Chapter 9 for the analysis from which these lessons were drawn.

pressure by the United Nations, the great powers, and other suppliers of external economic and military assistance. Even given the intractability of the conflict, perhaps if the Soviets had sufficiently shared Western anxiety to the point of cooperating by not introducing destabilizing arms and not trying to frustrate UN diplomacy, this might have inhibited the renewed outbreak of hostilities in 1956 or at least limited their potential scale and scope.

Given the profound, deep-seated basis for the Arab-Israeli quarrel, it is unknown if even unified great-power pressure would have forced the Arabs toward settlement, i.e., acceptance of Israel's continued existence. It is not even certain that such pressure could have succeeded in forcing one of the basic preconditions for such Arab reversal, i.e., Israeli agreement to repatriation and/or substantial compensation of Arab refugees. Nevertheless, some action might have been open to outsiders to make the resumption of hostilities less likely. Intense pressures on Israel might have resulted, even at this late stage, in readmission of at least a symbolic number of Arab refugees and compensation of others, particularly if international financial help were available. The pressure of international help on the Arab states might have brought about a start on resettlement of refugees, although this is more doubtful.

The threat of a unified boycott on the part of the Suez Canal users might have moved Egypt from its refusal to permit Israel's shipping through the canal. The Egyptian blockade of the Strait of Tiran might have been countered with the threat of military action by the maritime powers to enforce their right of free access to international waterways, and by airways users to force open a closed international air space.

Retention of British troops in the Suez Canal area might have served as a deterrent to aggression as well as a source of international intelligence about warlike preparations. If, for political reasons, British forces had had to leave the region, one possible surrogate for them might have been an expanded international presence to fill the vacuum. As for the existing UN truce supervision in the area, the United Nations was not as effective as it ought to have been in identifying, verifying, and condemning the *fedayin* raids or in following through on condemnation of Israel's Gaza incursions in reprisal. As a preventive of this kind of activity, the 1956 UNEF border watch was one war too late, so to speak. The clearly indicated preventive measure, both with respect to the raids and to the subsequent Israeli attack across the Sinai, would have been joint or third-party border patrols backed by strong international support and sanctions.

In this connection there was really no substitute (nor is there today) for sealing the border. Greater pressure ought to have been put on Israel to permit the United Nations within its boundaries. The United Nations should have physically sealed the border with barbed wire, ditches, etc., on all the land boundaries of Israel. The moats of the Middle Ages existed for good purpose, as did the "McNamara electronic barrier" in Vietnam, if it had ever been really implemented.

Propaganda warfare by Radio Cairo ought to have been severely condemned as violating a variety of UN resolutions about incitement to war. This should have been accompanied by efforts to increase the flow of factual information within the area, preferably by UN news broadcasts. This is also a good argument for considering a substantial strengthening of all UN information facilities, preferably with its own communications satellite facilities, in order to reach a maximum world-wide audience and to counter the sort of inflammatory propaganda in which Radio Cairo and others specialized.

The Soviet arms deal and the U.S. attempt to create an anti-Soviet alliance in the "northern tier" of Middle Eastern states (the former being a response to the latter) were also contributing background factors. Perhaps the chances are better today for a Soviet policy of restraint; but China may move in as a destabilizing factor as soon as it is able to. We place priority, however, on agreements among suppliers to restrict the sale of arms to states engaged in conflict. Perhaps more weight would attach to seeking such agreements if they were seen as one of the truly crucial problems of our times for which a high price should be paid, if need be, and high risks run to enforce.[1] If none of these measures was possible, the 1950 tripartite guarantee of borders needed to be enforced impartially and effectively.

The governments on both sides of the Arab-Israeli Conflict contributed to the acceleration of the slide toward renewed hostilities. Whatever private assurances both adversaries gave to the United States and other parties, the public posture of both was increasingly belligerent and intransigent. Perhaps manipulation of and involvement in the domestic affairs of both governments could have affected the personalities that eventually led both sides over the brink.

Practically all the above measures were relevant *after* the 1956 fighting and throughout the period leading up to the third round of hostilities in June of 1967. Perhaps the most depressing feature of this lugubrious—and bloody—cycle is that the prescription for conflict control for the latest period seems to be the same as before.

In retrospect, the 1967 hostilities suggest, however, some additional measures that might have been used for preventing the resumption of hostilities. Perhaps the most crucial of these continue to lie within the range of U.S.-Soviet diplomacy, above all the kind of price the former is willing to pay to persuade Moscow to abandon its conflict-breeding policies of influence and incursion into an area that would be best neutralized. But to keep the Cold War out of the Middle East requires an American willingness to abandon its own policy of obvious preference for Israel's side in all regional quarrels; U.S. impartiality among the Arab factions, notably an end to the traditional, oil-based policy of favoring the monarchies and sheikdoms at the expense of the more nationalistic or republicanized Arab states, is necessary. This requires a better American ability to distinguish genuine nationalism, however radical, from Communism, an ability notably lacking when the so-called Eisenhower Doctrine was formulated in early 1957.

[1] Lincoln P. Bloomfield and Amelia C. Leiss: "Arms Control and the Developing Countries," *World Politics,* October 1965.

A conflict-prevention-oriented U.S. policy would at the same time connect up far more coherently than in the recent past its commitments and its capabilities, plus its willingness to act. A credible American willingness to intervene without delay, preferably through UN frameworks but if necessarily unilaterally, in the event of overt Arab armed aggression, might have deterred both Nasser from precipitating the crisis by evicting UNEF and closing the Strait of Tiran, and Israel from launching a blitz attack on the basis of still-ambiguous evidence.

The UN performance in the Middle East during the 1956–1967 period was distinctly mixed, and decreasing attention was paid to settlement possibilities—although the UNEF presence was worth its weight in gold while it lasted. A better conflict-control strategy would have demanded extending UNEF to the Jordanian and Syrian borders as the price for entertaining the chronic complaints of both sides. It would have made a much greater and more public issue of mobilizing UNTSO plus whatever *ad hoc* assistance the latter required to undertake immediate, authoritative international fact-finding to check out the reports of Israeli concentrations on the Syrian border (reports made to Nasser by the Soviets).

The political atmosphere might have been helpfully altered if the UN Security Council had acted even-handedly toward both sides rather than appearing to condemn only Israel (due to the Soviet veto). The Security Council's reputation for justice should have demanded all steps to surmount the veto, including recourse to the General Assembly, accompanied by the same sort of potent Western and neutralist diplomacy that eschewed one-sided condemnations even in the several assembly sessions on the Middle East in 1967, whatever the other faults might have been of those sessions.

With full knowledge of the intractability of the central quarrel, a concerted effort to get at the roots of conflict between the second and third rounds might have tackled once again the gnawing issue of the Jordan waters—once so close to agreement; made concrete offers of financial and technical help in the resettlement and repatriation of refugees (a problem that, after the fighting, swelled to unmanageable proportions); reiterated the UN positions regarding opening the Suez Canal to all shipping, including Israeli, and keeping open the Strait of Tiran, with clear sanctions envisaged in the event of renewed stoppage.

Technological progress in fact made Persian Gulf oil and thus the Suez Canal matter less in 1967 than it had eleven years before. Further development of nuclear-fueled energy could help toward downgrading the importance of some of the more politically volatile areas of the modern world; in the same spirit, the crucial issue of water for both Israel and Jordan could be relieved without a formal settlement of the Jordan River problem if nuclear-powered desalination plants could be installed and made economical.

Though its mention might seem Machiavellian, it clearly was useful toward avoiding renewed warfare in Palestine for a significant portion of the Egyptian army to be bogged down in the shifting sands of the Yemen desert. The 1967 war followed the recent partial repatriation to Egypt of those 40,000 or so men. Other distractions might be invented by those interested in keeping expansionist or irredentist powers from being able to carry out their threatening rhetoric.

However impractical such advice may seem, politically, at a given moment, it would have assisted conflict control if Israel had been moving toward a secular state in which the Arabs already in residence there could have envisioned full integration and if Arab leaders discovered other bases for pan-Arab unity than implacable hatred of Israel.

A special kind of conflict-control measure comes from the capacity to make rational, soundly informed judgments about the costs of attaining national goals with existing capabilities. It might have altered Nasser's plans if he had had professional assistance in appraising the relative balance of forces in the Middle East. Similarly, better U.A.R. intelligence might have discredited the Soviet-sponsored reports of Israelis massing along the Syrian frontier.

A UN Secretary-General willing to act courageously and independently—as Hammarskjöld on occasion did in the face of possible criticism—might have temporized when Nasser demanded the immediate withdrawal of UNEF, even though some of his UN troops were defecting, in order to buy at least twenty-four hours in which international diplomatic pressures could have been brought to bear before the situation became irretrievable.

Terminating Resumed Hostilities

According to all our findings, it would have contributed to less intense hostilities if previously the military balance in the Middle East had been maintained at the lowest possible level, and if destabilizing weapons had been kept out of the area. At the same time, the quickest road to termination would have been an overwhelming advantage on one side, which may suggest the desirability of such weapons in the inventory of one side. The difficulty with this prescription is precisely that it makes hostilities more likely, because the disadvantaged side feels it must act before the other is ready to use its weapons efficiently. Great-power arms policy produced the worst of both worlds.

In the same spirit, the possibility of great-power involvement which our research—and intuition—proclaims to be generally a conflict-intensifying factor, can also act as a deterrent to prolonged local warfare and as a positive inducement to termination.

General conditions favoring early termination or, in any event, moderation throughout hostilities include the absence of irrationally nihilistic goals and the presence of pressures on the parties, particularly by the UN, to keep their goals limited. In this connection Jordan's commitment to join in battle if the U.A.R. were involved was unrealistic, and it warranted being discouraged.

The misreading of one another's intentions, not to say capabilities, was more acute in this case than in many others, perhaps because of the mischievous role of Moscow as *tertius gaudens*. It might help to find devices that can be set up in a hurry for quick communications to clarify intentions preferably before hostilities, but in any event as soon as they start. If Moscow and Washington can communicate for this purpose, so can other adversaries. Here perhaps a do-it-yourself "hot line" can be made available when needed by a neutral embassy, news service, etc.

The British-French-Egyptian Conflict

Keeping the Dispute Nonmilitary

The basic strategic aims involved in the Suez-Sinai war of 1956 could have been changed by developing strategic substitutes more appropriate to a postimperial and postcolonial era. The need for alternative energy sources for oil might have called forth more aggressive development of nuclear energy. There might have been further efforts to develop: long-range air-lift capabilities, sea-based and land-based long-range missile alternatives to foreign land bases; relocation of canal routes; and international regimes for vital waterways. These are policy measures that still have relevance to some of the strategic needs and political possibilities of the present.

Basic Western political strategy in the Middle East was, in retrospect, faulty—both Britain's strategy in Egypt and France's vis-à-vis Algeria (for which France came to blame Nasser and thus acquire a strong desire to overthrow him). This all gave to Soviet policy ready ways in which to exploit the situation. The combination of a traditional pattern of cultivating friendly relations among aristocratic feudal rulers and the attempt to tie them publicly to anti-Communist Western treaties seems guaranteed to excite negative popular passions in an age of resurgent nationalism. A preferred strategy would be the recognition of a sense of regional identity and independence and a policy that favors popularly supported regimes.

A major component of such a policy is to encourage constructive internal—and regional—development goals, while helping to strengthen the internal political, social, and economic fabric of a country to enable it to resist external blandishments and penetration attempts. In this connection, the effects of Secretary Dulles's cut-off aid to Egypt for the Aswan High Dam—which in turn was a reaction to Nasser's blackmail attempts—seems a powerful argument for multilateralizing significant aspects of external economic assistance. Such a program might even diminish the lure of a local demagogue by depriving him of identifiable "foreign devils."

Postwar U.S. policy in such regions as the Middle East has tended to accept rules of the game that take as given the existence of nonpopular regimes. The vicious conflict cycle often moves from there to a supportive policy involving the offering of arms to stave off threats to unpopular local rule. The unhappy experiences of the United States, Britain, France, and the Soviet Union (and perhaps even China one day) rationally suggest the value of a serious agreement among all external influences to abstain from securing special privileges or exacerbating local quarrels—a re-formed Open Door policy, backed by penalties, that would equalize the nonintervention of external states. It is difficult to think of a general approach that is more likely to be favored by the people who live in the countries concerned.

Preventing the Outbreak of Hostilities

The only thing more dangerous than forgetting the lessons of history is to misremember them. To Anthony Eden and Christian Pineau, Nasser was Hitler reincarnate—just as to some today Mao Tse-tung and Ho Chi Minh are Hitler's contemporary facsimiles. With his political brilliance, the danger of appeasing Nasser was not to be minimized. In retrospect, however, a greater evil was created by a Bourbon mentality blinded to the genuine forces of change that Nasser represented despite his charisma and demagogy. Given all this, the opposition to Eden, Pineau, and Ben Gurion should have been strongly—if clandestinely—encouraged, with the aim of either removing them from office or discrediting their militaristic policies.

Although the United States tried to act as a peacemaker, arbitrator, and inventor of time-stretching devices, U.S. diplomacy in fact contributed to the outbreak of the hostilities. For if all the other parties were made myopic by various cultural and character defects of their own, they themselves came to believe that the U.S. secretary of state was in fact misleading them and moving the situation from one ambiguity to another—to the point where U.S. credibility and, consequently, influence had virtually vanished. The results of the Dulles style would seem to suggest that some rather different qualities—chiefly candor in making explicit one's aims as well as the limits to one's intentions—might have helped to prevent catastrophic diplomatic miscalculations. Given candor in a case such as Suez, the U.S. refusal to countenance a forceful solution could have been believed and thus have served as the deterrent it was intended to be.

A strong case can be made that, if Secretary Dulles had been less certain of his personal diplomatic style, some possible avenues to peaceful settlement might have opened up. For example, at one stage during the summer of 1956, the U.A.R. gave indications that portions of the contested issues might be open to adjudication, perhaps by the International Court of Justice. Dulles chose to ignore the signal, as well as other possibilities that might have involved multilateralizing the essentially Western front against Nasser. U.S. diplomacy—as well as world peace—was thus deprived of the help of important existing diplomatic agencies and tools of action. In retrospect, Britain and France went through the pre-invasion UN exercise of October 1956 purely *pro forma;* but the United States even then could have done more to reinforce the efforts of the UN Secretary-General. In retrospect, good offices, negotiations, compromise, and international guarantees of any resulting agreement would have been an infinitely preferable road to the one followed.

The capacity of powers to make mischief for others is normally a function of the physical leverage they possess. Nasser straddled a vital Western artery that under international law represented in Western terms a "servitude" (*mot juste* for the Egyptian sentiments). Britain's ability to launch a fundamentally irrational assault was improved because it still had an imperial base in Cyprus. With full recognition that in some cases such bases are needed for self-defense or for protection of friends or allies, in principle the sooner overseas colonies are abandoned and foreign bases eliminated, the sooner some classic stimuli to conflict will have been lessened.

Typically, the Soviet intervention threats in Suez became thoroughly vocal and explicit only after the first really dangerous stage of the crisis had passed. Ironically, it might have been a helpful deterrent if Moscow had made its threats both early and credible.

Moderating/Terminating Hostilities

The British-French ultimatum, ostensibly aimed at halting hostilities, in effect broadened the war. More pointed deterrent threats by the great powers and the United Nations might have been useful, particularly if a UN force had been sent in promptly.

In retrospect, however likely renewed Israeli-Egyptian warfare may have been, its intensity was clearly increased by both the fact and the threat of growing stocks of arms supplies in the region—most particularly by Soviet-supplied aircraft in the hands of the U.A.R. A balancing policy (such as the United States has been following) would have sought to increase Israel's anti-aircraft defenses. But a more fundamental conflict-controlling policy would have pursued high-priority agreements for restraint among suppliers to the Middle East.

U.S.-Soviet convergence of interests continues to emerge as the prime conflict-control policy to be sought. Lacking that, it is then likely that the superpowers will act independently, and the U.S. will need to make its own pressures felt before the conflict is worsened by such Soviet conflict-control moves as the threat of invasion in the Suez case, however hollow that threat. It was probably U.S. pressure more than any other factor that turned the tide in this case, particularly U.S. leverage at the moment of the run on the pound (generally acknowledged as having been the crucial turning point of the Suez Conflict).

The second most potent agency for conflict control is the availability of UN machinery to give form and unity to pressures from states that it control conflict and also actually to create such conflict-control apparatus. Certainly the ability to create UNEF and to perform logistic miracles in fielding it provided both a pressure and a cover for a cease-fire and eventual withdrawal. Nothing could argue more eloquently for better stand-by peacekeeping capabilities or, at a minimum, for better developed contingency plans for rapid recruitment and deployment of the peacekeeping force.

Settling the Dispute

Terminating the Suez-Sinai hostilities and removing British and French troops both ended the British-French-Egyptian Conflict and settled the dispute over the canal. The measures to end the Arab-Israeli Conflict—which end is certainly not in sight yet—are discussed in earlier sections.

With hindsight one can re-examine recent cases of local conflict and see multiple opportunities to prevent, contain, and terminate violence—opportunities that were clouded at the time by imperfect information and the need for speed. We readily acknowledge that looking back on past events equips one with perfect knowledge of the consequences of an act or omission—something the harassed policy maker at the time can never hope to achieve.

But it is equally true that those in a position to exert a controlling influence in the direction of conflict control refrained from doing so, in some cases deliberately. They may, in fact, have been indifferent or even have directly or indirectly encouraged a conflict-promoting rather than a conflict-controlling course. From all the evidence, it seems clear that the single most crucial element in controlling local conflicts is the way in which great powers such as the United States view their interests, and the will and imagination with which they pursue them.

PART THREE

CHAPTER 11

United States Interests

Does the United States have a general interest in eliminating or controlling conflicts in the developing regions of the world? The answer might be thought self-evident. But U.S. interests can be interpreted in two strikingly different ways.

Perhaps the most common belief is that the United States, as an extraordinarily rich and strong power with a natural concern for international stability, ought to favor any reasonable means to stop conflict wherever it takes place despite whatever might be hoped to be gained by violence. The status quo probably suits this country as well as or better than any other nation in the world. In material and perhaps in political terms as well, the United States has more to lose and less to gain from chaos, instability, and unpredictability than any other nation. By this reasoning, it is clearly more consonant with U.S. interests to attain U.S. objectives by peaceful rather than by violent means. Logically, then, it is desirable that the numbers and effectiveness of nonviolent means of achieving national objectives be increased and strengthened. The United States should thus be in the forefront in advocating policies aimed at stabilizing local situations and minimizing outbreaks of violence.

Other observers, however, seeking to define a general U.S. attitude toward local conflict, arrive at a different conclusion. They do not rate U.S. interest in minimizing violence as paramount or exclusive. In their view, based on over two decades of

Cold War, the overriding U.S. interest in the world derives from its role as a committed competitor. In the years after World War II when the Communist bloc appeared united, U.S. interest lay in beating back the onslaught of a globally based conspiracy. As the Communist world became visibly fractured, and competition among its fragments began to grow in the developing areas, U.S. interest became defined as gaining victory over Communism, however fragmented, in that new arena; U.S. interest in a particular conflict situation (or dispute threatening to become a conflict) was often to prevent a Communist takeover, to preserve an alliance system, or to sustain a reputation for reliable assistance to beleaguered friends. Therefore, in its starkest and most extreme form, the notion of a Pax Americana, far from being a conflict-control strategy in the sense of giving first priority to minimizing violence, has represented a militant forward strategy of intervention with a goal of political and military victory.

The nature of—and sources for—conflicting U.S. interests can be seen more clearly by examining the U.S. approach to some contemporary situations of local conflict. Few of the following statements were applicable before 1941, all have been generally true since that time, and most of them seem likely to continue to be valid; some are consistent one with the other, others represent deep-seated inner tensions within the U.S. outlook that explain much of the confusion and malaise attendant on particular policy undertakings such as Vietnam.

(1) The lessons of the 1930's, indelibly imprinted in the minds of this generation of U.S. policy makers, call above all for discouraging armed aggression by nipping it in the bud.

(2) A generalized preference exists for an orderly international society in which differences are compromised by pacific means. But there is no effective world order able to enforce such a process. The fact that the United Nations cannot—and perhaps should not—act as a world government compounds American frustration.

(3) Recognition of the extreme dangers of resorting to nuclear weaponry encourages a strongly held desire to minimize

violence and avoid conflict intensification that would involve the great powers.

(4) The sense of being in a continuing historic conflict with various forms of Communism carries with it a willingness to employ unilateral force or to view some situations as irreconcilable—or some combination of both—when the United States believes that a major Communist advance would otherwise result.

(5) A profound conviction runs through all American history that the real revolutionary force in the world is the idea of human freedom and social justice. As Secretary of State Dean Rusk put it:

What we are pursuing . . . is not a static concept. For, unlike the Communists, we really believe in social revolution and not merely in power cloaked as revolution. We believe in constructive change and encourage it.[1]

(6) Equally in the American tradition is a traditional antipathy to dictatorial or tyrannical regimes, although this antipathy is not always acted upon.

(7) A persistent—though not necessarily dominant— national tradition insists that once U.S. forces are committed, there is no substitute for military victory.

(8) A deep-seated national desire for some form of isolation lingers, both as a residue of historic tradition and as a reaction to a growing sense of overcommitment abroad, fortified by the urgency of unsolved domestic problems.

The ways in which these ingredients interact to shape policy is not purely fortuitous. The bewildering riptides of contemporary U.S. policy arise largely from the clash between traditional American political and moral sentiments and the realities of exercising power and asserting responsibility.

Some significant patterns of national behavior can be discerned in the recent record of U.S. policy toward involvement in local

[1] Dean Rusk, Statement before the Senate Committee on Foreign Relations, as cited in the *Department of State Bulletin*, March 7, 1966, p. 352.

conflicts. The most striking are those in which U.S. military power has been substantially involved, directly or indirectly.

Of more than fifty local conflicts in the developing regions since 1945, U.S. military power was directly or indirectly present in twelve: the Greek Insurgency of the late 1940's, which was abetted by three Communist neighbors to the north; the Chinese Civil War that resulted in Mao's take-over in 1949; the Korean War of 1950–1953; the U.S.-sponsored overthrow of the left-wing Arbenz government in Guatemala in 1954; Communist China's efforts to seize control of the Nationalist-held offshore islands of Quemoy and Matsu in the middle 1950's; the Lebanon Crisis of 1958, in which both the U.S. Marines and the UN peacekeepers landed; the Congo collapse directly after independence in 1960, in which the United States backed up the United Nations and sent military missions several times to assist the Congolese government, evacuate whites, etc.; trouble and intervention in the Dominican Republic twice—in 1960, unrest under the dictator Trujillo, in 1965, U.S. intervention when Washington believed that internal crises seemed to be opening the door to power to local Communists; the Laotian civil war in 1960–1962; the American-planned and -supplied assault landings at the Bay of Pigs in Cuba in 1961, when Castro's new government seemed to drift toward the Soviet orbit; and Vietnam.

When—as in some of these twelve local conflicts—U.S. military forces have been *directly* and *openly* involved, special elements have certainly applied which grew out of the explicit commitment of U.S. prestige, power, and public opinion. And especially in those cases there has been recurrent tension between the pressures for victory and those that recognized limited war as part of a continuing power struggle in this age. The problem was summed up long ago by Alexis de Tocqueville when he wrote: "There are two things which a democratic people will always find very difficult—to begin a war and to end it."

Clearly, the more numerous local-conflict situations have

been those in which U.S. military forces were *not* significantly involved, directly or indirectly. With regard to these the United States has acted in the main as a suppressor of local conflict rather than as a fomenter or participant. As a rule it has disapproved, discouraged, disfavored, and sought to stop such conflicts, in general supporting what might be called a conflict-suppression policy. The characteristic view was stated by President Johnson when he said:

Here in the United States we do not like violence. . . . We regard it as a manifestation of failure. . . . Only when bargaining breaks off do we speak of failure. And so also in foreign policy. There, too, violence is one face of failure.[2]

In all cases, on the record the crucial variable factor inhibiting U.S. willingness to manipulate rather than suppress both internal and interstate conflicts has been and still is a perceived danger of great-power intensification. This is so both where the United States is relatively indifferent as to the outcome and where it is committed to victory for one side or the other. The point becomes clearer when one examines U.S. policy toward the two broad types of conflict, interstate and internal.[3]

THE UNITED STATES AND INTERSTATE CONFLICTS

U.S. interests toward local interstate wars usually converge with international norms in favoring *conflict control.* The United States has generally supported preventive diplomatic efforts. Examples are: the 1947 and 1965 fighting between India and Pakistan over Kashmir; the Palestine wars, including the Suez Conflict of 1956 and the 1967 outbreak; and the confrontation in the 1960's between Sukarno's Indonesia and Malaysia, de-

[2] President Johnson, Speech at Denver, Colorado, August 26, 1966, as cited in *The New York Times,* August 27, 1966.
[3] A schematic representation of the propositions that follow may be found in Appendix D.

spite the involvement of our British ally on the latter side. Day-to-day U.S. diplomacy has often shown real concern, when U.S. interests did not seem directly at stake, to settle disputes before they become serious, to suppress existing conflicts to the greatest extent possible, and to exercise maximum influence in terminating hostilities where actual violence has broken out.

The United States frequently—far more often than its critics give it credit for—has itself pursued a central role in activities aimed at tranquilizing situations in the developing regions before they burst into unwanted violence. The role of U.S. good offices in subduing the 1967 Cyprus flare-up and its role as mediator in the dispute between Britain and Guatemala over the ultimate disposition of the territory of Belize (British Honduras) are two examples out of many.

Typical of this thread in American policy was the doctrine of "renunciation of the use of force" which the Eisenhower administration pursued with respect to other people's quarrels, such as that in Suez. Another relevant policy doctrine that persists to this day is one of discouraging any change in political boundaries through the use of violence, which in turn is an accompaniment of a still more generalized policy of opposing the use of military force to achieve political objectives.

In this spirit, the United States has consistently spoken in favor of arrangements of international law and order aimed at implementing and making general this conflict-control preference. It has vigorously supported the formulation of rules that condemn conflict-provoking and conflict-producing policies. It has pronounced in favor of prohibitions on the violent crossing of political boundaries. It has invariably supported UN resolutions condemning intervention—making certain that they equally condemned "indirect aggression," such as subversion, terrorism, and the like.

The U.S. approach is different where it feels that crucial interests are at stake: At least until recently, the litmus-paper test has been the fear of major Soviet or Chinese advantage. In a few recent instances of interstate wars, one of the parties was a Communist state. U.S. policy in that type of situation has been generally conditioned by the assumption that an in-place cease-fire will probably result in an unacceptable political and psychological, if not military, victory for Communism. Instances in the postwar years were the Soviet-sponsored uprising in Azerbaijan in northern Iran in 1946 and, for a long time, Vietnam—but not Korea.

The next key, however, tells how far the United States is prepared to go to implement its general policy preference. If there appears a genuine danger of direct confrontation between U.S. and Soviet military power, both superpowers tend to place the avoidance of such intensification above all else. There are those who believe the U.S. might not have pressed its British and French allies so exigently to desist in their attempt to overthrow Nasser in 1956 had it not been for fear that Moscow's threat to intervene might be real. In the October–November 1956 Hungarian revolution, viewed in part as a conflict between Hungary and the Soviet Union, United States unwillingness to intervene because it feared to risk a direct clash with the Soviets outweighed earlier conflict-producing impulses that went under the label of "rollback" or "liberation." This reality again conditioned U.S. policy toward the Soviet invasion of Czechoslovakia in 1968.

Thus, where there has been a serious perceived danger of possible nuclear intensification—as in Hungary and Czechoslovakia—the United States has opted for termination, UN condemnation, and nonintervention. In Quemoy-Matsu, as another example, the United States officially spoke, during the 1955 bombardment, of a negotiated settlement, even hinting at a possible turnover of the offshore islands if fighting were once terminated. (That there was no follow-up is beside the point.) While the United States was unwilling to be frightened off when the Vietcong appeared about to win a *de facto* victory in Vietnam in 1965, despite the bombing and increase in troop strength it generally fought a limited action, seeking with increasing seriousness ways to terminate the fighting.

Where no serious intensification danger was perceived a hard U.S. line has usually persisted; e.g., Iran in 1946. But, if there is no danger of intensification, it does not of course necessarily follow that the U.S. will intervene, any more than that danger of intensification will automatically preclude intervention if the United States feels sufficiently compelled to protect or promote its interests. What *can* be said is that, if there is no fear of intensification in situations where the United States regards important interests to be at stake, U.S. intervention has been more likely. There is some evidence that the 1970's may see much greater reluctance on the part of the United States to intervene *militarily* than has been true in the past—a trend that places a premium on the development of effective nonmilitary conflict-control options.

If efforts to avoid hostilities fail, U.S. policy choices have seemed to be guided by asking whether there will be a direct, major, and measurable Soviet or Chinese gain from suppression of the fighting. If there is no such direct Communist advantage, U.S. policy activity tends to work toward the earliest possible cease-fire, using the United Nations or regional organizations to help bring this about. Examples from recent history are the Indian–Pakistani warfare in Kashmir, the several outbreaks of Arab-Israeli warfare in the Middle East, a little-noticed conflict between Honduras and Nicaragua, and the Egyptian–Saudi Arabian tug-of-war over Yemen in the late 1960's.

In cases where the stakes seemed relatively low, the United States has been more concerned with getting the fighting stopped than in dealing with the situations that generated it. It has usually hoped that procedures for peaceful settlement of disputes would then take over. But cease-fires are rarely made dependent on such solutions. Cases in recent history include the U.S. effort in 1957 (but not in 1967) to get Israel to withdraw from the Sinai Peninsula after winning it and to get India and Pakistan to stop fighting in 1965. In both cases, promises were implied of future justice for the claims involved; but, in fact, far less effort was invested in the pacific settlement of disputes than in the termination of hostilities.

THE UNITED STATES AND
INTERNAL CONFLICTS

In the case of most internal wars, U.S. interests have been invariably derived from strategic concerns—regional security, U.S.-Soviet-Chinese relations, modernization, etc. Rather than usually being subordinate to conflict-control policy, American interests have tended to depend on pragmatic assessments of the probability of success, the accessibility of the area, and the felt need for U.S. intervention. If Communist take-over does not appear to be a prime issue in internal conflicts, the United States is not likely to perceive a primary U.S. interest as to which faction wins, and favors ending the conflict. The Nigerian-Biafran conflict is a case in point.

Even in the internal category, a perhaps surprising American preference for stability and peace can be demonstrated. Before the outbreak of hostilities, this takes the form of policy activities generally lumped under the heading of assistance and modernization programs, combined with an increasing attention to preventive social policies that might be called "counter-pre-insurgency"; the strategy of economic assistance to developing countries has always rested on a belief in evolutionary progress toward ultimate political stability and peaceful orientation. That the United States does not always or consistently act on its insights is not due to a lack of desire to stabilize (and ultimately free itself of responsibility for) the areas in question. It is rather due to a built-in confusion of competing objectives in a pluralistic society—and government. The United States has in the main vigorously espoused economic- and political-development measures to ward off Communism's appeal and, if necessary, measures aimed at countering Communist take-over attempts. It has consequently supported UN resolutions condemning intervention.

But the United States has also considered that it has a strong interest in the outcome of political changes in some parts of the world, particularly in neighboring areas such as the Caribbean and Central America, an interest that could take precedence over conflict control. The United States is inevitably going to favor evolutionary change in much of the Communist world— Eastern Europe, Cuba, Communist Asia. And its commitment to the dynamic process of modernization throughout the under-developed regions is by definition a generator of new potential conflicts.

More pointed still, there were clearly internal situations with which the United States was unwilling to live, even at the cost of fomenting conflict. Obvious illustrations are Arbenz's Guate-mala in 1954, Castro's Cuba in 1961, and Tshombe's Katanga by 1963. Other cases where a U.S. conflict-generating impulse may have existed, although without overt action to support the impulse, were the Chinese Communists' crushing of the Tibetan revolt in 1959 and the situation in Trujillo's Dominican Repub-lic in 1961.

After the outbreak of hostilities, the United States character-istically recalculates the extent of its vital interests, if any, in the outcome. If no such vital interest is perceived—usually meaning in our times no perceived direct or primary Communist involve-ment—the U.S. posture is one of nonintervention, the encour-agement of pacification efforts, and a hope for reconciliation of contending factions. The United States may have "feelings" on the subject; but no significant commitment of blood or treasure to the outcome is to be looked for. Cases in point are numer-ous: Iraq's attempt in 1961 to take over Kuwait; the warfare in Cyprus, both in a colonial struggle against Britain in the mid-1950's and between Greek and Turkish Cypriots in the mid-1960's; the 1950–1954 Burmese-Taiwan dispute over National-ist Chinese troops in Northern Burma; the insurgent movements in Costa Rica in 1947; the Mau Mau in Kenya; India from 1945 to 1948; and—one is required to add—Batista's Cuba and Trujillo's Dominican Republic, whatever distaste the U.S. may have been felt for (non-Communist) dictatorships.

If, on the other hand, the U.S. feels it has a primary interest in which side wins, the U.S. preference for victory for its side typically overrides contrary desires for cease-fire, reconciliation, coalition governments, etc. The U.S. then seriously considers intervening with varying amounts of money, military hardware, and, in extreme situations, uniformed U.S. forces. In every one of the following cases the issue, real or fancied, was Communist take-over: the Greek Insurgency; the Venezuelan insurgency of the late 1950's and early 1960's; Laos; the Dominican Republic in 1965; the Bay of Pigs; Guatemala; the Communist terrorist and guerrilla operations in Malaya over a ten-year period; the Congo in 1960; Colombia in 1960; Lebanon in 1958; the Burmese Civil War after World War II; the insurgency movement of the Hukbalahaps (Huks) in the Philippines in the 1950's; and, of course, Vietnam in the 1950's and 1960's.

In internal wars, a primary key to American commitment is the degree of risk that might be involved in extending the fight in scope, scale, or time, rather than suppressing it. U.S. dissatisfaction with the Eastern European status quo in the late 1940's and early 1950's led this country to encourage expectations that many believe helped to foment the following major uprisings in our epoch: the June-1953 East German uprising; the Poznan riots in Poland in 1956; and, above all, the Hungarian revolution of 1956. (In a sense the Communists themselves fomented the situation in Czechoslovakia in 1968.) But the strategic risks in Hungary in 1956, in Laos in 1961–1962, and in Czechoslovakia in 1968 (though not in the Bay of Pigs) were evidently seen as sufficient to discourage an activist American policy. In the first case, the risks suggested a policy of strategic abstention along with rhetorical condemnation through the United Nations. In the second case, after several futile efforts to influence the situation in our favor, they led in 1962 to a policy of cease-fire and attempted reconciliation through the device of coalition government. The U.S. pursued a hands-off policy in Czechoslovakia.

When U.S. interests seem basically involved in insurgency situations, and where *no* serious danger of intensification is

perceived, the United States has not given priority to terminating hostilities or to a reconciliation policy. Postwar examples
are the insurgencies in Venezuela, Colombia, Malaya, and the
Philippines, and, above all, situations in which the United States
has physically intervened: Guatemala in 1954; Cuba in 1961;
and the Dominican Republic in 1965. In the Bay of Pigs there
was no serious concern over possible Soviet intervention if the
United States should succeed in overthrowing Castro and establishing a more congenial regime. The situation in Korea in
1950–1953, like Vietnam, involved a mixture of calculations
producing a policy of massive U.S. intervention although later a
readiness grew to terminate on compromise grounds out of fear
of the possible consequences.

The *desiderata* for U.S. policy naturally vary with the circumstances and call for quite different postures on the part of
the United States in the face of varying conflict threats. The
posture chosen probably represents the consensus in policy-
making circles. But that consensus can change. In some instances there may even be a succession of different postures
over time, as perceptions of the situation and, consequently,
definitions of U.S. interests change.

When it was feared, for example, that pro-Nasser Arab
radicals were seeking to seize power in Lebanon in 1958, the
United Nations first ran a conflict-control operation with a UN
Observer force. Then the United States ran a conflict-manipula-
tion operation with the landing of 8,000 U.S. soldiers and 6,000
marines. U.S. interests and perceptions had changed in the
interval. A similar sort of change occurred in the U.S. intervention in the Dominican Republic in 1965, when it later became desirable to introduce compromise-inducing OAS peace
forces and UN representation. In other conflicts, such as Laos
and Vietnam, the violent phases were entered into gradually
after starting out as political disputes. The post-Batista Cuban
situation followed this pattern to some degree. After Castro
ousted the Batista dictatorship, the U.S. posture toward Cuba
was at first a disinclination to foment conflict, followed by a
waiting period during which the United States watched the

revolution turn sour. The United States ultimately adopted a conflict-fomenting policy.

Since World War II, real or suspected Communist involvement has been the principal constant in U.S. policy toward local conflict. In the early postwar years there was ample reason for the United States to interpret local Communist take-over attempts as part of a unified worldwide conflict that was by definition unlimited. From the time of precipitate U.S. demobilization in 1945–1946 and Moscow's simultaneous reversion to a hard line, the Communists have been the primary *agents provocateurs* when it came to deliberate and willful initiation of conflict, and at root, the role the United States has played has been a reactive one. But this defensive, responsive U.S. strategy has sometimes been to foment a *counterconflict*.

To give an obvious example, the invasion of Cuba at the Bay of Pigs in 1961 by Cuban exiles recruited, trained, and armed by the United States represented a U.S.-fomented conflict in reaction to a Communist regime in the Western Hemisphere. The lengths to which the United States was prepared to go to respond forcibly to perceived challenges were illustrated again in the Dominican Republic in 1965. The other uses of U.S. force in recent years were in reaction to Communist initiatives. Both the Korean and Vietnam Wars involved U.S. power in response to attempted Communist take-overs. (This phenomenon has had a reciprocal aspect. Communist China probably would not tolerate a systemic reverse in North Korea or North Vietnam, nor, as the Soviet repressions of Hungary and Czechoslovakia demonstrated, will the Soviet Union in Eastern Europe.)

In a curious and troublesome historical irony, it has been increasingly true that the Soviet Union interprets U.S. policy toward local conflict precisely in compliance with Marxist expectations, reinforced by a number of instances when the United States behaved accordingly. As reported by one of the ablest American Sovietologists, on the basis of one hundred conversations in the Soviet Union and Eastern Europe in the fall of 1966,

Our improvisations are seen as fitting into a pattern of deliberate militancy reflecting a determination to intervene with force in any local situation where political trends are adverse to our interests.[4]

In part, this image of the U.S. as "unilateral interventionist gendarme" is a creation of Communist propaganda. But, in part, the fact is that the United States has sometimes over-reacted militarily to a politically ambiguous threat, as in Lebanon in 1958 and in the Dominican Republic in 1965. In part, also, these actions are the lot of any self-appointed gendarme, the consequence of which has been acute ambiguities in U.S. policy.

The varying attitudes of the United States toward specific conflict situations are obviously functions of its sense of involvement and commitment. One dilemma facing the United States—and the Soviet Union and perhaps also Communist China—is that what might be called their "impartial" (i.e., conflict-controlling) interests often compete with their "partial" (i.e., conflict-fomenting or conflict-manipulating) interests. A scale of partiality exists, marked by the degree to which threat is perceived. The avoidance of bloodshed in conflict situations has been not infrequently overridden by other considerations. The most egregious instances are cases of internal insurrections in which a status quo that was at least tolerable to the United States was threatened. In recent internal conflicts involving Bolivia, Panama, Colombia, and the Congo, Washington was willing in the end to give the status quo some measure of support ranging from tear gas to organization of a quasimilitary force.

In other cases it can be demonstrated that since World War II, a generalized U.S. preference has existed for conflict prevention, suppression, and termination. This has been true of virtually all colonial conflicts, most interstate local wars, and some internal conflicts—where Communism was not the prime issue. For most of these cases the clear U.S. preference was for minimum unilateral involvement consistent with its vital interests and

[4] Marshall Shulman, Washington *Post,* November 27, 1966.

international responsibilities (reinforced by C. L. Sulzberger's Fourth Cardinal Rule of Diplomacy[5]).

The difficulty arises in the instances where the given conflict *is* fomented, or abetted, by one or another Communist state. There may be no longer any international Communist conspiracy—and, by contrast with Peking, Hanoi, and Havana, Moscow may seem positively conservative in its foreign policy —but in other ways the Soviet Union appears to be increasingly adjusting its tactics and configuring its military forces for more effective manipulation and exploitation for Soviet benefit of local conflicts, particularly those in the Middle East.[6] Whether this trend was or was not provoked by the great recent increases in U.S. limited war and interventionist capabilities, Moscow can by no means be written off yet as a potential arsonist. As for the more adventurous Communist regimes, their dynamism and attempted export of messianism are too familiar to require documenting.

But to the extent that U.S. policy toward local conflicts *in general* tends only to be defined in terms of a Communist threat, it may no longer always be soundly based. It is striking that out of fifty-four local-conflict situations since World War II involving actual or potential application of force, forty-three were not primarily U.S.-Soviet or U.S.-Chinese confrontations. Contrary to common belief, by no means all insurgencies have been Communist-inspired. Of the overwhelming majority of them that have taken place in the developing areas, Communist elements were prominent in no more than 50 per cent.

The contrary assumption, even when partially disproven, continued to be fostered by political rhetoric, as well as by the fact that U.S. military strategy until recently was geared primarily to great-power confrontation. But we have discovered

[5] "Never get between a dog and a lamppost." *The New York Times,* May 27, 1957.

[6] Witness, for example, Soviet Union construction in 1967–1968 of its first aircraft carrier; the substantial Soviet naval power, including amphibious landing craft, operating in the Mediterranean for the first time in 1967; the display of helicopter assault forces in a Moscow air show in the summer of 1967; and the Soviet emergency air lift to supply the embattled Yemeni Republican forces in November and December 1967.

that, alongside their conflict-fomenting rhetoric and action, Communists also conform to realities of power, of timing, and, in the case of the Soviet Union, of the drain of messianic energy that comes with growing *embourgeoisement*. The Soviet Union practices a form of conflict control authentically stated in former Chairman Khrushchev's January 6, 1961, speech sancti-fying "wars of national liberation" but discouraging general—*and* limited—wars because of the danger of "escalation." And, even for the former, Russian "policy now is watch, help, but no deep involvement."[7]

Controlling a conflict that is defined by Communists as a "war of liberation" (or "people's war," in Peking phraseology) frequently turns out to mean, both to Communists and to those who counter their efforts, the manipulation of a fight in order to "win" without running unacceptable risks. For the period ahead, assuming the two Communist giants remain estranged, a much sharper distinction may well be made in U.S. eyes be-tween Soviet and Chinese involvement. If the Soviet Union has hovered, like Gertrude Stein's St. Theresa, between the indoors of status quo and the outdoors of revolution, Communist China has given the impression of acting on the revolutionary's belief that it can only gain from stirring up the established order of things, though it is not usually willing to run high risks. And Mao Tse-tung has demonstrated the use of what are in effect conflict-control doctrines and tactics as instruments of what might be called "safe victory." For at least as long as they are deterred by overwhelming strategic power in Western hands, both Peking and Moscow, their various belligerent utterances aside, may in general continue to behave as Bismarck was reputed to have done when asked if he wanted war: "Certainly not," he replied, "what I want is victory."

[7] Statement by Soviet agent (and British defector) Harold "Kim" Philby, interviewed in Moscow by *The New York Times,* December 19, 1967.

Toward a Strategy of Conflict Control

What have we learned from the analysis of conflict that can contribute to a purposeful strategy of conflict control? And what, from analysis of U.S. interests, that can lead to sound policy prescriptions?

First, some features of conflict clearly suggest patterns. Some of these patterns simply confirm the intuition of the experienced observer. For example, on the record, internal struggles have tended to be harder to control than interstate conflicts. Considerable great-power partiality has usually been a feature of those conflicts that have proven hard to control. The more intense that partiality has been, the more the conflicts have resisted prevention, moderation, or termination of hostilities. Furthermore, the geopolitical setting has related significantly to controllability, for difficult terrain and weather conditions, neighboring states that incite or support one side or the other, and political instability in a region have all correlated negatively with control. And finally, high commitments of will and resources by adversaries have tended to go with hostilities that are hard to bring to an end.

It may not be quite so obvious, however, that, both in terms of "causes" and also in terms of the kinds of policy activity that might minimize violence, the distinction between interstate and internal conflicts tends to become blurred, especially in regard to the involvement of third parties. And surely it is thought-provoking that the number and variety of plausibly available violence-minimizing measures is greatest in the pre-conflict phase, progressively declining as the conflict develops to the point of hostilities. The incidence of conflict-controlling policy activity that has been actually pursued is in inverse proportion to the chances of influencing events. Surely a crowning—and tragic—irony of modern diplomacy, quantitatively confirmed by the study of recent conflicts, is this paradox we reported earlier: only as realistic policy options dwindle does policy activity increase, often coming too late to act as a preventive and invariably trailing off again when fighting stops.

ELEMENTS OF A STRATEGY

In regard to specific policy measures aimed at preventing, containing, or terminating interstate and internal local conflict with a minimum of violence or danger of escalation, what does analysis suggest?

(1) A policy aimed at avoiding conflict must *stimulate and encourage economic, social, and political reforms* in the developing countries. For conflicts in the developing regions, there is no question that internal reform is a central element in a conflict-control strategy. The absence of reform invariably creates a role for extremists, frequently Communist. The cause-effect relationship here has perhaps been clearest where the issue was primarily colonial; it does not take a Sophocles to describe in advance the nature of the tragedy that could eventually ensue in the southern part of Africa unless the white man's ways are mended, in both his colonial and racial policies.

(2) The logic of conflict control also suggests a prescription of *strong, cohesive, and effective local government.* (The same nostrum applies in many local interstate conflicts.)

(3) Conflict prevention in the shape of *genuine reform must*

come early, preferably before disputes become military-type conflicts, if dynamic instabilities are not to be set in motion that later suppression—or reform—will not abate.

(4) Perhaps one of the most compelling needs in the prevention of internal conflicts is the one that encounters the greatest diplomatic sensitivity: it is highly desirable to *observe and comprehend a rebellion before it starts* or at least as close to its inception as possible. Domestically, *The Negro Family: A Case for National Action* (1965) by then-Assistant Secretary of Labor Daniel P. Moynihan should have served as a foundation of national policy. And the encouragement of sophisticated social-science research early on Vietnam—a well-done "Camelot" project, as it were—might have furnished better early warning and perhaps supplied better foundations to policies and commitments subsequently undertaken.

(5) A conflict-control policy will by definition seek to make military conflict less violent, destructive, or unmanageable. It is repeatedly shown that *unneeded national armaments are a source of potential danger to the peace,* a disturbing influence in the political and social life of a nation, and an unproductive burden on its economy. Some armaments are essential for paramount public purposes—for security and peace, for defense against subversion, and for internal stability. But to the extent that these purposes can be achieved either without arms, with fewer or less destructive arms, or with controlled arms, it seems to us to be clearly in the interests both of the country concerned and of the United States to reduce or limit them.

The supply of arms and military technology to developing countries has come under increasingly critical Congressional scrutiny. Perhaps Soviet policy makers have been equally concerned after the dismal performance of their Middle Eastern clients in 1967. Some arms-control measures might well be developed that could profitably be applied in various phases of local conflict.

Specific measures could take the form of: controlling the availability of arms, ammunition, spare parts, and supplies so as to set practical limits to a local war's duration—whether or not through formal disarmament agreements; discouraging competitive arming by substituting external agencies of security, national or multilateral; enforcing controls by arms suppliers; embargoing arms in the course of a given conflict; etc. The ideal here would be either to eliminate arms, or in any event not to use them (perhaps employing instead the so-called Brazilian method, whereby one side merely displays its dispositions and deployments, whereupon the adversary surrenders, the regime resigns, or whatever). One thing that *can* be done is to revive the most useful practice of the League of Nations in widely publicizing statistics and other facts about the arms trade. Communications have improved considerably since the interwar period; there might be few better sanctions than continuous publicity about arms races in places where they do not belong.

(6) Analysis of cases has repeatedly suggested instances when *more preventive conflict-controlling measures might have been taken through the United Nations and perhaps other international-organization machinery.* Vietnam of the early to mid-1950's is a good example. In reality, however, such multilateral processes are typically mobilized only in later, more acute stages of conflict, where the range of possible actions has become gravely restricted. Perhaps this is why the United Nations and regional organizations seem to be strained beyond measure, asked as they perpetually are to do what no one else can or will, usually after reason has fled.

(7) and (8) The tendency to work desperately for *early cease-fires in outbreaks of interstate hostilities,* regardless of the asserted justice of the claims, has contributed strongly to short-term conflict containment in the years since World War II. Peacekeeping activities remain a vital conflict-control tool. But a related policy measure that is rarely if ever undertaken successfully is what can be called *"peacemaking," i.e., bringing the underlying dispute to a successful peaceful resolution.*

The record here is very spotty. Until Israel invaded and held Arab territory in 1967 there was no serious follow-up either on the passage of Israeli ships through the Suez Canal, which was the 1956 issue, nor on the question of Israel's boundaries, which became the 1967 issue; the same thing is true of the promised plebiscite in Kashmir. U.S. policy emphasis has tended to rest on the aspect of control focused on cease-fire. It has given little real attention to peaceful change. This is due in part to the difficulties of peaceful change; in part it is reflective of the degree of interest the United States has in the outcome of the issues at stake in the given conflict. The United States often takes a relativistic and pragmatic approach to the detailed justice of the causes involved. With regard to other peoples' quarrels, U.S. diplomacy has tended to conform to Charles Thayer's definition of diplomacy as mediating "not between right and wrong but between conflicting interests."[1]

But, as pointed out elsewhere,[2] short-term cease-fire diplomacy represents only half of the policy of "cease-fire *and* peaceful change" frequently enunciated by the late Adlai E. Stevenson. If, according to a rational theory of conflict control, hostilities should be suppressed only in accompaniment with relief to legitimate interests at stake, even greater urgency attaches to development of better, workable, peaceful-change procedures.

(9) A conflict-control strategy may even contain arguments of U.S.-sponsored *intensification of a given conflict* under certain circumstances. If the United States could have been certain that it would not run an intolerably high risk of bringing China or the Soviet Union more directly into the Vietnam War, it might at least be arguable that the conflict could have been ended sooner by intensifying pressures on North Vietnam. An analogous situation existed in Korea in the early 1950's. (The same fear of uncontrolled intensification moderates recurrent temptations to prove to the Arabs once and for all that their ambition to drive Israel into the sea is unrealistic, or to let Pakistan demonstrate to India the necessity of self-determina-

---

[1] Charles Thayer: *Diplomat* (New York: Harper; 1959), p. 252.
[2] Lincoln P. Bloomfield: "Peacekeeping and Peacemaking," *Foreign Affairs,* July 1966.

tion for Kashmir. It remains an open question whether the interests of world peace would be advanced, considering the intensification potential in each case.)

But in general a strategy of conflict control *emphasizes political rather than military intervention.* It focuses on *prevention rather than suppression of conflict in the developing countries.* It calls for *more purposeful policies in the political, economic, and social realms* in order to lay the foundations of social and economic health, physical security, and political consensus. It also calls for *caring less about certain pieces of global real estate;* this in turn requires the *mobilizing of technology to create substitutes for bases and footholds* so that they matter less both strategically and economically.

(10) and (11) Something can be learned from instances of potential local conflict in which there was no great-power partiality and therefore "nothing happened"; as examples, the civil strife in Belgium or the Romanian-Hungarian dispute over Transylvania. On conflict-minimizing grounds a *purposeful policy of abstention or even collaboration with one's partial adversaries* might serve both national and common interests. Perhaps the United States, whatever its deeper sentiments may be, would serve its own interests by sometimes even feigning impartiality. Even better than this would be *agreements between the super powers on "spheres of abstention."* And even if that is not forthcoming, it will still be wise for the United States to ask of each incipient local conflict: Do we care?; Should we care?; and, Even if the Russians care, do we have to care?

(12) The other side of the coin is that a U.S. *conflict-control strategy will be interested in prevention and suppression even if Communist take-over is not involved.* In other ways it will act as often as possible in the name of minimizing violence instead of supporting ideology. But such a policy will be sterile and unavailing unless in the end something deeper, earlier, and more basic than most of the current prescriptions for meeting insurgencies is found. Policy toward the developing countries can find new validity in William James's prescription that

. . . what we now need to discover in the social realm is the moral equivalent of war: something heroic that will speak to men as universally as war does . . .[3]

Put in a more contemporary idiom, ways need to be found, particularly where there is hostility and alienation, of channeling the "militant enthusiasms" of the younger generation toward what Konrad Lorenz, in his search for substitutes for aggressive behavior, defines as "genuine causes that are worth serving in the modern world.[4] Reform, justice, modernization, education, health, and political freedoms all represent causes that Western democracy can genuinely espouse better than can any other system of values.

DILEMMAS OF CONFLICT CONTROL

No one—neither scholar nor diplomat—is entitled to pretend that the problem of local-conflict control is simple or straightforward. Far from it; it is complex and riddled with vexing dilemmas on almost every hand. Virtually each prescription in the preceding section contains complicating features requiring reflection—although not as an excuse for inaction.

A special dilemma arises from confusion over the nature of revolution and the position of the United States in a revolutionary world. As pointed out earlier, a theoretical argument can always be made that the United States, as the chief beneficiary of the established political, economic, and social orders in the world, has a kind of natural mission to use its power and resources wherever conflict emerges for the express purpose of shoring up that particular segment of the status quo. But this would always put the United States on the side of existing systems, always against revolution—scarcely a viable, not to say intelligent, policy.

[3] William James: *The Varieties of Religious Experience* (New York: Longmans, Green; 1923), p. 367.
[4] Konrad Lorenz: *On Aggression* (New York: Harcourt, Brace and World; 1966), p. 282.

The same ideological principle would also choose for the United States the side in an interstate conflict that was more likely to favor stability. The Moors and Turks successfully operated a conflict-suppression policy that encouraged stability for centuries. In this century many astute men have argued that, in the short term, conflict control may be made considerably easier if colonial or white or elite control is firmly retained. Undeniably, the reform of decolonization can accelerate the process of change and may temporarily increase instability and possibly violence.

But in terms of durable, longer-range stability, the shortcomings of a policy of repression or tyranny are surely obvious. For one thing, it may not always be true that measures directed against dissident groups will minimize the chance of violence. Repressive policies, unless accompanied by total social controls as in dictatorships, more often lead to new and more widespread political revolution (cf. those of 1776, 1789, and 1848, not to mention such contemporary instances as Cuba under Batista, the Dominican Republic under Trujillo, Indonesia under Sukarno, and Ghana under Nkrumah). Suppression has been a generally unsuccessful policy from the Holy Alliance through the era's Indian, Cypriot, Indonesian, Indochinese, and Algerian rebellions. Longer-term conflict-control goals are better served by political democracy and civil rights such as freedom of speech, assembly, and dissent than by short-term conflict suppression (unless the fear of intensification dominates superpower policy, as it did in Hungary in 1956 and Czechoslovakia in 1968).

Perplexing dilemmas also inhere in the attempt to minimize local conflicts by withholding, or balancing, or otherwise manipulating the supply of arms to the parties. The arms-control approach runs afoul of two perplexing uncertainties. Some, including the present authors,[5] have urged measures tending to reduce regional armaments to the level needed for internal-security purposes only, with assistance toward the latter end.

[5] Lincoln P. Bloomfield and Amelia C. Leiss: "Arms Control and the Developing Countries," *World Politics,* October 1965.

There are formidable problems of policy definition and execution in this formulation, but, if successful, it would ensure that whatever hostilities did break out would be conducted at a low level. There may be serious negative effects, however. A strong capability for internal policing may, by suppressing legitimate dissent, help to keep in power a tyrannical regime. Common experience indicates that, like colonial suppression, this policy tends to generate wider and more bitter later violence. And a capability for only internal security may help to make more likely external great-power interventions in the face of a later large-scale threat.

The other uncertainty concerns the balance to be established between local adversaries in interstate disputes. If the local situation appears to be in military imbalance, the side that believes itself stronger may be tempted to strike; if it does so, and if its assessment has been accurate, it is then likely that it will quickly overcome the victim (and violence will be ended). U.S. Middle Eastern policy has supplied arms to avoid such local imbalances. Rationally, the sides are supposed to be mutually deterred from starting anything. But if hostilities nevertheless ensue they might well be more destructive and dangerous, and speedy termination might be much harder to achieve. On a global scale this is of course the central dilemma of superpower mutual-deterrence policy. In the developing regions the same questions would be magnified manifold in the event that nuclear weapons were to proliferate.

The United Nations and other international-organization machinery obviously have a central role to play in conflict prevention, given sufficient will on the part of their members. The ability of the UN to cope is dependent on that will. More precisely, whether the UN can play a major role in control of local conflict is a function of the policy of the superpowers, the United States no less than the Soviet Union. Regional organizations such as OAS, OAU, and NATO reflect the partial interests of their most influential members and thus find it hard to deal with disparity within their regions. International organizations generally have proven unable to cope with the new format of internal conflict—subversion, terror, insurgency, and a whole catalog of conflict types that continue to baffle the international community. The reason is in part the legal and constitutional rules under which the international system presently operates. But it is also because of the insistence of one or both of the two superpowers that they have an interest at stake. The UN Congo operation was a notable exception in which the UN responded to an internal collapse in the face of great-power competition. But the UN inaction in the face of Vietnam demonstrated that the problem remains fundamentally unsolved.[6]

We are thus led inescapably to question the very international system as presently organized. International law and organization are still shaped by classic notions of nation-states, sovereign equality, and legally impregnable barriers to intervention unless and until uniformed soldiers of one state cross the national boundaries of another. In regard to the old-fashioned type of interstate conflict, the international system is geared to provide a framework for intervention in the name of both law and order. At the other extreme (particularly until the racial conflicts of southern Africa were rechristened "international" in the 1960's by a growing UN majority), the system generally prohibited intervention in civil wars (themselves now rechristened "insurgencies"). That the latter type of conflict appears to be more uncontrollable than the interstate conflict probably reflects the weaknesses of the international system as much as it does any uniquely intractable quality of wars of brother against brother.

With regard to peaceful change, the dilemma is equally obvious. It is reasonable to ask whether a policy of suppression of violence should be expected to deal with anything beyond the short-run silencing of guns. After all, conflict control can be achieved temporarily by a policy of colonial suppression (as in Palestine in 1946 or Kenya and Cyprus in the 1950's) or by

[6] Lincoln P. Bloomfield: *The UN and Vietnam* (New York: Carnegie Endowment for International Peace; 1968), particularly Chap. I.

military victory in which one side or the other is defeated (as in Hungary in 1956). It was with this contradiction in mind that John Foster Dulles insisted on adding the words "and justice" to Article 2, paragraph 3 of the United Nations Charter; "All Members should settle their international disputes by peaceful means in such a manner that international peace and security, and justice, are not in danger."[7] It is evident that a vexing dilemma exists in balancing the urgency of stopping potential escalation against a fair settlement.

But the most vexing dilemma of all is how to measure the suppression of violence, as a governing principle of U.S. foreign policy, against other overarching principles and goals. Would simple conflict *avoidance* have been a reasonable alternative to the postwar response made by the United States and others to take-over attempts by violence and terror in Greece, in Korea, and in Vietnam? Nonviolence is not the only value to be cherished. The issue for the United States must never be posed in terms of suppressing violence at the expense of freedom. At root, this dilemma is moral and ethical in nature and carries with it inherent limits to the pursuit of any strategy that is overweighted in favor of a single value.

John Stuart Mill made clear a century ago the painful dilemma that above all others drives the United States perpetually to consider unilateral intervention, however unplanned or unwanted. He wrote:

The doctrine of non-intervention, to be a legitimate principle of morality, must be accepted by all governments. The despots must consent to be bound by it as well as the free States. Unless they do, the profession of it by free countries comes but to this miserable issue, that the wrong side may help the wrong, but the right must not help the right.[8]

---

[7] John Foster Dulles considered this defect the prime tragedy leading to World War II; others have identified it as the gravest gap in modern international machinery; Dulles: *War, Peace and Change* (New York: Harpers; 1939), pp. 81–5. See also Lincoln P. Bloomfield: *Evolution or Revolution—The UN and the Problem of Peaceful Territorial Change* (Cambridge: Harvard University Press; 1957).

[8] John Stuart Mill: "A Few Words on Non-Intervention," in *Dissertations and Discussions* (London: Longmans, Greene, Reader, and Dyer;

At the same time, one of the most intriguing facts about local conflicts is the rather low batting average of the superpowers in directly intervening with the aim of scoring a clear-cut win. In many ways the U.S.-sponsored attack on Cuba at the Bay of Pigs was a mirror image of the Soviet attempt to subvert and take over Iran in 1945–1946. Behind both was a wider political conflict of which the case in point was merely one sector or front. In both cases, one of the superpowers was a close neighbor. In both cases the neighboring superpower fomented internal conflict through subversive guerrilla forces inside, in addition to training and introducing additional indigenous subversives from without. In both cases, justification for intervention was found in historic precedents and frameworks (spheres-of-influence treaties in Iran and the Monroe Doctrine in Cuba). In both instances, current international law, including the UN Charter, expressly forbade the policies the superpowers pursued. And in both instances the superpowers were unsuccessful in their aim of overthrowing the neighboring regime.

Even in less dramatic instances of U.S.-Soviet or U.S.-Chinese proxy struggles for control or influence or for countering the influence of the other it is by no means clear that unopposed attempts to "penetrate" bring much reward in this day of sensitive nationalist emotions. Is the Soviet Union really better off with a resentful, troublemaking ally in Cuba that costs $1 million a day to support, with little to show in return, ideological or economic? Would it have advanced either U.S. interests or the prospects for regional peace if the United States had reacted massively in opposition to Chinese Communist attempts to penetrate certain African countries in the early 1960's, attempts that almost uniformly backfired?[9] Here, too, the key is *selective* intervention—and equally deliberate selective nonintervention. Here, too, the strategic framework for

---

1867), pp. 176–7; originally published in *Fraser's Magazine,* December 1859.

[9] As Soviet agent Harold Philby put it (regarding deep Soviet involvement in Africa, in particular Ghana), it was "millions of rubles down the drain." Interview with *The New York Times,* December 19, 1967.

policy should give equal weight to opposing clear-cut acts of aggression and to supporting conflict-control activity.

THE WAY AHEAD

It is not easy to find a posture for the United States toward local conflict that will be either always consistent or always successful. The former may be undesirable and the latter impossible. U.S. foreign policy takes its cues not only from what it wants of the world but also from the complex nature of the international scene and of the forces and pressures that play across it. This in turn gives rise to conflicting interpretations of events and to the setting of frequently incompatible goals and priorities.

Having suggested a broad range of potential control measures (ELEMENTS OF A STRATEGY), the question remains as to whether the United States ought or ought not to sponsor some or all of them. Some might, if they are taken, disadvantage the United States in the pursuit of its particular objectives as seen at the time. Other measures will, if taken, clearly support the nation's general interest in stability and peace. Still others may appear to be disadvantageous, but actually may have the effect of sparing the United States from committing what looks in retrospect like a blunder.

The changing international scene is bound to affect the policy calculations the United States will be making on this issue in the period ahead. The nature and intensity of U.S. interests in local conflicts has been defined so far largely by the extent of the entanglement of those conflicts in the Cold War. If both the Communist and the Western worlds continue to grow more pluralistic, and if new political issues, new centers of military power and political activity, and new patterns of conflict and alignment arise to complicate or even subordinate Cold War issues, U.S. policies and strategies of intervention and conflict control will have to become much more selective and diversified.

But even in today's ambiguous world the options open to the

United States are not necessarily mutually antagonistic. A selective strategy of conflict control would not necessarily compete or clash at all points with other legitimate American strategies. Moreover, there is nothing innate or eternally valid about the particular way the United States has played its world role in the 1940's, 1950's, and 1960's.

Historically, there have been two ways for this country to play that role. One flourished in the 1920's and 1930's and took the form of a pretense that the United States had *no* role to play. Generally, it followed Mark Twain's precept that "to do good is noble. To tell others to do good is also noble and a lot less trouble." Disregarding any analogies to Vietnam, it remains everlastingly true that Hitler and Imperial Japan in the 1930's were thus encouraged to believe that no significant obstacles lay in their paths of conquest.

The second way, shaped by the shock of emergence from isolation, was for this country to project its power to deter aggression, oppose injustice, support friends, and police disorder. But this active mode of national behavior has within it two further options: One is for the United States to project its power with partiality (taking sides in local disputes and conflicts in the developing areas), on the assumption that U.S. interests are vitally involved in virtually all substantive outcomes; the other would be to project U.S. power as a form of influence aimed above all at the goal of preventing, moderating, and terminating local conflict, always with regard for justice, but with lessened partiality. Both are forms of intervention. Indeed, a strategy of conflict control is far from isolationist, or passive. As we have tried to show, it may at times call for intervention with economic, social, political, diplomatic, perhaps military, tools even on occasions when no Communist elements are involved and the United States is thus not directly challenged or threatened. At other times, the prescription may be for a strategy of withdrawal or abstention as much as for one of participation, depending on the effect a given act by an external power is likely to have on the probable course of the conflict. In short, it calls for selective intervention or nonintervention in accordance with conflict-control criteria, and above all it emphasizes political rather than military intervention. The latter requirement is urgently underscored by the reactions to the Vietnam War.

The United States is not alone in the world. Even if it were to adopt a conflict-control strategy as a guiding principle, as long as other great powers chose to challenge and threaten, there might still be occasions when this country would feel itself obliged to resort to unilateral military intervention in local-conflict situations.

The most crucial element in local-conflict control for the future is thus the degree to which not only the United States but also the Soviet Union and China view their vital interests as seriously involved; equally important is the degree to which they can view a given conflict impartially rather than favor one side. Perhaps the most important task of diplomacy in the years ahead will be to minimize the former and strengthen the latter. American policy can contribute to this high purpose by constantly re-examining the premises of its own actions.

In the end, policy will still operate in the gray areas, unable —for sound reasons—to occupy either the black or white. Freedom and justice will remain the highest values of political ethics. But they may sometimes become confused with power and prestige. Both world peace and the deepest American values can be served by a strategy of conflict control that vigorously seeks to support freedom and justice in ways that purposefully minimize violence.

APPENDIXES

Appendix A

Phase of Conflict	Threshold of Transition Between Phases	Description of Phase or Transition
Ph. I		Dispute, not perceived in military terms by either party
	I–II	Introduction of military option by one or both parties
Ph. II		Conflict, perceived in military terms by one or both parties
	II–III	Outbreak of hostilities
Ph. III		Hostilities
	III–IV	Termination of hostilities
Ph. IV		Post-hostilities, but conflict still perceived in potentially military terms by at least one party
	IV–V	End of conflict
Ph. V		Dispute, not perceived in military terms by either party
	S	Settlement of dispute

The Structure of Local Conflict

Crucial Factors Bearing on Transition		Pre-Dispute
Toward Conflict Control (Away from Violence)	**Away from Conflict Control (Toward Violence)**	
• Tending to keep dispute nonmilitary • Tending toward settlement	• Tending to introduce military option • Tending away from settlement	
(Factors operating during Phase I have combined to push the dispute across the threshold to Phase II, making it a conflict.)		
• Inhibiting the outbreak of hostilities • Restricting the scale/scope of potential hostilities • Tending toward settlement	• Promoting the outbreak of hostilities • Expanding the scale/scope of potential hostilities • Tending away from settlement	
(Factors operating during Phase II have combined to push the conflict across the threshold to Phase III, generating hostilities.)		
• Moderating hostilities • Terminating hostilities • Tending toward settlement	• Intensifying hostilities • Continuing hostilities • Tending away from settlement	
(Factors operating during Phase III have combined to push the conflict across the threshold to Phase IV, terminating actual fighting.)		
• Inhibiting the resumption of hostilities • Restricting the scale/scope of potential hostilities • Tending toward settlement	• Promoting the resumption of hostilities • Expanding the scale/scope of potential hostilities • Tending away from settlement	
(Factors operating during previous phases have combined to remove the military option of both adversaries, but the underlying dispute remains.)		
• Tending to keep dispute nonmilitary • Tending toward settlement	• Tending to introduce military option • Tending away from settlement	
(Factors operating during previous phases—or factors unrelated to the conflict itself—have combined to bring the underlying dispute to settlement.)		

Pre-Dispute

PRE-HOSTILITIES

DISPUTE — CONFLICT — HOSTILITIES

POST-HOSTILITIES

Dispute Settled

The Structure of Local-Conflict Control

Phase of Conflict	Threshold of Transition Between Phases	Description of Phase or Transition
Ph. I		Dispute, not perceived in military terms by either party
	I–II	Introduction of military option by one or both parties
Ph. II		Conflict, perceived in military terms by one or both parties
	II–III	Outbreak of hostilities
Ph. III		Hostilities
	III–IV	Termination of hostilities
Ph. IV		Post-hostilities, but conflict still perceived in potentially military terms by at least one party
	IV–V	End of conflict
Ph. V		Dispute, not perceived in military terms by either party
	S	Settlement of dispute

Crucial Factors Bearing on Transition		Conflict-Control Policy Objectives	Pre-Dispute
Toward Conflict Control (Away from Violence)	Away from Conflict Control (Toward Violence)		
• Tending to keep dispute nonmilitary • Tending toward settlement	• Tending to introduce military option • Tending away from settlement	• Keeping dispute nonmilitary • Settling the dispute	
(Factors operating during Phase I have combined to push the dispute across the threshold to Phase II, making it a conflict.)			
• Inhibiting the outbreak of hostilities • Restricting the scale/scope of potential hostilities • Tending toward settlement	• Promoting the outbreak of hostilities • Expanding the scale/scope of potential hostilities • Tending away from settlement	• Preventing the outbreak of hostilities • Restricting the scale/scope of potential hostilities • Settling the dispute	PRE-HOSTILITIES
(Factors operating during Phase II have combined to push the conflict across the threshold to Phase III, generating hostilities.)			
• Moderating hostilities • Terminating hostilities • Tending toward settlement	• Intensifying hostilities • Continuing hostilities • Tending away from settlement	• Moderating hostilities • Terminating hostilities • Settling the dispute	HOSTILITIES
(Factors operating during Phase III have combined to push the conflict across the threshold to Phase IV, terminating actual fighting.)			
• Inhibiting the resumption of hostilities • Restricting the scale/scope of potential hostilities • Tending toward settlement	• Promoting the resumption of hostilities • Expanding the scale/scope of potential hostilities • Tending away from settlement	• Preventing the resumption of hostilities • Restricting the scale/scope of potential hostilities • Settling the dispute	POST-HOSTILITIES
(Factors operating during the previous phases have combined to remove the military option of both adversaries, but the underlying dispute remains.)			
• Tending to keep dispute nonmilitary • Tending toward settlement	• Tending to introduce military option • Tending away from settlement	• Keeping dispute nonmilitary • Settling the dispute	
(Factors operating during previous phases—or factors unrelated to the conflict itself—have combined to bring the underlying dispute to settlement.)			

Dispute Settled

Appendix C

The Fifty-four Local Conflicts

Conventional Interstate	Unconventional Interstate	Internal with Significant External Involvement	Primarily Internal	Colonial
○ Aden-Yemen, 1954–1959	◇ Indonesia-Malaysia, 1963–1965	□ Bay of Pigs, 1960–1961	◇ Chinese Civil War, 1945–1949	△ Algeria, 1954–1962
△ Algeria-Morocco, 1962–1963	◇ Vietnam, 1959		□ Colombia, 1960–	△ Angola, 1961–
○ Arabs-Israel, 1967		◇ Burma–Nationalist China, 1950–1954	△ Congo, 1960–1964	○ Cyprus, 1952–1959
□ Honduras-Nicaragua, 1957		◇ Burmese Civil War, 1948–1954	□ Costa Rica, 1947	△ French Cameroun, 1955–1960
◇ India-China, 1954–1962		△ Congo (Katanga), 1961–1964	□ Cuba, 1958–1959	△ French Morocco, 1952–1956
◇ Kashmir, 1947–1949		□ Costa Rica, 1955	□ Dominican Republic, 1961–1962	◇ Goa, 1961–1962
◇ Kashmir, 1965		○ Cyprus, 1963–	◇ India, 1945–1948	◇ Indochina, 1945–1954
◇ Korea, 1950–1953			○ Iraq (Kurds), 1959–1963	◇ Indonesia, 1945–1949

○ Kuwait-Iraq, 1961

△ Morocco–Spanish Morocco, 1957–1958

○ Palestine, 1945–1948

◇ Quemoy-Matsu, 1954–1958

△ Somalia-Ethiopia-Kenya, 1960–1964

○ Soviet-Iran, 1941–1947

○ Suez, 1956

□ Dominican Republic, 1965

Greece, 1944–1949

□ Guatemala, 1954

◇ Laos, 1959–1961

◇ Malaya, 1948–1960

△ Nigeria, 1967

◇ Tibet, 1955–1959

□ Venezuela, 1960–1963

○ Yemen, 1962–

○ Lebanon, 1958

◇ Philippines, 1948–1954

△ Kenya, 1952–1958

△ Madagascar, 1947

○ Muscat-Oman, 1956–1958

◇ West Irian, 1962–1963

Legend: △ Africa   ◇ Asia   □ Latin America   ○ Middle East

INTERSTATE CONFLICTS ▶

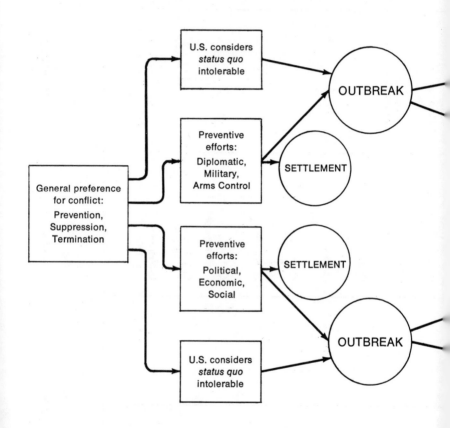

INTERNAL CONFLICTS ▶

| Phase of Conflict | Ph. I: Dispute
Pre-Military | Ph. II: Conflict
Pre-Hostilities | Ph. III: Conflict
Hostilities |

Model of U.S. Policy Preferences and Activities
Toward Local Conflicts Outside Europe

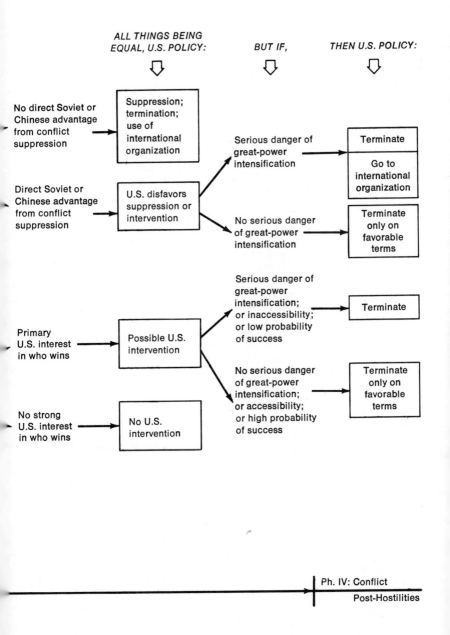

INDEX

A NOTE ABOUT THE AUTHORS

Lincoln P. Bloomfield and Amelia C. Leiss are political scientists working at the MIT Center for International Studies. Both have published widely. Professor Bloomfield, a former State Department planner who is now director of MIT's Arms Control Project, is the author or co-author of six books in the fields of foreign policy and international security, among them The United Nations and U.S. Foreign Policy, International Military Forces, *and* Khrushchev and the Arms Race, *as well as numerous articles that have appeared in* Foreign Affairs, World Politics, *and the* American Political Science Review. *Miss Leiss is the author of* Apartheid and United Nations Collective Measures *and co-author of* European Peace Treaties After World War II. Controlling Small Wars *is derived from their joint research sponsored by the U.S. Arms Control and Disarmament Agency.*

A NOTE ON THE TYPE

The text of this book was set on the Linotype in a face called TIMES ROMAN, designed by STANLEY MORISON for The Times (London), and first introduced by that newspaper in 1932.

Among typographers and designers of the twentieth century, Stanley Morison has been a strong forming influence, as typographical adviser to the English Monotype Corporation, as a director of two distinguished English publishing houses, and as a writer of sensibility, erudition, and keen practical sense.

In 1930 Morison wrote: "Type design moves at the pace of the most conservative reader. The good type-designer therefore realises that, for a new fount to be successful, it has to be so good that only very few recognise its novelty. If readers do not notice the consummate reticence and rare discipline of a new type, it is probably a good letter." It is now generally recognized that in the creation of Times Roman Morison successfully met the qualifications of this theoretical doctrine.

Composed by H. Wolff Book Manufacturing Co., New York.
Printed by Universal Lithographers, Timonium, Maryland.
Bound by L. H. Jenkins, Richmond, Virginia.
Typography and binding design by Winston Potter.